AGE 4

God Made the World

AUTHORS
Sisters of Notre Dame
Chardon, Ohio

LOYOLAPRESS.
A JESUIT MINISTRY
Chicago

Imprimatur: Reverend John F. Canary, S.T.L., D. Min., Vicar General, Archdiocese of Chicago, September 17, 2008

In accordance with c. 827, permission to publish in the Archdiocese of Chicago has been granted by the Very Reverend John F. Canary, Vicar General, on September 17, 2008. This means that the material has been found free from doctrinal or moral error, and does not imply that the one granting this permission agrees with the content, opinions, or statements expressed therein. Nor is any legal responsibility assumed by the Archdiocese of Chicago by granting this permission.

God Made the World of the *God Made Everything* Series
found to be in conformity

The Ad Hoc Committee to Oversee the Use of the Catechism, United States Conference of Catholic Bishops, has found the doctrinal content of this manual, copyright 2010, to be in conformity with the *Catechism of the Catholic Church.*

ACKNOWLEDGMENTS

Excerpts from the *New American Bible* with Revised New Testament and Psalms Copyright © 1991, 1986, 1970 Confraternity of Christian Doctrine, Inc., Washington, DC. All rights reserved. No portion of the *New American Bible* may be reprinted without permission in writing from the copyright holder.

Excerpts from the English translation of *The Roman Missal* © 1973, International Committee on English in the Liturgy, Inc. (ICEL). All rights reserved.

Excerpts from *Catechism of the Catholic Church.* English translation of the *Catechism of the Catholic Church* for the United States of America copyright © 1994, United States Catholic Conference, Inc.—Libreria Editrice Vaticana.

Loyola Press has made every effort to locate the copyright holders for the cited works used in this publication and to make full acknowledgment for their use. In the case of any omissions, the publisher will be pleased to make suitable acknowledgments in future editions.

Art credits are supplied in sequence, left to right, top to bottom. Page positions are abbreviated as follows: (t) top, (c) center, (b) bottom, (l) left, (r) right.

Photography OV-5 ©iStockphoto.com/Vladimir Melnikov, OV-7 ©iStockphoto.com/Craig Veltri, OV-8 ©iStockphoto.com/Monika Adamczyk, OV-12–OV-13 ©iStockphoto.com/René Mansi, OV-14 Jose Luis Pelaez/Iconica/Getty Images, OV-16 ©iStockphoto.com/Ekaterina Monakhova, T1 ©iStockphoto.com/Ekaterina Monakhova, T40(t) ©iStockphoto.com/Matthew Apps, T295 ©iStockphoto.com/René Mansi, T296 ©iStockphoto.com/Paul Tessier, T305 ©iStockphoto.com/KMITU, T325 ©iStockphoto.com/ Ekaterina Monakhova, T326 ©iStockphoto.com/Dieter Hawlan, T327 ©iStockphoto.com/Nicole S. Young

Illustration T265 Susan Tolonen, T267(t) ©iStockphoto.com/John Woodcock, T193, T267(b) ©iStockphoto.com/Marguerite Voisey, T279 Susan Tolonen, **Cutouts** Kathleen M. Burke, Phyllis Pollema Cahill, Renée Daily, Diana Magnuson, and Robert Masheris

Tapestry OV-194 © 2003 John Nava/Cathedral of Our Lady of the Angels, Los Angeles California

Photos and illustrations not acknowledged above are either owned by Loyola Press or from royalty-free sources including but not limited to Agnus, Alamy, Comstock, Corbis, Creatas, Fotosearch, Getty Images, Imagestate, iStock, Jupiter Images, Punchstock, Rubberball, and Veer. Loyola Press has made every effort to locate the copyright holders for the cited works used in this publication and to make full acknowledgment for their use. In the case of any omissions, the Publisher will be pleased to make suitable acknowledgments in future editions.

Acknowledgments continued on page T335

Designer: Maggie Hong
Art Director: Judine O'Shea
Cover Artist: Susan Tolonen

Project Editor: Nicola S. Caso
Catechetical Consultant: Susan Anderson

ISBN 10: 0-8294-2803-8, ISBN 13: 978-0-8294-2803-2

Manufactured in the United States of America.
08 09 10 11 12 13 14 Bang 10 9 8 7 6 5 4 3 2 1

LOYOLAPRESS.
A JESUIT MINISTRY

3441 N. Ashland Avenue
Chicago, Illinois 60657
(800) 621-1008
www.loyolapress.com

DEDICATION

THE SISTERS OF NOTRE DAME GRATEFULLY REMEMBER
PERSONS FROM THEIR PAST WHOSE MINISTRY
OF CATECHESIS THEY ARE PRIVILEGED TO CONTINUE
IN THE PRESENT.

Sister Maria Aloysia Wolbring (1828–1889) foundress of the Sisters of Notre Dame of Coesfeld, Germany, and the first sisters of this new community, were formed in the spiritual and pedagogical tradition of Reverend Bernard Overberg. God, our loving and provident Father, was presented not only as caring for persons more than anyone else ever could, but also as challenging them to a responsible love for themselves, for all other people, and for creation. One of Sister Aloysia's students recalled: "Her religious instructions meant more to us than the sermons preached in church. She spoke from deepest conviction and tried to direct our hearts to God alone. Best of all, she did not require too much piety of us. 'Children,' she would say, 'always follow the golden middle way—not too little, not too much.'"

Reverend Bernard Overberg (1754–1826) began his life work of shaping teacher formation and catechesis in 1783 in the diocese of Munster, Germany. Reverend Overberg sought to present the Church's faith and teaching in such a way as to lead children and adults toward a deep, mature relationship with God in Jesus Christ. Faith, experienced through the lens of salvation history and related to everyday life, was to touch both the mind and the heart, calling forth reflection, prayer, and active response. His approach to catechesis was the way the Coesfeld Sisters of Notre Dame were led to know God in their childhood, and how they were later formed as catechists.

Saint Julie Billiart (1751–1816), foundress of the Sisters of Notre Dame de Namur, was the source of the Rule by which the Coesfeld Sisters of Notre Dame were formed. With Christian education designated as the main work of the congregation, the sisters had a framework within which to continue the mission they had begun as lay teachers. As they learned more about Julie, the sisters were inspired by the story of how this simple French woman became a remarkable catechist who helped renew the people's faith after the chaos of the French Revolution. As a young girl, Julie's deep faith and love impelled her to share the Good News with others. During a 12-year period in which she suffered a crippling illness, Julie devoted herself to catechizing women and children. Julie's confidence in the goodness and provident care of God remained unshaken in the face of misunderstandings on the part of some bishops, priests, and even her own sisters. Always open to the Spirit, she courageously carried out her ministry and taught others to proclaim the Good News. The more the Coesfeld Sisters of Notre Dame came to know about Julie, the more they desired to make known God's goodness. "How good God is." Today they regard her as their spiritual mother.

Contents

God Made the World

Unit 1: God Made People

Unit 2: God Made Holy Things

Unit 3: God Made the Earth

Unit 4: God Made Living Things

Music 'n Motion   T265

Catechist's Handbook   T295

Cutouts

Scripture Cards

Helping Young Children Know That...

God Made Everything

The *God Made Everything* series is a comprehensive early childhood program complete with all the components and catechist support you need to nurture and enrich the faith and spiritual lives of children ages three, four, and five. Each developmentally appropriate curriculum is carefully planned so that at completion, the children are ready to continue their faith journey into first grade and beyond.

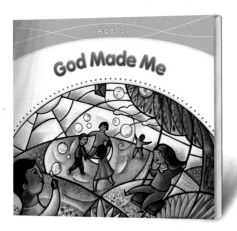

God Made Me
Child's Book for Pre-K, Age 3

Through this curriculum, three-year-olds understand that God created them and made them good, happy, active, and special. The children's own abilities serve as the central springboard for each chapter.

God Made the World
Child's Book for Pre-K, Age 4

In this curriculum, four-year-olds learn that God made living things, including people, holy things, the earth, and other wonderful surprises. A unique aspect of God's creation is the main focus of each chapter.

God Loves Us
Student Book for Kindergarten

Five-year-olds explore God's love as they are introduced to God's goodness shown through words, actions, feelings, people, places, and things. Learning, growing, sharing, and celebrating provide the foundation for each chapter. One special aspect of God's goodness is the focus of each chapter.

God Made the World

Child's Book and Materials

Created especially for four-year-olds, *God Made the World* helps our youngest faithful grow and develop with lessons and activities suited just for them.

- The Child's Book includes **lessons and activity pages** for five units with five chapters in each unit.

- Life and faith are celebrated as children have fun learning about **special seasons and days with activities** for Halloween/ Feast of All Saints, Advent, Christmas, Lent, Easter, Pentecost, Thanksgiving, Valentine's Day, Mother's Day, Father's Day, Birthdays, and Last Class/Summer.

- **Appealing illustrations and photographs** serve as a springboard for discussion and an introduction to the faith theme.

- **Discussion of the art** helps the children tap prior knowledge, develop ideas and understanding, and prepare to hear the faith message.

- **Scripture** serves as a powerful tool to explain the foundation of our Catholic faith, create a sense of identity and belonging, and enrich the faith of the children.

- **Active learning** reinforces chapter concepts as the children talk, move, play games, color, cut, glue, draw, or create to express themselves and their ideas.

- **Prayer** coincides with active learning to guide the children to reflect upon ideas and grow in their faith.

- Once the chapter is complete, the children take home their page and are invited to engage in **Family Time** with their loved ones.

Music 'n Motion CD

Music 'n Motion provides a setting for young children to imagine, dream, mime, move, and express their ideas and emotions. Exercise of the creative imagination through movement, music, and drama helps lay the groundwork for development of the religious imagination.

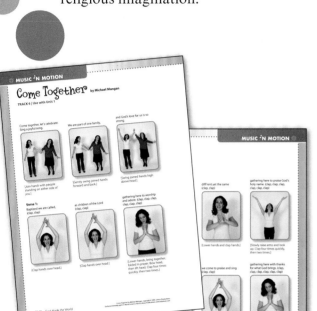

Eighteen engaging songs introduce and reinforce important concepts from *God Made Me* and *God Made the World*.

Fun rhythms and melodies invite the children to sing, dance, and move with their catechist as guide.

Special-occasion songs are provided for Halloween/Feast of All Saints, Thanksgiving, Christmas, Valentine's Day, Easter, Birthdays, and Last Class/Summer.

Research-Based!

"*. . . music in the lives of young children is a highly effective means of delivering vital information . . .*"

MENC: The National Association for Music Education, National Association for the Education of Young Children, and the U.S. Department of Education, and supported by Texaco, Inc. Washington D.C., June 14–16, 2000.

Child's Book and Materials *continued*

Living and experiencing faith at home is key to a child's faith formation.
Family Time provides essential tools to help parents guide their child and
live their faith together as a family.

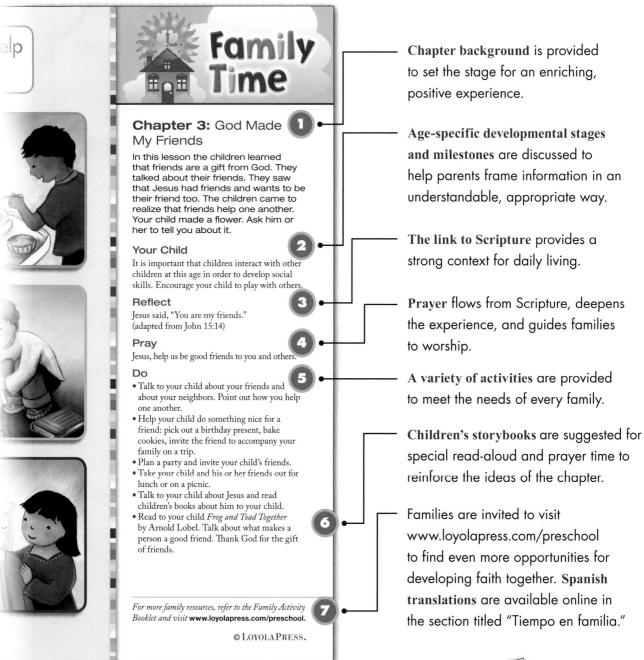

Family Time

Chapter 3: God Made **1**
My Friends

In this lesson the children learned
that friends are a gift from God. They
talked about their friends. They saw
that Jesus had friends and wants to be
their friend too. The children came to
realize that friends help one another.
Your child made a flower. Ask him or
her to tell you about it.

Your Child **2**
It is important that children interact with other
children at this age in order to develop social
skills. Encourage your child to play with others.

Reflect **3**
Jesus said, "You are my friends."
(adapted from John 15:14)

Pray **4**
Jesus, help us be good friends to you and others.

Do **5**
• Talk to your child about your friends and
  about your neighbors. Point out how you help
  one another.
• Help your child do something nice for a
  friend: pick out a birthday present, bake
  cookies, invite the friend to accompany your
  family on a trip.
• Plan a party and invite your child's friends.
• Take your child and his or her friends out for
  lunch or on a picnic.
• Talk to your child about Jesus and read
  children's books about him to your child.
• Read to your child *Frog and Toad Together*
  by Arnold Lobel. Talk about what makes a **6**
  person a good friend. Thank God for the gift
  of friends.

For more family resources, refer to the Family Activity
Booklet and visit **www.loyolapress.com/preschool.** **7**

© LOYOLAPRESS.

Chapter background is provided
to set the stage for an enriching,
positive experience.

Age-specific developmental stages
and milestones are discussed to
help parents frame information in an
understandable, appropriate way.

The link to Scripture provides a
strong context for daily living.

Prayer flows from Scripture, deepens
the experience, and guides families
to worship.

A variety of activities are provided
to meet the needs of every family.

Children's storybooks are suggested for
special read-aloud and prayer time to
reinforce the ideas of the chapter.

Families are invited to visit
www.loyolapress.com/preschool
to find even more opportunities for
developing faith together. **Spanish**
translations are available online in
the section titled "Tiempo en familia."

The **Family Activity Booklet** *is sent home*
at the beginning of the year for additional
support and family-time fun. Family members
can reference the activities, poems, and
songs learned in the preschool program.

God Made the World Catechist Manual

Catechist Manual and Materials

Ample background, support, and clear direction provide success for catechists of every experience level.

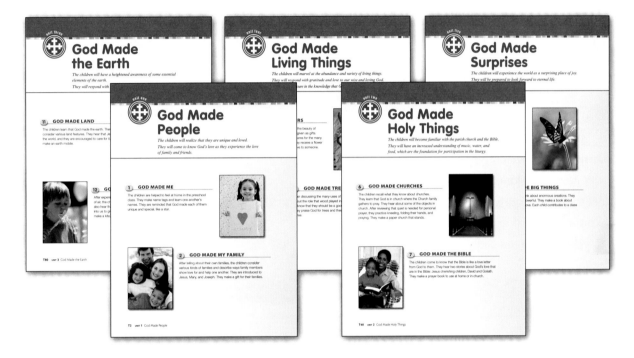

Five Units of Five Chapters Each

The Catechist Manual follows the Child's Book with five units of five chapters each. Each chapter includes the following elements:

- **Catechist preparation** through listening, reflecting, and responding to Scripture

- **Comprehensive lesson plan** that includes references to Scripture and the *Catechism of the Catholic Church*, materials list of program components and classroom supplies, preparation tips, music references, extension ideas to enrich the faith experience, children's storybook suggestions, and snack ideas

- **Alternative scheduling options** offer flexibility

- Clear **learning outcomes** and **child development background** for teaching success

- **Step-by-step lesson plans** that follow an easy three-step model

- **Checkpoints** to assess and gauge learning

- **Enriching the faith experience** with suggestions for additional activities

Teaching as Easy as 1, 2, 3

The three-step teaching method—Centering, Sharing, Acting—provides children with routine and repetition to aid in understanding the content and learning to pray.

Step-by-step directions clearly show the progression of each step in the chapter. These numbered steps guide new and experienced catechists through the chapter.

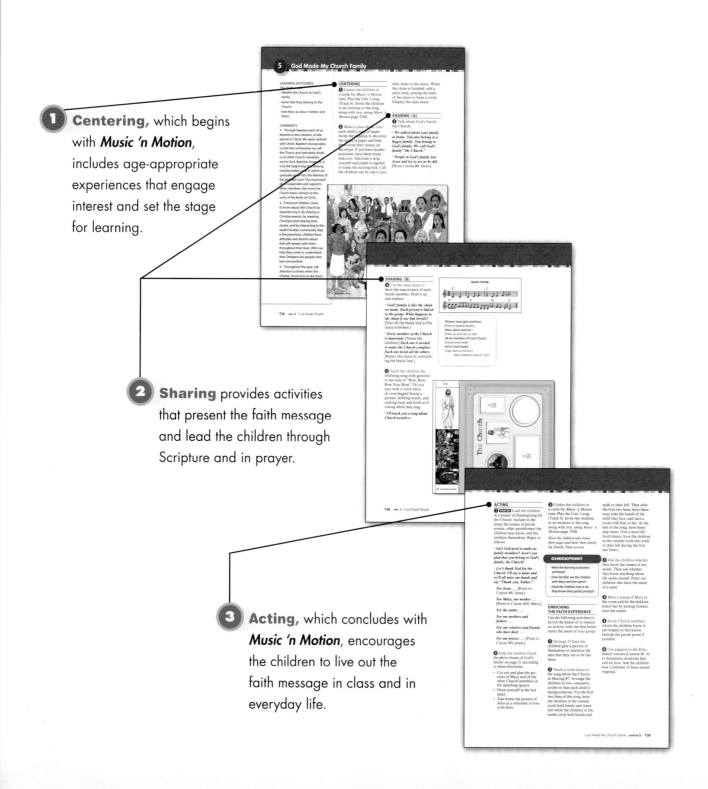

1 Centering, which begins with *Music 'n Motion,* includes age-appropriate experiences that engage interest and set the stage for learning.

2 Sharing provides activities that present the faith message and lead the children through Scripture and in prayer.

3 Acting, which concludes with *Music 'n Motion,* encourages the children to live out the faith message in class and in everyday life.

Even More Ideas and Support

The Catechist Manual provides even more ideas and support for lively and effective catechesis.

Music 'n Motion *Support Materials*

The *Music 'n Motion* CD is supported with the following materials:

- **Professional-development** article by choreographer Nancy Marcheschi, nationally known for her leadership in the area of performing arts as prayer and ministry

- **Movement and motion guide** picturing key movements for songs on the CD

Additional Support

Additional lessons and supplements include the following elements to provide further background for teaching success:

- The **Special Seasons and Days** section provides additional lessons to celebrate important times throughout the year.

- Resources and support for a successful **Parent-Catechist Meeting**

- Comprehensive **Catechist's Handbook** with child development background, ideas for meeting individual needs, teaching methodology, and additional resources

- An **index** of Scripture passages, games, finger plays, poems, and songs

- **Scripture cards** that adapt Scripture to make it comprehensible to young children

- **Cutouts** to make learning interactive

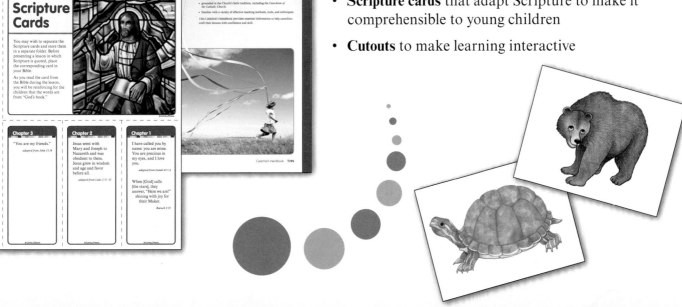

Unit and Chapter Background

The *God Made Everything* series uses a holistic approach to early childhood faith formation. A variety of methods and techniques ensures that the Good News is conveyed in ways suited to different ages, learning styles, and teaching approaches.

Each chapter in *God Made the World* opens and ends with a song and dance or song and finger play from the *Music 'n Motion* CD. Additional music selections are provided for those who wish to include more music in their lessons.

Each unit has five chapters. The chapters are crafted to be taught once a week for approximately 60 minutes. Alternative program schedules are provided for each chapter in the **Preparing the Faith Experience** section. Activities from the **Enriching the Faith Experience** section at the end of the chapter can be used to adapt the chapter to better meet the children's needs.

Because young children need structure and delight in predictability, the weekly chapters have a similar pattern:

* **experiences** leading to a faith message

* presentation of **faith message** and **Scripture** readings

* developmentally appropriate **prayer** experiences to express and internalize the faith message

* **creative activities** to bring faith to life

The format of each chapter is generally the same. The chapter introduces the experiences from which the theme is drawn. Then the faith message is presented and extended or deepened through Scripture, activities, songs, and stories. The children are led in prayer at various times throughout the chapter.

" . . . young children are active learners who need to learn through a variety of hands-on activities."

"Preschool for All: A First-Class Learning Initiative."
California Department of Education, January 2005.

Preparing for the Year

Complete the **Planning Calendar** on pages OV-12 and OV-13 to develop general plans based on your program calendar and the year's activities, liturgical seasons, and feasts.

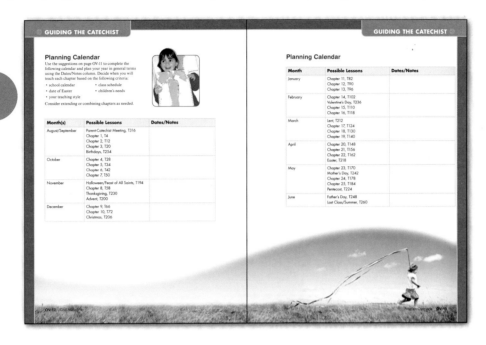

Consider the following recommendations as you plan:

1. Determine a day early in the year to schedule a **Parent-Catechist Meeting** to help parents effectively guide their children in living the Catholic faith. Record the date and planning notes on the Planning Calendar. See pages T316–T319 for meeting outline and planning tips.

2. Read the **Table of Contents** and review the **units** and **chapters** to determine the week during which you will teach each chapter. Determine how to incorporate these into your calendar.

3. Study the chapters for **Special Seasons and Days** on pages T192–T264 of this manual. The special season and feast day chapters can be taught on or near the appropriate date. Special Day chapters are optional. Determine how to integrate these into your calendar.

4. Detach and organize the **Scripture cards** and **cutouts,** placing them in a folder or envelope in order of use.

Suggestions for Pacing

Your class may not meet enough times to cover all the chapters in this program. If so, some chapters can be combined so that you can focus on the most important material.

The following chapters are closely related in content and can be combined if necessary:

- 3 and 4
- 16 and 17
- 22 and 23

Planning Calendar

Use the suggestions on page OV-11 to complete the following calendar and plan your year in general terms using the Dates/Notes column. Decide when you will teach each chapter based on the following criteria:

- school calendar
- date of Easter
- your teaching style
- class schedule
- children's needs

Consider extending or combining chapters as needed.

Month(s)	Possible Lessons	Dates/Notes
August/September	Parent-Catechist Meeting, T316 Chapter 1, T4 Chapter 2, T12 Chapter 3, T20 Birthdays, T254	
October	Chapter 4, T28 Chapter 5, T34 Chapter 6, T42 Chapter 7, T50	
November	Halloween/Feast of All Saints, T194 Chapter 8, T58 Thanksgiving, T230 Advent, T200	
December	Chapter 9, T66 Chapter 10, T72 Christmas, T206	

Planning Calendar

Month	Possible Lessons	Dates/Notes
January	Chapter 11, T82 Chapter 12, T90 Chapter 13, T96	
February	Chapter 14, T102 Valentine's Day, T236 Chapter 15, T110 Chapter 16, T118	
March	Lent, T212 Chapter 17, T124 Chapter 18, T130 Chapter 19, T140	
April	Chapter 20, T148 Chapter 21, T156 Chapter 22, T162 Easter, T218	
May	Chapter 23, T170 Mother's Day, T242 Chapter 24, T178 Chapter 25, T184 Pentecost, T224	
June	Father's Day, T248 Last Class/Summer, T260	

Prepare and Teach

For each chapter, your manual presents material for preparation and personal reflection called **Preparing the Faith Experience.** This section is followed by the lesson plan for the chapter. It is important to consider carefully the lesson plans and ideas before and during teaching.

In Advance

1. Prayerfully read the **Listening** and **Reflecting** sections.

2. Consider the question found in the **Responding** section, perhaps writing your response in a prayer journal. Continue in prayer, using your own words or the suggested prayer.

3. Use the suggested Scripture references and the paragraphs from the *Catechism of the Catholic Church* for further insights or clarification.

4. Read the chapter and study the Child's Book pages.

Before You Teach

1. Read the **Learning Outcomes** and lesson plan, including the **Comments,** which provide important background information on the content to be taught as well as helpful teaching tips.

2. Read **Enriching the Faith Experience** at the end of the chapter. Activities from this section can be substituted for activities found in the chapter or can be used to extend the lesson. Decide which options best meet the needs of the children.

3. Annotate your manual. Make notes that will help the flow of the lesson. Use a highlighter to set off sections you plan to use.

4. Familiarize yourself with the scripted teacher-talk in boldface italics so you can present the lesson in your own words as you teach. Avoid reading from the manual.

5. Gather necessary **Materials** for the chapter and review the preparation notes.

6. Review and gather **Books to Share** to incorporate into your lesson or to read aloud if you have extra time at the end of class. Visit www.loyolapress.com/preschool to find additional ideas for using storybooks in your lessons.

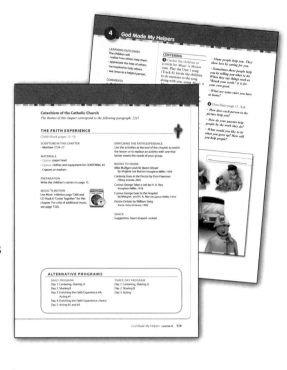

Teaching Tips

1. Follow tips from the **Catechist's Handbook.**

2. Prepare for each class as soon as possible after the previous class. Allow time to shape the lesson and to make it your own.

3. Pray frequently to the Holy Spirit, your partner and guide.

4. Write notes or an outline of your plan on a note card for easy reference.

After You Teach

1. Evaluate your session using the **Checkpoint** at the end of the lesson to assess whether the outcomes of the lesson have been met.

2. Write follow-up comments on the lesson plan in your manual. Record ideas for improvement. Consult helpers, parents, and the children who participated in class to help determine which activities worked well and which could be improved.

3. Consider revisiting ideas and presenting information in a different way if children seemed to lack understanding at the end of the lesson.

the Family Time section.

CHECKPOINT

- *Were the learning outcomes achieved?*
- *How familiar are the children with Mary and the saints?*
- *Have the children met or do they know their parish priest(s)?*

ENRICHING THE FAITH EXPERIENCE

Use the following activities to

God Made the World

Introduction

The *God Made the World* preschool program develops religious awareness in four-year-old children by capitalizing on their natural sensitivity and wonder. It is designed to draw preschoolers to know and love God by focusing on the world God has created. As they study and experience the wonders of creation, the children are filled with awe and come to realize not only the goodness, power, and wisdom of God but also God's love for them. The goal of the program is to shape attitudes in the children that will prepare them to be committed Catholics who comprehend the truths of our faith and live by them. The lessons include a variety of activities geared to the learning styles and abilities of four-year-olds: play, games, sensory experiences, manipulative activities, stories, poems, and songs.

As they participate in the lesson activities, the children come to feel at home in a community, laying the foundation for a deeper life within the Christian community later.

References to Jesus as friend, the Bible, Christian symbols, and the importance of love are woven throughout the program, preparing the children for a more complete comprehension of these things when they are older. The lessons evoke a response of prayer that frequently involves song and ritual.

In **Unit 1** the children begin to explore and ponder God's gifts, starting with themselves, their families, friends, and the wider community of the parish. They come to see themselves as special and loved, and they learn of God's love for them through the love of others.

In **Unit 2** the children are introduced to features that play a role in the spiritual life of Catholics: the parish church; the Bible; hymns; the baptismal symbol of water; and the importance of food, in particular bread, a basic symbol of our great commemorative meal, the Eucharist. The children are invited to pray and learn some of the dynamics of praying.

In **Unit 3** the children have experiences with basic elements of the world: land, air, light, color, and weather. They learn that the universe is filled with gifts waiting to be discovered, and they are helped to feel responsible for the world.

In **Unit 4** the children are led to be amazed at the wonderful variety of creations: flowers, trees, animals, birds, and fish. They praise and thank God who made everything and who cares for them above all other creatures.

In **Unit 5** the children delight in the surprises God put on earth: butterflies, big and little things, people in great diversity, and the capacity for joy and laughter. They are prepared to better comprehend the greatest surprise of all: eternal life.

The **Special Seasons and Days** supplement offers twelve additional lessons with activities to help children learn about and celebrate the seasons and feast days of the Church year, as well as other special days.

God Made People

The children will realize that they are unique and loved.
They will come to know God's love as they experience the love
of family and friends.

 1 GOD MADE ME

The children are helped to feel at home in the preschool class. They make name tags and learn one another's names. They are reminded that God made each of them unique and special, like a star.

2 GOD MADE MY FAMILY

After telling about their own families, the children consider various kinds of families and describe ways family members show love for and help one another. They are introduced to Jesus, Mary, and Joseph. They make a gift for their families.

3 GOD MADE MY FRIENDS

The children learn through a game and a story that friends help one another. They are introduced to Jesus as someone who wants to be their friend. They make a flower to remind them that friends are wonderful and beautiful.

4 GOD MADE MY HELPERS

The children enumerate the many people who help them. They are led to realize that God helps them through others and to understand that rules are made for their own good. They make a thank-you card for someone who helps them.

5 GOD MADE MY CHURCH FAMILY

The children are introduced to their Church family, people who love Jesus and try to live like him. Through the experience of making a paper chain, they learn the importance of each member. They learn about the special roles of priests and Mary and hear about the saints. They make a photo frame of Church members, including themselves.

Chapter 1
God Made Me

FAITH FOCUS

God made us.

Genesis 1:26–31; Psalm 8; Psalm 139:13–14

PREPARING THE FAITH EXPERIENCE

LISTENING

Thus says the LORD,
who created you and formed you:
Fear not, for I have called you by
name: you are mine.
You are precious in my eyes
and glorious, and I love you.

Adapted from Isaiah 43:1,4

REFLECTING

God, in great wisdom and love, called us into life, making us images of our Creator. Each person has dignity and deserves to be reverenced and cherished. Like God, we can think and love. God is a personal God who not only loves us but also invites us to love in return. With the psalmist who knew well the fundamental truth that each of us is made by God, we sing:

You formed my inmost being;
you knit me in my mother's womb.
I praise you, so wonderfully you made me;
wonderful are your works!

Psalm 139:13–14

Our faith assures us that our origin was beautiful and our destiny magnificent. We believe and trust God, who for all eternity lives in unapproachable light. According to God's plan, we will spend eternity caught up in the joyful vision of God's light and love. In humble wonder we recognize God's goodness to us:

What are humans that you are mindful of them,
mere mortals that you care for them?
Yet you have made them little less than a god,
crowned them with glory and honor.

Psalm 8:5–6

Although we are made to praise and serve God, we have the freedom to believe in God and to love him. We have the ability and the responsibility to express God's loving, forgiving care for each person. We are free to decide to develop the gifts and abilities God has given us. We can choose to use them to serve others. When we are the best persons we can be, then we are praising and thanking God, our Creator. As Saint Irenaeus expressed it, the person fully alive is the glory of God.

At the Eucharist we come to the Father as the human family. With grateful hearts, in the name of every creature on earth, we praise and thank God. We celebrate at this sacred meal the mystery of Christ that renewed our friendship with God after we had shattered it. There we are inspired and empowered to work for the betterment of a world in which many are deprived of their human rights. There we find the grace to use our gifts to try to lead all people to God's kingdom.

RESPONDING

Having reflected upon God's Word, take some time now to continue to respond to God in prayer. You might wish to use a journal to record your responses throughout this year.

- In what ways do I treat each of the children as a precious child of God?

  God, make your image apparent in me and in those in my care.

Catechism of the Catholic Church

The themes of this chapter correspond to the following paragraphs: 355, 362.

THE FAITH EXPERIENCE

Child's Book pages 1–4

SCRIPTURE IN THIS CHAPTER

• *Isaiah 43:1,4*

• *Baruch 3:35*

MATERIALS

• Chapter 1 Scripture card
• Bible
• Option: Cutout #66, star, (or a picture of stars)
• Crayons or markers
• Glitter
• Glue
• 24-inch pieces of yarn or ribbon, one for each child
• Hole punch
• Scissors
• Large ball (or a beanbag)
• Flashlight
• Stamp pad and star stamp (or star stickers)

PREPARATION

• Write the children's names on page 1. If you wish, precut the stars.
• Write the children's names on page 3.
• Separate the Scripture cards at the back of this manual and put them in a folder for future use during the year
• Place the Chapter 1 Scripture card for SHARING #2 and #4 in the Bible.

MUSIC 'N MOTION

Use *Music 'n Motion* page T268 and CD Track 6 "Come Together" for this chapter. For a list of additional music, see page T320.

ENRICHING THE FAITH EXPERIENCE

Use the activities at the end of the chapter to enrich the lesson or to replace an activity with one that better meets the needs of your group.

BOOKS TO SHARE

The Day of Ahmed's Secret by Florence Parry Heide and Judith Heide Gilliland (HarperTrophy, 1995)

Leo the Late Bloomer by Robert Kraus (HarperTrophy, 1994)

Me I Am! by Jack Prelutsky (Farrar, Straus & Giroux, 2007)

William's Doll by Charlotte Zolotow (HarperTrophy, 1985)

SNACK

Suggestion: star-shaped cookies

ALTERNATIVE PROGRAMS

DAILY PROGRAM

Day 1: Centering, Sharing A
Day 2: Sharing B
Day 3: Acting #1 and #2
Day 4: Enriching the Faith Experience choice
Day 5: Enriching the Faith Experience #2 or
　　　 #3, Acting #3–5

THREE-DAY PROGRAM

Day 1: Centering, Sharing A
Day 2: Sharing B
Day 3: Acting

LEARNING OUTCOMES

The children will
- know that God made all people.
- be grateful that God made them.
- grow in self-esteem.
- respect all people.

COMMENTS

1. Our attitudes toward God and toward other people are greatly influenced by our self-concepts. Children who are helped to form healthy self-concepts at an early age are better able to relate to others and to develop their own potential. In God's eye, every human being is of value and a unique creation worthy of being saved by Jesus and of having eternal life. One task of a catechist is to instill in the children a sense of self-worth. Another is to teach them to value all other people.

2. The children readily and enthusiastically praise and thank God. Build on their natural inclination to pray by using opportunities that arise during class to pray spontaneously. For example, if a child tells about something wonderful, invite the class to join in thanking God for it. Prayers of praise and thanks are most suited to preschool children's developmental stages, while a more complete understanding of prayers of petition and contrition develops later.

3. Children will grasp that the Bible is a sacred book by the reverent way you handle it. By reading from the Bible whenever a Scripture passage is used in the lesson, you will reinforce that God speaks to the children through this book. Most of the Scripture passages have been adapted for young children. The Scripture cards at the back of this manual are a resource for including the Bible in the lessons.

1 God Made the World

Page 2 is blank.

CENTERING

1 Welcome the children as they arrive. Gather them in a circle for *Music 'n Motion* time. Play the Unit 1 song (Track 6). Invite the children to do motions to the song along with you, using *Music 'n Motion* page T268.

2 Direct the children to the table on which you have placed supplies for making the name tags from page 1. Help the children do the following:

- Decorate the star, using crayons or markers.
- Place glue on the star and sprinkle on glitter.
- Cut out the star.
- Punch a hole in the star and string yarn through it.
- Knot the ends of the yarn together.
- Put on the star name tag.

3 Ask the children to gather around you. Introduce the preschool program.

• *You are here to learn about yourself, the world, and God, who made everything. You are also here to have fun. So that everyone enjoys our time together, let's keep this rule: Be kind. How can you be kind to the other children here?* (Listen when they speak. Say or do nothing to hurt them. Help them. Share toys and supplies.)

• *Today we will talk about a very special person. If you look at your star, you will see the name of this person. Who is it?*

SHARING [A]

1 Tell the children that God created them.

• *Each one of you is special because you belong to God. God made you. You are God's child.*

• *Sometimes things are marked "Made by George Flores" or "Made by the Brown Company." If you were marked, what would the tag say?* (Made by God)

• *God loves you very much.*

2 **SCRIPTURE** Read about God's love (adapted from Isaiah 43:1,4) from the Scripture card in the Bible.

• *God has a message for you in this great book, God's book. Listen. God says,*

> *"I have called you by name: you are mine. You are precious in my eyes, and I love you."*

• *God tells you that you are precious. God knows your name. We like it when someone knows and uses our name. Let's learn one another's names.*

3 Play the "Name Game." Invite the children to sit in a circle. Say "My name is [name]" and roll a ball on the floor to a child. That child says his or her name and rolls the ball to someone else, who does the same. After a while, as the ball is rolled, have everyone say the name of the child to whom the ball has been rolled. (If you wish, have the children toss a beanbag instead of rolling a ball.)

SHARING [B]

4 **SCRIPTURE** Talk about shining for God like a star. [Option: Show Cutout #66, star, or a picture of stars.] Read about God calling the stars (Baruch 3:35) from the Scripture card in the Bible.

• *God made us, and God made the stars. God's book says,*

> *"When* [God] *calls* [the stars]*, they answer, 'Here we are!' shining with joy for their Maker."*

• *You can shine for God too. You shine for God when you do the best you can.*

5 Have the children show what they can do. As each child performs, shine a flashlight on him or her.

• *God made you so you can do many wonderful things. You can make beautiful things such as your name tag. Who can clap? Who can hop on one foot?* [Let children demonstrate one at a time.] *Who can turn a somersault? Who can clap?* [Let children demonstrate one at a time.] *What else can you do?*

6 **PRAYER** Lead the children to express thanks to God.

• *God knew we would enjoy doing these things. Isn't God good for making us so we can do them? Let's thank God for making us so wonderful. Let's say*

"Thank you, God, for making me wonderful." [Children repeat.]

7 Distribute page 3 and point out that every person is special.

• *Look at the children in the picture. Are any of them exactly the same?* (No.) *Each person is special. God made and loves each one of them.*

• *Look at the stars you made. Each one is different. You are special too. No one looks just like you. No one can do exactly what you can do.*

ACTING

1 Tell the story of Saint Thérèse and the stars.

• *I'll tell you a story about a little girl who knew that God loved her. She knew that she was special. Her name was Thérèse.*

Saint Thérèse and the Stars

One night Thérèse went for a walk with her father. The sky was full of stars. All of a sudden Thérèse cried out, "Look, Father. There's a *T* for my name in the sky." Sure enough, some of the stars were in the shape of a *T*, which was the first letter of Thérèse's name.

Thérèse always tried to shine for God. She lived a good life, and now she is with God in heaven.

2 Invite the children to draw stars in the sky on page 4. They may use a crayon or put dots of glue on the page and sprinkle on glitter. Invite the children to write the first letter of their name. They may refer to their name tags.

Name_____

3 God Made the World

3 **PRAYER** Lead a celebration giving praise to God. Use a stamp or stickers to put a star on each child. Explain:

• *God is good to make us so wonderful. Let's praise God for making us. When I call one of you to come to me, we'll all pray "Praise you, God, for . . ." and say your name. I will put a star on your hand because you are special.*

4 Collect the name tags so they can be used in the next few classes.

5 Gather the children in a circle for *Music 'n Motion* time. Play the Unit 1 song (Track 6). Invite the children to do motions to the song along with you, using *Music 'n Motion* page T268.

Have the children take home their pages and show their family the Family Time section.

CHECKPOINT

• *Were the learning outcomes achieved?*

• *Were the children comfortable in the class?*

• *Which children seem to need special attention and care?*

• *Did the children seem to be familiar with God and prayer?*

Put stars in the sky. Make the first letter of your name.

4 God Made the World

© LOYOLAPRESS.

Family Time

Chapter 1: God Made Me

In this lesson the children learned that God made them and that they are precious in God's sight. They heard that they are special and can do wonderful things. Your child made a star-shaped name tag because we are like stars shining for God when we try to do our best.

Your Child
Children's self-concepts are formed primarily in the home. Ask your child to tell how he or she is special and to demonstrate one of his or her own gifts. Praise your child frequently.

Reflect
I have called you by name: you are mine. You are precious in my eyes, and I love you. (adapted from Isaiah 43:1,4)

Pray
God, help us always remember that we are your precious children.

Do
• Tell your child why he or she is special to you.
• Think of a particular talent your child has and then plan how to develop it.
• Take your child outside to look at the stars. You may have to go to an unlighted spot in order to see them well.
• Pray with your child, thanking God for your child's special gifts as well as for his or her eyes, ears, nose, arms, and legs.
• Read to your child *Me I Am!* by Jack Prelutsky. Help your child identify traits and gifts that make him or her special and unique. Praise God for making each of us special.

For more family resources, refer to the Family Activity Booklet and visit **www.loyolapress.com/preschool.**

ENRICHING THE FAITH EXPERIENCE

Use the following activities to enrich the lesson or to replace an activity with one that better meets the needs of your group.

1 Cut an apple in half horizontally and show the children the star shape in the middle of the apple. Suggest that whenever they eat an apple, they think about how they can "shine" for God like a star. Provide apple slices for a snack after this activity.

2 Teach the children the following songs (with motions), the first sung to the tune of "Twinkle, Twinkle, Little Star" and the second to the tune of "I'm a Little Teapot."

You may wish to let the children take turns demonstrating their ability to run, skip, sing, or whistle after they have sung "I'm a Child of God."

Twinkle, Twinkle, Little Star

Twinkle, twinkle, little star,
[Open and close fists raised high.]
God has made us what we are.
Though a million stars I see,
[Sweep arm from left to right.]
You are special just like me.
[Point thumb at self.]
Twinkle, twinkle, little star,
[Open and close fists raised high.]
God has made us what we are.
    Mary Kathleen Glavich, S.N.D.

I'm a Child of God

I'm a child of God from head to toe.
[Gesture from head to toe.]
God made me special. This I do know.
[Put thumbs in shoulders.]
If you want to see what makes me so.
[Point to audience.]
Just watch: My special gift I will show.
[Move arms to the side with both hands open.]
    Mary Kathleen Glavich, S.N.D.

3 Teach this poem with the motions given. You might sing it to the tune of "Hark the Herald Angels Sing."

> I have two eyes that wink and blink, [Wink.]
> I have a mind to make me think, [Point to head.]
> I have two hands that clap for fun, [Clap.]
> I have two feet that jump and run,
> [Jump and run in place.]
> I have two ears to hear a song,
> [Cup ears with hands.]
> Two lips to praise God all day long,
> [Point to lips.]
> I have a body strong and good,
> [Put hands out at sides.]
> To use for Jesus as I should.

4 Take pictures of the children on the first day of class. Make a poster from the pictures or put them on a bulletin board.

5 Use Cutout #3, Patty (or a doll), to lead the children to consider the gifts of their bodies. Point to her eyes, ears, mouth, nose, arms, hands, legs, and heart and have the children tell what Patty and they can do with these parts.

6 Give each child a large sheet of shelf paper. Have the children lie on the paper while you or an aide traces them. Then help the children draw their faces and clothes and color the picture. You might provide a large mirror for the children.

7 Invite the children to dance to music. Make comments about how each child's dance is different.

8 Using finger paint, have the children make handprints on construction paper. Make sure to write the children's names on the papers.

Chapter 2
God Made My Family

FAITH FOCUS

God's plan is for family members to live and grow together in love. Genesis 1:27–28; Ephesians 6:1–3

PREPARING THE FAITH EXPERIENCE

LISTENING

He [Jesus] went down with them [Mary and Joseph] and came to Nazareth, and was obedient to them; and his mother kept all these things in her heart. And Jesus advanced [in] wisdom and age and favor before God and man.

Luke 2:51–52

REFLECTING

Robert Frost wrote "Home is the place where, when you have to go there, / They have to take you in." (from "The Death of the Hired Man") God planned for us to grow and learn within a circle of people who accept us and who have bonded with us in a special way—our family. Ideally parents nurture, protect, and teach children how to live. Parents not only train their children how to walk, talk, and eat, but also share their values and principles with them. Parents are the primary educators of their children. Most important, they pass on to their children the Catholic faith.

Belief in God, Father, Son, and Holy Spirit, begins in the home. There children first learn the prayers, truths, traditions, and customs of the Catholic faith. The family is called the domestic church. Like the Church, it is meant to reflect the love and unity that bind together the members of the Trinity.

Through family relationships children should come to understand that God loves and cares for them. Not without reason did Jesus tell us to call God "Abba," or "Father." Like a father, God is our source of life, the one upon whom we depend. Like a loving father, God protects us, provides for us, and forgives us.

Calling God "Father" implies that we are all brothers and sisters. The mutual care and concern that family members have for one another are meant to be extended to all our brothers and sisters in Christ.

Jesus in his life on earth served as a model for us. Although God might have used other means for saving the human race, he chose to become a member of a family. He knew the give-and-take involved in living under the same roof and in sharing meals. He and his family experienced together joys, sorrows, and hardships. He learned from Mary and Joseph and served them; he also was served by them.

Scripture says, "Children, obey your parents in everything, for this is pleasing to the Lord." (Colossians 3:20) Children are to honor their parents and obey them. All members of the family should demonstrate selfless love. When children love and are loved in a family, they are better prepared to live the Christian life in which we are exhorted to "love one another with mutual affection; anticipate one another in showing honor." (Romans 12:10)

RESPONDING

God's Word calls us to respond in love. Respond to God now in the quiet of your heart, and perhaps through a journal that you are keeping this year.

- Are there family situations that call for my awareness and sensitivity?

  Our Father, bless the families of the children and make them holy.

Catechism of the Catholic Church

The themes of this chapter correspond to the following paragraphs: 360–361, 437.

THE FAITH EXPERIENCE

Child's Book pages 5–10

SCRIPTURE IN THIS CHAPTER

• *Luke 2:51–52*

MATERIALS

• Cutouts: #1, father; #2, mother; #3, Patty; #4, Joe (the Riley family)
• Name tags from the previous chapter
• Option: family photograph, perhaps one of your own family
• Option: clothes and equipment for playing house
• Crayons
• Tempera paint
• Pieces of sponge
• Clip clothespins

PREPARATION

• Write the children's names on page 5.
• Place the Chapter 2 Scripture card for SHARING #6 in the Bible.
• Cover the area for painting with newspapers.

MUSIC 'N MOTION

Use *Music 'n Motion* page T268 and CD Track 6 "Come Together" for this chapter. For a list of additional music, see page T320.

ENRICHING THE FAITH EXPERIENCE

Use the activities at the end of the chapter to enrich the lesson or to replace an activity with one that better meets the needs of your group.

BOOKS TO SHARE

All Kinds of Families by Norma Simon
    (Albert Whitman & Co., 1976)

Nobody Asked Me If I Wanted a Baby Sister by Martha Alexander (Charlesbridge Publishing, 2005)

The Patchwork Quilt by Valerie Flournoy (Dial, 1985)

My Grandpa and I by P.K. Hallinan
    (Candy Cane Press, 2002)

On Mother's Lap by Ann Herbert Scott
    (Clarion Books, 1992)

Love Is a Family by Roma Downey
    (HarperEntertainment, 2001)

Tell Me Again About the Night I Was Born by Jamie Lee Curtis (HarperTrophy, 2000)

I Love You Like Crazy Cakes by Rose A. Lewis
    (Little, Brown Young Readers, 2000)

SNACK

Suggestion: cheesy crackers

ALTERNATIVE PROGRAMS

DAILY PROGRAM

Day 1: Centering, Sharing A
Day 2: Sharing B
Day 3: Acting #1
Day 4: Enriching the Faith Experience choice
Day 5: Acting #2 and #3

THREE-DAY PROGRAM

Day 1: Centering, Sharing A
Day 2: Sharing B
Day 3: Acting

LEARNING OUTCOMES

The children will

- understand how family members love and help one another.
- know that Jesus, Mary, and Joseph are the Holy Family.
- appreciate what individual family members do for them.
- desire to show love and concern for their family members.

COMMENTS

1. Ordinarily God's love is communicated to children through their parents and other family members. Reflecting on their families enhances children's sense of identity as individuals and as part of a family. It prepares them for taking their place in the wider family of the Christian community.

2. Children usually enjoy talking about their homes and families, the only world many children have known before beginning preschool. So that children who come from nontraditional families are not made to feel uncomfortable, be especially sensitive to their needs during the discussion. Remember too that some children are looking for someone to accept them and to show them affection.

CENTERING

1 As the children enter the room, help them find their name tags. Gather the children in a circle for *Music 'n Motion* time. Play the Unit 1 song (Track 6). Invite the children to do motions to the song along with you, using *Music 'n Motion* page T268.

2 Have the children play house in small groups, choosing their own roles.

SHARING [A]

1 Let the children tell about their families. [Option: Show a family photo and tell about it.] Ask:

- *God gave each of us a family. Who are the people in your family?*

- *What are some things that you do together with your family at home?*

- *Who cooks the meals?*

- *Where do you go together?*

- *Isn't God good to give us people to live with?*

2 Introduce the Riley family. (Cutouts: #1, father;

Name_____

5 God Made the World

#2, mother; #3, Patty; #4, Joe)

• *This is the Riley family. The members of the family love one another. They care for one another. Each member does many things to help the family.*

3 Suggest or have the children suggest what each member of the Riley family does to help the family. Have the children stand and pantomime the actions. Examples:

- Mr. Riley: drives the family to church, cooks, washes clothes
- Mrs. Riley: irons clothes, cuts the grass
- Patty: dusts the furniture, folds the clothes
- Joe: sets the table, feeds the dog

4 Ask the children what they do to show love for their family members.

SHARING [B]

5 Distribute page 5 and talk about the picture.

• *What families do you see in the picture?* (Human beings, birds, rabbits, squirrels, butterflies, ducks, fish)

• *The little squirrel belongs to the squirrel family. The fish belongs to the fish family. The children in the picture belong to a human family. You belong to a family too.*

6 **SCRIPTURE** Have the children look at page 6. Discuss the Holy Family. Read about Jesus and his family (adapted from Luke 2:51–52) from the Scripture card in the Bible.

• *Does anyone know the family in the picture?* (The Holy Family: Jesus, Mary, and Joseph)

• *Jesus was a great man who loved us and showed us how to live. Jesus belonged to a family as you do. His mother was Mary, and the father in his family was Joseph. They all loved one another very much.*

• *What do you think Jesus did to show Mary and Joseph that he loved them?* (He helped them, obeyed them, and gave them gifts.)

• *Listen to what the Bible tells us about Jesus and his family:*

> *"Jesus was obedient to Mary and Joseph. Jesus grew in wisdom and age and favor before all."*

7 **PRAYER** Use each child's name to pray a litany of thanks for families. ("For [name]'s family . . . ") Have the children respond "We thank you, God."

8 Direct the children to finish drawing the bouquet on page 6.

Draw flowers in Jesus' hand.

6 God Made the World

Family Time

Chapter 2: God Made My Family

In this lesson the children learned that God gave them families. Families are people who live together and love one another. Families vary—some are large, some small; some have just one parent; some include grandparents. Family members try to help one another. Your child made a picture as a gift for your family. Display it in a prominent place. Ask your child to tell who the people are in the picture on this page.

Your Child
Children need to know about their family background. Tell your child stories about yourself and other relatives, including grandparents, aunts, and uncles.

Reflect
Jesus went with Mary and Joseph to Nazareth and was obedient to them. Jesus grew in wisdom and age and favor before all.
(adapted from Luke 2:51–52)

Pray
Loving God, help our family grow in love and holiness.

Do
- Talk with your child about the ways each member of your family helps the others. Point out how your child contributes to the family.
- Visit or call family members.
- Go through a family album with your child or, if you don't have one, start one.
- Plan a family night once a week.
- Develop in your child the habit of praying for family members each night before going to bed.
- Read to your child *All Kinds of Families* by Norma Simon. Talk about the people who are part of your family. Together ask God to bless each person in your family.

For more family resources, refer to the Family Activity Booklet and visit www.loyolapress.com/preschool.

© LOYOLAPRESS.

ACTING

1 Distribute page 7, "A Kitten's Tale," and have the children fold it in half to make a book. To review how family members help one another, read the book while the children follow the pictures. Then discuss the poem:

• *What did Mrs. Cat do for her family in the story?* (She hung a picture, comforted Kitty, helped look for the mitten, and knit a mitten.)

• *What did Mr. Cat do for the family?* (He cooked and helped look for the mitten.)

• *What did Tom do?* (He went out and looked for the mitten.)

• *In a family everyone cares for everyone else. Kitty's family tried to help her. They tried to make her feel better.*

• *What did Kitty do for someone in her family?* (She thanked her mother and gave her a hug.) *How do you think her mother felt?* (Happy)

A Kitten's Tale

So a mitten for her kitten Mother sat and knit. When Kitty tried it on she found it was a PURRfect fit. "Oh, thank you, Mom," she said at once, giving her a hug.

Then ready for a catnap, Kitty curled up on the rug.

Kitty Cat and brother Tom came home one day from school.

Mr. Cat was cooking. Mom was working with a tool.

"Oh, no!" meowed poor Kitty Cat. "It seems I've lost a mitten."

Her whiskers twitched. Her eyes filled up. She cried. Poor, little kitten.

4

1

7 God Made the World

Name_____

2 Distribute page 9 and have the children make a gift for their family. Invite them to make a picture or design, using a sponge held with a clip clothespin and dipped in tempera paint. Write the child's name below the picture, unless the child can do it. As an alternative for decorating page 9, have the children glue pieces of fabric or torn tissue paper to it.

3 Gather the children in a circle for *Music 'n Motion* time. Play the Unit 1 song (Track 6). Invite the children to do motions to the song along with you, using *Music 'n Motion* page T268.

Have the children take home the pages and show their family the Family Time section.

"Don't cry, my dear," said Kitty's mom. "It's no catastrophe."

Tom purred, "Don't worry. I'll go back and see where it can be."

Mom gave Kitty catnip, and Dad made her some tea.

He said, "We'll find your mitten. Just you wait and see."

Through some catalogs they looked. One mitten no one sold.

They looked all through the rag bag and found one that was too old.

Tom came back with empty paws; no mitten could he find.

"I'll knit a mitten," Mother said, "and make it the same kind."

2

3

© LOYOLAPRESS.

ENRICHING THE FAITH EXPERIENCE

Use the following activities to enrich the lesson or to replace an activity with one that better meets the needs of your group.

1 Have the children draw pictures of their families on drawing paper. Put the pictures back to back in plastic zipper bags in which you have punched three holes in the side. Put the bags in a three-ring binder to make an album of the children's families.

2 Help the children make coupons that say "This coupon entitles you to one hug from me." Invite the children to give their coupons to family members.

9 God Made the World

By

Page 10 is blank.

3 Introduce the Hand family: Thumbkin, Pointer, Tall One, Ringer, and Pinky. Point out that each finger does something different. Together the fingers do many things. Teach the children the following words to the tune of "Frère Jacques," substituting each finger's name for successive verses.

Where Is Thumbkin?

Where is Thumbkin?
Where is Thumbkin?
Here I am. Here I am.
[Hold up one thumb at a time.]
How are you this morning?
[Bend one thumb to the other.]
Very well, I thank you.
[Bend the other thumb to the first.]
Run and hide. Run and hide.
[Put hands behind back one at a time.]

4 Play "The Farmer in the Dell." The children hold hands and form a circle. Choose a child to stand in the middle as the farmer. The children walk around in a circle as they sing. The farmer chooses a wife, who joins him in the middle. The wife chooses a child, and the game continues according to the words of the song. After the cheese is chosen, one person after another returns to the circle as the respective verse is sung until only the cheese is left.

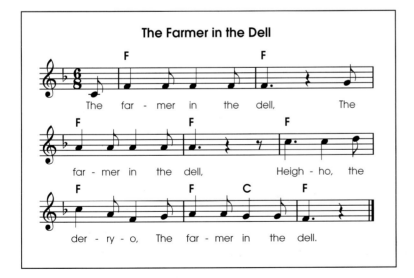

The Farmer in the Dell

The farmer takes a wife.
The farmer takes a wife.
Heigh-ho the derry-o,
The farmer takes a wife.

The wife takes a child . . .
The child takes a nurse . . .
The nurse takes a dog . . .
The dog takes a cat . . .
The cat takes a rat . . .
The rat takes the cheese . . .

The farmer goes home . . .
The wife goes home . . .
The child goes home . . .
The nurse goes home . . .
The dog goes home . . .
The cat goes home . . .
The rat goes home . . .
The cheese stands alone . . .

FAITH FOCUS

God, who gave us friends, is our best friend.

John 11:1–5; John 15:10–16; 1 Corinthians 13:1–7

PREPARING THE FAITH EXPERIENCE

LISTENING

No one has greater love than this, to lay down one's life for one's friends. You are my friends if you do what I command you. I no longer call you slaves, because a slave does not know what his master is doing. I have called you friends, because I have told you everything I have heard from my Father. It was not you who chose me, but I who chose you and appointed you to go and bear fruit that will remain, so that whatever you ask the Father in my name he may give you.

John 15:13–16

REFLECTING

One of the greatest joys of being human is having friends. Throughout life we encounter kindred souls who share our values, ideals, and interests. With some of these people, we develop a special relationship in which we support each other. Scripture says,

*A faithful friend is a sturdy shelter;
he who finds one finds a treasure.*

Sirach 6:14

True friends are one with us in times of joy and sorrow. They listen, sympathize, encourage, and challenge us. We do the same for them. God planned that we help one another in this way.

Jesus too, when he lived on earth, enjoyed special relationships. Out of his 12 chosen companions, he singled out Peter, James, and John for the privilege of being with him during crucial times—at the raising of Jairus's daughter from the dead, at the Transfiguration, and during his agony in the garden. Periodically Jesus sought rest and refreshment at the home of Lazarus and his two sisters, Martha and

Mary. He loved this family and enjoyed their company.

Jesus is our friend no matter what. A friend has been defined as someone who knows all your faults but likes you anyway. No one knows us better than Jesus. He wants to share our lives with us—our failures, hardships, and worries as well as our successes. He wants us to spend time with him. As with any friend, Jesus expects us to turn to him for help, understanding, and comfort. Even when we disappoint and fail him, he is always willing to forgive us and build our relationship anew.

We strengthen our bonds with Jesus through prayer and the sacraments—especially the Eucharist, in which we celebrate Jesus' greatest gift, the sacrifice of his life for us. In the sacraments we meet Jesus and get to know him better. He shares his very life with us, and we become what we were made to be—more worthy of sharing divinity for all eternity with him in heaven.

RESPONDING

Having been nourished by God's Word, we are able to respond to God's great love for us. In prayer, respond to God's call to you to share his Word with others. You may also wish to respond in your prayer journal.

- What friendships has God given me for the enrichment of my life?

Jesus, help the children be good friends to you and to others.

Catechism of the Catholic Church

The themes of this chapter correspond to the following paragraph: 396.

THE FAITH EXPERIENCE

Child's Book pages 11–14

SCRIPTURE IN THIS CHAPTER

• *John 15:14*

MATERIALS

• Children's name tags
• Beanbag
• Option: card from a friend
• Cutouts: #5, buttercup; #6, bee; #7, beehive; #8, Jesus
• Crayons or markers
• Scissors
• Glue

PREPARATION

• Write the children's names on page 11.
• If you wish, use a paper cutter to cut off the stems on page 13 for the children.

MUSIC 'N MOTION

Use *Music 'n Motion* page T268 and CD Track 6 "Come Together" for this chapter. For a list of additional music, see page T320.

ENRICHING THE FAITH EXPERIENCE

Use the activities at the end of the chapter to enrich the lesson or to replace an activity with one that better meets the needs of your group.

BOOKS TO SHARE

We Are Best Friends by Aliki (HarperTrophy, 1987)

A Friend Is Someone Who Likes You by Joan Walsh Anglund (Harcourt Children's Books, 1983)

Will I Have a Friend? by Miriam Cohen (Aladdin, 1989)

Best Friends by Steven Kellogg (Dial, 1986)

Frog and Toad Together by Arnold Lobel (HarperFestival, 1999)

George and Martha: The Complete Stories of Two Best Friends by James Marshall (Houghton Mifflin, 1997)

SNACK

Suggestion: graham crackers

ALTERNATIVE PROGRAMS

DAILY PROGRAM

Day 1: Centering, Sharing A
Day 2: Sharing B
Day 3: Acting #1, Enriching the Faith Experience #1
Day 4: Enriching the Faith Experience choice
Day 5: Acting #2 and #3

THREE-DAY PROGRAM

Day 1: Centering, Sharing A
Day 2: Sharing B
Day 3: Acting

LEARNING OUTCOMES

The children will
• know what a friend is.
• be grateful for their friends.
• consider Jesus a friend.
• try to be a good friend to others.

COMMENTS

1. Four-year-old children, who are emerging from an egocentric stage, are beginning to relate to others. They are ready to develop certain social skills and to learn how to be a friend. Praise the children for actions that spring from love for a friend. Show them that you are their friend.

2. Jesus as a friend is a concept that is understandable and appealing to children, as well as to adults. It is consoling to know that when no one else seems to care about us, Jesus cares. When we seem to be all alone, Jesus is with us. When no one else has the power to help us, Jesus can help. As time passes, the children should become aware of God as their friend above all others.

CENTERING

❶ Gather the children in a circle for *Music 'n Motion* time. Play the Unit 1 song (Track 6). Invite the children to do motions to the song along with you, using *Music 'n Motion* page T268.

❷ Have the children put on their name tags and play or talk with a friend.

❸ Play "Find the Beanbag." Explain the game:

• *Today some of you will have a chance to find a beanbag. Because we are all friends, we will help the child who is looking for a beanbag by clapping.*

Whenever he or she gets close to the hiding place, we will clap louder. [Choose a child to leave the room while you hide a beanbag. Repeat the game several times.]

❹ Discuss the game.

• *We helped children find the beanbags, and we were happy when they found them. We are friends. What is a friend?* (Someone who likes you, helps you, cares about you, plays with you) [Option: Show the card from a friend.]

• *Friends are a gift from God. God is so good to give us friends.*

Name _____

⓫ God Made the World

The Two Yellow Friends

Once upon a time there was a yellow bee named Dizzy. Every day when it wasn't raining, Dizzy flew through the woods and fields, looking for flowers. Bees need flowers in order to make honey, and some flowers need bees in order to make seeds. One day Dizzy flew and flew, but he didn't see many blossoms. Dizzy was worried. If he couldn't find enough flowers, the bees wouldn't be able to make honey.

Suddenly as he flew up over a hill, he saw a big field full of yellow flowers. He was so excited that he buzzed around and around before swooping down to talk to a beautiful flower near the edge of the field.

"Hello," he said. "I am a bee, and my name is Dizzy."

"I can see that you are," said the flower, "both a bee and dizzy. My name is Buttercup."

As the wind blew Buttercup back and forth, she said, "I like living here with my flower friends and dancing in the breeze, but it must be wonderful to be able to fly around and see the world."

"Yes, it is," said Dizzy, and he told his new friend wonderful stories about things he had seen. He told her too about his hive and all of his bee friends. "I am going home now," he said, "to tell the other bees where to find this field of flowers. But I promise I'll be back."

Before long Dizzy returned with the other bees, who began to gather sweet nectar from the flowers to take back to the hive to make honey. "There sure is a lot of buzzing and talking in this field," said Buttercup to Dizzy.

"That's because we're so happy," Dizzy said. "Thanks for helping us."

"My pleasure. That's what friends are for," said Buttercup.

SHARING [A]

1 Tell the story "The Two Yellow Friends," using Cutouts #5–7.

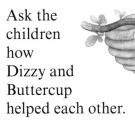

Ask the children how Dizzy and Buttercup helped each other.

2 Distribute page 11 and invite the children to tell how friends are helping each other in the picture.

3 Have the children draw lines on page 12 to match how a child can be a friend to others. Ask:

• *How can you be a good friend to the children in this class?*

Draw a line from the person who needs help to a friend who is helping.

12 God Made the World

© LOYOLA PRESS.

Family Time

Chapter 3: God Made My Friends

In this lesson the children learned that friends are a gift from God. They talked about their friends. They saw that Jesus had friends and wants to be their friend too. The children came to realize that friends help one another. Your child made a flower. Ask him or her to tell you about it.

Your Child
It is important that children interact with other children at this age in order to develop social skills. Encourage your child to play with others.

Reflect
Jesus said, "You are my friends."
(adapted from John 15:14)

Pray
Jesus, help us be good friends to you and others.

Do
• Talk to your child about your friends and about your neighbors. Point out how you help one another.
• Help your child do something nice for a friend: pick out a birthday present, bake cookies, invite the friend to accompany your family on a trip.
• Plan a party and invite your child's friends.
• Take your child and his or her friends out for lunch or on a picnic.
• Talk to your child about Jesus and read children's books about him to your child.
• Read to your child *Frog and Toad Together* by Arnold Lobel. Talk about what makes a person a good friend. Thank God for the gift of friends.

For more family resources, refer to the Family Activity Booklet and visit **www.loyolapress.com/preschool.**

SHARING [B]

4 Talk about Jesus' friends. [Show Cutout #8, Jesus.]

• Jesus had friends too. He had 12 good friends who followed him from town to town and helped him teach people. Jesus especially liked a man called Lazarus and his two sisters, Martha and Mary. When Jesus needed a rest from his work, he went to their house. They enjoyed talking and eating together. Once when Lazarus was very sick, Jesus made him well. Then everyone was happy again.

5 **SCRIPTURE** Tell the children that Jesus is their friend. Read the adaptation of John 15:14 from the Scripture card in the Bible.

• A friend makes you happy. Jesus is your friend. He wants to make you happy. Listen to what Jesus says in the Bible:

"You are my friends."

• Jesus is always with you. He cares for you and protects you. He loves you very much and wants to be your friend for ever and ever.

*• **PRAYER** You can talk to your friend Jesus anytime. Let's look at his picture and thank him right now for being our friend. Repeat after me,*

"Thank you, Jesus, for being my friend."

6 Teach the children the first verse of the song "The More We Are Together." (See page T25.) Have them stand in a circle, hold hands, and then swing their hands in time with the music.

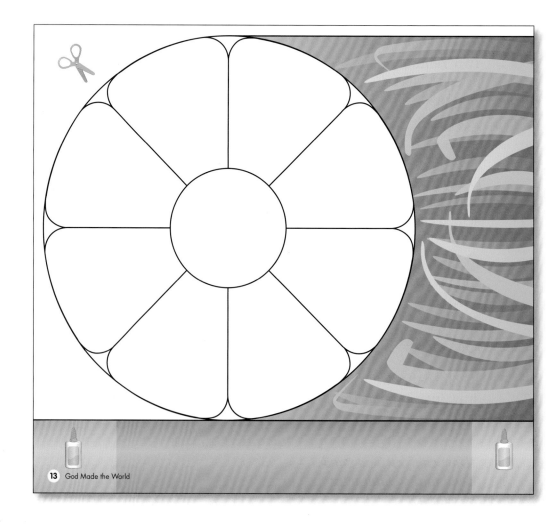

13 God Made the World

The More We Are Together

Here are two more verses you may wish to teach the children for enrichment.

2. The more we work together,
 together, together,
 The more we work together,
 the happier we'll be.
 For working together is having
 fun together,
 The more we work together,
 the happier we'll be.

3. The more we share together,
 together, together,
 The more we share together,
 the happier we'll be.
 For sharing is caring, and caring
 is sharing,
 The more we share together,
 the happier we'll be.

name _____

I love you.

ACTING

1 Ask the children in what ways they have been a good friend to someone and in what ways someone has been a good friend to them.

2 Have the children make a flower from page 13. Introduce the activity:

• *Friends are wonderful and beautiful, like flowers. Think about your friends. Today you will make a flower, and then we will all celebrate being friends.*

Help the children follow these directions:

- Write your name under the words "I love you" on the back of the flower.
- Color the flower.
- Cut off the stem.
- Cut the line between the flower and grass.
- Finish cutting out the flower.
- Glue the grass and flower to the stem.

For more elaborate flowers, have the children glue small pieces of colored construction paper or confetti to the centers of the flowers. Or you may wish to cut out three or four circles of colored tissue paper for each child and staple them to the center of the flower. Have the children pull the paper up around the staple to make ruffles.

Post the flowers as a "field of friends" on a wall or a bulletin board in the classroom. Remind the children that we are all friends.

3 Gather the children in a circle for *Music 'n Motion* time. Play the Unit 1 song (Track 6). Invite the children to do motions to the song along with you, using *Music 'n Motion* page T268.

Have the children take home their pages and show their family the Family Time section.

ENRICHING
THE FAITH EXPERIENCE

Use the following activities to enrich the lesson or to replace an activity with one that better meets the needs of your group.

1 Teach the children the other verses of "The More We Are Together" in SHARING #6.

2 Teach the children the song "Oh, How I Love Jesus."

3 Play "Pass the Ring" or another game in which the children depend on others to win. Thread a ring onto a long piece of string (or yarn) and tie the ends of the string together. Seat the children in a circle and have each child hold on to the string with both hands. Have them pass the ring around the circle by lifting the string and letting go with one hand. When you say "Stop," the child who has the ring is the winner.

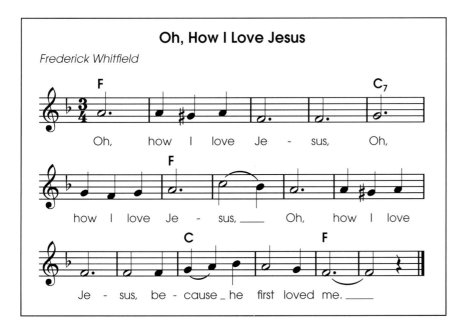

Oh, How I Love Jesus

Frederick Whitfield

Oh, how I love Je - sus, Oh,
how I love Je - sus, Oh, how I love
Je - sus, be - cause he first loved me.

FAITH FOCUS

People help us in many ways.

1 Corinthians 12:4–7,27–30

PREPARING THE FAITH EXPERIENCE

LISTENING

There are different kinds of spiritual gifts but the same Spirit; there are different forms of service but the same Lord; there are different workings but the same God who produces all of them in everyone. To each individual the manifestation of the Spirit is given for some benefit.

1 Corinthians 12:4–7

REFLECTING

In God's grand design we survive on earth through interdependence. Each person is sustained by others and in turn is called upon to contribute to the well-being and progress of humankind.

Throughout our lives we are helped by others. We depend on them for food, clothing, shelter, health care, safety, and entertainment. We also depend on others for support, encouragement, sympathy, and advice. Sometimes we take this care for granted, forgetting that it is a manifestation of the goodness and providence of our loving God.

We each use our gifts and talents in a career, ministry, or apostolic service in which we minister to others—at least indirectly. As Christians, our service is not just utilitarian or philanthropic. Jesus explained that when we love others and care for them, it is as though we are caring for and loving him.

Jesus experienced the help of others, primarily that of his parents. He showed his appreciation with obedience and love. He showed respect for civil and religious authority and expected his followers to do likewise. Jesus was helped in his work by the apostles and disciples. Once

he was even helped by a young boy who, by giving him his loaves and fish, enabled Jesus to feed a crowd. At the end of Jesus' life, Simon helped him carry his cross to Calvary, and Joseph of Arimathea provided his tomb.

Today as we carry out our work or perform Spiritual and Corporal Works of Mercy, we too are helping Christ.

As a body is one though it has many parts, and all the parts of the body, though many, are one body, so also Christ. For in one Spirit we were all baptized into one body . . .

1 Corinthians 12:12–13

RESPONDING

God's Word moves us to respond in word and action. Let God's Spirit work within you as you prayerfully consider how you are being called to respond to God's message to you today. Responding through a journal may help to strengthen your response.

- Who has helped me today?

  God, make the children thankful for those who help them.

Catechism of the Catholic Church

The themes of this chapter correspond to the following paragraph: 2217.

THE FAITH EXPERIENCE

Child's Book pages 15–18

SCRIPTURE IN THIS CHAPTER

• *Matthew 17:24–27*

MATERIALS

• Option: paper heart
• Option: clothes and equipment for CENTERING #2
• Crayons or markers

PREPARATION

Write the children's names on page 15.

MUSIC 'N MOTION

Use *Music 'n Motion* page T268 and CD Track 6 "Come Together" for this chapter. For a list of additional music, see page T320.

ENRICHING THE FAITH EXPERIENCE

Use the activities at the end of the chapter to enrich the lesson or to replace an activity with one that better meets the needs of your group.

BOOKS TO SHARE

Mike Mulligan and His Steam Shovel by Virginia Lee Burton (Houghton Mifflin, 1939)

Corduroy Goes to the Doctor by Don Freeman (Viking Juvenile, 2005)

Curious George Takes a Job by H. A. Rey (Houghton Mifflin, 1974)

Curious George Goes to the Hospital by Margret and H. A. Rey (Houghton Mifflin, 1973)

Doctor DeSoto by William Steig (Farrar, Straus & Giroux, 1990)

SNACK

Suggestion: heart-shaped cookies

ALTERNATIVE PROGRAMS

DAILY PROGRAM

Day 1: Centering, Sharing A
Day 2: Sharing B
Day 3: Enriching the Faith Experience #4, Acting #1
Day 4: Enriching the Faith Experience choice
Day 5: Acting #2 and #3

THREE-DAY PROGRAM

Day 1: Centering, Sharing A
Day 2: Sharing B
Day 3: Acting

LEARNING OUTCOMES

The children will
- realize how others help them.
- appreciate the help of others.
- be inspired to help others.
- see Jesus as a helpful person.

COMMENTS

1. By thinking about people who serve them, the children are preparing for a later understanding of the role of leaders. Leaders exercise a ministry to others, whom they are responsible for serving. We as followers must obey their authority. In discussing how we are to listen to those in authority, avoid leading the children to think that they should blindly follow the orders of all adults—unfortunately it is not always safe or wise for children to do so.

2. Children love to help, a natural tendency that should be cultivated. Involve the children as much as possible in setting up the classroom and in cleaning it up. Acknowledge their efforts by showing your gratitude. Service and cooperation are hallmarks of the Christian community.

CENTERING

❶ Gather the children in a circle for *Music 'n Motion* time. Play the Unit 1 song (Track 6). Invite the children to do motions to the song along with you, using *Music 'n Motion* page T268.

❷ Have the children engage in free play in which they pretend to be a helping person, such as a doctor, nurse, firefighter, or police officer.

SHARING [A]

❶ Comment on people who help the children. [Option: Show the paper heart.]

- *Many people help you. They show love by caring for you.*

- *Sometimes these people help you by telling you what to do. When they say things such as "Brush your teeth," it is for your own good.*

- *What are some rules you have at home?*

❷ Distribute page 15. Ask:

- *How does each person in the picture help you?*

- *How do your parents help people by the work they do?*

- *What would you like to be when you grow up? How will you help people?*

15 God Made My World

3 Have the children circle anyone on page 16 who has helped them.

SHARING [B]

4 Tell the children that Jesus was a helping person.

• *Jesus helped people. He made them well and fed them. He taught them about God. He taught them how to live.*

• *I'll tell you about one of the times Jesus helped someone.*

5 SCRIPTURE Read the following echo pantomime (adapted from Matthew 17:24–27) and perform the accompanying actions. Have the children repeat each line and do the things that you are doing.

• *A man came to Peter, Jesus' friend.*
[Walk in place.]

• *He said, "You owe tax money. So does Jesus."*
[Point.]

• *Peter went into the house to find Jesus.*
[Open door.]

• *Jesus said, "Go fishing and you will find the money."*
[Place arms akimbo.]

• *Peter went fishing and caught a fish.*
[Throw out line.]

• *He opened the fish's mouth and found a coin.*
[Pull out coin.]

6 Explain to the children how Jesus helps them.

• *Jesus helps you by sending others to help you.*

• *Doing the good things these people tell you to do will make you healthy and happy.*

7 PRAYER Pray a litany of thanksgiving for helpers.

• *Let's thank God for the wonderful people he sends to help us. Anyone here can name someone who helps, and we'll say together,*

  "Thank you, God."

ACTING

1 Have the children guess whom you are describing.

• *If something is on fire, I put the fire out.* (Firefighter)

• *If you want to buy something, I help you.* (Salesperson)

• *If you need to cross the street, I help you cross safely.* (Crossing guard)

• *If you want to know about God, I talk to you.* (Priest)

• *If you want to learn to read, I teach you.* (Teacher)

• *If you are sick, I help you feel better.* (Doctor, nurse)

• *If you need to go somewhere, I take you.* (Driver)

Circle anyone who has helped you.

Family Time

Chapter 4: God Made My Helpers

In this lesson the children learned about many people who help them. They were guided to obey these helpers. They thought about how their parents assist people through their work. The children heard that Jesus helped many people and that he still helps us today through others. Your child made a card for someone who helps him or her. Let your child tell you about this card. Help him or her deliver it if necessary.

Your Child
Praise your child's efforts to be a helper at home.

Reflect
To each individual the manifestation of the Spirit is given for some benefit.
(1 Corinthians 12:7)

Pray
Holy Spirit, help us use our gifts to help others.

Do
• Take your child to work with you one day.
• Talk about the helpers in your child's life and what they do.
• Make a book of helpers with your child, using magazine and newspaper pictures.
• Try to name with your child all the people who made possible one meal on your table.
• Teach your child to say "please" and "thank you" for others' help.
• Let your child help with tasks, such as making beds, picking up toys, and folding laundry.
• Read to your child a book in the *Curious George* series by Margret and H. A. Rey in which George visits someone in a helping profession. Recall an experience your child has had with a person who helps others. Ask God to show you ways to be a helper to others.

For more family resources, refer to the Family Activity Booklet and visit **www.loyolapress.com/preschool.**

16 God Made the World

© LOYOLAPRESS.

- *If you eat at a restaurant, I serve you.* (Server)

- *If you want a book from the library, I help you.* (Librarian)

- *If you want strong, healthy teeth, I help you.* (Dentist)

- *If you are lost, I help you find your way.* (Police officer)

2 Have the children make a trophy card from page 17 to give to a helper in their lives. Help each child write his or her name inside the card. Introduce the activity:

- *Today you will make a card for someone who helps. That person might be a police officer, your babysitter, your mail carrier, or your doctor. The card has a trophy on it. A trophy is an award for doing something well. Inside the card reads, "Thank you for helping me."*

Help the children follow these directions:

- Fold the card in half.
- Inside the card, draw a picture of the person who helps you.
- Write your name inside the card.

3 Gather the children in a circle for *Music 'n Motion* time. Play the Unit 1 song (Track 6). Invite the children to do motions to the song along with you, using *Music 'n Motion* page T268.

Have the children take home their pages and show their family the Family Time section.

CHECKPOINT

- *Were the learning outcomes achieved?*
- *How easy was it for the children to decide to whom to give their cards?*

ENRICHING THE FAITH EXPERIENCE

Use the following activities to enrich the lesson or to replace an activity with one that better meets the needs of your group.

1 Ask someone who has a career in human services, such as a nurse, firefighter, or mail carrier, to speak to the children about his or her work. If you know of a child's relative who works in this field, consider inviting that person to come to class.

2 Play the game "Follow Simon." Perform actions and have the children imitate you.

3 Teach the children the song on page T33 to the tune of "The Muffin Man." If you wish, after each verse add a response beginning "Oh yes, I know the . . ."

17 God Made the World

You're the best!

1. Oh, do you know the
   police officer,
   The police officer, the
   police officer,
   Oh, do you know the
   police officer,
   Who keeps you safe from
   harm?

2. Oh, do you know the
   doctor and nurse . . .
   Who help you to be well?

3. Oh, do you know the mail
   carrier . . .
   Who brings and takes your
   mail?

4. Oh, do you know the
   storekeeper . . .
   Who sells you things you
   need?

Mary Kathleen Glavich, S.N.D.

❹ Tell the story of Rosie
Raccoon and then ask
the children how Rosie
was a helper.

Rosie Raccoon

Rosie Raccoon was happy. She was going shopping with her mother.
On their way out the door, they met the mail carrier. He handed Rosie's
mother some letters. Rosie thought, "I'd like to be a mail carrier and help
bring raccoons letters every day." Rosie's mother gave her the letters and
said, "Would you please put these on the table while I find the car keys?"
Rosie did what her mother asked.

As they drove along, Rosie's mother said, "Hear how quiet the
engine is. Didn't the raccoons at the repair shop do a good job fixing
the car?" Rosie said yes and thought, "I'd like to fix cars someday." Her
mother said, "Honey, can you find my sunglasses in my purse? I can't see
well without them." Rosie did what her mother asked.

At the store while Rosie pushed the cart, Rosie's mother filled it
with food. At the checkout line, a raccoon filled bags for them. Rosie
thought, "I'd like to work in a store someday and help raccoons with
their groceries." Rosie's mother said, "Would you help me carry the bags
out to the car, Rosie?" Rosie did what her mother asked.

On the way home, Rosie said, "I wish I were grown up. Then I could
be a mail carrier or fix cars or work in a store and help others."

"Why Rosie, " said her mother. "You don't have to be grown up to be
a helper. You are a big help to me already." Rosie smiled.

Thank you for helping me.

Name_____

Chapter 5
God Made My Church Family

FAITH FOCUS

The Church is God's family, and Mary is our mother.   John 15:1–5; John 19:25–27; Ephesians 3:14–21

PREPARING THE FAITH EXPERIENCE

LISTENING

Standing by the cross of Jesus were his mother and his mother's sister, Mary the wife of Clopas, and Mary of Magdala. When Jesus saw his mother and the disciple there whom he loved, he said to his mother, "Woman, behold, your son." Then he said to the disciple, "Behold, your mother." And from that hour the disciple took her into his home.

John 19:25–27

REFLECTING

According to one tradition, the birth of the Church occurred at the Crucifixion when the soldier's lance pierced the side of Christ and blood and water flowed out. Through the redemptive action of Christ, all men and women again became children of God and heirs to heaven. We could again call God "Father" and hope to live with him in our eternal home.

Church members are people, living and dead, who believe and love God. They include three groups: the Church Triumphant—the saints in heaven; the Church Suffering—the souls in purgatory; and the Church Militant—people on earth. All of us are mysteriously linked in what is called the Communion of Saints. We are like branches on a vine, one with Christ, our head. We draw our life from him. He leads us on earth through the pope, bishops, priests, and deacons.

We honor Mary, the mother of Jesus. She is also Mother of the Church and our mother. As Mary loved and cared for her divine Son, she now loves and cares for us, his mystical body. Mary is a model for us of what it means to be a disciple of Jesus Christ.

On earth our unity as the Church is particularly expressed and strengthened when we gather for the Eucharist. There, in union with Christ, Mary, and the angels and saints, we praise and thank God the Father. There we celebrate and participate in the sacrifice of God's Son, a sacrifice that made eternal life a possibility for us.

As we live our Christian way of life and strive to bring others to share in the richness and beauty of our faith, we rely for guidance on the Holy Spirit and on the prayers of Mary, Mother of the Church. We await the new heaven and new earth described in Scripture:

"Behold, God's dwelling is with the human race. He will dwell with them and they will be his people and God himself will always be with them [as their God]. He will wipe every tear from their eyes, and there shall be no more death or mourning, wailing or pain, [for] the old order has passed away."

Revelation 21:3–4

RESPONDING

Having reflected upon God's Word, take some time now to continue to respond to God in prayer. You might wish to use a journal to record your responses throughout this year.

- How can I become a more vibrant member of the Church?

  Holy Spirit, implant a great love for the Church in the hearts of the children.

Catechism of the Catholic Church

The themes of this chapter correspond to the following paragraphs: 781, 828, 963, 1563.

THE FAITH EXPERIENCE

Child's Book pages 19–22

SCRIPTURE IN THIS CHAPTER

• *John 13:35*

MATERIALS

• Chapter 5 Scripture card
• Bible
• Cutouts: #8, Jesus; #9, priest; #10, Mary
• Option: photo of a parish activity
• 9-inch strips of construction paper—one more than the number of participants
• Stapler
• Crayons or markers
• Scissors
• Glue

PREPARATION

• Write the children's names on pages 19, 20, and 22.
• Place the Chapter 5 Scripture card for SHARING #2 in the Bible.
• If you wish, use a paper cutter to cut off the strip of pictures on page 21 for the children. You might save the extra pictures of Jesus to distribute as gifts in another lesson instead of having the children take them home after this lesson.

MUSIC 'N MOTION

Use *Music 'n Motion* page T268 and CD Track 6 "Come Together" for this chapter. For a list of additional music, see page T320.

ENRICHING THE FAITH EXPERIENCE

Use the activities at the end of the chapter to enrich the lesson or to replace an activity with one that better meets the needs of your group.

BOOKS TO SHARE

The Relatives Came by Cynthia Rylant (Aladdin, 1993)

In My Family/En mi familia by Carmen Lomas Garza
(Children's Book Press; Bilingual edition, 2000)

Family-Time Bible in Pictures by Kenneth N. Taylor
(Tyndale House Publishers, 2007)

SNACK

Suggestion: gingerbread-people cookies

ALTERNATIVE PROGRAMS

DAILY PROGRAM

Day 1: Centering, Sharing A
Day 2: Sharing B
Day 3: Enriching the Faith Experience #3, Acting #1
Day 4: Enriching the Faith Experience choice
Day 5: Acting #2 and #3

THREE-DAY PROGRAM

Day 1: Centering, Sharing A
Day 2: Sharing B
Day 3: Acting

LEARNING OUTCOMES

The children will

- identify the Church as God's family.
- know that they belong to the Church.
- love Mary as Jesus' mother and theirs.

COMMENTS

1. Through Baptism each of us became a new creation, a new person in Christ. We were clothed with Christ. Baptism incorporates us into the community we call the Church and intimately binds us to other Church members and to God. Baptism, however, is only the beginning of a lifelong transformation, one in which we gradually grow into the likeness of the glorified Lord. The more each of us cooperates and supports other members, the more the Church bears witness to the unity of the Body of Christ.

2. Preschool children come to know about the Church by experiencing it. By sharing in Christian events, by meeting Christians and hearing their stories, and by interacting in the small Christian community that is the preschool, children form attitudes and absorb values that will remain with them throughout their lives. With our help they come to understand that Christians are people who love one another.

3. Throughout the year, call attention to times when the children show love as did Jesus.

CENTERING

1 Gather the children in a circle for *Music 'n Motion* time. Play the Unit 1 song (Track 6). Invite the children to do motions to the song along with you, using *Music 'n Motion* page T268.

2 Make a class chain. Give each child a strip of paper. Invite the children to decorate the strips of paper and help them write their names on the strips. If you have teacher assistants, have them make links too. Decorate a strip yourself and staple it together to make the starting link. Call the children one by one to join their links to the chain. When the chain is finished, add a plain strip, joining the ends of the chain to form a circle. Display the class chain.

SHARING [A]

1 Talk about God's family, the Church.

- *We talked about your family at home. You also belong to a bigger family. You belong to God's family. We call God's family "the Church."*

- *People in God's family love Jesus and try to act as he did.* [Show Cutout #8, Jesus.]

19 God Made the World

Name _____

Init1.indd 19   10/29/08 11:30:50 AM

- *Some of God's family belong to* [name of your local church] *parish.* [Option: Show a photo of a parish activity.]

2 **SCRIPTURE** Read the adaptation of John 13:35 from the Scripture card in the Bible.

- *Listen to what Jesus said about the Church:*

  "Everyone will know you are my followers, if you love one another."

3 Distribute page 19 and discuss the picture.

- *You see some of God's family in this picture. There are millions of people in God's family, the Church. Can you name some?*

- *Look at the last man in the procession. Do you know what he is?* (A priest) *Priests help the other members of the Church in special ways.* [Show Cutout #9, priest.] *What is the name of our parish priest?*

- *Church members who have died are with God in heaven now. We call these Church members saints. Maybe your great-grandmother or great-grandfather is a saint.*

4 Introduce Mary as Mother of the Church.

- *Families usually have a mother. God's family has a mother too. Do you know who she is?* (Mary) [Show Cutout #10, Mary.]

Mary is Jesus' mother, but she is also the Mother of the Church. She is our mother too.

- *What does your mother at home do for you?*

- *Your mother Mary in heaven does good things for you too. She prays for you, watches over you, and helps you. Mary loves you.*

- *We love our mother Mary. We honor her by putting flowers by her statue or picture. We sing and pray to her.*

- *Jesus is happy when we show love for Mary, his mother.*

5 Help the children work page 20.

- *Some of the children in the pictures are acting like good members of the Church. They are loving like Jesus. Let's see whether you can tell who is a follower of Jesus.*

Color the heart next to each child who is loving like Jesus.

Family Time

Chapter 5: God Made My Church Family

In this lesson the children learned that the Church is God's family and that every member is important. They heard that Church members follow Jesus and try to love as he did. They know that priests serve the Church, the saints are members who are in heaven, and Mary is God's mother and theirs too. Ask your child to explain the photo frame he or she made.

Your Child

Children should know that the people they love who have died are in heaven with God and continue to care for their loved ones. Give your child a sense of belonging to the parish by introducing him or her to the priests and parishioners.

Reflect

Jesus said, "Everyone will know you are my followers, if you love one another." (adapted from John 13:35)

Pray

Jesus, help us love others as you taught.

Do

- Display a picture of Mary or set up a shrine in her honor.
- Share with your child what Mary means to you.
- Take your child to parish activities.
- Read to your child *The Relatives Came* by Cynthia Rylant. Discuss how all members of a family are important to one another. Thank God for making us part of the Church family.

For more family resources, refer to the Family Activity Booklet and visit **www.loyolapress.com/preschool.**

20 God Made the World

© LOYOLAPRESS.

SHARING [B]

6 Use the class chain to show the importance of each family member. Hold it up and explain:

• *God's family is like the chain we made. Each person is linked to the group. What happens to the chain if one link breaks?* [Tear off the blank link.] (The chain is broken.)

• *Every member of the Church is important.* [Name the children.] *Each one is needed to make the Church complete. Each one needs all the others.* [Repair the chain by reattaching the blank link.]

7 Teach the children the following song with gestures to the tune of "Row, Row, Row Your Boat." Or you may wish to have them sit cross-legged facing a partner, holding hands, and rocking back and forth as if rowing while they sing.

• *I'll teach you a song about Church members.*

God's Family

Women, men, girls, and boys,
[Point to several people.]
Mary, saints, and me—
[Point up and then to self.]
All are members of God's Church.
[Extend arms wide.]
We're God's family.
[Clap twice at the end.]
Mary Kathleen Glavich, S.N.D.

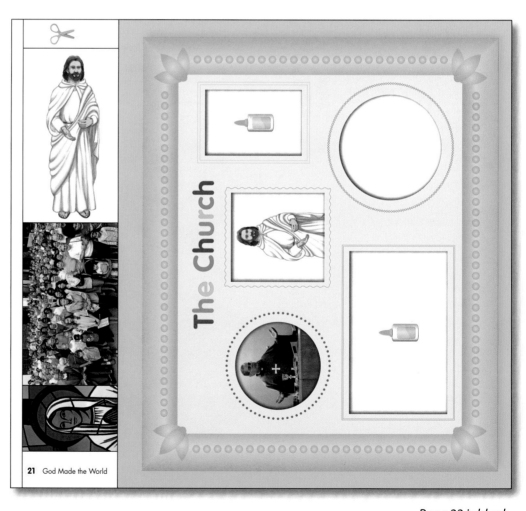

21 God Made the World

Page 22 is blank.

ACTING

1 PRAYER Lead the children in a prayer of thanksgiving for the Church. Include in the litany the names of parish priests, other parishioners the children may know, and the children themselves. Begin as follows:

• *Isn't God good to make us family members? Aren't you glad that you belong to God's family, the Church?*

• *Let's thank God for the Church. I'll say a name and we'll all raise our hands and say "Thank you, Father."*

> *For Jesus . . .* [Point to Cutout #8, Jesus.]
>
> *For Mary, our mother . . .* [Point to Cutout #10, Mary.]
>
> *For the saints . . .*
>
> *For our mothers and fathers . . .*
>
> *For our relatives and friends who have died . . .*
>
> *For our priests . . .* [Point to Cutout #9, priest.]

2 Help the children finish the photo frame of God's family on page 21 according to these directions:

• Cut out and glue the pictures of Mary and of the other Church members in the matching spaces.
• Draw yourself in the last space.
• Take home the picture of Jesus as a reminder to love as he does.

3 Gather the children in a circle for *Music 'n Motion* time. Play the Unit 1 song (Track 6). Invite the children to do motions to the song along with you, using *Music 'n Motion* page T268.

Have the children take home their pages and show their family the Family Time section.

CHECKPOINT

• *Were the learning outcomes achieved?*
• *How familiar are the children with Mary and the saints?*
• *Have the children met or do they know their parish priest(s)?*

ENRICHING THE FAITH EXPERIENCE

Use the following activities to enrich the lesson or to replace an activity with one that better meets the needs of your group.

1 On page 22 have the children glue a picture of themselves to reinforce the idea that they are to be like Jesus.

2 Teach a circle dance to the song about the Church in Sharing #7. Arrange the children in two concentric circles so that each child is facing someone. For the first two lines of the song, have the children in the outside circle hold hands and stand still while the children in the inside circle hold hands and walk to their left. Then after the first two lines, have them stop, take the hands of the child they face, and turn a circle with him or her. At the end of the song, have them clap twice. (For a more difficult dance, have the children in the outside circle also walk to their left during the first two lines.)

3 Ask the children whether they know the names of any saints. Then ask whether they know anything about the saints named. Point out children who have the name of a saint.

4 Have a statue of Mary in the room and let the children honor her by putting flowers near the statue.

5 Invite Church members whom the children know to participate in this lesson. Include the parish priest if possible.

6 Use puppets or the Riley family cutouts (Cutouts #1–4) to dramatize situations that call for love. Ask the children how a follower of Jesus would respond.

God Made Holy Things

The children will become familiar with the parish church and the Bible. They will have an increased understanding of music, water, and food, which are the foundation for participation in the liturgy.

6 GOD MADE CHURCHES

The children recall what they know about churches. They learn that God is in church where the Church family gathers to pray. They hear about some of the objects in church. After reviewing that quiet is needed for personal prayer, they practice kneeling, folding their hands, and praying. They make a paper church that stands.

7 GOD MADE THE BIBLE

The children come to know that the Bible is like a love letter from God to them. They hear two stories about God's love that are in the Bible: Jesus cherishing children, David and Goliath. They make a prayer book to use at home or in church.

8 GOD MADE MUSIC

The children learn that songs can be prayers. They meet David again, this time as the writer of song-prayers. They make a banner and march and sing to honor God.

9 GOD MADE WATER

The children have experiences with water, which prepare them for its use in the liturgy. They hear about holy water and are blessed with it. They are encouraged not to waste water and to keep it clean. They make a water scene to remind them to take care of God's gift of water.

10 GOD MADE FOOD

After talking about the importance of good food, the children learn about bread as well as other foods made from flour. They reflect on special meals as a preparation for the sacred meal—the Eucharist—that we celebrate as Christians. They make a place mat as a reminder to thank God for food.

God Made Churches

PREPARING THE FAITH EXPERIENCE

LISTENING

Jesus entered the temple area and drove out all those engaged in selling and buying there. He overturned the tables of the money changers and the seats of those who were selling doves. And he said to them, "It is written:

'My house shall be a house of prayer,'

but you are making it a den of thieves."

Matthew 21:12–13

REFLECTING

Churches are sacred spaces. When God appeared to Moses in the burning bush, God said, "Remove the sandals from your feet, for the place where you stand is holy ground." (Exodus 3:5) Our churches are holy ground because God is present in them. Someone once remarked to a Catholic, "If I believed what you Catholics believe about God being in the tabernacle, I would go down the aisle of your church on my knees."

Certain places have always been designated as holy. Since ancient times the Jewish people have worshiped at the Temple in Jerusalem, a sacred place to which all who were able once were obliged to journey for the celebration of great feasts. According to Scripture, mountains were a special place for encounters with God. Moses spoke to God face-to-face on a mountain; Jesus was transfigured on a mountain and often went up on a mountain to pray.

Every Catholic church is a place of encounter with God. The sanctuary light signals God's presence. Catholics assemble at church to worship God in the celebration of the Eucharist. Church is where we celebrate key events in our lives: baptisms, weddings, and funerals. It is where we gather to celebrate and strengthen

our faith. It is a place to be alone with God and a place to be before God as one of God's people. It is a place of refuge, a place of self-examination, a place of resolution. It is where we do what we were created to do: adore the one God, the source of all life and goodness.

In church are signs of God's holiness. Incense, bells, candles, holy water, the crucifix, statues, and stained-glass windows, as well as silence, beauty, and space, remind us of God and of our life with Christ. They invite and inspire us to pray.

Whether it be a magnificent cathedral or a one-room chapel, a Catholic church is none other than the house of God and the gate of heaven.

RESPONDING

God's Word calls us to respond in love. Respond to God now in the quiet of your heart, and perhaps through the journal that you are keeping this year.

- How well do I know the history and features of my parish church?

   God, may all the children worship you with their whole hearts.

Catechism of the Catholic Church

The themes of this chapter correspond to the following paragraphs: 1180–1186, 2650.

THE FAITH EXPERIENCE

Child's Book pages 23–26

SCRIPTURE IN THIS CHAPTER
- *Psalm 122:1*
- *John 2:13–17*

MATERIALS
- Chapter 6 Scripture card
- Bible
- Cutout #11: Tillie Mouse, taped to a pencil or a craft stick
- Option: picture of your parish church
- Candle
- Sacramentary and lectionary
- Crucifix
- Crayons or markers
- Scissors
- Glue

PREPARATION
- Write the children's names on pages 23 and 26.
- Place the Chapter 6 Scripture card for SHARING #1 in the Bible.
- If you wish, use a paper cutter to cut off the strip of pictures on page 25 for the children.
- You might take photos of features of your parish church to show during SHARING #3.

MUSIC 'N MOTION
Use *Music 'n Motion* page T270 and CD Track 7 "Stand Up!" for this chapter. For a list of additional music, see page T320.

ENRICHING THE FAITH EXPERIENCE
Use the activities at the end of the chapter to enrich the lesson or to replace an activity with one that better meets the needs of your group.

BOOKS TO SHARE
A Peek Into My Church by Wendy Goody and Veronica Kelly (Whippersnapper, 1999)

Come Worship With Me: A Journey Through the Church Year by Ruth L. Boling and Tracey Dahle Carrier (Carrier Press, 2001)

SNACK
Suggestion: curved pretzels (These "praying hands" originated as a Lenten food.)

ALTERNATIVE PROGRAMS

DAILY PROGRAM
Day 1: Centering, Sharing #1 and #2, Enriching the Faith Experience #4
Day 2: Sharing #3 and #4, Acting #1
Day 3: Sharing B
Day 4: Enriching the Faith Experience choice
Day 5: Acting #2 and #3

THREE-DAY PROGRAM
Day 1: Centering, Sharing A
Day 2: Sharing B, Acting #1
Day 3: Acting #2 and #3

LEARNING OUTCOMES

The children will

- identify the church building as God's house.
- be quiet in church in the presence of God.
- become familiar with some characteristics of a church.
- learn to pray quietly in their hearts.

COMMENTS

1. King David desired to build a house for God, but God reserved that task for David's son, King Solomon, who built the first of the grand temples in Jerusalem. We Catholics are privileged to have God dwelling with us in the Blessed Sacrament—not just in one building but in countless churches ranging from majestic basilicas to one-room chapels. Our contemporary places of worship vary a great deal. There are large churches with ornate architecture and numerous statues of the saints. There are also churches that resemble auditoriums, as well as churches that are simple and bare. Whatever its shape, style, or furnishings, a church is still God's house and the center of faith for a community.

2. Some children may already be familiar with a church, but some may not. Learning about a church helps the children be more at home in it.

CENTERING

❶ Gather the children in a circle for *Music 'n Motion* time. Play the Unit 2 song (Track 7). Invite the children to do motions to the song along with you, using *Music 'n Motion* page T270.

❷ Distribute page 23 and discuss the pictures.

- *What do you see in the pictures?* (Two churches)

- *How do you know they are churches?* (They have crosses, stained-glass windows, steeples, and bells.)

- *Some churches are big and some are small.*

- *Have you ever been in a church? What did you see there?*

SHARING [A]

❶ **SCRIPTURE** Talk about churches. Read the psalm (adapted from Psalm 122:1) from the Scripture card in the Bible. [Option: Show the picture of your church.]

- *God is everywhere, but the church is God's house. God is in a church in a special way. Members of God's family gather in church to pray together. We try to make our churches beautiful because God is there, and God is so wonderful.*

Name_____

23 God Made the World

• *Listen to this prayer from the Bible: "I am glad when I go to God's house."*

• *We are quiet in church because people go to church to talk to God. It is easier to talk to God and to listen to God when we are quiet. Talking with God is called praying.*

2 Have the children stand and sing the song about the Church that they learned in Chapter 5. If you have not already done so, teach them the circle dance for it in Enriching the Faith Experience #2 on page T39.

3 Use Cutout #11, Tillie Mouse, to introduce objects in the church. Show any objects or pictures you may have. Adapt the following to your parish church:

• *Hi! I'm Tillie. I live in your church. I'd like to tell you about it.*

• *There are special things in the church that make people think of God and help them pray.*

• *A cross is a sign of God's love. Usually there are crosses inside and outside a church.*

• *Candles shine brightly. They are signs that God is good and that God is holy.*

• *In the beautiful colored windows, we can see pictures of Jesus, the saints, and Mary. Sometimes the pictures tell stories about God.*

• *Big, important books help people pray to God.*

• *The priest stands behind a big table called an altar when he leads God's family in praying together at Mass.*

• *I especially love the church on weekends. People of all ages come to church. They sing and pray to our good God who made all of us.*

4 Guide the children in completing the pictures on page 24.

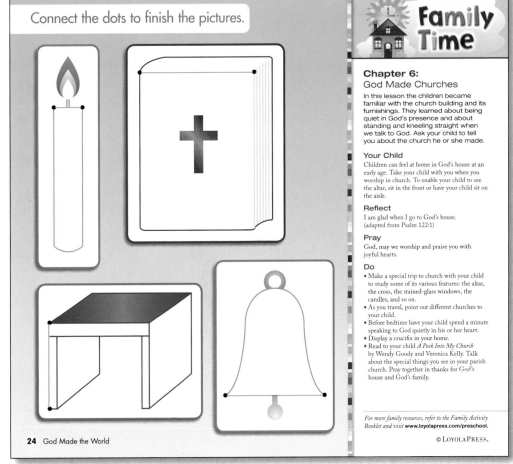

Connect the dots to finish the pictures.

Family Time

Chapter 6:
God Made Churches

In this lesson the children became familiar with the church building and its furnishings. They learned about being quiet in God's presence and about standing and kneeling straight when we talk to God. Ask your child to tell you about the church he or she made.

Your Child
Children can feel at home in God's house at an early age. Take your child with you when you worship in church. To enable your child to see the altar, sit in the front or have your child sit on the aisle.

Reflect
I am glad when I go to God's house. (adapted from Psalm 122:1)

Pray
God, may we worship and praise you with joyful hearts.

Do
• Make a special trip to church with your child to study some of its various features: the altar, the cross, the stained-glass windows, the candles, and so on.
• As you travel, point out different churches to your child.
• Before bedtime have your child spend a minute speaking to God quietly in his or her heart.
• Display a crucifix in your home.
• Read to your child *A Peek Into My Church* by Wendy Goody and Veronica Kelly. Talk about the special things you see in your parish church. Pray together in thanks for God's house and God's family.

For more family resources, refer to the Family Activity Booklet and visit **www.loyolapress.com/preschool.**

24 God Made the World

© LOYOLA PRESS.

SHARING [B]

5 Explain kneeling.

• *God is so great and wonderful that when we pray to God, sometimes we kneel like this.* [Demonstrate.] *We stand or kneel as straight as we can. Then we are praising God with our whole body. Let's see how you kneel.* [Have the children kneel. Gestures can and should be adapted when necessary to accommodate different needs, such as bowing instead of kneeling.]

• *Usually when we talk to God we fold our hands like this.* [Demonstrate.] *Now fold your hands.*

• *At night you may kneel by your bed and thank God for the good things that happened during the day.*

6 **PRAYER** Lead the children in prayer.

• *Let's talk to God right now.*

• *Everyone tiptoe quietly to a different spot in the room.*

• *You may kneel if you wish.*

• *Fold your hands. Close your eyes and be very quiet, so quiet that you can hear yourself breathing.*

• *Tell God quietly in your heart,*

   "God, you are good." [Pause.]

• *Tell God,*

   "I love you." [Pause.]

• *Thank God for something.* [Pause.]

ACTING

1 Have the children tell what they like about their church.

2 Have the children make the church from page 25. Help them follow these directions:

• Cut out the altar and the cross.
• Glue the cross in place on the back of the page.
• Glue the altar in front of the priest.
• Fold the church in thirds so that it stands.

25 God Made the World

• Cut the doors on the black lines and fold them on the dotted lines so that they open.

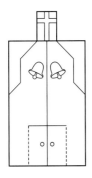

❸ Gather the children in a circle for *Music 'n Motion* time. Play the Unit 2 song (Track 7). Invite the children to do motions to the song along with you, using *Music 'n Motion* page T270.

Have the children take home their pages and show their family the Family Time section.

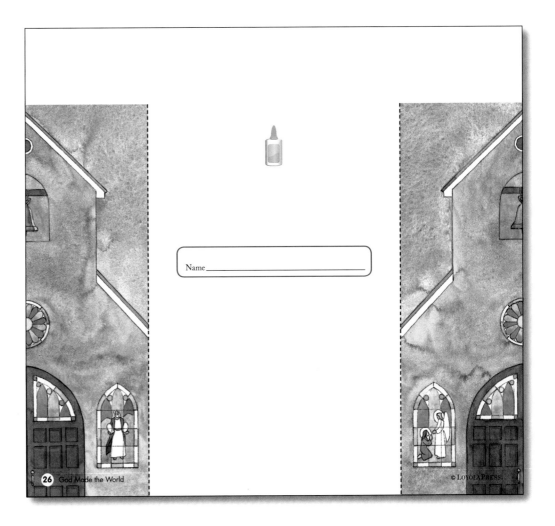

Name

26 God Made the World

© LOYOLA PRESS.

ENRICHING THE FAITH EXPERIENCE

Use the following activities to enrich the lesson or to replace an activity with one that better meets the needs of your group.

① Take the children to visit a church or a chapel. Point out features they talked about during the lesson. Have them sit or stand quietly for a few moments to say "I love you" to God and to thank God for something. (Most four-year-olds are too small to kneel in the pews.) After the visit, talk about some of the things the children noticed in church.

② Play "Doggie and Bone." Choose a child to sit backwards before the group so that he or she cannot see the rest of the children. Set an eraser, a beanbag, or a block behind the child. Choose another child to tiptoe up quietly, take the object, and be seated again with the object hidden behind him or her. The children ask in unison, "Doggie, Doggie, who has your bone?" The child in front of the group guesses who took the object until he or she guesses correctly. The child who took the object then becomes the next "doggie."

③ Conduct other quiet activities.

- Stand some distance from the children and tell them you will softly call each of them to come to you. They must be very quiet so that they can hear their name. Call each child by whispering his or her name.

- Have the children be quiet for a minute and listen for sounds. At the end of the minute, let them tell what they heard.

- Teach the children to sit down and repeat "I'm as quiet as a mouse," each time saying it more softly until they cannot be heard. This is a good activity for settling the children.

④ **SCRIPTURE** Tell the children about Jesus in God's house. Read the adaptation of John 2:13–17 from the Chapter 6 Scripture card placed in the Bible. Discuss some of the ways we pray in church.

Once Jesus went to God's house to pray. Some people were doing things there that they shouldn't have been doing. Jesus chased those people out. Jesus said, "God's house should be a place of prayer."

⑤ Help the children make stained-glass windows, using colored tissue paper and yarn of different lengths. Mix equal parts of white glue and water in a bowl. Direct the children to soak pieces of yarn in the glue mixture and then to squeeze out the excess glue through their fingers. Have them press the yarn to the tissue paper, making designs.

6 Teach the following finger play.

Here is the church.
[Interlace fingers with knuckles on top, fingers tucked under palms, and thumbs together, pointing up.]

Here is the steeple.
[Point index fingers up, fingertips touching, to form a steeple.]

Open the doors
[Turn hands over with fingers still interlaced.]

And see all the people.
[Wiggle fingers.]

Chapter 7

God Made the Bible

FAITH FOCUS

The Bible is God's love letter to us.

Psalm 119:105; 2 Timothy 3:16–17; 2 Peter 1:19–21

PREPARING THE FAITH EXPERIENCE

LISTENING

When I found your words, I devoured them; they became my joy and the happiness of my heart[.]

Jeremiah 15:16

REFLECTING

Scripture is the Word of God. *The Constitution on Divine Revelation* states, "In the sacred books the Father who is in heaven comes lovingly to meet his children, and talks with them." (21) God inspired human beings to write down what God wanted made known to us. Through the inspiration of the Holy Spirit, the Church determined the books that we accept as Sacred Scripture. Just as God spoke to us in the Word made flesh, Jesus Christ, God speaks to us in the written Word, the Bible.

Reading Scripture, then, is communicating with God. We use the Bible in personal prayer. Scripture speaks to our hearts. When we turn expectantly to Scripture for comfort, encouragement, inspiration, or guidance, we are never disappointed. Meditating on the verses leads to peace and a holy life. We pay particular attention to the Gospels, in which we have accounts of Jesus' life and teachings. There is truth in the saying "A person whose Bible is falling apart usually isn't."

We also use the Bible in liturgy. Since the time of the first Christians, the Eucharist has included listening to God's Word and an explanation of it. The words of Scripture may strike us as an intensely personal message. In Jeremiah 23:29 God asks "Is not my word like fire . . . like a hammer shattering rocks?" We sometimes find that it is.

We read the Bible to learn about our history as a Church, to learn about ourselves, and most of all to learn about God. The one overwhelming message of the Bible is that God loves us. When the great Protestant theologian Karl Barth, who wrote some 80 books on God's Word, was asked to summarize his writings, he merely said, "Jesus loves me. This I know, for the Bible tells me so."

We read the Bible for enlightenment. As someone once said, "Scripture tells us not so much how the heavens go, but how to go to heaven." Through Scripture God lets us know how to live:

Your word is a lamp for my feet, a light for my path.

Psalm 119:105

The more we open our hearts to Scripture, the more we come to know and love Jesus, the Word made flesh.

RESPONDING

Having been nourished by God's Word, we are able to respond to God's great love for us. In prayer, respond to God's call to you to share his Word with others. You may also wish to respond in your prayer journal.

- How can I develop the habit of daily Bible reading?

Holy Spirit, give the children a love for the Bible.

Catechism of the Catholic Church

The themes of this chapter correspond to the following paragraph: 104.

THE FAITH EXPERIENCE

Child's Book pages 27–32

SCRIPTURE IN THIS CHAPTER

- *Matthew 18:2–3*
- *1 Samuel 17*
- *Isaiah 54:10*

MATERIALS

- Chapter 7 Scripture card
- Bible
- Table for the Bible
- Cloth to cover the table
- Option: flowers
- Tape or stickers
- Crayons or markers

PREPARATION

- Write the children's names on page 27.
- To enthrone the Bible, set up a table covered with a cloth. If you wish, place flowers on the table.
- Place the Chapter 7 Scripture card for SHARING #3 and ACTING #2 in the Bible.

MUSIC 'N MOTION

Use *Music 'n Motion* page T270 and CD Track 7 "Stand Up!" for this chapter. For a list of additional music, see page T320.

ENRICHING THE FAITH EXPERIENCE

Use the activities at the end of the chapter to enrich the lesson or to replace an activity with one that better meets the needs of your group.

BOOKS TO SHARE

Ira Sleeps Over by Bernard Waber
(Houghton Mifflin/Walter Lorraine Books, 1975)

I May Be Little: The Story of David's Growth by Marilyn Lashbrook (Through the Bible Publishers, 1987)

Tomie dePaola's Book of Bible Stories by Tomie dePaola (Putnam Juvenile, 2002)

SNACK

Suggestion: sugar cookies (God's Word is sweet.)

ALTERNATIVE PROGRAMS

DAILY PROGRAM
Day 1: Centering, Sharing A
Day 2: Sharing B
Day 3: Acting #1 and #2
Day 4: Acting #3–5
Day 5: Enriching the Faith Experience choice

THREE-DAY PROGRAM
Day 1: Centering, Sharing A
Day 2: Sharing B
Day 3: Acting

LEARNING OUTCOMES

The children will

• know that the Bible is God's book.

• treat the Bible with respect and love.

• enjoy a story from the Bible.

• desire to speak to God.

COMMENTS

1. Children, as well as adults, may be more moved by what they see than by what they hear. A beautifully covered Bible enthroned on a table with flowers communicates that this book deserves special respect. The table may be covered with a cloth that is changed to correspond to the liturgical seasons.

2. If you wish, each week you may place the optional items suggested for the lesson on the enthronement table.

CENTERING

1 Gather the children in a circle for *Music 'n Motion* time. Play the Unit 2 song (Track 7). Invite the children to do motions to the song along with you, using *Music 'n Motion* page T270.

2 Talk about letters.

• *Have any of you ever received a letter or a card? Do you like to get letters and cards?*

• *Today I have a letter for you.*

3 Distribute page 29 and help the children finish their letters from God, according to these directions:

• Help each child write his or her name on the front and back of the letter.

• Cut off the side strip and fold and tape the letters closed.

• Read to the children what the letter says on each side.

Name_____

27 God Made the World

SHARING [A]

1 Show the Bible and explain that it is God's book.

• *This book is a special book. It is God's book. Do you know what it is called?* (The Bible)

• *God gave us the Bible as a message to us.*

• *In the Bible, God often says what was written in your letter. What was that?* (I love you.)

• *The Bible is like a very long love letter to us from God.*

• *Because the Bible is God's book, we handle it carefully.*

2 Tell the children that the Bible is read in church.

• *When God's family meets in church to pray, someone reads aloud from the Bible.*

• *All the people listen very carefully. They know that God speaks to them through the Bible.*

• *The priest kisses the Bible because it is God's holy book.*

3 Distribute page 27 and tell the children how much Jesus loves them.

• **SCRIPTURE** *Look at the picture on this page. You see Jesus with some children. The Bible tells how much Jesus loved children.* [Read the following adaptation of Matthew 18:2–3 from the Scripture card placed in the Bible.]

"One day Jesus set a child before all the people. He said, 'Only people who are like this child will be with me in heaven forever.'"

• *Jesus loved children. He talked to them and blessed them.*

Draw yellow light around David to show that God is with him.

Family Time

Chapter 7: God Made the Bible

In this lesson the children learned that the Bible is the Word of God in which God tells us over and over, "I love you." They learned how we show reverence for Sacred Scripture. They listened to the famous biblical story of David and Goliath. Ask your child to explain to you the prayer book he or she made. Use it to pray with your child.

Your Child
The Bible contains our Sacred Tradition and stories. Although much of the Bible is beyond the comprehension of children and not suitable for them, they ought to be exposed to what they can understand, for it is God's Word to them too. Tell your child Bible stories and verses that pertain to his or her life. For example, if your child is afraid of the dark, quote God's reassuring words in Isaiah, "Do not be afraid; I am with you." (adapted from Isaiah 41:10)

Reflect
Your word is a lamp for my feet,
 a light for my path. (Psalm 119:105)

Pray
God, open our hearts to your loving Word.

Do
• Show your child the family Bible. (If you don't have a family Bible, this would be a good time to purchase one.)
• Establish a family tradition of reading the Bible together for a few minutes at least once a week, perhaps before or after a meal or on Sunday.
• Read to your child *Tomie dePaola's Book of Bible Stories* by Tomie dePaola or read from a children's Bible. Talk about why the Bible is special. Pray together, giving thanks for God's Word.

For more family resources, refer to the Family Activity Booklet and visit **www.loyolapress.com/preschool.**

28 God Made the World

© LOYOLAPRESS.

❹ Teach the children the song "Jesus Loves Me." Add sign language for the words "Yes, Jesus loves me."

Jesus Loves Me

Anna B. Warner   Wm. B. Bradbury

Je - sus loves me, this I know, For the Bi - ble tells me so. Lit - tle ones to him be - long, They are weak, but he is strong. Yes, Je - sus loves me! Yes, Je - sus loves me! Yes, Je - sus loves me! The Bi - ble tells me so.

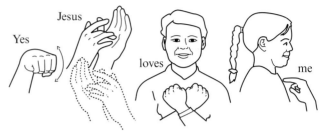

Yes—Shake the right "S" up and down in front of you.

Jesus—Place the tip of the middle finger of the right open hand into the left palm and reverse.

loves—The "S" hands are crossed at the wrist and pressed to the heart.

me—Point the right index finger at yourself.

SHARING [B]

❺ **SCRIPTURE** Tell the story "David and Goliath" on page T55 (adapted from 1 Samuel 17) while the children look at the picture on page 28.

• *The Bible has many stories about God's love. I'll tell you a favorite one. It's a story about one of Jesus' relatives. Look at the picture on page 28.*

29

David and Goliath

A long time ago there was a boy named David. He had seven older brothers. David took care of his family's sheep. Once he killed a lion that was trying to carry away a sheep. Another time he killed a bear.

One day David went to visit his brothers, who were soldiers in the king's army. In the enemy army there was a giant named Goliath. Goliath had said that he would fight one person from the king's army. Whoever won would win the war for his country. David went to the king and offered to fight the giant Goliath.

On the day of the fight, Goliath wore armor to protect himself. The king gave David his armor to wear, but David wasn't used to it. He took it off.

Then David found five stones. Carrying these stones and a sling to throw them, David went to face Goliath. David was sure that God would help him win the fight.

When Goliath saw young David, he made fun of him. David put one stone in his slingshot. He threw the stone, and it hit Goliath on the forehead. The giant fell to the ground. God loved David and saved him from Goliath.

ACTING

1 **PRAYER** Hold a procession as the Bible is taken to the table. [Option: Let the children place flowers on the table.] Give these instructions:

• *Let's show God that we are glad to have the Bible. Let's have a parade to thank God.*

• *I'll carry the Bible high, the way it is sometimes carried in church. You may follow me in a line with your hands folded.*

• *We'll sing "Jesus Loves Me."*

• *When we get to the table, I'll set the Bible on it and bow. You may go to the Bible too, one by one, and bow.*

6 Direct the children to draw yellow light around David on page 28 to show that God was with him.

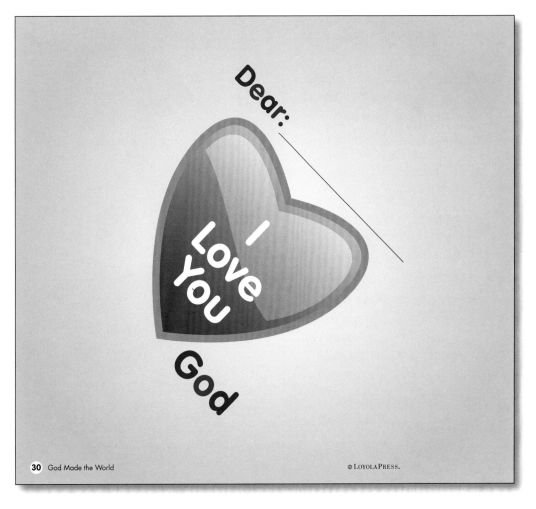

2 **SCRIPTURE** Read the adaptation of Isaiah 54:10 from the Scripture card in the Bible.

• *Now I will read something God says to us:*

    "I will love you forever and ever."

• *God is so good to speak to us in the Bible. Are you happy to hear God say "I love you"?*

• *Let's clap because we are happy.* [Clap.]

3 Have the children make prayer books from page 31. Help them fold the page in half and write their name on the front. Explain to the children what the book is.

• *This is your very own prayer book. It will help you talk to God.*

• *Open the book, and on the first page you see wonderful things that God has made. Look at them and in your heart say to God, "I praise you."*

• *On the next page you see some wonderful people that God put in your life. Look at them and say to God, "I thank you."*

• *On the back of the book you see Jesus. The red heart tells you that Jesus loves you. In your heart say to God, "I love you."*

• *You can use this book to talk to God at home or in church.*

4 Have the children draw a picture of themselves next to Jesus on the back of the prayer book.

5 Gather the children in a circle for *Music 'n Motion* time. Play the Unit 2 song (Track 7). Invite the children to do motions to the song along with you, using *Music 'n Motion* page T270.

Have the children take home their pages and show their family the Family Time section.

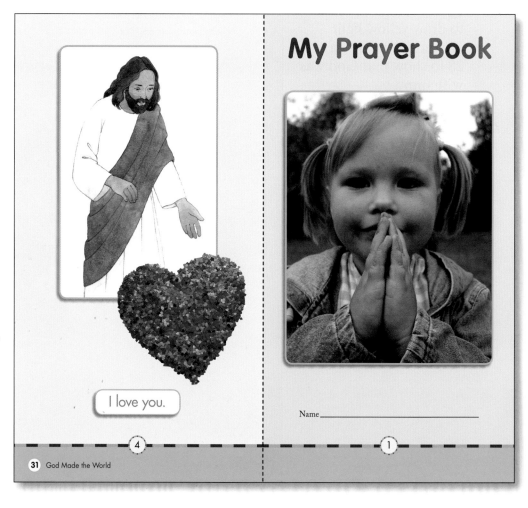

I love you.

31 God Made the World

4

My Prayer Book

Name_____

1

ENRICHING THE FAITH EXPERIENCE

Use the following activities to enrich the lesson or to replace an activity with one that better meets the needs of your group.

1 Pray a Bible litany. Have the children respond "Thanks be to God" after each line. Tell them that this is a way of saying thank you.

> *God gave us the Bible.*
>
> *The Bible is the Word of God.*
>
> *The Bible tells us about Jesus.*
>
> *God speaks to us in the Bible.*
>
> *God says "I love you" in the Bible.*

2 Give the children time in class to pray with their prayer books.

3 Read selections from *A Child's Book of Miracles* and *A Child's Book of Parables* by Mary Kathleen Glavich, S.N.D. (Loyola Press, 1994).

4 Teach the children a prayer from the Bible. Here are some suggestions:

> *I will praise you, LORD, with all my heart*[.] (Psalm 9:2)
>
> *"How good our God has been to me!"* (Psalm 13:6)
>
> *Keep me as the apple of your eye*[.] (Psalm 17:8)
>
> *I love you, LORD, my strength*[.] (Psalm 18:2)
>
> *O LORD, my God, forever will I give you thanks.* (Psalm 30:13)
>
> *[A]t the works of your hands I shout for joy.* (Psalm 92:5)

I praise you.

I thank you.

2

3

FAITH FOCUS

Making music can praise God.

1 Samuel 16:14–23; Psalm 150

PREPARING THE FAITH EXPERIENCE

LISTENING

*Shout with joy to the LORD, all the earth;
  break into song; sing praise.
Sing praise to the LORD with the harp,
  with the harp and melodious song.
With trumpets and the sound of the horn
  shout with joy to the King, the LORD.*

Psalm 98:4–6

REFLECTING

Music is a gift from God. Creation is filled with musical sounds, such as the rhythmic crashing of waves, the rustling of leaves, the cheerful babbling of brooks, and the beautiful and varied songs of birds. Perhaps the most glorious sounds in the world are those that human beings produce: a symphony, an aria, a choral work. The joy of hearing beautiful music is equalled only by the joy of contributing to its creation.

Music calms and soothes the heart, creates good feelings, and expresses what is in our souls. The human voice used in song is a vehicle for our loving adoration of God. Saint Augustine said, "Singing well is praying twice." No wonder that our liturgies are laced with song, both vocal and instrumental.

Music has a history of being used in worship. Our Jewish ancestors in the faith wrote the psalms, the 150 song-prayers that are in Scripture, and which we continue to sing and pray today. King David, Israel's greatest king, danced to the sound of the horn before the Ark of the Covenant. Other religions make music part of their worship too, from the resounding drums of Native Americans to the emotive pipes of Hindus.

The unity of a choir or an orchestra is a good analogy for the unity that Jesus desires for his Church. When everyone contributes and is sensitive to the other members of the group, the result is marvelous.

As we strive to stay in tune with others, we look forward to that day in heaven when we will sing the praises of God forever. In recording his vision of the Lamb and the 144,000 who had the name of the Lamb and of his Father written on their foreheads, the Scripture writer stated:

I heard a sound from heaven like the sound of rushing water or a loud peal of thunder. The sound I heard was like that of harpists playing their harps. They were singing [what seemed to be] a new hymn before the throne[.]

Revelation 14:2–3

It is consoling to know that when we are saints in heaven, our voices will be lovely too.

RESPONDING

God's Word moves us to respond in word and action. Let God's Spirit work within you as you prayerfully consider how you are being called to respond to God's message to you today. Responding through your journal may help to strengthen your response.

• Do I use my voice and the musical talent I have to praise God?

Jesus, let the children know the joy of music.

Catechism of the Catholic Church

The themes of this chapter correspond to the following paragraphs: 1156, 1162, 2579, 2585–2589.

THE FAITH EXPERIENCE

Child's Book pages 33–36

SCRIPTURE IN THIS CHAPTER

- *Psalm 98:1,4*
- *2 Samuel 6:14–15*

MATERIALS

- Chapter 8 Scripture card
- Bible
- Recording of a lively religious song for CENTERING #2
- Cutout #12, harp
- Option: musical instrument
- Recording of a beautiful piece of music for ACTING #1
- Option: scarves, streamers of ribbon, or crepe paper
- Crayons or markers
- Scissors
- Pencils
- Tape or stapler

PREPARATION

- Write the children's names on page 33.
- If you wish, use a paper cutter to cut apart the banner on page 35 for the children.
- Place the Chapter 8 Scripture card for SHARING #6 in the Bible.

MUSIC 'N MOTION

Use *Music 'n Motion* page T270 and CD Track 7 "Stand Up!" for this chapter. For a list of additional music, see page T320.

ENRICHING THE FAITH EXPERIENCE

Use the activities at the end of the chapter to enrich the lesson or to replace an activity with one that better meets the needs of your group.

BOOKS TO SHARE

The Wheels on the Bus by Paul O. Zelinsky
(Dutton Juvenile, 1990)

The First Song Ever Sung by Laura Krauss Melmed
(HarperCollins Publishers, 1993)

Music, Music for Everyone by Vera B. Williams
(HarperTrophy, 1988)

Song and Dance Man by Karen Ackerman
(Knopf Books for Young Readers, 2003)

Ben's Trumpet by Rachel Isadora (Live Oak Media,1998)

SNACK

Suggestion: pretzel rods (shaped like flutes or drumsticks)

ALTERNATIVE PROGRAMS

DAILY PROGRAM

Day 1: Centering, Sharing A
Day 2: Sharing B, Acting #1
Day 3: Enriching the Faith Experience choice
Day 4: Enriching the Faith Experience choice
Day 5: Acting #2–4

THREE-DAY PROGRAM

Day 1: Centering, Sharing A
Day 2: Sharing B
Day 3: Acting

LEARNING OUTCOMES

The children will
- know that song and music can praise God.
- enjoy singing and playing instruments.
- be proud of their musical abilities.

COMMENT

Most children love music, and they should be encouraged to express themselves in song and dance. Their experiences with music will prepare them to participate fully in liturgies in which singing, playing instruments, and dancing are important aspects of our worship. Not only do the participants praise God with their skills, but they also minister to the other worshipers. They provide an aesthetically pleasing experience that is conducive to prayer.

CENTERING

1 Gather the children in a circle for *Music 'n Motion* time. Play the Unit 2 song (Track 7). Invite the children to do motions to the song along with you, using *Music 'n Motion* page T270.

2 Play some music and let the children dance to it. You might give them scarves or streamers of ribbon or crepe paper to wave as they dance. Set the ground rule that the children may not touch one another during the dancing.

3 Comment on music.

- *God gave us the gift of music. We use it to praise God.*

SHARING [A]

1 Distribute page 33 and talk about music. [Option: Show and play an instrument.]

- *Music is a wonderful gift. What are some of the things you see on the page that help us make music?*

- *When do you like to hear music?*

- *Some music is so beautiful that it makes us think of God. In church we often pray to God with music.*

Name _____

33 God Made the World

2 Talk about ways in which we can make music. Let a few children demonstrate.

• *How can we make music with our hands?* (By clapping) *with our feet?* (By stamping them)

• *How else can we make music?* (By singing and whistling)

• *We can make sounds like instruments. How does a drum sound? a flute? a triangle? cymbals? a trumpet?*

3 SCRIPTURE Use page 34 to talk about David who praised God with music and dancing. (2 Samuel 6:14–15) Introduce the psalms as song-prayers found in the Bible.

• *Do you remember David? Who was he?* (A relative of Jesus')

• *One day, in a parade people were having for God, David danced for God.*

• *David also made beautiful music. Some of his songs were prayers. We call them psalms. Some of David's psalms are in the Bible.* [Show the Bible.]

4 Have the children finish the harp on page 34. Show them Cutout #12, harp, as a model.

• *David played the harp. The harp you see in the picture needs strings. Connect the dots that are the same color to put strings on the harp.*

5 Play "Follow Simon," giving commands that are related to music. For example, you might command the children to whistle, to pretend to beat a drum, or to play a piano or a trumpet. Give the command, perform the action, and then have the children imitate you.

Draw strings on the harp by connecting the dots.

Family Time

Chapter 8:
God Made Music

In this lesson the children were led to appreciate the gift of music and to understand that we praise God with music. They sang and danced. They learned that David sang and danced and wrote songs that are in the Bible. Ask your child to show you the banner that he or she made.

Your Child

Develop your child's love of music. Play different kinds of music in your home. Think about arranging for your child to learn to play an instrument or to take dancing lessons.

Reflect

Sing to the Lord a new song. Sing joyfully to the LORD, all the earth.
(adapted from Psalm 98:1,4)

Pray

Gracious God, may we sing your praises with joy forever.

Do

• Teach your child some of the Mass responses that are sung in your parish.
• Take your child to various Masses at which different kinds of music are sung.
• Help your child memorize this adaptation of Psalm 98:1,4, which was read aloud: "Sing to the LORD a new song. Sing joyfully to the LORD all the earth."
• Go to a concert with your child.
• Read to your child *The First Song Ever Sung* by Laura Krauss Melmed. Ask your child to name or sing some favorite songs. Choose a song or hymn to sing together as a prayer to God.

For more family resources, refer to the Family Activity Booklet and visit **www.loyolapress.com/preschool.**

© LOYOLAPRESS.

34 God Made the World

6 **SCRIPTURE** Introduce and read from the Scripture card in the Bible the following adaptation of Psalm 98:1,4:

• *I'll read you part of one of David's psalms.*

  Sing to the Lord a new song.

  Sing joyfully to the Lord, all the earth.

• *Say it after me.*

  Sing to the Lord a new song.
  [Children repeat.]

  Sing joyfully to the Lord, all the earth.
  [Children repeat.]

7 Teach the song "His Banner over Me Is Love."

• *Let's sing a new song to the Lord. It's called "His Banner over Me Is Love."*

• *A banner is like a flag. It can show the person you belong to.*

His Banner over Me Is Love

ACTING

1 **PRAYER** Play a beautiful piece of music and invite the children to think of God and give thanks for the gift of music.

2 Have the children make the banner on page 35. Help them follow these directions:

- Decorate the banner.

- Cut out the banner. (The children who are able may cut the banner along the diagonal lines.)

- Starting with one corner, roll the green strip of paper around a pencil and tape it together. Remove the pencil. Use the rolled-up piece of paper as a stick. (Instead of paper, pencils or cardboard tubes from dry-cleaning hangers may be used for sticks.)

- Tape or staple the banner to the "stick."

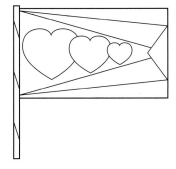

3 Invite the children to make music for the Lord by singing "His Banner over Me Is Love." Lead them in a march and have them wave their banners.

4 Gather the children in a circle for *Music 'n Motion* time. Play the Unit 2 song (Track 7). Invite the children to do motions to the song along with you, using *Music 'n Motion* page T270.

Have the children take home their pages and show their family the Family Time section.

CHECKPOINT

- *Were the learning outcomes achieved?*

- *Did the children enjoy this lesson?*

Name_____

ENRICHING THE FAITH EXPERIENCE

Use the following activities to enrich the lesson or to replace an activity with one that better meets the needs of your group.

❶ Record the children as they make music and then play the music back for them.

❷ Play a psalm set to music, preferably one the children would hear in their parish church.

❸ Ask the children to choose a song to sing that they learned in a previous lesson.

❹ Play "Musical Chairs." Place chairs back-to-back, one less than the number of children. Play music and have the children walk around the chairs. When the music stops, each child should sit on a chair. One child will be without a chair and will be out of the game. Remove a chair and continue to play the game until only one child is left. Let those who are "out" play an instrument to accompany those still playing the game. You might choose not to remove any chairs or to eliminate any children from the game. The children will still enjoy it.

❺ Have the children make "harps" with rubber bands or strings around corrugated cardboard or empty boxes of facial tissue. Help the children make simple instruments. They can use the instruments to accompany songs in future lessons.

Horn—Cut one end of a plastic straw to form a peak. Blow through that end.

Kazoo—Punch a hole about an inch from the end of a cardboard tube. Cover this end with wax paper and hold it in place with a rubber band. Hum through the opposite end of the tube.

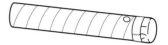

Tambourine—Punch six holes around the edge of an aluminum-foil pan. Put an opened paper clip through each hole. Twist the paper clips closed.

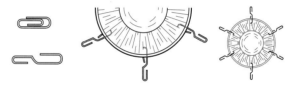

Maracas—Put some beans or gravel inside a plastic container, that has a long neck to serve as a handle, such as a shampoo bottle.

Drum—Seal the lid onto a coffee can, a round ice-cream container, or an oatmeal box. Tap it with fingers or plastic spoons.

Shaker—Put rice inside a small plastic container, such as a yogurt cup. Tape the lid on.

Rhythm sticks—Use two thick, unsharpened pencils.

PREPARING THE FAITH EXPERIENCE

LISTENING

Jesus answered and said to her, "If you knew the gift of God and who is saying to you, 'Give me a drink,' you would have asked him and he would have given you living water." [The woman] said to him, "Sir, you do not even have a bucket and the cistern is deep; where then can you get this living water? Are you greater than our father Jacob, who gave us this cistern and drank from it himself with his children and his flocks?" Jesus answered and said to her, "Everyone who drinks this water will be thirsty again; but whoever drinks the water I shall give will never thirst; the water I shall give will become in him a spring of water welling up to eternal life."

John 4:10–14

REFLECTING

Life-giving water is essential to our physical and spiritual well-being. Water makes up three-fourths of our planet and 90 percent of our bodies. Water serves us in many ways, and none of us can live long without it. We use water to wash ourselves and our possessions, to quench our thirst, to cook our food, to swim in for recreation, and to satisfy our longing for beauty.

Water is also a powerful sacramental sign. During the Easter Vigil, the priest blesses water by praying:

> At the very dawn of creation
> your Spirit breathed on the waters,
> making them the wellspring of all holiness.

Water was essential to our Jewish spiritual ancestors, who were nomads in the desert. A climactic moment in their history occurred when Moses led them to freedom through the parted waters of the Red Sea. They were sustained in the desert when Moses called forth water from rock.

In the Gospel of John, Jesus tells Nicodemus that "no one can enter the kingdom of God without being born of water and Spirit." (John 3:5) Through Baptism with water, we are born to new life in Christ. Jesus says "Let anyone who thirsts come to me and drink." (John 7:37) In the saving waters of Baptism, we are cleansed of original sin and flooded with divine life, which Jesus won for us. We receive the opportunity to live forever. Jesus says that whoever believes in him will have rivers of living water flowing from within. (John 7:38) We show gratitude for our salvation whenever we reverently make the Sign of the Cross with holy water, a reminder of our Baptism.

Saint Francis, in his great prayer Canticle of the Sun, called water "Sister Water, so useful, lowly, precious, and pure." It is said that Francis was even careful not to step in water on the ground because of his reverence for it. We show similar reverence when we strive to make our oceans, lakes, and rivers pure.

RESPONDING

Having reflected upon God's Word, take some time now to continue to respond to God in prayer. You might wish to record your responses in your journal.

- How do I regard the gift of water?

Lord, may the children always thirst for you.

Catechism of the Catholic Church

The themes of this chapter correspond to the following paragraphs: 337, 694, 2415.

THE FAITH EXPERIENCE

Child's Book pages 37–40

SCRIPTURE IN THIS CHAPTER
• *Luke 5:4–6*

MATERIALS
• Cutouts: #8, Jesus; #13–17, raindrops
• Option: cup or pitcher of water
• Song for the blessing in ACTING #2
• Water in tubs, pails, dishpans, or a swimming pool
• Water toys such as detergent bottles, funnels, sieves, corks, cups, bulb basters, and sponges
• Towels
• Holy water
• Crayons or markers
• Blue yarn of various lengths
• White glue mixed with water

PREPARATION
• Write the children's names on pages 36, 37, and 39.
• Protect the area where the children will play with water.
• Cover the painting area with newspapers.

MUSIC 'N MOTION
Use *Music 'n Motion* page T270 and CD Track 7 "Stand Up!" for this chapter. For a list of additional music, see page T320.

ENRICHING THE FAITH EXPERIENCE
Use the activities at the end of the chapter to enrich the lesson or to replace an activity with one that better meets the needs of your group.

BOOKS TO SHARE
Where Does the Butterfly Go When It Rains? by May Garelick (Mondo Publishing, 1997)

Down Comes the Rain by Franklyn M. Branley (HarperTrophy, 1997)

A Fish Out of Water by Helen Palmer (Random House Books for Young Readers, 1961)

King Bidgood's in the Bathtub by Audrey Wood (Harcourt Big Books, 1993)

Why Should I Save Water? by Jen Green (Barron's Educational Series, 2005)

SNACK
Suggestion: graham crackers

ALTERNATIVE PROGRAMS

DAILY PROGRAM
Day 1: Centering, Sharing A
Day 2: Sharing B
Day 3: Enriching the Faith Experience choice
Day 4: Enriching the Faith Experience choice, Acting #1 and #2
Day 5: Acting #3–5

THREE-DAY PROGRAM
Day 1: Centering, Sharing A
Day 2: Sharing B
Day 3: Acting

LEARNING OUTCOMES

The children will
- appreciate the gift of water.
- associate water with life.
- know that water is used in church.

COMMENTS

1. The children's experiences with water in this lesson will prepare them for understanding water's meaning as a liturgical symbol. Water is appropriately the primary symbol of Baptism, for water speaks strongly of cleansing, newness, and life. Throughout our lives we will experience water used ritually in blessings, reminding us of the new creation we became when, at the baptismal font, we were united with Christ through his Death and Resurrection.

2. Make a water-snake puppet out of an old sock. Sew buttons on the toe for eyes and make a mouth with a red marker. You may use Walter the Water Snake to teach SHARING A and parts of later lessons.

CENTERING

❶ Gather the children in a circle for *Music 'n Motion* time. Play the Unit 2 song (Track 7). Invite the children to do motions to the song along with you, using *Music 'n Motion* page T270.

❷ Let the children play in water with the water toys.

SHARING [A]

❶ Distribute page 37 and talk about water. [Option: Show the cup or pitcher of water.]

• *God made water for us. Water is wonderful. It comes in many different forms. What kinds of water do you see in the picture?*

• *Which of these do you like best?*

❷ Tell the story "The Five Raindrops" on page T69. Show a raindrop (Cutouts #13–17) each time one is mentioned.

• *How could Herbie become part of you?* (When I drink water)

❸ Have the children draw lines on page 38 to connect each item to the form of water to which it corresponds.

❹ Ask the children to look at the pictures on page 38 and tell about the various ways in which water is used.

Name_____

37 God Made the World

SHARING [B]

5 Teach the children the song "Looby Loo." Introduce it:

• Long ago many children used to take baths only once a week, on Saturday night. This song was made up to tell about getting into the tub.

The Five Raindrops

Once upon a time there were five raindrops who lived in a cloud. Their names were Splish, Splash, Drip, Drop, and Herbie. A day came when it grew cold, the winds blew, and the drops knew it was time to leave the cloud and go to Earth. One by one they let go and went falling through the sky.

Splish landed in a birdbath. Later in the day a sparrow was happily splashing around in the cool water.

Splash fell onto a windowpane. He slid all the way down the window and into a flower bed. Into the ground he sank until he came to the thirsty roots of a tulip.

Drip fell into a swimming pool. After the storm, children went outside and played in the pool.

Drop landed in a little stream. He traveled down the stream and joined a big river. The river took him into the great ocean where ships sailed back and forth.

Herbie dropped into a lake. Then he flowed into a special building where he was cleaned up. Pipes took him into your home. The next time you turn on your faucet, Herbie will be there at your service. Someday Herbie might even become part of you!

All the raindrops were happy because they helped to make others happy.

Looby Loo

Here we go loo - by loo. Here we go loo - by lye. Here we go loo - by loo, all on a Sat - ur - day night. I put my right hand in. _____ I take my right hand out. _____ I give my right hand a shake, shake, shake, and turn my - self a - bout.

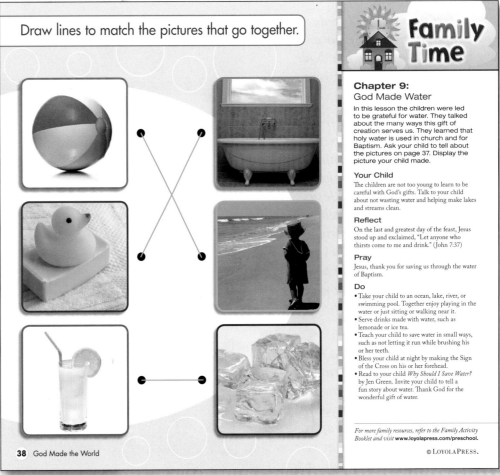

Draw lines to match the pictures that go together.

38 God Made the World

Family Time

Chapter 9:
God Made Water

In this lesson the children were led to be grateful for water. They talked about the many ways this gift of creation serves us. They learned that holy water is used in church and for Baptism. Ask your child to tell about the pictures on page 37. Display the picture your child made.

Your Child
The children are not too young to learn to be careful with God's gifts. Talk to your child about not wasting water and helping make lakes and streams clean.

Reflect
On the last and greatest day of the feast, Jesus stood up and exclaimed, "Let anyone who thirsts come to me and drink." (John 7:37)

Pray
Jesus, thank you for saving us through the water of Baptism.

Do
• Take your child to an ocean, lake, river, or swimming pool. Together enjoy playing in the water or just sitting or walking near it.
• Serve drinks made with water, such as lemonade or ice tea.
• Teach your child to save water in small ways, such as not letting it run while brushing his or her teeth.
• Bless your child at night by making the Sign of the Cross on his or her forehead.
• Read to your child *Why Should I Save Water?* by Jen Green. Invite your child to tell a fun story about water. Thank God for the wonderful gift of water.

For more family resources, refer to the Family Activity Booklet and visit **www.loyolapress.com/preschool.**

6 Talk about holy water.

• *Because water is so important in our lives, we use it in church. The priest blesses the water when he prays that God will work through the water. Holy water is water that a priest has blessed.*

• *We use holy water as a sign that we belong to Jesus. Have you ever seen people put holy water on themselves when they go into a church? Sometimes the priest blesses us by putting holy water on us. He prays that God will work in us.*

7 **SCRIPTURE** Tell the children about Jesus and water and the story of the great catch of fish. (adapted from Luke 5:4–6) [Show Cutout #8, Jesus.]

• *Jesus must have loved water. Jesus lived near a sea and was often in a boat with his friends, who were fishermen.*

• *Listen to this story from the Bible. One day the friends of Jesus had been fishing for a long time, but they had not caught any fish. Jesus told them to lower their nets again. When Jesus' friends pulled up the nets, they had so many fish that the nets were tearing. Somehow Jesus always knew where the fish were.*

• *Jesus chose water to be used in Baptism, when someone becomes a member of his Church. Have you ever seen a person being baptized? What happens?* (Water is poured on the person, or the person goes into water.)

ACTING

1 **PRAYER** Pray a litany of water. Have the children sing the response: "We thank you, God." Give each of five children a raindrop cutout to raise every time the response is sung.

• *Let's thank God for giving us the gift of water. I'll say something for which we thank God, and then you sing like this.* [Demonstrate.]

> *For beautiful lakes . . .*
> (We thank you, God.)

> *For great and wonderful oceans . . .*

> *For bubbly brooks and fish-filled streams . . .*

For rain that makes things grow . . .

For puddles to play in . . .

For fresh, clean water that comes into our homes . . .

For holy water . . .

2 Bless each child by making the Sign of the Cross with holy water on his or her forehead and saying "God bless you, [name]." Play a song as background music. Or you might sprinkle the group with holy water, using a leafy branch. Tell the children that the drops are like God's love falling on them.

Name_____

39 God Made the World

Page 40 is blank.

3 Using blue yarn, help the children complete the water scene on page 39. Have them dip each piece of yarn into a mixture of water and white glue, squeeze the yarn through their fingers to get rid of the excess glue, and arrange the yarn on the paper to represent curvy waves. Instead of using yarn, the children could paint or color the water.

4 Talk about being responsible for water.

• *How can we take care of God's gift of water?* (Don't waste it. Keep it clean.)

• *When you look at your picture, thank God for the gift of water. Remember to take care of water.*

5 Gather the children in a circle for *Music 'n Motion* time. Play the Unit 2 song (Track 7). Invite the children to do motions to the song along with you, using *Music 'n Motion* page T270.

Have the children take home their pages and show their family the Family Time section.

CHECKPOINT

• *Were the learning outcomes achieved?*

• *Which children need to be drawn into the group more?*

ENRICHING THE FAITH EXPERIENCE

Use the following activities to enrich the lesson or to replace an activity with one that better meets the needs of your group.

1 From a roll of aluminum foil, tear off pieces that are the width of the roll by five inches. Have the children fold the foil in half to make a boat to float on water. Demonstrate how the ends can be folded up and pinched together and the bottom flattened.

2 Teach this finger play:

Pitter-pat, pitter-pat,
[Drum fingers on the floor.]
The rain goes on for hours.
And though it keeps me in the house,
It's very good for flowers.
[Open fists and raise hands.]

3 Teach the children the following words to the melody of "Here We Go 'Round the Mulberry Bush." Add appropriate motions.

1. This is the way we wash our clothes,
   wash our clothes, wash our clothes.
   This is the way we wash our clothes,
   with the gift of water.
2. This is the way we water the yard . . .
3. This is the way we brush our teeth . . .
4. This is the way we quench our thirst . . .
5. This is the way we cook our food . . .
6. This is the way we swim in the pool . . .

4 Let the children make designs with water on the sidewalk or playground. Then have them watch the water evaporate.

Chapter 10
God Made Food

FAITH FOCUS

God feeds us.

John 6:32–40; 1 Corinthians 11:23–26

PREPARING THE FAITH EXPERIENCE

LISTENING

"[M]y Father gives you the true bread from heaven. For the bread of God is that which comes down from heaven and gives life to the world."

So they said to him, "Sir, give us this bread always." Jesus said to them, "I am the bread of life; whoever comes to me will never hunger, and whoever believes in me will never thirst."

John 6:32–35

REFLECTING

Long ago, God fed the Israelites on their journey to the Promised Land with manna, bread from heaven. Later, Jesus multiplied bread to feed a hungry crowd. God still works the miracle of providing a wonderful bread to save and nourish people today—the Eucharist.

Jesus' choice to be with us always in the form of bread and wine is appropriate. Food is essential for life. Our daily food helps us grow physically. The Eucharist helps us grow spiritually so that we may become holy. Jesus becomes one with us in the Eucharist, making us more like himself. We become his very self. The many grains that make the one bread and the many grapes that make the wine are like us, the members of Christ, who are one in him.

The ritual of eating is linked with celebration across cultures. We eat in the intimate circle of our families and give banquets to mark and commemorate special events. As Catholics, our greatest celebration is the Eucharist, where we partake of the Body and Blood of Christ and offer him to the Father. We do this to remember the Death and Resurrection of Jesus, which saved us from death and gave us eternal life. The Eucharist reminds us of our dependence on God and God's goodness.

We look to God for our daily bread to nourish our bodies and for the food of the Eucharist to sustain our spiritual lives. When God designed the world, it was God's plan to provide enough food for all to live. God depends on us, however, to use the earth's resources well so that none of our brothers and sisters starve. Christ says that when we feed those who are hungry, we are feeding him.

Jesus spoke of heaven as a banquet to which all are invited. The Eucharist is a foretaste of that heavenly banquet at which all will be united in love and joy, forever celebrating God's glory. On the feast of the Body and Blood of Christ, we pray:

> **Lord Jesus Christ,**
> **you gave us your body and blood**
> **in the Eucharist**
> **as a sign that even now we share your life.**
>
> **May we come to possess it completely**
> **in the kingdom**
> **where you live for ever and ever.**

Prayer after Communion

RESPONDING

God's Word calls us to respond in love. Respond to God now in the quiet of your heart, and perhaps through the journal that you are keeping this year.

- How can I deepen my experience of the Eucharist?

Jesus, may the children always hunger for you.

Catechism of the Catholic Church

The themes of this chapter correspond to the following paragraphs: 1333, 1392.

THE FAITH EXPERIENCE

Child's Book pages 41–46

SCRIPTURE IN THIS CHAPTER
• *Psalm 33:5*

MATERIALS
• Chapter 10 Scripture card
• Bible
• Option: samples of bread
• Cutout #18, baby
• Crayons or markers
• Decorations for a special meal: tablecloth, place mats, napkins, centerpiece
• 2-inch yellow paper circle (to represent a cracker) for each child
• Tape
• Cloth for a blindfold
• Scissors
• Paint

PREPARATION
• Write the children's names on pages 41, 44, and 45.
• Prepare the "crackers" for the "Feed the Baby" game by putting a piece of rolled tape on the back of each paper circle.
• Place the Chapter 10 Scripture card for SHARING #5 in the Bible.
• Protect the painting area with newspapers.
• Set the tables for a special meal.

MUSIC 'N MOTION
Use *Music 'n Motion* page T270 and CD Track 7 "Stand Up!" for this chapter. For a list of additional music, see page T320.

ENRICHING THE FAITH EXPERIENCE
Use the activities at the end of the chapter to enrich the lesson or to replace an activity with one that better meets the needs of your group.

BOOKS TO SHARE
The Pigeon Finds a Hot Dog! by Mo Willems (Hyperion, 2004)

Stone Soup by Marcia Brown (Aladdin, 2005)

Pancakes, Pancakes! by Eric Carle (Aladdin, 2005)

Pancakes for Breakfast by Tomie dePaola (Voyager Books, 1978)

Growing Vegetable Soup by Lois Ehlert (Harcourt Big Books, 1991)

Bread and Jam for Frances by Russell Hoban (HarperTrophy, 1986)

SNACK
Suggestion: cheese-flavored crackers

ALTERNATIVE PROGRAMS

DAILY PROGRAM
Day 1: Centering, Enriching the Faith Experience #2, Sharing #1
Day 2: Sharing #2 and #3
Day 3: Sharing B
Day 4: Enriching the Faith Experience choice
Day 5: Acting

THREE-DAY PROGRAM
Day 1: Centering, Sharing A
Day 2: Sharing B
Day 3: Acting

LEARNING OUTCOMES

The children will
- be grateful for the food God gives us.
- know that the Mass is a festive meal.
- desire to feed those who are hungry.

COMMENT

Talking about food and the experience of sharing meals prepares the children to comprehend at a later time our great commemorative meal, the Eucharist. What Christ did once and for all in his Paschal Mystery (Passion, Death, Resurrection, and Ascension) is again made present when we partake of this holy meal. The Eucharist is both a meal and a sacrifice, a memorial celebration that involves us in the present moment while we anticipate the fulfillment of the mystery at the end of time.

CENTERING

❶ Gather the children in a circle for *Music 'n Motion* time. Play the Unit 2 song (Track 7). Invite the children to do motions to the song along with you, using *Music 'n Motion* page T270.

❷ Read or recite the nursery rhyme "Little Miss Muffet," "Little Jack Horner," or "Sing a Song of Sixpence" to the children. Have them join you in reciting it. (See Enriching The Faith Experience #4 for the words to the rhymes.)

SHARING [A]

❶ Explain that food is a gift from God.

- *Why do we need food?* (To live and grow, to be strong and healthy)

- *God is good to give us all kinds of food.*

- *It's important to eat good food, such as fruits and vegetables, not just candy, soda pop, and snacks.*

- *We thank God for the gift of food by eating what is on our plates and by not wasting it.*

- *Some people don't have enough food. They are hungry. What can people who have food do to help hungry people?* (Share with them)

Name_____

41 God Made the World

❷ Give the children page 45, "The Story of Flour," and have them fold it to make a book. Before you read the story to the children, introduce it:

• *A food that almost everyone eats is bread.* [Option: Show samples of bread.] *There are many kinds of bread. Which ones can you name?* (White, brown, black, rye, pumpernickel, pita, tortillas, wheat) *Bread is made from flour. Flour is also used to make many other good things to eat.*

• *Your book tells about flour. Let's read that story now.*

❸ Present the snacks as a special meal by using a tablecloth or place mats, a centerpiece, and napkins.

SHARING [B]

❹ Play "Feed the Baby." Display Cutout #18, baby, and give each child a cracker (a circle of paper) with rolled tape on the back. Blindfold the children one at a time and invite them to put the cracker on the cutout. See who can put the cracker nearest the mouth.

❺ **SCRIPTURE** Distribute page 41 and have the children tell what foods come from each plant and animal pictured. Introduce the activity and read the psalm (adapted from Psalm 33:5) from the Scripture card in the Bible:

> *God planned our world so that many plants and animals become our food. Listen to this prayer from the Bible: "The earth is full of the goodness of the Lord."*

❻ Discuss special meals, using the pictures on page 42.

• *Sometimes we have special meals. Why do you think the family in the top picture is having a special meal?* (It is Thanksgiving, Christmas, or someone's birthday.)

• *When God's people go to church, they usually have a special meal too. Look at the bottom picture. What do you see that is also at the family's meal?* (Table, flowers, candles)

• *At church God's family eats a very special bread and drinks a special drink. When you are old enough, you may share in this meal.*

❼ Have the children color the centerpiece on page 42.

Color the centerpiece on the table.

42 God Made the World

© LOYOLA PRESS.

Family Time

Chapter 10:
God Made Food

In this lesson the children reflected on the gift of food. The foundation was laid for the gift of the Eucharist. The children talked about having meals of celebration and feeding those who are poor. Ask your child to tell you about the book he or she made. Set the place mat made by your child on your table or save it for Sunday meals.

Your Child
Children respond to the needs of others. They should learn about those who are hungry and should want to help them.

Reflect
The earth is full of the goodness of the LORD. (adapted from Psalm 33:5)

Pray
Bless us, O Lord, and these your gifts which we are about to receive from your bounty through Christ our Lord. Amen.

Do
• Begin or renew the custom of praying before meals. You might pray the Grace Before Meals shown above.
• Let your child help you make his or her favorite meal.
• Have your child help choose food to donate to those who are poor.
• Invite your child's friends for a meal.
• Begin using a certain serving plate for special family meals.
• Make dinner pleasant by having each person tell good news.
• Read to your child *The Pigeon Finds a Hot Dog!* by Mo Willems. Ask your child to name some favorite foods and talk about how each is made. Thank God for giving us good food to eat.

For more family resources, refer to the Family Activity Booklet and visit **www.loyolapress.com/preschool.**

ACTING

1 **PRAYER** Lead the children in prayer.

• *We can pray for hungry people. Let's pray now for them. Repeat after me.*

> *God, thank you for my food.*
> [Children repeat.]
>
> *Please take care of hungry people,*
> [Children repeat.]
>
> *especially hungry children.*
> [Children repeat.]

2 Have the children make page 43 into a place mat to use at home for family meals, especially on Sunday. Read aloud the sentence on the mat. Tell the children that their place mats will remind their families to thank God for their food. Have the children decorate the mats by painting them.

3 Children who can use scissors well might make fringe along the edges, or cut wavy or jagged sides. You might let the children decorate the place mats with finger paints. Some children might like to make designs on the mats, using the end of a pencil, a glue stick, or other object dipped in paint.

4 Gather the children in a circle for *Music 'n Motion* time. Play the Unit 2 song (Track 7). Invite the children to do motions to the song along with you, using *Music 'n Motion* page T270.

Have the children take home their pages and show their family the Family Time section.

CHECKPOINT

• *Were the learning outcomes achieved?*

• *Do any of the children appear to be poorly nourished?*

Thank you, God.

43 God Made the World

Page 44 is blank.

ENRICHING THE FAITH EXPERIENCE

Use the following activities to enrich the lesson or to replace an activity with one that better meets the needs of your group.

1 Let the children name their favorite foods.

2 Have the children draw their favorite meal on paper plates or glue pictures cut from magazines to the plates.

3 Arrange for the children to share the experience of making bread or biscuits. Prepared bread dough may be used.

4 Read or recite one of the nursery rhymes you did not present in Centering #2.

Little Miss Muffet

Little Miss Muffet
Sat on a tuffet,
Eating her curds and whey.
Along came a spider
And sat down beside her
And frightened Miss Muffet away.

Little Jack Horner

Little Jack Horner
Sat in a corner,
Eating his Christmas pie.
He stuck in his thumb
And pulled out a plum
And said, "What a good boy am I!"

Sing a Song of Sixpence

Sing a song of sixpence,
A pocketful of rye.
Four and twenty blackbirds
Baked in a pie.
When the pie was opened,
The birds began to sing.
Wasn't that a dainty dish
To set before a king!

The Story of Flour

A farmer plants seeds.

The seeds grow into wheat.

Name _____

①

Flour is used to make many good things.

④

㊺ God Made the World

The farmer cuts the wheat.

The wheat goes to a mill where it is ground into flour.

2

3

© LOYOLAPRESS.

God Made the Earth

The children will have a heightened awareness of some essential elements of the earth.

They will respond with awe and love to God, Creator of the earth.

11 GOD MADE LAND

The children learn that God made the earth. They consider various land features. They hear that Jesus loved the world, and they are encouraged to care for it. They make an earth mobile.

12 GOD MADE AIR

After experiencing and recalling the characteristics and uses of air, the children learn that God is like air—all around us. They also hear that according to a story in the Bible, God breathed into us to give us life. They thank God for the gift of life and make a kite.

13 GOD MADE LIGHT

The children talk about different kinds of light and learn that God made light. They hear the story of Jesus curing the man who was blind. They make paper candles as reminders that Jesus is our light.

14 GOD MADE COLOR

The children delight in the different colors in our world. They begin to learn that colors have meaning and can evoke certain responses in us. This prepares them for understanding the use of liturgical colors. They make a color booklet and pray a litany of thanks to God for color.

15 GOD MADE WEATHER

The children study different types of weather and their effect on us. They are reminded to dress for the weather. They hear the song of the three men who called on weather to praise God. They make a weather wheel to set according to the daily weather.

Chapter 11
God Made Land

FAITH FOCUS

God made the world.

Job 38:4–7; Psalm 95:1–5

PREPARING THE FAITH EXPERIENCE

LISTENING

*For the L*ORD *is the great God,*
 the great king over all gods,
Whose hand holds the depths of the earth;
 who owns the tops of the mountains.
The sea and dry land belong to God,
 who made them, formed them by hand.

Psalm 95:3–5

REFLECTING

Genesis tells of God stepping out from eternal silence and calling forth matter into being. At God's Word the world took shape, its features an amazing, intricate system of interdependence capable of sustaining life, our life. In "Pied Beauty" Gerard Manley Hopkins wrote of God, "He fathers-forth whose beauty is past change: Praise Him." In awe at the grandeur of the earth and of the creativity and cleverness of our all-powerful God who designed it, we invoke all creatures to join us in praising our Creator:

Let the earth bless the Lord,
 praise and exalt him above all forever.
Mountains and hills, bless the Lord;
 praise and exalt him above all forever.

Daniel 3:74–75

The beauty of our earth-home is breathtaking. We love to view its majestic mountains, wind-rippled fields, serene lakes, and green, fertile valleys. No wonder Edna St. Vincent Millay exclaimed in her poem "God's World," "O World, I cannot hold thee close enough!" Yet all is but a foretaste of eternal beauty.

Throughout our earthbound existence, we work out our salvation. We search for God who speaks to us in the whispering winds, in the lapping of waves, in rich, life-giving soil, and in the overwhelming silence of rock. We strive to share our priceless possessions, the land and its fruits, with all People of God. We do our best not to abuse the earth and to use it for the good of all.

Jesus is the Savior of all creation, including our planet. His presence on the earth sanctified it. His delight in earthly things and his use of them in the sacraments and in prayers underlines the conviction expressed in Genesis that over and over as God made the earth, "God saw how good it was."

RESPONDING

Having been nourished by God's Word, we are able to respond to God's great love for us. In prayer, respond to God's call to you to share his Word with others. You may also wish to respond in your prayer journal.

- How can I contribute to the beauty of the earth?

 Holy Spirit, teach the children to care for the earth and to share it.

Catechism of the Catholic Church

The themes of this chapter correspond to the following paragraphs: 32, 290–294.

THE FAITH EXPERIENCE

Child's Book pages 47–50

SCRIPTURE IN THIS CHAPTER
• *Psalm 95:3–5*

MATERIALS
• Chapter 11 Scripture card
• Bible
• Clay (or sand on a sensory table)
• Option: rock
• Cutout #19, Mr. Sparrow
• Colored chalk or a large sheet of paper
• Crayons or markers
• Option: magazine pictures of geographical features
• Hole punch
• 12-inch piece of yarn or ribbon for each child
• Glue

PREPARATION
• Write the children's names on pages 47 and 49.
• Place the Chapter 11 Scripture card for SHARING #6 in the Bible.

MUSIC 'N MOTION
Use *Music 'n Motion* page T272 and CD Track 8 "Windy Days" for this chapter. For a list of additional music, see page T320.

ENRICHING THE FAITH EXPERIENCE
Use the activities at the end of the chapter to enrich the lesson or to replace an activity with one that better meets the needs of your group.

BOOKS TO SHARE
Where the Forest Meets the Sea by Jeannie Baker
  (Greenwillow, 1988)

Junglewalk by Nancy Tafuri (Greenwillow, 1988)

Nature's Green Umbrella by Gail Gibbons
  (HarperTrophy, 1997)

It's Earth Day! by Mercer Mayer (HarperFestival, 2008)

SNACK
Suggestion: rock candy

ALTERNATIVE PROGRAMS

DAILY PROGRAM
Day 1: Centering, Sharing A
Day 2: Sharing B, Acting #1
Day 3: Enriching the Faith Experience choice
Day 4: Enriching the Faith Experience choice
Day 5: Acting #2 and #3

THREE-DAY PROGRAM
Day 1: Centering, Sharing A
Day 2: Sharing B, Acting #1
Day 3: Acting #2 and #3

LEARNING OUTCOMES

The children will
• know that God made the earth.
• marvel at certain land features.
• desire to keep the earth beautiful.

COMMENTS

1. This lesson lays the foundation for the children to respect and care for the earth as they marvel at its wonders and express gratitude to God for it. Only lately have we begun to understand that the gifts of our planet must be protected and used with care. Now that the rain forests, the Everglades, the great pine forests, and our lakes and seas are in danger, we realize that we must exercise prudent stewardship over this wonderful world we call home. Its treasures and beauties are not inexhaustible.

2. If there is a large rock outdoors near the school, you might have the children sit on it or, if practical, bring a rock into the classroom.

CENTERING

❶ Gather the children in a circle for *Music 'n Motion* time. Play the Unit 3 song (Track 8). Invite the children to do motions to the song along with you, using *Music 'n Motion* page T272.

❷ Let the children make things out of clay or have them play with sand on a sensory table. Comment:

• *The clay* [sand] *you have been playing with is part of the earth. God gave us the earth as our home. God filled it with things that we need and enjoy.* [Option: Show the rock and talk about the use of rocks in building.]

SHARING [A]

❶ Tell the children the story "Mr. Sparrow's Travels," on page T85, using Cutout #19, Mr. Sparrow.
As you talk, illustrate the story with colored chalk on the board or by drawing on a sheet of paper.

47 God Made the World

Mr. Sparrow's Travels

Hi! I'm Mr. Sparrow. I just returned from a trip. Let me tell you what I saw as I flew.

At first the land seemed flat. Farmers had planted crops. In some places there were forests. Then the land became hilly. The hills had green valleys in between them where people had built houses. Then I flew over a wide, wide river that curved like a snake. There were more hills on the other side. In the distance I could see a beautiful blue lake sparkling in the sun. After the hills came mountains so high that they had snow on their tops. On the other side of the mountains was a desert where desert flowers were in bloom.

As I flew, I thought about how very powerful and wise God is to make such a wonderful place as the earth.

2 Talk about the story.

• *Have you ever seen any of the things Mr. Sparrow saw?*

• *What is the land like where you live? Is it flat or hilly? Do you live near a mountain, lake, desert, or river?*

SHARING [B]

3 Play "Follow the Leader." Pretend to climb a mountain, swim a river, run down a hill, and leap from rock to rock to cross a brook.

4 Distribute page 47 and talk about how children play on the earth.

• *How are the children playing on the earth in the picture?*

• *What activities in the picture do you especially like to do?*

5 Tell how Jesus loved the earth.

• *Jesus loved the earth. He took many long journeys, walking from town to town. He spent time in the desert, but he lived near a lake and a river. He liked to go up a mountain to pray.*

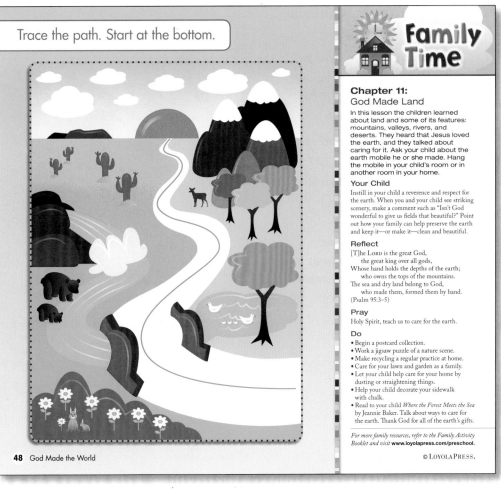

Trace the path. Start at the bottom.

48 God Made the World

Family Time

**Chapter 11:
God Made Land**

In this lesson the children learned about land and some of its features: mountains, valleys, rivers, and deserts. They heard that Jesus loved the earth, and they talked about caring for it. Ask your child about the earth mobile he or she made. Hang the mobile in your child's room or in another room in your home.

Your Child

Instill in your child a reverence and respect for the earth. When you and your child see striking scenery, make a comment such as "Isn't God wonderful to give us fields that beautiful?" Point out how your family can help preserve the earth and keep it—or make it—clean and beautiful.

Reflect

[T]he Lord is the great God,
   the great king over all gods,
Whose hand holds the depths of the earth;
   who owns the tops of the mountains.
The sea and dry land belong to God,
   who made them, formed them by hand.
(Psalm 95:3–5)

Pray

Holy Spirit, teach us to care for the earth.

Do

• Begin a postcard collection.
• Work a jigsaw puzzle of a nature scene.
• Make recycling a regular practice at home.
• Care for your lawn and garden as a family.
• Let your child help care for your home by dusting or straightening things.
• Help your child decorate your sidewalk with chalk.
• Read to your child *Where the Forest Meets the Sea* by Jeannie Baker. Talk about ways to care for the earth. Thank God for all of the earth's gifts.

For more family resources, refer to the Family Activity Booklet and visit **www.loyolapress.com/preschool.**

© LOYOLA PRESS.

6 **SCRIPTURE** Introduce and then read Psalm 95:3–5 from the Scripture card in the Bible.

• *Jesus praised and thanked God for the wonderful things on the earth. Maybe Jesus prayed this prayer that is in the Bible:*

> *The Lord is the great God, the great king over all gods,*
>
> *Whose hand holds the depths of the earth;*
>
> *who owns the tops of the mountains.*
>
> *The sea and dry land belong to God,*
>
> *who made them, formed them by hand.*

7 Encourage the children to care for the earth.

• *God is so good to give us the earth to live on. We can thank God for this gift by taking good care of it.*

• *What can we do to keep the earth beautiful?* (Put garbage where it belongs, pick up litter, plant flowers, don't write on walls)

• *We can keep our own corners of the world neat and clean. What is your corner of the world?* (My room, our home, our yard)

ACTING

1 **PRAYER** Have the children trace the path on page 48, starting at the bottom. Invite the children to pray. Suggest that they pray, "I praise you, God" silently in their hearts as they look at the beautiful and interesting things that God made.

2 Help the children make the mobile on page 49 by following these directions:

• If you wish, cut out the picture of the earth.

• Draw or glue pictures of land features (forests, fields, mountains) in the four sections on the back.

• Punch a hole in the top of the mobile.

• String either yarn or ribbon through the hole to form a loop.

• Invite the children to hang up their mobiles at home, where everyone can see them and remember to care for God's gift of the earth.

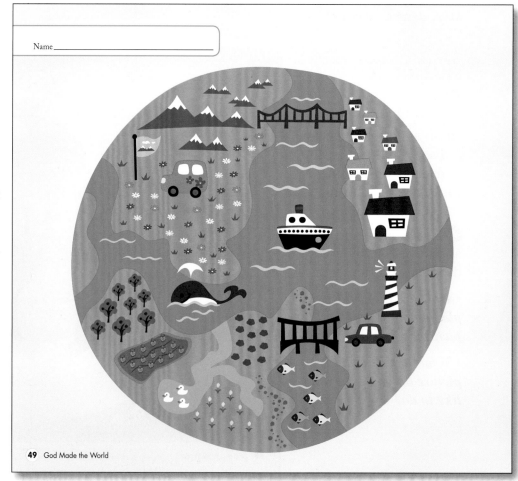

Name

49 God Made the World

3 Gather the children in a circle for *Music 'n Motion* time. Play the Unit 3 song (Track 8). Invite the children to do motions to the song along with you, using *Music 'n Motion* page T272.

Have the children take home their pages and show their family the Family Time section.

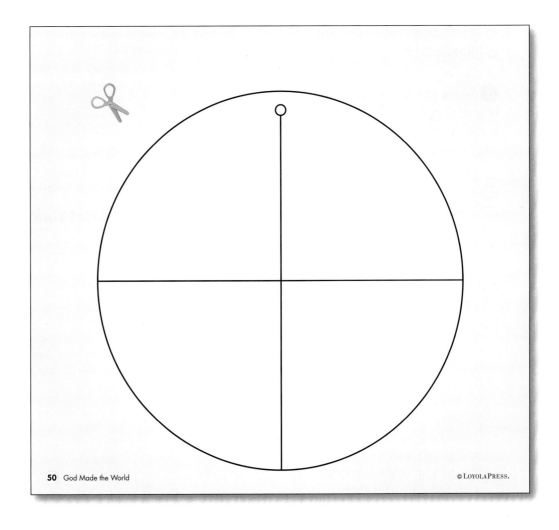

50 God Made the World   © LOYOLAPRESS.

ENRICHING THE FAITH EXPERIENCE

Use the following activities to enrich the lesson or to replace an activity with one that better meets the needs of your group.

1 Take the children on a walk and have them collect stones, leaves, and other mementos to display in the classroom.

2 Encourage the children to begin a rock collection. Give each child a pretty stone or rock, or display a collection of rocks on a table and allow each child to choose one. You might purchase a bag of "river rocks" from a garden supply store. Wash the rocks first to show their true color and brilliance.

3 Show photos of beautiful scenery. After each photo have the children say "We praise you, O God."

4 Dye sand. Add food coloring to water and then pour it into a cup of sand. After 15 minutes, drain the water and spread the sand out on paper towels to dry. Use the sand for the following activities:

• Have the children spoon the colored sand into small jars with lids to form layers that look like mountains and valleys.
• Give the children construction paper and white glue. Have them draw something with the glue and then sprinkle on the sand, one item and one color at a time.

5 Teach the children the song "He's Got the Whole World," using the sentences that follow for additional verses:

2. He's got the towering mountains in his hands.
3. He's got the peaceful valleys in his hands.
4. He's got the busy cities in his hands.
5. He's got the lovely farmlands in his hands.
6. He's got the hot, dry deserts in his hands.

6 Teach the children the poem "The Grand Old Duke of York." Have them march and make the indicated motions.

The Grand Old Duke of York

The grand old Duke of York
He had ten thousand men.
He marched them up a very high hill,
And he marched them down again.
And when they were up, they were up.
[Stand tall.]
And when they were down, they were down.
[Stoop low.]
And when they were only half way up,
[Stoop halfway.]
They were neither up nor down.
[Quickly stand tall and stoop.]

7 Teach the children the song "My God Is So Great." They may make up and add motions.

My God Is So Great

God Made Air

FAITH FOCUS

Air is like God's life.

John 20:19–23

PREPARING THE FAITH EXPERIENCE

LISTENING

[T]he LORD God formed man out of the clay of the ground and blew into his nostrils the breath of life, and so man became a living being.

Genesis 2:7

REFLECTING

According to one Creation story in Genesis, God brought the first human being to life by breathing into him. Breath is equivalent to life. God's divine life, then, animates us.

Later in Salvation History, Jesus appeared to his disciples after the Resurrection and imparted the Holy Spirit. Again the breath of God played a role in the conferring of new life:

[Jesus] said to them again, "Peace be with you. As the Father has sent me, so I send you." And when he had said this, he breathed on them and said to them, "Receive the holy Spirit."

John 20:21–22

A story is told that one night a little girl who was afraid of the dark called for her mother. To comfort her daughter, the mother reminded her, "God loves you. God is everywhere and watches over you." "I know that," the girl responded, "but tonight I want someone with skin."

Air is a good analogy for God. Like God, air is invisible and all around us. In the form of wind, air is very powerful, as typhoons and tornadoes demonstrate. The most striking comparison is that air, like God, is essential for life. Besides keeping us alive, air serves us in many ways. It is a source of energy and protects us from the sun's rays. It fills our tires, sails our boats, and flies our kites. On sweltering days gentle breezes are a delight to hear

and feel. In autumn a brisk wind puts a spring into our steps. In all these ways, air is a sign of God's love.

Scripture highlights the obvious relationship between God and air. In the Old Testament, God spoke to the prophet Elijah in the form of a breeze. (1 Kings 19:11–13) In the New Testament the Holy Spirit descended on the apostles on Pentecost like a strong, driving wind. (Acts of the Apostles 2:1–2) Hoping to experience the same divine life, we pray Saint Augustine's prayer:

> **Breathe into me, Holy Spirit,**
> **that my mind may turn to what is holy.**
> **Move me, Holy Spirit,**
> **that I may do what is holy.**
> **Stir me, Holy Spirit,**
> **that I may love what is holy.**
> **Strengthen me, Holy Spirit,**
> **that I may preserve what is holy.**
> **Protect me, Holy Spirit,**
> **that I may never lose what is holy.**

RESPONDING

God's Word moves us to respond in word and action. Let God's Spirit work within you as you prayerfully consider how you are being called to respond to God's message to you today. Responding through your journal may help to strengthen your response.

- When have I last delighted in God's gift of air?

Holy Spirit, be with me as I speak to the children about you.

Catechism of the Catholic Church

The themes of this chapter correspond to the following paragraphs: 41, 362, 691.

THE FAITH EXPERIENCE

Child's Book pages 51–54

SCRIPTURE IN THIS CHAPTER
• *Genesis 2:7*

MATERIALS
• Chapter 12 Scripture card
• Bible
• Balloon
• Electric or hand fan
• Option: bubbles
• Option: woodwind instrument
• Crayons or markers
• 10-inch piece of string or yarn for each child
• Scissors
• Transparent tape

PREPARATION
• Write the children's names on page 51.
• Place the Chapter 12 Scripture card for SHARING #8 in the Bible.
• If you wish, cut out the multicolored strip on page 53.

MUSIC'N MOTION
Use *Music 'n Motion* page T272 and CD Track 8 "Windy Days" for this chapter. For a list of additional music, see page T320.

ENRICHING THE FAITH EXPERIENCE
Use the activities at the end of the chapter to enrich the lesson or to replace an activity with one that better meets the needs of your group.

BOOKS TO SHARE
Gilberto and the Wind by Marie Hall Ets (Puffin, 1978)

The Wind Blew by Pat Hutchins (Aladdin, 1993)

Feel the Wind by Arthur Dorros (HarperTrophy, 1990)

Little Cloud by Eric Carle (Putnam Juvenile, 2001)

SNACK
Suggestion: popcorn

ALTERNATIVE PROGRAMS

DAILY PROGRAM
Day 1: Centering, Sharing A
Day 2: Enriching the Faith Experience choice
Day 3: Sharing B, Acting #1
Day 4: Enriching the Faith Experience choice
Day 5: Acting #2 and #3

THREE-DAY PROGRAM
Day 1: Centering, Sharing A
Day 2: Sharing B, Acting #1
Day 3: Acting #2 and #3

LEARNING OUTCOMES

The children will
- know what air does for us.
- appreciate the gift of air.
- associate air with God and God's life.

COMMENT

Four-year-old children can grasp simple analogies. Comparing God to air prepares them for a better understanding of God, especially the powerful work of the Holy Spirit. Of the Three Persons of the Trinity, it is the Holy Spirit to whom we attribute the work of sanctification. The Holy Spirit dwelling within us gently moves our minds and hearts but sometimes shakes us with hurricane force to bring about our holiness.

CENTERING

❶ Gather the children in a circle for *Music 'n Motion* time. Play the Unit 3 song (Track 8). Invite the children to do motions to the song along with you, using *Music 'n Motion* page T272.

❷ Whistle for the children or play a woodwind instrument, such as a flute or a recorder. Let several children whistle. Ask:

- **What makes the music when we whistle?** (Air, our breath)

❸ Have the children pay attention to their breathing.

- *Listen to your breathing. Hear how you take air in and then let it out.*

- *Today we will talk about God's gift of air.*

SHARING [A]

❶ Talk about some of the characteristics of air.

- *We can't see air, but it is all around us. Air is powerful. What do we call air when it is moving?* (Wind)

- *What have you seen strong wind do?* (Bend trees, blow off hats, make waves)

- *Let's see what air can do.*

Name _____

51 God Made the World

2 Blow up a balloon at some distance from the children and then release it, letting it fly around the room to show what air can do.

3 Blow air gently on the children with a fan. Comment:

• *When we are too hot, moving air makes us feel good.*

4 Compare the air to God.

• *The air is like God. It is all around us. God is everywhere. We can't see air. We can't see God either. Air is strong. God is strong too. Air gives us life. God gives us life.*

5 Distribute page 51 and use it to talk about air.

• *What is the boy doing in the picture?* (Blowing seeds off a dandelion) *The wind will carry the seeds away so that they can find someplace to grow.*

• *What do you think the girl is pumping into her bike tire?* (Air)

• *What is helping the plane stay up?* (Air)

• *What is pushing the sailboat?* (Air)

• *Have you ever seen a bird gliding or swooping in the air?*

6 Have the children look at the toys on page 52. Ask:

• *Air helps you play. Which toys in the picture use air?* (Bicycle, kite, bubble maker, balloon, pool toy) [Option: Have a child blow bubbles.]

7 Invite the children to trace the missing parts of the toys on page 52.

SHARING [B]

8 **SCRIPTURE** Introduce and then read the adaptation of Genesis 2:7 from the Scripture card in the Bible.

• *Long ago, people told a story about how God made the first human being. Now it is in the Bible. I will read it to you:*

> *"The Lord God formed man out of the clay of the ground. Then God blew breath into the man, and the man came to life."*

• *In this story what made the man come to life?* (God's breath)

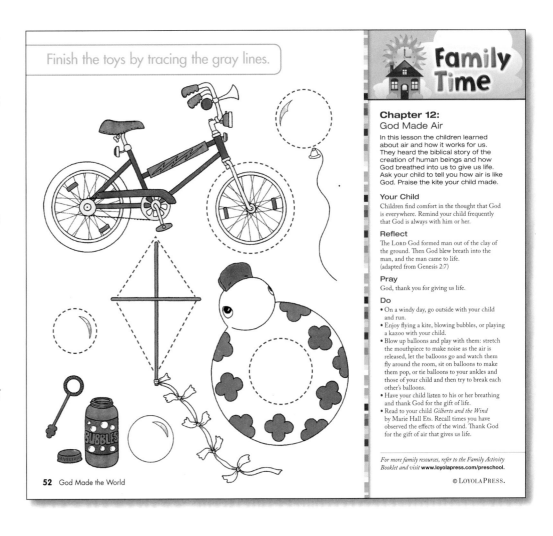

Finish the toys by tracing the gray lines.

Family Time

Chapter 12:
God Made Air

In this lesson the children learned about air and how it works for us. They heard the biblical story of the creation of human beings and how God breathed into us to give us life. Ask your child to tell you how air is like God. Praise the kite your child made.

Your Child
Children find comfort in the thought that God is everywhere. Remind your child frequently that God is always with him or her.

Reflect
The Lord God formed man out of the clay of the ground. Then God blew breath into the man, and the man came to life. (adapted from Genesis 2:7)

Pray
God, thank you for giving us life.

Do
• On a windy day, go outside with your child and run.
• Enjoy flying a kite, blowing bubbles, or playing a kazoo with your child.
• Blow up balloons and play with them: stretch the mouthpiece to make noise as the air is released, let the balloons go and watch them fly around the room, sit on balloons to make them pop, or tie balloons to your ankles and those of your child and then try to break each other's balloons.
• Have your child listen to his or her breathing and thank God for the gift of life.
• Read to your child *Gilberto and the Wind* by Marie Hall Ets. Recall times you have observed the effects of the wind. Thank God for the gift of air that gives us life.

For more family resources, refer to the Family Activity Booklet and visit **www.loyolapress.com/preschool.**

52 God Made the World

© LOYOLA PRESS.

9 Have the children act out the story.

• *Let's act out this story.*

• *Pretend that God has just made you from clay. Lie on the floor perfectly still. Don't move. Don't even breathe.*

• *Now pretend that God comes and breathes air into you. Take a deep breath. Now you are alive. Get up and move.*

• *Do something that you can do because you are alive: hop, skip, jump, or clap.*

10 Talk about the relationship of air to life.

• *We breathe air all the time. We need air to stay alive. What happens if we can't breathe?* (We faint.)

• *When someone has almost drowned, what does a lifeguard do to save the person's life?* (Breathes air into the person)

___

ACTING

1 **PRAYER** Pray a prayer to thank God for life.

• *Let's thank God for giving us life. Close your eyes and think about God in your heart. Take a deep breath.*

• *Thank you, God, for giving us air. Thank you for giving us life. May we always praise you with our lives. May the air we breathe make us think of you.*

2 Have the children make the kite on page 53. Help them follow these directions:

• Make designs or pictures on the yellow part.

• Cut off the multicolored strip.

• Fold the two blue sides to meet in the back and tape them together.

• Cut off the white triangle at the bottom.

• Tape the multicolored strip to the bottom to make the kite's tail.

• Tape the string or yarn to the multicolored strip.

• Run or twirl around with the kite to make it fly.

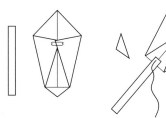

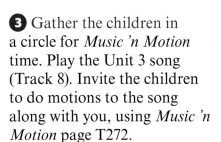

3 Gather the children in a circle for *Music 'n Motion* time. Play the Unit 3 song (Track 8). Invite the children to do motions to the song along with you, using *Music 'n Motion* page T272.

Have the children take home their pages and show their family the Family Time section.

Page 54 is blank.

CHECKPOINT

• *Were the learning outcomes achieved?*

• *Did any children express fear of the wind?*

ENRICHING THE FAITH EXPERIENCE

Use the following activities to enrich the lesson or to replace an activity with one that better meets the needs of your group.

1 Cut a one-inch hole in the side of a flat box. Set a feather (or a piece of plastic-foam packing) in front of the hole. Show the children the empty box. Push down on the box like a bellows, which will blow the feather or plastic-foam away. Ask what was in the box. (Air)

2 Teach the children this poem. You might wish to sing it to the tune of "Jingle Bells."

The wind tells me,
[Sway.]
The birds tell me,
[Flap arms.]
The Bible tells me too,
[Open hands like a book.]
How much our Father loves us all,
[Stretch out arms.]
And now I'm telling you!
[Point to self and then point out.]

3 Read to the children the poem "The March Wind."

The March Wind

I come to work as well as
    play;
I'll tell you what I do;
I whistle all the live-long day,
"Woo-oo-oo-oo! Woo-oo!"

I toss the branches up and
    down
And shake them to and fro,
I whirl the leaves in flocks of
    brown,
And send them high and
    low.

I strew the twigs upon the
    ground,
The frozen earth I sweep;
I blow the children round
    and round
And wake the flowers from
    sleep.

4 Teach the children the song "Praise the Lord Together."

5 Have the children create art with air by blowing through a straw. Cover the work area with newspapers. Give each child a sheet of paper and a straw. Tell the children to put a drop of paint somewhere on the paper and to use the straw to blow the paint gently to make it move and leave a trail. Let the children add drops of different colored paints to form various designs.

6 Have the children make the sounds of air: a gentle breeze, a strong wind, a howling wind, a whistling teakettle.

7 Give the children balloons that adults have blown up. Have the children decorate the balloons with paint or markers.

God Made Air **CHAPTER 12** **T95**

PREPARING THE FAITH EXPERIENCE

LISTENING

Jesus spoke to them again, saying, "I am the light of the world. Whoever follows me will not walk in darkness, but will have the light of life."

John 8:12

REFLECTING

One of the most beautiful and powerful images for God is light. According to the Book of Genesis, God called forth light on the first day. Light is a lovely creation. Who has not stopped to admire sunlight playing on a lake or stream, or filtering through green leaves in a forest? As a poet once remarked, light lends loveliness to all other created things.

Light is both practical and symbolic. It dispels darkness and enables us to see. It is a primordial symbol for goodness that triumphs over evil. Heaven is described as a place of unending light, of eternal day.

Jesus, the Son of God, is truly our sun. He called himself our light, echoing Zechariah, who had prophesied that

*". . .the daybreak from on high will visit us to shine on those who sit in darkness and
death's shadow,
to guide our feet into the path of peace."*

Luke 1:78–79

Jesus also fulfilled Simeon's prophecy by being "a light for revelation to the Gentiles." (Luke 2:32)

Without Jesus we are lost in darkness and sin. We grope and stumble, prey to many dangers. Just as Jesus gave sight to many who were blind, he floods our lives with the light of his life. When we are depressed and despairing, he brightens our days. When we need direction,

he illuminates the way. When we are confused, he gives us the certainty of eternal truth. He sheds light on the mysteries of life. Best of all, Jesus enables us to see the Father.

Jesus tells us that we are to be light for the world. The closer we are to him, the Son of God, the more we will radiate his love. During the Easter Vigil, the celebration of light calls us to reflect on the many ways in which light symbolizes Christ. As the priest holds high the paschal candle, a symbol of Christ, he chants "Light of Christ." Grateful for the gift of Jesus, we respond "Thanks be to God." Then our own tapers are lighted from the large Christ candle.

Let us pray with John Henry Cardinal Newman:

> *Penetrate and possess my whole being so completely that my life may only be a radiance of yours. Shine through me, and be so in me that everyone with whom I come into contact may feel your presence within me. Let them look up and no longer see me, but only you, Jesus.*

RESPONDING

Having reflected upon God's Word, take some time now to continue to respond to God in prayer. You might record your responses in your journal.

- What is my favorite image or name for God?

Jesus, may the children live in your light.

Catechism of the Catholic Church

The themes of this chapter correspond to the following paragraphs: 257, 298.

THE FAITH EXPERIENCE

Child's Book pages 55–58

SCRIPTURE IN THIS CHAPTER
- *Genesis 1:3–4*
- *John 9:1–7*

MATERIALS
- Chapter 13 Scripture card
- Bible
- Lights (such as flashlight, electric candle, night-light, lantern)
- Cutouts: #8, Jesus; #20, sun
- Crayons or markers
- Scissors
- Glue
- Transparent tape

PREPARATION
- Write the children's names on pages 54 and 55.
- Place the Chapter 13 Scripture card for SHARING #1 in the Bible.
- If you wish, use a paper cutter to cut off the strip with the flame on page 57 for the children.

MUSIC'N MOTION
Use *Music 'n Motion* page T272 and CD Track 8 "Windy Days" for this chapter. For a list of additional music, see page T320.

ENRICHING THE FAITH EXPERIENCE
Use the activities at the end of the chapter to enrich the lesson or to replace an activity with one that better meets the needs of your group.

BOOKS TO SHARE
Sunshine: A Book About Sunlight by Josepha Sherman (Picture Window Books, 2003)

Sun Bread by Elisa Kleven (Puffin, 2004)

Arrow to the Sun: A Pueblo Indian Tale by Gerald McDermott (Puffin, 1977)

Sun Up, Sun Down by Gail Gibbons (Voyager Books, 1987)

SNACK
Suggestion: oranges, with the slices arranged to look like the sun's rays.

ALTERNATIVE PROGRAMS

DAILY PROGRAM
Day 1: Centering, Sharing A
Day 2: Enriching the Faith Experience choice
Day 3: Sharing B, Acting #1
Day 4: Acting #2 and #3
Day 5: Enriching the Faith Experience #5

THREE-DAY PROGRAM
Day 1: Centering, Sharing A
Day 2: Sharing B, Acting #1
Day 3: Acting #2 and #3

LEARNING OUTCOMES

The children will

- be grateful to God for the gift of light.
- identify Jesus as light.
- know that Jesus had the power to heal.

COMMENT

The use of candles in Christian worship has its roots in Roman practices and is another instance of the Church "baptizing" pagan customs. In this case it is a wonderful adaptation because light is such a beautiful and fitting symbol for Christ. By the time of Constantine, many candles were being used around the altar, adding splendor to the liturgy. Today at least two candles are to be on or near the altar when the Eucharist is celebrated. The Church blesses candles on February 2, the feast of the Presentation of the Lord, which has become known as Candlemas.

CENTERING

❶ Gather the children in a circle for *Music 'n Motion* time. Play the Unit 3 song (Track 8). Invite the children to do motions to the song along with you, using *Music 'n Motion* page T272.

❷ Display various kinds of lights, such as a flashlight, an electric candle, a night-light, or a lantern. Have individual children take turns holding the lights as they tell how each type of light is used.

❸ Pose a riddle.

• *All these things give us light. But there is something that gives us more light than anything else. It is something very big, bright, round. Can you guess what it is?* (The sun) [Show Cutout #20, sun.]

SHARING [A]

❶ **SCRIPTURE** Read about the creation of light (Genesis 1:3–4) from the Scripture card in the Bible.

• *The Bible tells us that light was the first thing that God made: "God said, 'Let there be light,' and there was light. God saw how good the light was."*

Name _____

2 Distribute page 55 and have the children talk about the light in the picture.

• *What makes this picture so pretty?* (The light)

• *Have you ever seen beautiful light? Where?*

• *Light is a wonderful gift from God.*

• *What happens when there is no light?* (It is dark. We can't see.)

• *Light helps us see.*

3 Talk about Jesus as the light of the world.

• *Jesus tells us that he is the light of the world. He helps us know what to do. He makes us happy.* [Place Cutout #8, Jesus, next to or over the cutout of the sun.]

• *When we are friends of Jesus, we too are like light. We shine.*

4 Teach the children the song "Rise and Shine." Have them march in place.

Rise and Shine

Rise __ and shine __ and give God the glo - ry, glo - ry.

Rise __ and shine __ and give God the glo - ry, glo - ry.

Rise and shine and (clap) give God the glo - ry, glo - ry,

child - ren of the Lord.

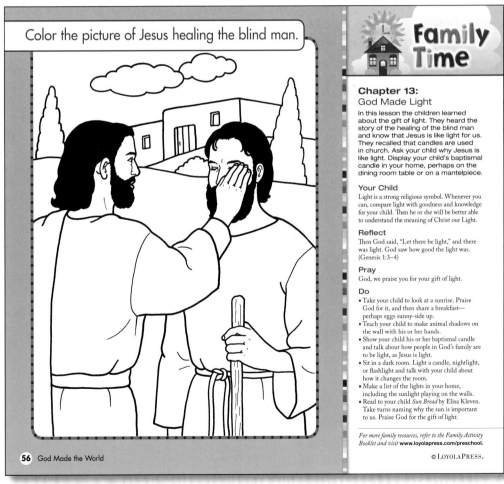

Color the picture of Jesus healing the blind man.

Family Time

Chapter 13:
God Made Light

In this lesson the children learned about the gift of light. They heard the story of the healing of the blind man and know that Jesus is like light for us. They recalled that candles are used in church. Ask your child why Jesus is like light. Display your child's baptismal candle in your home, perhaps on the dining room table or on a mantelpiece.

Your Child
Light is a strong religious symbol. Whenever you can, compare light with goodness and knowledge for your child. Then he or she will be better able to understand the meaning of Christ our Light.

Reflect
Then God said, "Let there be light," and there was light. God saw how good the light was. (Genesis 1:3–4)

Pray
God, we praise you for your gift of light.

Do
• Take your child to look at a sunrise. Praise God for it, and then share a breakfast—perhaps eggs sunny-side up.
• Teach your child to make animal shadows on the wall with his or her hands.
• Show your child his or her baptismal candle and talk about how people in God's family are to be light, as Jesus is light.
• Sit in a dark room. Light a candle, nightlight, or flashlight and talk with your child about how it changes the room.
• Make a list of the lights in your home, including the sunlight playing on the walls.
• Read to your child *Sun Bread* by Elisa Kleven. Take turns naming why the sun is important to us. Praise God for the gift of light.

For more family resources, refer to the Family Activity Booklet and visit www.loyolapress.com/preschool.

56 God Made the World

© LOYOLAPRESS.

SHARING [B]

5 **SCRIPTURE** With the children looking at page 56, tell the story of Jesus healing the man who was blind. (adapted from John 9:1–7)

• *Close your eyes. Do you see darkness? If you were blind, that is all you would see. Listen to this story from the Bible about how Jesus helped a man who could not see.*

> One day, Jesus was walking and saw a man who was blind. Jesus' friends saw the man, too. The man had always been blind. From the time he was born, he could not see. Jesus said, "I am the light of the world." Then Jesus made clay by mixing his spit with dirt on the ground. He put the clay on the man's eyes and told him to wash in a certain pool. The man did what Jesus said. After he washed in the pool, the man was able to see.

• *Wasn't Jesus good to help the man see? Jesus was like light for the man.*

6 On page 56 have the children color the picture of Jesus healing the man who was blind.

7 Talk about the use of candles in church.

• *Because Jesus is the light of the world, we use candles in church. Sometimes we use a very large candle to remind us of Jesus.*

• *Where have you seen candles in church?* (On or near the altar, in front of statues and pictures, in a procession)

ACTING

1 **PRAYER** Lead the children in a prayer based on the picture on page 55.

• *Let's thank God for the wonderful gift of light. Look at the beautiful picture on the page. Imagine that you are there in the picture in the light. The light is all around you. It is like God. God's love is all around you. Let's talk to God now.*

Thank you, God, for giving us light. Thank you for Jesus, who is like light. Thank you for letting us see.

2 Have the children make the paper candle on page 57. Tell them that the candle will remind them that Jesus is the light. Help them follow these directions:

- Color the flowers.
- Write your name on the line above the flowers.
- Cut off the strip with the flame on it.
- Roll the large piece of the page and tape it together.
- Glue or tape the flame to the top of the candle.

57 God Made the World

3 Gather the children in a circle for *Music 'n Motion* time. Play the Unit 3 song (Track 8). Invite the children to do motions to the song along with you, using *Music 'n Motion* page T272.

Have the children take home their pages and show their family the Family Time section.

CHECKPOINT

- Were the learning outcomes achieved?
- How did the children respond to the story of Jesus healing the man who was blind?

ENRICHING THE FAITH EXPERIENCE

Use the following activities to enrich the lesson or to replace an activity with one that better meets the needs of your group.

1 Play "I Spy." Describe various objects in the room. Have the children guess what you are describing.

2 Have the children act out the story of Jesus healing the man who was blind.

3 Hold a procession with the paper candles that the children made. Display on a table a picture of Jesus. Play music and have the children march around the room, pausing periodically and raising the paper candles to Jesus. Let the children set their paper candles around the picture.

4 Let the children shine reflected sunlight on the walls using aluminum pie tins, aluminum foil, metal camp mirrors, or unbreakable mirrors.

5 Create some shadows. Explain that they are made by light shining on and around an object. Then pair the children. Have one stand behind the other and be a "shadow." Tell the children in the front to move, standing in one spot, and then have the "shadows" imitate their movements. Have the children exchange roles.

God Made Color

FAITH FOCUS

God made the world in color.

Psalm 104:24; Ezekiel 1:26–28

PREPARING THE FAITH EXPERIENCE

LISTENING

Above the firmament over their heads something like a throne could be seen, looking like sapphire. Upon it was seated, up above, one who had the appearance of a man. Upward from what resembled his waist I saw what gleamed like electrum; downward from what resembled his waist I saw what looked like fire; he was surrounded with splendor. Like the bow which appears in the clouds on a rainy day was the splendor that surrounded him. Such was the vision of the likeness of the glory of the LORD.

Ezekiel 1:26–28

REFLECTING

In Ezekiel's vision, God's glory appears like a rainbow. In the Book of Genesis, a rainbow is given as the sign of God's love and promise to never again destroy the world by water. Seeing a rainbow across the sky is always an exciting, magical moment. No matter what our age, it gives us a feeling of awe and wonder.

The seven colors of the rainbow and other colors made from combining them occur throughout the natural world. Sometimes as we view lavish splashes of color in our environment, we may feel that we are living in a gigantic kaleidoscope. The Divine Artist has painted creation with remarkable hues, from the delicate pink of a seashell to the vivid purple of an orchid. God has also delighted in presenting colors in stripes and zigzags, plaids, and polka dots.

Colors evoke certain feelings in us and have come to symbolize certain things. Mindful of our response to color, the Church has integrated colors into its celebrations. Red, the color of blood, stands for martyrs and for the Sacred Heart. Green, the sign of life and hope, is the color of Ordinary Time. Purple or violet signify penance and sorrow, as well as royalty. It is used during Lent and Advent. And white, the color of glory and joy, is especially visible during the Easter season. It is also the color of baptismal garments, a girl's First Communion clothes, and wedding dresses. Lovely blue has become the color of Our Lady, Mother of God.

White stands for all things pure. In eternity may we be in the throng John saw standing before the throne and before the Lamb, having "washed their robes and made them white in the blood of the Lamb." (Revelation 7:14)

RESPONDING

God's Word calls us to respond in love. Respond to God now in the quiet of your heart, and perhaps through your journal.

- When did I last take time to revel in the colorful world God has created?

Good God, may the children always appreciate your efforts to make them happy.

Catechism of the Catholic Church

The themes of this chapter correspond to the following paragraph: 1146.

THE FAITH EXPERIENCE

Child's Book pages 59–62

SCRIPTURE IN THIS CHAPTER
• *Sirach 43:11*

MATERIALS
• Chapter 14 Scripture Card
• Bible
• Cutouts: #21, red and green circle; #22–28, color cards
• Option: set of paints or crayons
• Crayons or markers
• Option: prism
• Option: small cards for tickets

PREPARATION
• Write the children's names on pages 59 and 61.
• Place the Chapter 14 Scripture card for SHARING #2 in the Bible.

MUSIC'N MOTION
Use *Music 'n Motion* page T272 and CD Track 8 "Windy Days" for this chapter. For a list of additional music, see page T320.

ENRICHING THE FAITH EXPERIENCE
Use the activities at the end of the chapter to enrich the lesson or to replace an activity with one that better meets the needs of your group.

BOOKS TO SHARE
The Mixed-Up Chameleon by Eric Carle
(HarperTrophy, 1988)

Green Eggs and Ham by Dr. Seuss
(Random House Books for Young Readers, 1960)

Harold and the Purple Crayon by Crockett Johnson
(HarperCollins, 1998)

Little Blue and Little Yellow by Leo Lionni
(HarperTrophy, 1995)

Caps for Sale by Esphyr Slobodkina (HarperTrophy, 1996)

The Color Kittens by Margaret Wise Brown
(Golden Books, 2003)

White Rabbit's Color Book by Alan Baker
(Kingfisher, 1999)

SNACK
Suggestion: any colorful food, such as fruit salad with strawberries, blueberries, and melon

ALTERNATIVE PROGRAMS

DAILY PROGRAM
Day 1: Centering, Sharing A
Day 2: Enriching the Faith Experience choice
Day 3: Sharing B
Day 4: Enriching the Faith Experience choice
Day 5: Acting

THREE-DAY PROGRAM
Day 1: Centering, Sharing A
Day 2: Sharing B
Day 3: Acting

LEARNING OUTCOMES

The children will
- realize that God designed the world full of color.
- appreciate the many colors in the world.
- understand that various colors can mean different things.

COMMENTS

1. This lesson prepares the children to understand the liturgical colors used in Church worship. We celebrate the seasons and feasts of the liturgical year with different colors. Green is the liturgical color for Ordinary Time. Red is for Palm Sunday of the Lord's Passion, Good Friday, Pentecost, apostles, evangelists, and martyrs. White is for the Easter and Christmas seasons, celebrations of the Lord other than his Passion, of Mary, and of the saints. Violet, or purple, is the color for Advent and Lent. At Masses for the dead, violet or purple may be worn; white or black vestments may also be used.

2. Pair children who cannot yet identify colors with children who can. Have the pairs work as partners, using the color cards to practice identifying colors.

3. Be aware of the fact that some children may have a deficiency in color perception, sometimes called color blindness. If you believe that a child has this problem, you may wish to discuss it with the school nurse or with the child's parents.

CENTERING

1 Gather the children in a circle for *Music 'n Motion* time. Play the Unit 3 song (Track 8). Invite the children to do motions to the song along with you, using *Music 'n Motion* page T272.

2 Tell the children the story "Ethan's Green Day" on page T105.

SHARING [A]

1 Ask the children to tell their favorite color. Group them according to these colors and have one child in each group hold the appropriate color card, using Cutouts #22–28, color cards. Have the children give examples of items they like in that particular color (a yellow house, flower, and so on).

2 **SCRIPTURE** Distribute page 59 and talk about God's gift of color.

• Look at the two pictures. God could have made everything in the world the same color. But God knew that we would enjoy the world much more if it had many different colors.

• What things do you see in the picture that are not always the same colors?

Name _____

59 God Made the World

- *God also made people with skin of different colors.*

- *Colors make the world both beautiful and interesting.*

- *God filled the world with hundreds of colors.* [Option: Show the paints or crayons.]

- *God must have liked to play with colors. Using many colors, God made some things spotted or striped. Sometimes God mixed a lot of colors together to make new colors.*

- [Read the adaptation of Sirach 43:11 from the Scripture card in the Bible.] *We see many of the colors God made when we see a rainbow. Listen to what the Bible says about the rainbow: "Look at the rainbow! Then bless God who made it."*

3 Have the children color the rainbow on page 60, making the bars match the paintbrushes at the bottom. Tell the children that the rainbow has all the main colors. [Option: Using a prism, make rainbows for the children.]

Ethan's Green Day

Ethan was a little boy who loved green. He made every picture he colored green. His green crayon was always worn down before the others in his crayon box.

One summer day Ethan fell asleep outside. When he woke up, he couldn't believe his eyes. Everything was green. Ethan blinked a few times. Everything was still green. The grass, of course, was green. So were the leaves on the trees. But now the sky and the clouds were green too. All the flowers in the yard were green and so was his bicycle.

Ethan pinched his green arm to see if he was sleeping. The pinch hurt and should have awakened him, but everything was still green.

Ethan ran into his green house, calling, "Mom, Mom!"

"What is it?" asked his mom. She was sitting in the green kitchen wearing a green dress. Her face was green too.

"Mom," gasped Ethan. "Everything has turned green."

"Silly boy," said Ethan's mom. "You have your sunglasses on."

Sure enough, Ethan had fallen asleep wearing his green sunglasses. He took them off, and the kitchen was once again filled with different colors.

"I like green," exclaimed Ethan, "but not that much!"

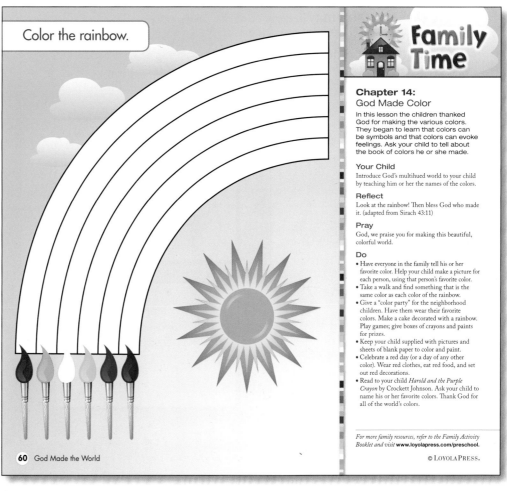

Color the rainbow.

Family Time

Chapter 14:
God Made Color

In this lesson the children thanked God for making the various colors. They began to learn that colors can be symbols and that colors can evoke feelings. Ask your child to tell about the book of colors he or she made.

Your Child
Introduce God's multihued world to your child by teaching him or her the names of the colors.

Reflect
Look at the rainbow! Then bless God who made it. (adapted from Sirach 43:11)

Pray
God, we praise you for making this beautiful, colorful world.

Do
- Have everyone in the family tell his or her favorite color. Help your child make a picture for each person, using that person's favorite color.
- Take a walk and find something that is the same color as each color of the rainbow.
- Give a "color party" for the neighborhood children. Have them wear their favorite colors. Make a cake decorated with a rainbow. Play games; give boxes of crayons and paints for prizes.
- Keep your child supplied with pictures and sheets of blank paper to color and paint.
- Celebrate a red day (or a day of any other color). Wear red clothes, eat red food, and set out red decorations.
- Read to your child *Harold and the Purple Crayon* by Crockett Johnson. Ask your child to name his or her favorite colors. Thank God for all of the world's colors.

*For more family resources, refer to the Family Activity Booklet and visit **www.loyolapress.com/preschool**.*

60 God Made the World

© LOYOLAPRESS.

SHARING [B]

4 Tell the children that colors can have meaning.

• *Sometimes colors mean certain things. When someone is driving a car and comes to a red traffic light, what does red mean?* (Stop) *What does green mean?* (Go)

5 Play "Stop and Go" with Cutout #21, red/green circle. Have the children walk around the room (or pretend to be driving cars) as long as you show the green circle. When you turn the card to the red circle, have the children stop where they are. You may wish to give "tickets" to those children who do not stop.

6 Discuss how certain colors make us feel. Show the color cards as you mention each color. Not all children will feel the same way about the colors.

• *Colors can make us feel certain ways. Yellow is bright and reminds us of the sun. How does it make you feel?* (Good, happy)

• *Blue is soft and pretty. How does it make you feel?* (Calm, peaceful)

• *How does red make you feel?* (Excited, happy)

• *Green may make us feel alive. Plants and trees are green. Green is a sign of life.*

7 Introduce the idea of liturgical colors.

• *Sometimes in church we use colors to help us celebrate certain things. The priest even wears different-colored clothes to mean different things. He wears white to show joy and green to show life. Sometimes the large table called the altar is covered with the same color cloth to match.*

ACTING

1 Have the children make a color booklet from pages 61–62. Help them follow these directions:

- Fold the page in half on the dotted line.

- On each page, color the picture the same color as the balloon beside or above it.

- Draw more things that are the color of the balloon. Draw things that belong to you.

2 **PRAYER** Pray a prayer of thanks to God for the gift of color. Say "Thank you, God, for [name of color]." Have the children add the names of the things they drew in their booklets, preceded by that color. For example:

- Catechist: Thank you, God, for blue.

- Child 1: For blue flowers

- Child 2: For blue sky

3 Gather the children in a circle for *Music 'n Motion* time. Play the Unit 3 song (Track 8). Invite the children to do motions to the song along with you, using *Music 'n Motion* page T272.

Have the children take home their pages and show their family the Family Time section.

62 God Made the World

© LOYOLA PRESS.

ENRICHING THE FAITH EXPERIENCE

Use the following activities to enrich the lesson or to replace an activity with one that better meets the needs of your group.

1 Help the children make a collage using items that are their favorite color. Provide the children with colored buttons, scraps of material, yarn, and pieces of paper. Have the children select items of their chosen color and glue them onto construction paper.

2 Hold a "color hunt." Ask the children to find things in the room that are the same color.

3 Have the children make a design with tempera paint or watercolors, using stripes, zigzags, or spots.

4 Have the children make handprints on construction paper using their favorite color of paint.

5 Let the children mix red and blue paint, yellow and red paint, and yellow and blue paint on paper to discover the colors created by combining the paints.

6 Have the children drip various colored paints on paper, place the paper in a box, and spin the box. The paint will run, creating designs.

7 Read the poem "Colors" to the children and have them listen for their favorite color. Hold up the color card that corresponds to each verse.

Colors

Red, red, roses are red.
Red is the hair on Jeremy's head.
Cherries are red and strawberries too.
I like red apples. How about you?

Orange, orange, oranges are good.
I'd like one now—I certainly would!
A gorgeous orange is the setting sun.
I think orange is a lot of fun.

Yellow, yellow, butter is yellow,
So is the cap on that little fellow.
Bees and lemons, bananas, the sun.
Want a happy color? Yellow is the one.

Green, green, grass is green,
Green trees and grass—a lovely scene.
Lettuce, peas, and beans and such,
God must like green very much.

Blue, blue, the sky is blue—
Light blue, dark blue, dazzling too.
Bluebirds, blueberries, oceans and lakes.
A bit of blue a pretty world makes.

Brown, brown, mud is brown.
Mud on the rug makes Mom and Dad frown.
Brown is the color of things that are nice,
Like chocolate, puppies, birds, and mice.

Purple, purple, grapes are fine.
Pansies, violets, plums, and wine.
Pale and soft or deep and rich.
Purple's my favorite; I'll not switch.

Mary Kathleen Glavich, S.N.D

FAITH FOCUS

God made weather for our good.

Sirach 43

PREPARING THE FAITH EXPERIENCE

LISTENING

The clear vault of the sky shines forth
 like heaven itself, a vision of glory.
The orb of the sun, resplendent at its rising:
 what a wonderful work of the Most High!

Behold the rainbow! Then bless its Maker,
 for majestic indeed is its splendor;
It spans the heavens with its glory,
 this bow bent by the mighty hand of God.

When the mountain growth is scorched
   with heat,
 and the flowering plains as though by flames,
The dripping clouds restore them all. . .

Sirach 43:1–2,11–12,22–23

REFLECTING

Sirach 43 is a song of praise to the Lord of weather. With infinite ingenuity, God designed the world with a remarkable balance of forces. The sun's rays, rain, snow, and ice sustain and nurture the life forms of the earth.

Weather phenomena can be magnificent displays of power and beauty. To explain natural occurrences—such as sunrise, sunset, and lightning—people in ancient pagan cultures installed in the heavens various deities, each in charge of an element of weather. Apollo was the sun-god who drove his chariot across the sky every day, Zeus controlled thunder and lightning, Isis was the goddess of the rainbow, and Aeolus guarded the winds.

As Christians we believe with our Jewish spiritual ancestors in the one God who created everything. Christians also believe that Jesus redeemed creation and became Lord of creation. His are the sun and the winds, the rain and the snow. His are the seasons. The same God who called forth the world into being and who once commanded a storm on the Sea of Galilee to cease is still the master of all creation.

The powerful natural forces testify to God's goodness and wisdom. Wisdom 13:5 states "[F]rom the greatness and the beauty of created things / their original author, by analogy, is seen."

RESPONDING

Having been nourished by God's Word, we are able to respond to God's great love for us. In prayer, respond to God's call to you to share his Word with others. You may also wish to respond in your prayer journal.

- What image in nature best represents God for me?

  Lord of all, help the children find you through your works.

Catechism of the Catholic Church

The themes of this chapter correspond to the following paragraph: 344.

THE FAITH EXPERIENCE

Child's Book pages 63–66

SCRIPTURE IN THIS CHAPTER
• *Daniel 3:62,64–65,67–70,73*

MATERIALS
• Chapter 15 Scripture card
• Bible
• Cutouts: #13–17, raindrops; #20, sun; #29, snowflake; #30, cloud
• Crayons or markers
• Music for dancing in SHARING #4
• Scissors

PREPARATION
• Write the children's names on pages 63 and 65.
• Place the Chapter 15 Scripture card for SHARING #6 in the Bible.
• If you wish, use a paper cutter to cut off the strip of pictures on page 65 for the children.
• Make slits in the weather wheels with a utility or hobby knife.

MUSIC 'N MOTION
Use *Music 'n Motion* page T272 and CD Track 8 "Windy Days" for this chapter. For a list of additional music, see page T320.

ENRICHING THE FAITH EXPERIENCE
Use the activities at the end of the chapter to enrich the lesson or to replace an activity with one that better meets the needs of your group.

BOOKS TO SHARE
Katy and the Big Snow by Virginia Lee Burton (Houghton Mifflin, 1974)

The Big Snow by Berta and Elmer Hader (Macmillan, 1994)

The Snowy Day by Ezra Jack Keats (Puffin, 1976)

Snowsong Whistling by Karen E. Lotz (Dutton, 1993)

Listen to the Rain by Bill Martin Jr. and John Archambault (Holt, 1988)

Umbrella by Taro Yashima (Puffin, 1977)

SNACK
Suggestion: iced tea (sun tea if possible); cookies with smiling sun faces made with icing or chocolate chips

---

ALTERNATIVE PROGRAMS

DAILY PROGRAM
Day 1: Centering, Sharing A
Day 2: Enriching the Faith Experience choice
Day 3: Sharing B
Day 4: Enriching the Faith Experience choice
Day 5: Acting

THREE-DAY PROGRAM
Day 1: Centering, Sharing A
Day 2: Sharing B
Day 3: Acting

LEARNING OUTCOMES

The children will

- know that God made weather.
- understand that weather is both good and necessary.
- thank God for weather.

COMMENTS

1. In this lesson the children learn that we are dependent on God for the weather. Through reflecting on the various kinds of weather, they come to realize more deeply how powerful and how good God is. Not without reason are theophanies (manifestations) of God in Scripture accompanied by thunder, lightning, and clouds. Avoid giving children the impression, however, that God is directly responsible for the weather. Otherwise they will conclude that God causes tornadoes, hurricanes, and floods that do damage and destroy life.

2. Four-year-old children are beginning to identify their feelings, but they do not have the vocabulary to express what they feel. Use this lesson and other opportunities to help the children verbalize their emotions. Make comments (to individuals), such as "I see that you are upset this morning" or "I feel very happy today because I enjoy being with you."

CENTERING

❶ Gather the children in a circle for *Music 'n Motion* time. Play the Unit 3 song (Track 8). Invite the children to do motions to the song along with you, using *Music 'n Motion* page T272.

❷ Tell the story "Miguel's Mixed-Up Day."

Miguel's Mixed-Up Day

One morning, bright sunshine shone through Miguel's window. As soon as he could, Miguel ran outside to play. Later, the wind began to blow. At first it felt good, but then it became stronger. The sun went away, and dark clouds filled the sky. A raindrop fell on Miguel's nose. He put away his toys and ran inside.

From his window, Miguel watched the rain fill up the birdbath and make puddles on the sidewalk. Lightning flashed and thunder roared. Suddenly little bits of hail started hitting the window. Miguel was glad that he was inside.

Soon the storm clouds moved away and the sun came out. Miguel's big sister Sara called, "Miguel, there's a beautiful rainbow outside. Come and see."

As they looked at the rainbow, Miguel said, "Sara, today we had every kind of weather except snow. What a mixed-up day!" That night at dinner Mom made snow cones for dessert. "Wow," said Miguel. "Now I've seen everything!"

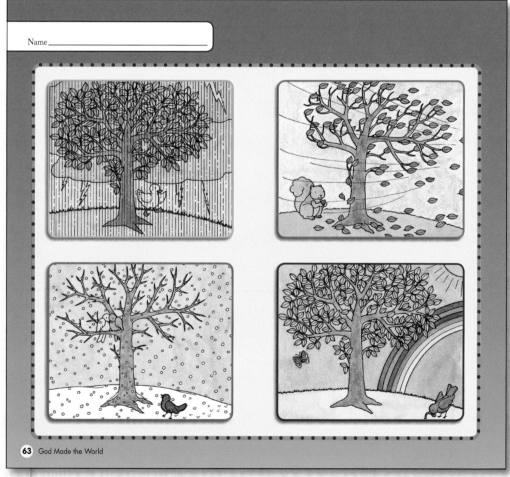

Name

SHARING [A]

① Distribute page 63. Have the children tell what weather the tree is experiencing in each picture. Ask:

- *What is the weather like today?*

② Discuss the weather, using Cutouts #13–17, raindrops, #20, sun, and #29 and #30, snowflake and cloud. Comment: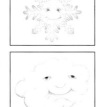

- *God is very wise. God made weather to help things grow.*

- *Sadie Sunbeam makes plants strong and healthy. She gives us energy.*

- *Connor Cloud protects us from the sun's rays. Benny also gives us rain and snow.*

- *Ricky Raindrop waters the thirsty plants and fills our lakes and rivers.*

- *Susie Snowflake makes the earth look beautiful. When she melts, she also gives us water to make things grow.*

- *What kind of weather do you like? Why?*

- *Isn't God good to give us so many different kinds of weather?*

③ Have the children draw lines on page 64 to connect the type of weather with the proper attire. Encourage them to dress appropriately for the weather in order to stay healthy.

SHARING [B]

④ Have the children do a "weather dance." First teach them motions for the following types of weather. Then play music and have the children dance. Call out the words *sunbeams, raindrops,* and *snowflakes* in random order to direct the children's motions.

- Sparkling as sunbeams: opening and closing hands
- Pitter-pattering as rain-drops: walking on tiptoe
- Floating as snowflakes: twirling around

⑤ Talk about how weather sometimes can make us feel happy or sad. Show each weather cutout and ask the children how they might feel during such weather. Ask why they might feel that way.

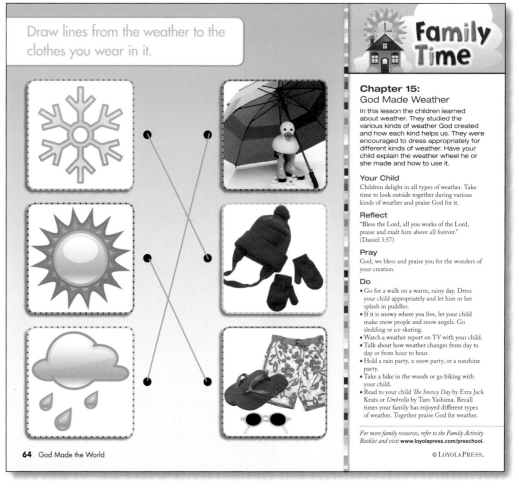

Draw lines from the weather to the clothes you wear in it.

Family Time

Chapter 15:
God Made Weather

In this lesson the children learned about weather. They studied the various kinds of weather God created and how each kind helps us. They were encouraged to dress appropriately for different kinds of weather. Have your child explain the weather wheel he or she made and how to use it.

Your Child

Children delight in all types of weather. Take time to look outside together during various kinds of weather and praise God for it.

Reflect

"Bless the Lord, all you works of the Lord, praise and exalt him above all forever." (Daniel 3:57)

Pray

God, we bless and praise you for the wonders of your creation.

Do

- Go for a walk on a warm, rainy day. Dress your child appropriately and let him or her splash in puddles.
- If it is snowy where you live, let your child make snow people and snow angels. Go sledding or ice skating.
- Watch a weather report on TV with your child.
- Talk about how weather changes from day to day or from hour to hour.
- Hold a rain party, a snow party, or a sunshine party.
- Take a hike in the woods or go biking with your child.
- Read to your child *The Snowy Day* by Ezra Jack Keats or *Umbrella* by Taro Yashima. Recall times your family has enjoyed different types of weather. Together praise God for weather.

For more family resources, refer to the Family Activity Booklet and visit www.loyolapress.com/preschool.

64 God Made the World

© LOYOLAPRESS.

6 SCRIPTURE Introduce the story of the three young men who praised God. Then read the verses from Daniel 3:62,64–65,67–70,73 from the Scripture card in the Bible.

• *In the Bible there is a story about how God once saved the lives of three young men. The men were so happy that they called on all types of weather to praise God. Again and again they said "bless the Lord," which means "praise the Lord." This is what they sang* [If you wish, sing the words]:

• *Sun and moon, bless the Lord . . .*

• *Every shower and dew, bless the Lord . . .*

• *All you winds, bless the Lord . . .*

• *Cold and chill, bless the Lord . . .*

• *Dew and rain, bless the Lord . . .*

• *Frost and chill, bless the Lord . . .*

• *Ice and snow, bless the Lord . . .*

• *Lightnings and clouds, bless the Lord . . .*

ACTING

1 PRAYER Lead the children to thank God for weather. Let individuals choose a weather cutout and say "For [cutout's name]." Then have the class sing in response on one note, "Thank you, God." Add or let the children add lines such as the following:

• *For sunshine and blue skies . . .*

• *For warm days . . .*

• *For fluffy white clouds . . .*

• *For gentle rain . . .*

• *For cool days . . .*

• *For thunder and lightning . . .*

• *For soft, beautiful snow . . .*

• *For hail . . .*

• *For frost . . .*

• *For little breezes . . .*

• *For powerful winds . . .*

2 Have the children make a weather wheel, using page 65. Help them follow these directions:

• Cut slits in the wheel along the lines.

• Color the sun yellow.

• Color the raindrops blue.

• Cut the strip from the page.

• Fold the page on the dotted line so that it stands.

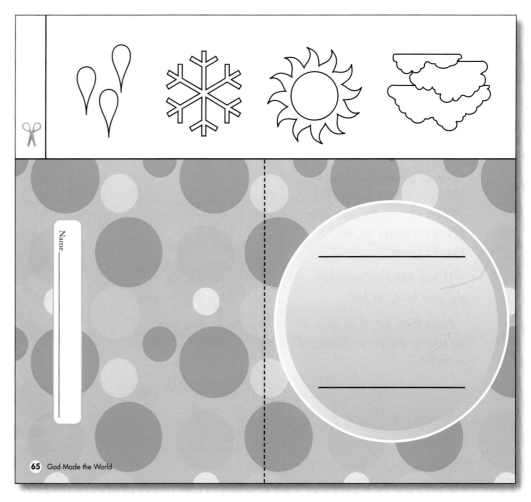

Name

65 God Made the World

Page 66 is blank.

- Put the ends of the strip through the slits in the wheel. (The strip should slide back and forth to show the pictures.)

❸ Tell the children how to use the weather wheel.

• *Each morning when you wake up, thank God for the new day. Then look out the window to see what the weather is and make your weather wheel match it.*

❹ Gather the children in a circle for *Music 'n Motion* time. Play the Unit 3 song (Track 8). Invite the children to do motions to the song along with you, using *Music 'n Motion* page T272.

Have the children take home their pages and show their family the Family Time section.

CHECKPOINT

- *Were the learning outcomes achieved?*
- *Do any of the children seem abnormally fearful of storms?*

ENRICHING THE FAITH EXPERIENCE

Use the following activities to enrich the lesson or to replace an activity with one that better meets the needs of your group.

❶ Have clothes for various kinds of weather in the dress-up/play pretend corner of your room: boots, raincoats, scarves, mittens, shorts, hats, umbrellas. Let the children play with them.

❷ For one month keep a classroom chart of the weather, drawing appropriate symbols on a large calendar that you have posted on a bulletin board.

❸ Make a classroom weather wheel showing various types of weather. Attach an arrow to the center with a brass fastener and point the arrow at the representation of the day's weather.

❹ Have the children make a winter scene, using white crayon on blue construction paper. They might make a snowstorm by painting on dark paper with an object dipped in white tempera paint or by gluing cotton balls onto the paper.

God Made Living Things

The children will marvel at the abundance and variety of living things.

They will respond with gratitude and love to our wise and loving God.

They will feel secure in the knowledge that God loves and cares for them.

16 GOD MADE FLOWERS

The children experience and talk about the beauty of flowers and learn that flowers are often given as gifts. They hear that Jesus told us that God cares for the many flowers and cares even more for us. They receive a flower and then make a basket of flowers to give to someone.

17 GOD MADE TREES

After discussing the many uses of trees, the children hear about the role that wood played in the life of Jesus. They come to know that they should be a good tree and bear good fruit. They praise God for trees and then complete a picture of a tree.

18 GOD MADE ANIMALS

After making animals from clay, the children learn that God made all the animals. They talk about ways that animals help us, and they are encouraged to care for animals. They make a box decorated with animals.

19 GOD MADE BIRDS

The children name various birds and then recall that God made and cares for all of them. They hear that Jesus told us that God cares for us more than for the sparrows. They dance to express thanks to God. They make a bird mobile.

20 GOD MADE FISH

The children name various sea creatures and praise the Lord for them. They hear the story of the large catch of fish and learn that they are like a fish that Jesus caught. They color a large fish.

PREPARING THE FAITH EXPERIENCE

LISTENING

"For see, the winter is past,
  the rains are over and gone.
The flowers appear on the earth,
  the time of pruning the vines
    has come,
  and the song of the dove is
    heard in our land.
The fig tree puts forth its figs,
  and the vines, in bloom, give
    forth fragrance."

Song of Songs 2:11–13

REFLECTING

God placed the first man and woman in a garden, the Garden of Eden. We can only imagine the luxurious plants and flowers that bloomed there. Apparently God delighted in this garden, for Scripture describes God as "moving about in the garden at the breezy time of the day." (Genesis 3:8) Although we cannot go to the Garden of Eden, we still can enjoy the beautiful flowers that enhance our planet with their fragrance and loveliness. In describing creation, Donald Culross Peattie wrote:

The beauty of a butterfly's wing, the beauty of all things, is not slave to purpose, a drudge sold to futurity. It is excrescence, superabundance, random ebullience, and sheer delightful waste to be enjoyed in its own right.

An Almanac for Moderns

Jesus must have loved the flowers of Palestine. In teaching he once referred to God's caring for all the flowers of the field, commenting

that not even Solomon in all his glory was arrayed as one of them. Jesus' lesson was that we should trust in our Father to care for us even as he cares for these less important creations.

Mary, the mother of Jesus, is known as "a lily among thorns," a title from Song of Songs 2:2. Another title for Mary, one that is in the Litany of Loreto, is Mystical Rose. Mary must have loved flowers. Recall that Our Lady of Guadalupe gave roses to Juan Diego in December to prove to the bishop that Juan's visions were real.

We present bouquets and corsages to one another as tokens of love and respect. How God must love us to give us a whole world filled with flowers!

RESPONDING

God's Word moves us to respond in word and action. Let God's Spirit work within you as you prayerfully consider how you are being called to respond to God's message to you today. Responding through your journal may help to strengthen your response.

- When have flowers reminded me of God's love?

God, may the children's trust in you grow.

Catechism of the Catholic Church

The themes of this chapter correspond to the following paragraphs: 270, 303–305.

THE FAITH EXPERIENCE

Child's Book pages 67–70

SCRIPTURE IN THIS CHAPTER
• *Luke 12:27–28*

MATERIALS
• Chapter 16 Scripture card
• Bible
• Cutouts: #31, rose; #32, bouquet
• Option: vase of flowers
• Music for dancing for Sharing #5
• Real or artificial flower for each child
• Crayons or markers
• Scissors
• Stapler

PREPARATION
• Write the children's names on pages 67 and 70.
• Place the Chapter 16 Scripture card for SHARING #4 in the Bible.
• If you wish, use a paper cutter to cut off the strip on page 69 for the children.

MUSIC 'N MOTION
Use *Music 'n Motion* page T274 and CD Track 9 "Praise and Glorify" for this chapter. For a list of additional music, see page T320.

ENRICHING THE FAITH EXPERIENCE
Use the activities at the end of the chapter to enrich the lesson or to replace an activity with one that better meets the needs of your group.

BOOKS TO SHARE
Miss Rumphius by Barbara Cooney (Puffin, 1985)

The Story of Ferdinand by Munro Leaf (Puffin, 2007)

No Roses for Harry! by Gene Zion (HarperTrophy, 1976)

The Rose in My Garden by Arnold Lobel (HarperTrophy, 1993)

SNACK
Suggestion: apple slices or orange segments fanned out above celery sticks to look like flowers

---

ALTERNATIVE PROGRAMS

DAILY PROGRAM
Day 1: Centering, Sharing A
Day 2: Enriching the Faith Experience choice
Day 3: Sharing B, Acting #1
Day 4: Enriching the Faith Experience choice
Day 5: Acting #2 and #3

THREE-DAY PROGRAM
Day 1: Centering, Sharing A
Day 2: Sharing B, Acting #1
Day 3: Acting #2 and #3

LEARNING OUTCOMES

The children will

- know that God made a variety of flowers.
- realize that creation demonstrates God's goodness and wisdom.
- appreciate God's gift of flowers.

COMMENTS

1. In this lesson the children reflect on the beautiful flowers. They learn that God cares for human beings much more than for flowers. We use flowers to adorn our churches, giving back in a way a gift that God gave to us. Lovely flowers enhance celebrations. The lily has become associated with our celebration of Easter, and the poinsettia with our celebration of Christmas.

2. If this lesson does not occur during a flower season in your region, you might teach it at another time.

3. You might make the flowers you give the children in ACTING #1 out of facial tissue and then spray perfume on them.

CENTERING

1 Gather the children in a circle for *Music 'n Motion* time. Play the Unit 4 song (Track 9). Invite the children to do motions to the song along with you, using *Music 'n Motion* page T274.

2 Have the children play "Ring-around-the-Rosy."

Explain that posies are flowers. Help the children make a ring (form a circle) and hold hands. Place Cutout #31, rose, in the middle of the circle. As they sing the song, have the children walk and then fall to the floor on the last line.

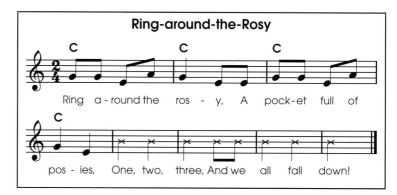

Ring-around-the-Rosy

Ring a-round the ros-y, A pock-et full of pos-ies, One, two, three, And we all fall down!

Name

67 God Made the World

3 Introduce the topic of flowers.

• *How many flowers can you name?* [Option: show the vase of flowers.]

• *God made all the flowers in the world.*

• *Today we will talk about God's gift of flowers.*

SHARING [A]

1 Distribute page 67 and talk about flowers.

• *Look at all the beautiful flowers in the picture.*

• *What flower do you like best?*

• *Do you have flowers in your yard? What kind? Have you seen flowers in a park? What kind?*

• *Flowers smell good too. They smell like perfume. If you put flowers in a room, soon the whole room smells good.*

• *Flowers make the world more beautiful. God is good to give us flowers to look at and smell.* [Option: Carry a vase of flowers around to the children so that they can see and smell them.]

2 Help the children circle the flower in each row that is different from the other flowers on page 68.

SHARING [B]

3 Talk about what flowers must have in order to grow.

• *What do flowers need in order to grow?* (Sun, good soil, water)

• *Do you ever help care for flowers at home? What do you do?* (Plant flowers, water them, pull weeds)

4 **SCRIPTURE** Read from the Scripture card in the Bible about God's care for flowers. (adapted from Luke 12:27–28)

• *Jesus once used flowers to teach people. Listen.*

• *One day Jesus was telling people about how God loves us. He said, "Look at the flowers. They don't work, but God clothes them in clothes more beautiful than a king's. God will take care of you just as God takes care of the flowers. You don't have to worry."*

• *Who sends the rain and the sun that help the flowers grow?* (God)

• *Who made all the flowers?* (God)

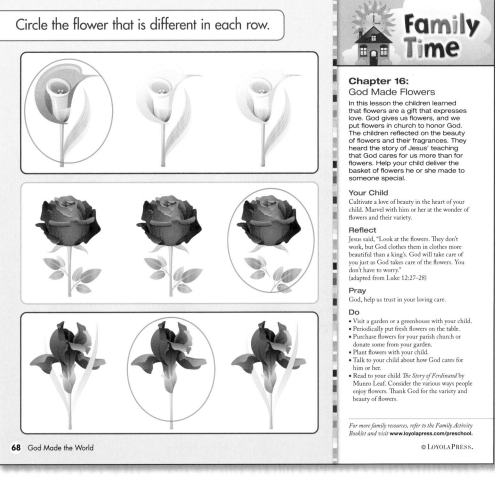

Circle the flower that is different in each row.

68 God Made the World

Family Time

Chapter 16:
God Made Flowers

In this lesson the children learned that flowers are a gift that expresses love. God gives us flowers, and we put flowers in church to honor God. The children reflected on the beauty of flowers and their fragrances. They heard the story of Jesus' teaching that God cares for us more than for flowers. Help your child deliver the basket of flowers he or she made to someone special.

Your Child
Cultivate a love of beauty in the heart of your child. Marvel with him or her at the wonder of flowers and their variety.

Reflect
Jesus said, "Look at the flowers. They don't work, but God clothes them in clothes more beautiful than a king's. God will take care of you just as God takes care of the flowers. You don't have to worry."
(adapted from Luke 12:27–28)

Pray
God, help us trust in your loving care.

Do
• Visit a garden or a greenhouse with your child.
• Periodically put fresh flowers on the table.
• Purchase flowers for your parish church or donate some from your garden.
• Plant flowers with your child.
• Talk to your child about how God cares for him or her.
• Read to your child *The Story of Ferdinand* by Munro Leaf. Consider the various ways people enjoy flowers. Thank God for the variety and beauty of flowers.

For more family resources, refer to the Family Activity Booklet and visit **www.loyolapress.com/preschool.**

© LOYOLAPRESS.

5 **PRAYER** Invite the children to pray. Suggest that the children pretend to be any flower they wish. Let them "dance" in the breeze to music. Tell them to make their dance a prayer of praise to God who always takes care of us. Set the ground rule that they are not to touch anyone else as they dance.

6 Show Cutout #32, bouquet, and talk about flowers as gifts.

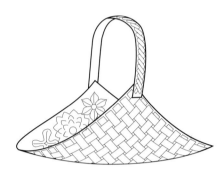

• *In church you usually see flowers. We put them there to praise and honor God.*

• *We give flowers to Mary, God's mother, too.*

ACTING

1 Give each child a flower, either real or artificial. Explain:

• *This flower is a gift from me. It shows that I like you. When you look at this flower, think about how much God loves you. God gave us all the flowers in the world.*

2 Have the children make the basket of flowers on page 69 to give to someone they love. Help them follow these directions:

• Color the flowers.

• Cut off the strip at the side.

• Staple one end of the strip to the corner of the large square where there is a blue dot.

• Staple the other end to the blue dot at the opposite corner so that the ends of the square are pulled up to form a basket.

3 Gather the children in a circle for *Music 'n Motion* time. Play the Unit 4 song (Track 9). Invite the children to do motions to the song along with you, using *Music 'n Motion* page T274.

Have the children take home their pages and show their family the Family Time section.

CHECKPOINT

• *Were the learning outcomes achieved?*

• *How have the children demonstrated that they understand the significance of your gift of a flower?*

69 God Made the World

ENRICHING THE FAITH EXPERIENCE

Use the following activities to enrich the lesson or to replace an activity with one that better meets the needs of your group.

1 Have the children make pictures of flowers. Give them small paper drinking cups, cupcake/muffin foils, or buttons to glue on as centers of the flowers.

2 Have the children make flowers out of six 5-inch circles of tissue paper stapled together in the middle and pulled up to form petals. These flowers may be glued on paper or attached to a craft stem.

3 Teach the children the following finger play. You might sing it to the tune of "On Top of Old Smokey."

> This is my garden.
> [Extend hand, palm up.]
> I'll rake it with care.
> [Make pulling motion with hands.]
> And plant some flower seeds
> [Make planting motions with thumb and index finger.]
> Right in there.
> The sun will shine,
> [Circle arms above head.]
> The rain will fall.
> [Flutter fingers downward.]
> And my garden will blossom
> [Cup hands; raise them.]
> And grow straight and tall.
> [Bring arms down to sides.]

4 Cut apart the sections of egg cartons and fill them with potting soil. Let each child have one section to plant seeds. Place the sections in a well-lit place. Keep the soil moist. Have the children observe the plants' growth.

5 Have the children gather small flowers. Press them between paper towels inside of large books. Help the children glue the dried flowers onto paper or press them between two pieces of clear contact paper.

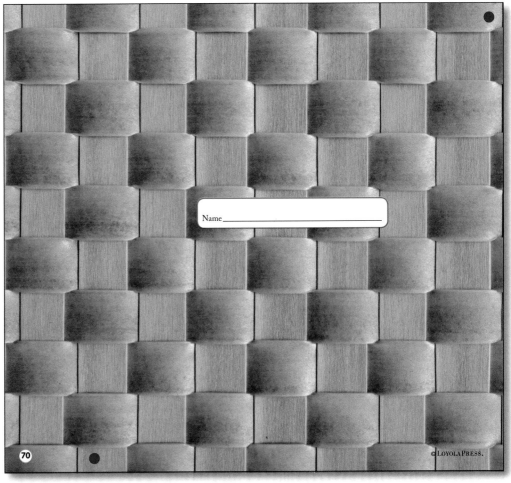

Name _____

70

God Made Trees

FAITH FOCUS

God's gift of trees serves us in many ways.

Luke 6:43–45

PREPARING THE FAITH EXPERIENCE

LISTENING

Out of the ground the LORD God made various trees grow that were delightful to look at and good for food, with the tree of life in the middle of the garden and the tree of the knowledge of good and bad.

Genesis 2:9

REFLECTING

Joyce Kilmer concludes his popular poem "Trees" with the lines "Poems are made by fools like me, / But only God can make a tree." Who has not been in awe of the majesty of the gigantic trees in the redwood forest, the delicate beauty of maples laced with ice, and the stately grace of white birches? Who has not marveled at the glory of a brilliant autumn landscape with its flaming red, yellow, and orange trees? And who has not been transfixed by the beauty of bare tree branches against a winter sky? Trees are one of God's finest creations.

Not only are trees beautiful to behold, but they also have practical uses. Their fruits and nuts provide us with food. With their wood we make our homes, furniture, boats, and paper. Trees even shade us from the burning sun, and the sound of a rustling breeze soothes us.

According to Scripture, trees play a significant role in salvation history. In Genesis, fruit plucked from the tree of the knowledge of good and evil led to the fall of the human race. In the Gospels the death of Jesus on a cross made from the wood of a tree brought about our redemption. In Revelation the tree of life grows in the new city and produces fruit each month. Its leaves serve as medicine. (Revelation 22:2)

To teach moral lessons in Scripture, trees are compared to human beings. Psalm 1 describes those who keep God's law:

*They are like a tree
planted near streams
of water,
that yields its fruit in season;
Its leaves never wither;
whatever they do prospers.*

Psalm 1:3

Jesus pointed out, "A good tree does not bear rotten fruit, nor does a rotten tree bear good fruit. For every tree is known by its own fruit." (Luke 6:43–44)

Then there is the tree of Zacchaeus, which enabled him to see Jesus and ultimately brought him salvation. May we all be childlike and adventurous enough to climb trees and go out on a limb to see Jesus.

RESPONDING

Having reflected upon God's Word, take some time now to continue to respond to God in prayer. You might wish to record your responses in your journal.

- How appreciative am I of trees and other wonders of creation?

Jesus, let trees speak to the children of your love.

Catechism of the Catholic Church

The themes of this chapter correspond to the following paragraph: 339.

THE FAITH EXPERIENCE

Child's Book pages 71–74

SCRIPTURE IN THIS CHAPTER
• *Genesis 2:9*
• *Luke 6:43–44*

MATERIALS
• Chapter 17 Scripture card
• Bible
• Blocks or toys made of wood
• Option: an arrangement of branches, leaves, nuts, and pinecones
• Crayons or markers
• Option: sponges, tempera paint, glue, tissue paper, construction paper, fabric, leaves

PREPARATION
• Write the children's names on pages 71 and 73.
• Place the Chapter 17 Scripture card for CENTERING #3 in the Bible.

MUSIC 'N MOTION

Use *Music 'n Motion* page T274 and CD Track 9 "Praise and Glorify" for this chapter. For a list of additional music, see page T320.

ENRICHING THE FAITH EXPERIENCE
Use the activities at the end of the chapter to enrich the lesson or to replace an activity with one that better meets the needs of your group.

BOOKS TO SHARE
The Great Kapok Tree: A Tale of the Amazon Rain Forest by Lynne Cherry (Voyager Books, 2000)

Oak Tree by Gordon Morrison (Houghton Mifflin/Walter Lorraine Books, 2005)

The Giving Tree by Shel Silverstein (HarperCollins, 1964)

A Tree Is Nice by Janice May Udry (HarperTrophy, 1987)

SNACK
Suggestion: apple slices, orange segments, or fruit cocktail

ALTERNATIVE PROGRAMS

DAILY PROGRAM
Day 1: Centering, Sharing A
Day 2: Enriching the Faith Experience choice
Day 3: Sharing B
Day 4: Enriching the Faith Experience choice
Day 5: Acting

THREE-DAY PROGRAM
Day 1: Centering, Sharing A
Day 2: Sharing B
Day 3: Acting

LEARNING OUTCOMES

The children will

- know that God made trees.

- appreciate the many uses
of trees.

- enjoy trees.

COMMENT

This lesson continues to teach the children about God's goodness, demonstrated by the gifts of creation. It also describes the role of wood in the life of Jesus, the carpenter, thereby relating Jesus more closely to our world. Because Jesus was nailed to a cross, wood is forever exalted. On Good Friday the Church sings: "This is the wood of the cross, on which hung the Savior of the world. Come, let us worship."

CENTERING

❶ Gather the children in a circle for *Music 'n Motion* time. Play the Unit 4 song (Track 9). Invite the children to do motions to the song along with you, using *Music 'n Motion* page T274.

❷ Have the children engage in free play with wooden blocks or other wooden toys.

❸ **SCRIPTURE** Read from the Scripture card in the Bible about how God made trees. (adapted from Genesis 2:9)

• *Out of the ground the LORD God made different kinds of trees grow that were delightful to look at and good for food.* [Option: Point out the arrangement of items that come from trees.]

• *The toys you played with are made of wood from trees. God gave us trees for many reasons. Trees are a great gift from God.*

SHARING [A]

❶ Distribute page 71 and talk about trees and their many uses.

• *How are the children enjoying the trees?* (Swinging from a tree, picking fruit, playing in a tree house, raking leaves,

Name_____

71 God Made the World

sitting by a fireplace, making things out of paper)

• *What animals live in trees?* (Birds, opossums, squirrels, bees)

• *Trees are marvelous to see, especially in the fall in areas where the leaves turn color. Trees make our world more beautiful.*

• *There are many kinds of trees. Some trees are tall and some are short. Some have leaves and some have needles. Some have dark wood and some have light wood.*

• *Do you have trees in your yard or neighborhood? What special trees have you seen?*

• *What food comes from trees?* (Fruits: apples, oranges, pears, grapefruit, bananas; nuts: walnuts, pecans, cashews)

• *What else do trees give us?* (Wood, paper, shade, maple syrup)

❷ Have the children find and circle what is hidden in and around the tree on page 72 (two squirrels, two birds, a nest, and a girl).

SHARING [B]

❸ Direct the children to stand by wooden things in the room. Have each child tell what the object is.

❹ Talk about Jesus and wood.

• *Jesus used wood too. When he was born, his mother, Mary, laid him in a wooden box called a manger. Joseph was a carpenter. He probably taught Jesus how to make things out of wood. The boats Jesus used to travel across the lake were made of wood. The cross, the sign of Jesus' love for us, was made of wood.*

❺ **SCRIPTURE** Tell how Jesus compared a good tree to a good person. (Luke 6:43–44)

• *What kind of apples will an old, rotten tree have?* (Small, sour) *What kind of apples will a healthy, strong, apple tree have?* (Large, sweet)

• *Jesus once said that a good tree bears good fruit. That was his way of telling us that a good person is like a good tree. A good person does good things and says good things. Jesus wants us to be good and loving like him.*

Find and circle two squirrels, two birds, a nest, and a girl.

Family Time

Chapter 17:
God Made Trees

In this lesson the children reflected on one of God's magnificent creations—trees. They talked about the many uses of trees and the role trees played in Jesus' life. They heard Jesus' teaching about a good tree bearing good fruit. Ask your child how he or she could "bear good fruit," that is, do good deeds. Show appreciation of the picture of the tree your child made.

Your Child
Children, like all of us, can be led to know God and about God through creation. Point out to your child that God is very wise to make trees, which are useful in so many ways.

Reflect
Out of the ground the LORD God made different kinds of trees grow that were delightful to look at and good for food.
(adapted from Genesis 2:9)

Pray
Jesus, make our lives bear good fruit for you.

Do
• Take a walk through the woods with your child and name different kinds of trees.
• Share together some food that came from trees: fruits or nuts or both.
• Talk about wooden things that are in your home and how they help you.
• Help your child climb a tree, sit in a tree, swing from a tree, or play in leaves.
• Read to your child *A Tree Is Nice* by Janice May Udry. Talk about why trees are important to us. Together praise God for the gift of trees and their many uses.

For more family resources, refer to the Family Activity Booklet and visit www.loyolapress.com/preschool.

© LOYOLAPRESS.

72 God Made the World

ACTING

1 **PRAYER** Lead the children in an echo prayer of praise to God for trees. Have the children stand and raise their arms to heaven like tree branches reaching for the sky. Then tell the children to repeat each line after you.

> *I thank you, God,*
> *for your gift of trees:*
> *for the huge oak trees*
> *and the tiny pine trees,*
> *for Christmas trees*
> *and flowering dogwood trees,*
> *for trees that give us nuts*
> *and trees that give us fruit.*
> *Thank you, God,*
> *for making beautiful trees.*

2 Have the children add leaves to the tree on page 73 with crayons or markers. For a more exciting activity, the children may dip sponges in tempera paint and press them to the branches. Or have the children glue on pieces of green or red, yellow, and orange tissue paper, torn construction paper, or fabric. The children might also add real leaves.

3 Gather the children in a circle for *Music 'n Motion* time. Play the Unit 4 song (Track 9). Invite the children to do motions to the song along with you, using *Music 'n Motion* page T274.

Have the children take home their pages and show their family the Family Time section.

CHECKPOINT

• *Were the learning outcomes achieved?*

• *What signs were there that the children were impressed by the many ways in which trees serve us?*

Name

73 God Made the World

Page 74 is blank.

ENRICHING THE FAITH EXPERIENCE

Use the following activities to enrich the lesson or to replace an activity with one that better meets the needs of your group.

1 Go for a walk with the children and look at trees. You might hug a tree and encourage the children to do the same.

2 Have the children do leaf rubbings using leaves and white paper. Tell them to cover the leaves with the paper and rub over them with the side of a crayon. You might put a leaf in an envelope for each child and have the children make rubbings on their envelopes.

3 Have the children make crayon rubbings of tree bark.

4 Invite the children to bring leaves to class. Iron them between pieces of wax paper.

5 Obtain small chunks of wood, perhaps from a carpenter or a home-improvement store, and have the children glue pieces together to make sculptures.

6 Bring in a wooden toy designed with holes to accommodate wooden pegs. Then have the children pound in the pegs with a rubber mallet.

7 Let the children use Cutouts #1–4, the Riley family, to act out ways to say and do good and loving things.

8 Sing for the children "I Had a Little Nut Tree."

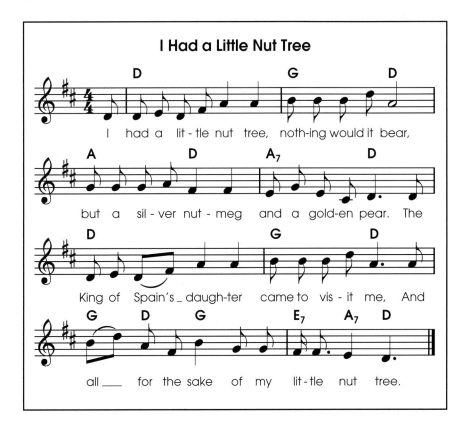

I Had a Little Nut Tree

I had a lit-tle nut tree, noth-ing would it bear, but a sil-ver nut-meg and a gold-en pear. The King of Spain's daugh-ter came to vis-it me, And all ___ for the sake of my lit-tle nut tree.

PREPARING THE FAITH EXPERIENCE

LISTENING

How varied are your works, LORD!
  In wisdom you have wrought
   them all;
  the earth is full of your
   creatures.

Psalm 104:24

REFLECTING

A visit to a zoo can be a spiritual experience, for there in one place is a sampling of the myriad creatures that have come from the hand of our incredible and playful God. All the animals—from the gentle lamb to the strong, powerful lion, from the tiny toad to the towering giraffe—cause us to marvel at the ingenuity of the Creator. We praise God's power and wisdom that fashioned such unique and fascinating creatures.

In the first Creation story in Genesis, God gives human beings dominion over all animals. The second Creation story shows Adam naming the creatures that God had formed out of the earth. To name something is to have power over it. Animals serve us in numerous ways, providing us with food and clothing and, in some cases, acting as our companions. Animals once transported us and plowed our fields; in some countries they still perform these tasks. Along with our dominion over these creatures, we have responsibility for the animals that share the earth with us. God cares for them through us.

There is a bond between animals and humans. We are part animal and part spirit. Like animals we have bodies and senses. Our call to respect life includes respecting animal life.

As the poet Samuel Taylor Coleridge pointed out in "The Rime of the Ancient Mariner,"

  He prayeth well who loveth well

  Both man and bird and beast.

Creatures praise their Creator by doing well what they were made to do. A bird's song praises God. So does an elephant's trumpeting. In Psalm 148 we sing,

Praise the LORD from the earth,
  you sea monsters and all deep waters; . . .
You animals wild and tame,
  you creatures that crawl and fly[.]

Psalm 148:7,10

Some animals are much stronger than we are, some have better vision, and some can run faster. But no animal is as fortunate as we are, for we are made in the image and likeness of God.

RESPONDING

God's Word calls us to respond in love. Respond to God now in the quiet of your heart, and perhaps through your journal.

- When can I take time to marvel over the unique animals that God made?

  God, fill the children with awe at the wonders you have created.

Catechism of the Catholic Church

The themes of this chapter correspond to the following paragraphs: 340–343, 2415–2418.

THE FAITH EXPERIENCE

Child's Book pages 75–82

SCRIPTURE IN THIS CHAPTER
• *Genesis 2:19*

MATERIALS
• Chapter 18 Scripture card
• Bible
• Option: live animal
• Cutouts: #11, Tillie Mouse; #33, monkey; #34, lion; #35, elephant; #36, horse; #37, turtle; #38, bear; #39, rabbit; #40, dog
• Clay
• Option: beanbag
• Scissors
• Transparent tape

PREPARATION
• Write the children's names on pages 75 and 77.
• Place the Chapter 18 Scripture card for SHARING #1 in the Bible.
• If you wish, cut out the four yellow squares of page 82 for the children.

MUSIC 'N MOTION

Use *Music 'n Motion* page T274 and CD Track 9 "Praise and Glorify" for this chapter. For a list of additional music, see page T320.

ENRICHING THE FAITH EXPERIENCE
Use the activities at the end of the chapter to enrich the lesson or to replace an activity with one that better meets the needs of your group.

BOOKS TO SHARE
Charlie Needs a Cloak by Tomie dePaola (Aladdin, 1982)

The Adventures of Curious George by H. A. Rey (Houghton Mifflin Company, 1995)

Where the Wild Things Are by Maurice Sendak (HarperCollins, 1976)

Harry the Dirty Dog by Gene Zion (HarperCollins, 1976)

SNACK
Suggestion: a "monkey treat" (dried banana slices mixed with raisins) or animal crackers

---

ALTERNATIVE PROGRAMS

DAILY PROGRAM
Day 1: Centering, Sharing A
Day 2: Enriching the Faith Experience choice
Day 3: Sharing B, Acting #1
Day 4: Enriching the Faith Experience choice
Day 5: Acting #2–4

THREE-DAY PROGRAM
Day 1: Centering, Sharing A
Day 2: Sharing B, Acting #1
Day 3: Acting #2–4

LEARNING OUTCOMES

The children will

- know that God made the animals.
- wonder at the variety of animals God made.
- praise and thank God for animals.
- respect and care for animals.

COMMENTS

1. Children are intrigued by living creatures and show concern for them. Worms, birds, and small animals fascinate them. At an early age children can be taught to respect all forms of life, which is a reflection of respect for their Creator. Perhaps no one is more known for kindness to animals than the beloved Saint Francis of Assisi. He recognized the importance of all creatures and even called them his brothers and sisters. Some parishes celebrate his feast day, October 4, with a blessing for children's pets.

2. Before this lesson you might invite the children to bring a stuffed animal to share with the class. You might consider arranging for one child to bring in a live pet, or you might plan to bring in your own pet if you have one.

CENTERING

1 Gather the children in a circle for *Music 'n Motion* time. Play the Unit 4 song (Track 9). Invite the children to do motions to the song along with you, using *Music 'n Motion* page T274.

2 Have the children make animals out of clay. Display Cutouts #11 and #33–40, animals, so that the children may use them as models.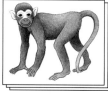

SHARING [A]

1 **SCRIPTURE** Tell the children that God made the animals. Read from the Scripture card in the Bible. (adapted from Genesis 2:19)

- *You made many different animals out of clay. Who made the real animals?* (God)

- *The Bible tells us this. It says "God formed animals and birds out of the ground and brought them to the first man to give them names. Whatever the man called each animal was its name."*

- *Let's see whether you know the names of some animals.*

75 God Made the World

2 Distribute page 75 and have the children name the animals pictured and tell where they live. Talk about the various animals. [Option: Show a live animal.] Conclude:

• *God made many different kinds of animals. Isn't God smart?*

• *God made the animals for us. Animals help us in many ways.*

3 Have the children identify each animal on page 76 from the parts shown. Ask what each animal does for us.

• Cow—gives us milk and meat

• Chicken—gives us eggs and meat

• Pig—gives us meat

• Cat—keeps us company

• Horse—gives us rides and pulls carts

• Sheep—gives us meat and wool for clothing

• Goose—gives us eggs, meat, and feathers

• Goat—gives us milk

SHARING [B]

4 Play "Guess the Animal." Place Cutouts #11 and #33–40, animals, on the floor facedown. Have the children take turns choosing a card (or tossing a beanbag on one) and acting and sounding like the animal shown. Let the other children guess what animal is being represented and then ask them all to imitate that animal.

5 Talk about caring for animals.

• *God loves and cares for animals. People who love God care for the animals God made. One of God's friends was Saint Martin, who was a doctor. When Martin found a sick cat or dog or other animal, he took it to his sister's house and cared for it. His sister's house became a hospital for animals.*

• *Who has a pet at home? What is it? What do you do to take care of your pet?*

What animals do you see in the picture?

Family Time

Chapter 18:
God Made Animals

In this lesson the children studied the wide variety of animals God created and learned how many of them help us. They also talked about caring for animals. Ask your child to tell about the animals on the animal box he or she made. Read the story "Tommy's Just-Right Pet" to your child or have him or her tell you about it.

Your Child

Reverence for all living things is something children should learn. If your child does not have a pet, you might consider getting one. Your child should share the responsibility of caring for the pet.

Reflect

God formed animals and birds out of the ground and brought them to the first man to give them names. Whatever the man called each animal was its name.
(adapted from Genesis 2:19)

Pray

God, help us care for all the animals you made.

Do

• Visit a zoo. Take pictures of various animals and make an animal photo album.
• Teach your child the names and habitats of various animals.
• Look for TV shows about animals and watch them with your child.
• Help your child become an expert on a particular favorite animal. Read aloud stories or nonfiction books about that animal.
• Read to your child *Harry the Dirty Dog* by Gene Zion. Discuss ways to care for animals. Thank God for all of the earth's animals and ask for help in caring for them.

For more family resources, refer to the Family Activity Booklet and visit **www.loyolapress.com/preschool.**

© LOYOLAPRESS.

76 God Made the World

ACTING

1 Distribute pages 77 and 79. Direct the children to place the pages so that page 77 is on top of page 79. Then have them fold the pages in half. Read aloud the story "Tommy's Just-Right Pet" as the children follow along, looking at the pictures.

2 **PRAYER** Lead the children in a prayer for the animals.

• *Because animals can't thank God, let's do it for them. I'll say something about an animal, and you say "Thank you, God."*

> *For a porcupine's sharp quills that protect it from other animals . . .*

> *For an elephant's tusks that help it get food . . .*

> *For a zebra's stripes that help it hide from enemies . . .*

> *For a bear's fur that keeps it warm in winter when it's sleeping . . .*

> *For a lion's powerful roar that makes it king of the jungle . . .*

> *For a monkey's long tail that helps it swing through trees . . .*

Tommy went home with the puppy and thanked God for his pet.

8

77 God Made the World

Tommy's Just-Right Pet

Tommy was looking for a pet. He went to a farm, and a cow said, "I'll be your pet." But Tommy said, "You would give me milk, but you need a barn."

Name_____

1

3 Distribute page 81 and help the children make an animal box, following these directions:

- Cut out the four yellow squares on page 82.

- Fold up each side so that the color green is inside. Tape the sides together.

- Fold the four yellow squares along the diagonal and stand the animals in the box.

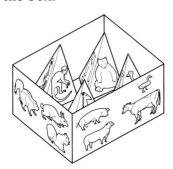

4 Gather the children in a circle for *Music 'n Motion* time. Play the Unit 4 song (Track 9). Invite the children to do motions to the song along with you, using *Music 'n Motion* book page T274.

Have the children take home their pages and show their family the Family Time section.

Tommy went to the jungle, and a lion said, "I'll be your pet." But Tommy said, "You would protect me, but you would frighten the neighbors."

Then Tommy went down to the animal shelter. A black-and-white puppy said, "I'll be your pet." And Tommy said, "You are just right. You will be my friend. I'll take good care of you."

2

7

78 God Made the World

© LOYOLA PRESS.

ENRICHING THE FAITH EXPERIENCE

Use the following activities to enrich the lesson or to replace an activity with one that better meets the needs of your group.

1 Tell the story of *Henny Penny/Chicken Little.* Various versions are available at your local library.

2 Teach this finger play:

Five little monkeys jumping on the bed.
[Bounce the fingers of one hand on the other palm.]
One fell off and bumped his head.
[Rub head.]
Mama called the doctor, and the doctor said,
[Hold "phone" to ear.]
"That's what you get for jumping on the bed."
[Shake finger.]
Four little monkeys . . .
[Bounce four fingers.]
Three little monkeys . . .
[Bounce three fingers.]
Two little monkeys . . .
[Bounce two fingers.]
One little monkey jumping on the bed.
[Bounce one finger.]
He fell off and bumped his head.
[Rub head.]
Mama called the doctor, and the doctor said,
[Hold "phone" to ear.]
"No more monkeys jumping on the bed."

Tommy went to a forest, and a skunk said, "I'll be your pet." But Tommy said, "You are pretty, but my mother wouldn't like your perfume."

6

79 God Made the World

Tommy went to the zoo, and a giraffe said, "I'll be your pet." But Tommy said, "You would help me reach for things, but our house isn't high enough for you."

3

3 Teach the following poem:

Teddy bear, Teddy bear,
    turn around.
Teddy bear, Teddy bear,
    touch the ground.
Teddy bear, Teddy bear,
    go upstairs.
Teddy bear, Teddy bear,
    say your prayers.
Teddy bear, Teddy bear,
    turn out the light.
Teddy bear, Teddy bear,
    say good-night.

4 Let the children come to class dressed as animals.

5 Hold a three-ring circus. Arrange the children in three groups and let each group imitate a different animal. Let them act like that animal for a short time and then ask them to pretend to be another animal of their choice.

6 Teach the following finger play, adding snapping gestures with the thumb and fingers of one hand when the turtle snaps:

There was a little turtle.
    He lived in a box.
He swam in a puddle.
    He climbed on the rocks.
He snapped at a mosquito.
    He snapped at a flea.
He snapped at a minnow,
    and he snapped at me.
He caught the mosquito.
    He caught the flea.
He caught the minnow,
    but he didn't catch me.

Tommy went to the circus, and a monkey said, "I'll be your pet." But Tommy said, "You would be fun to play with, but we have no trees for you."

Tommy went to the desert, and a camel said, "I'll be your pet." But Tommy said, "You would be good to ride, but your hump won't fit through our door."

4

5

80 God Made the World

© LOYOLAPRESS.

God Made Animals **CHAPTER 18** **T137**

7 Have the children make puppet pets by drawing an animal's face on a sock or on a round piece of paper and then gluing it onto the bottom of a brown paper lunch bag.

8 Sing for the children or teach them the song "Animal Fair."

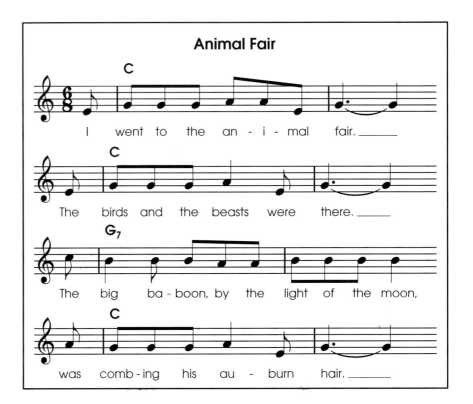

Animal Fair

I went to the an-i-mal fair. _____

The birds and the beasts were there. _____

The big ba-boon, by the light of the moon,

was comb-ing his au-burn hair. _____

81 God Made the World

You ought to have seen the monk; _____

He climbed up the el - e - phant's trunk. _____

The el - e - phant sneezed and fell on her knees,

and what be - came of the monk?

82 God Made the World

FAITH FOCUS

We can trust God to care for us as God cares for birds. Matthew 23:37

PREPARING THE FAITH EXPERIENCE

LISTENING

Are not five sparrows sold for two small coins? Yet not one of them has escaped the notice of God. Even the hairs of your head have all been counted. Do not be afraid. You are worth more than many sparrows.

He said to [his] disciples, "Therefore I tell you, do not worry about your life and what you will eat, or about your body and what you will wear. For life is more than food and the body is more than clothing. Notice the ravens: they do not sow or reap; they have neither storehouse nor barn, yet God feeds them. How much more important are you than birds!"

Luke 12:6–7,22–24

REFLECTING

How wonderful it would be if we could fly like a bird, soaring through the sky, swooping over lakes, and gliding on the wind. Although we may envy the birds' ability to fly, we need not envy God's care of them. God instills instinct in these creatures, watches over their nest-building and migratory flights, and provides food for them. This same God promises us tender care. Jesus assured us that we are more precious in God's sight than the birds are.

In Scripture, birds are signs of hope. Jesus used the image of a bird to convey his desire to protect people. In Matthew 23:37 we read that Jesus longed to hold the people of Jerusalem close to himself, just as a mother hen enfolds her chicks under her wings. In the Old Testament too, we find God symbolizing his protection through bird imagery. In Psalm 17:8

we pray "hide me in the shadow of your wings. . ." In Psalm 91:3–4 we are consoled, "God . . . [w]ill shelter you with pinions, / spread wings that you may take refuge."

Isaiah tells us that

They that hope in the
LORD will renew
their strength,
they will soar as with
eagles' wings . . .

Isaiah 40:31

An anonymous writer put it this way:

When we walk to the edge of all of life we have and take that step into the darkness of the unknown, we must believe that one of two things will happen: There will be something solid for us to stand on, or we will be taught to fly.

RESPONDING

Having been nourished by God's Word, we are able to respond to God's great love for us. In prayer, respond to God's call to you to share his Word with others. You may also wish to respond in your prayer journal.

- How firm is my trust in the Lord who loves me?

  Loving God, may the children always turn trustingly to you.

Catechism of the Catholic Church

The themes of this chapter correspond to the following paragraphs: 303–305, 2415–2418.

THE FAITH EXPERIENCE

Child's Book pages 83–86

SCRIPTURE IN THIS CHAPTER
- *Genesis 1:20–22*
- *Luke 12:6–7, 22–24*

MATERIALS
- Chapter 19 Scripture card
- Bible
- Cutout #19, Mr. Sparrow, taped to the end of a pencil or craft stick
- Option: feather or bird (real or artificial)
- Recording of joyful music for ACTING #1
- Scissors
- Crayons or markers
- Four pieces of yarn or string of varying lengths for each child
- Hole punch
- Transparent tape

PREPARATION
- Write the children's names on page 83.
- Place the Chapter 19 Scripture card for SHARING #3 in the Bible.
- If you wish, use a paper cutter to cut apart the sections on page 85 for the children.

MUSIC 'N MOTION

Use *Music 'n Motion* page T274 and CD Track 9 "Praise and Glorify" for this chapter. For a list of additional music, see page T320.

ENRICHING THE FAITH EXPERIENCE
Use the activities at the end of the chapter to enrich the lesson or to replace an activity with one that better meets the needs of your group.

BOOKS TO SHARE
Good-Night, Owl! by Pat Hutchins (Aladdin, 1990)

Tree of Birds by Susan Meddaugh
    (Houghton Mifflin/Walter Lorraine Books, 1994)

Owl Moon by Jane Yolen (Philomel, 1987)

Make Way for Ducklings by Robert McCloskey
    (Viking Juvenile, 1941)

SNACK
Suggestion: thumbprint (bird's nest) cookies

ALTERNATIVE PROGRAMS

DAILY PROGRAM
Day 1: Centering, Sharing A
Day 2: Enriching the Faith Experience choice
Day 3: Sharing B
Day 4: Enriching the Faith Experience choice
Day 5: Acting

THREE-DAY PROGRAM
Day 1: Centering, Sharing A
Day 2: Sharing B
Day 3: Acting

LEARNING OUTCOMES

The children will

- know that God made the birds.
- realize that God cares for all creation.
- believe that God takes care of them.

COMMENT

Trust is the hallmark of a Christian. Young children can understand God's loving care and can learn to look to God for help. Jesus assures us that even the hairs on our head are counted. (Matthew 10:30) God knows us and our needs and will provide for us. Divine Providence directs our lives. Even though our lives sometimes unfold in mysterious and puzzling ways, we can trust that in the end all will be well. God is the source of all good and draws good from evil. Eventually everything works together for the good.

CENTERING

❶ Gather the children in a circle for *Music 'n Motion* time. Play the Unit 4 song (Track 9). Invite the children to do motions to the song along with you, using *Music 'n Motion* page T274.

❷ Play "Bluebird, Bluebird." Tell the children that they will pretend to be birds and fly in and out "windows." Have them form a circle, hold hands, and then raise their hands.

Choose a child to be the first bird, who weaves in and out under the children's arms as the class sings the first four lines. (See page T143.) At the words "Pick a little bird and tap it on the shoulder," the first bird stops behind a child and taps his or her shoulders in time to the music. As the song is begun again, the second child holds the hand of the first, and the two go "through my window."

Continue the game, adding birds to the line until all the children have had a turn.

Name _____

83   God Made the World

Bluebird, Bluebird

Blue - bird, blue - bird, go through my win - dow.

Blue - bird, blue - bird, go through my win - dow.

Blue - bird, blue - bird, go through my win - dow.

Oh, John - ny, aren't you tired? _____

Pick a lit - tle bird and tap it on the shoul - der.

Pick a lit - tle bird and tap it on the shoul - der.

Pick a lit - tle bird and tap it on the shoul - der.

Oh, John - ny, aren't you tired? _____

Trace the path of the mother bird to her babies.

Family Time

Chapter 19:
God Made Birds

In this lesson the children learned about birds and how our good God takes special care of them. They heard how Jesus taught us that God takes even better care of us. Help your child identify the birds on page 83. Hang in your child's room the mobile he or she made as a reminder of God's care.

Your Child

Children are fascinated by birds and for good reason. Not only can birds fly, but the relationship between the parent birds and baby birds is unique. The parents build the nest, feed the babies, and then teach them to fly. Compare the birds' care for their young with the tender care God has for us.

Reflect

[Jesus said,] "Are not five sparrows sold for two small coins? Yet not one of them has escaped the notice of God. Even the hairs of your head have all been counted. Do not be afraid. You are worth more than many sparrows."
(Luke 12:6–7)

Pray

God, we thank you for your love and care.

Do

• Let your child feed the birds in your yard or in a park. You might set up a bird feeder or birdbath and watch the birds with your child.
• Give your child binoculars to have close-up views of the birds.
• Help your child distinguish the various bird songs and birdcalls.
• Read to your child *Good-Night, Owl!* by Pat Hutchins. Consider the great variety of birds and how God cares for them. Thank God for caring for us.

For more family resources, refer to the Family Activity Booklet and visit www.loyolapress.com/preschool.

© LOYOLAPRESS.

SHARING [A]

❶ Talk about birds and show Cutout #19, Mr. Sparrow. [Option: Show the feather or bird.]

• *Did you like pretending to be a bird?*

• *Would you like to be a bird? Why?*

• *Name some kinds of birds.*

❷ Distribute page 83. Have the children name as many birds as they can. (Hummingbird, ostrich, parrot, eagle, goose, woodpecker, cardinal, blue jay, crow, duck, penguin, pelican) Ask:

• *Who made the birds?* (God)

❸ **SCRIPTURE** Read the adaptation of Genesis 1:20–22 from the Scripture card in the Bible.

• *"God said, 'Let birds fly in the sky.' And God made all kinds of winged birds. God blessed them."*

• *Why do you think God made birds fly?* (So that they could find food and get away from enemies)

• *God takes care of all the birds. They find enough to eat. They build soft, safe nests for their babies. When winter is coming, many birds know that they should fly south to a warm place. God gave the birds songs to sing.*

• *God is good to make so many birds for us to enjoy. God is good to take care of the birds.*

SHARING [B]

❹ Have the children trace the path from the mother bird to the nest on page 84.

❺ **PRAYER** Teach the children this prayer. Have them stand and add the motions. You might sing this prayer to the tune of "London Bridge."

Thank you for the world so sweet,
[Put out right hand.]

Thank you for the food we eat,
[Put out left hand.]

Thank you for the birds that sing,
[Raise hands.]

Thank you, God, for everything.
[Extend hands to side.]

85 God Made the World

6 SCRIPTURE Tell how Jesus described God's care. (adapted from Luke 12:6–7,22–24) Show the Bible.

• *Jesus once said that God cares for us more than for the sparrows.*

• *God gives us good people to take care of us. God feeds us and keeps us from harm. God is like a mother bird that watches over all her babies.*

ACTING

1 PRAYER Lead the children in a dance of prayer. Play joyful music as they dance.

• *Let's thank God for making birds. Let's thank God for taking care of birds and for taking care of us. We can do this by dancing for God.*

• *You can fly or hop like a bird to the music. Make your dance beautiful for God. As you dance, think about how good God is.*

2 Distribute page 85 and have the children make a bird mobile. Help them follow these directions:

• Cut apart the three sections.

• Tape an end of a piece of yarn to each bird.

• Tape the other ends of the yarn to the strip.

• Punch a hole in the top of the strip.

• Thread yarn through the hole and tie it to make a loop for hanging the mobile.

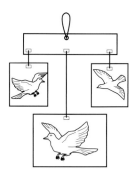

3 Tell the children to hang the mobile in their rooms as a reminder that God cares for them.

86 God Made the World

© LOYOLAPRESS.

Name

4 Gather the children in a circle for *Music 'n Motion* time. Play the Unit 4 song (Track 9). Invite the children to do motions to the song along with you, using *Music 'n Motion* page T274.

Have the children take home their pages and show their family the Family Time section.

CHECKPOINT

- *Were the learning outcomes achieved?*
- *What signs are there that the children have a sense of God's providence?*

ENRICHING THE FAITH EXPERIENCE

Use the following activities to enrich the lesson or to replace an activity with one that better meets the needs of your group.

1 Ask the children to flap their arms when what you say is true. Then make statements such as "Pigeons fly. Zebras fly. Robins fly. Penguins fly. Elephants fly. Bees fly."

2 Help the children make bird feeders. Remember to be aware of peanut or other food allergies.

- Punch three or four holes around the edge of a plastic lid. Thread yarn or ribbon through the holes and tie it so that the lid can be hung. On the lid, smear soy butter and add popcorn, birdseed, or other things birds eat. (An orange rind or a small paper plate can be used instead of a lid.)

- Tie string around a pine-cone, put soy butter and birdseed on it, and hang it outside.

- Thread doughnut-shaped cereal onto a piece of yarn or string. Hang the strand of cereal outside.

3 Lead the children in a bird chorus. Teach them what various birds say (tweet-tweet, caw, quack, coo) and then let groups make the sounds when you point to them. Sometimes have two or more groups make their sounds simultaneously.

4 Play "Duck, Duck, Goose." Have the children stand in a circle. One child who is "It" goes around the outside of the circle, tapping children on the head and saying "duck." "It" taps one child and says "goose." That child tries to tag "It" before he or she gets to the child's place. If the child doesn't tag "It," the child becomes the next "It."

5 Teach this finger play:

> Two little blackbirds sitting on a hill,
> [Hold up the index finger of each hand.]
> One named Jack,
> [Bend right finger.]
> The other named Jill.
> [Bend left finger.]
> Fly away, Jack.
> [Put right hand behind your back.]
> Fly away, Jill.
> [Put left hand behind your back.]
> Come back, Jack.
> [Hold up right finger.]
> Come back, Jill.
> [Hold up left finger.]

6 Read the following poem to the children and have them fill in the missing words. Talk about the food, clothes, and homes God has given us.

I love to watch God's birds fly by,
Gliding smoothly in the _____ (sky).
God gives them bugs and worms so sweet,
Because that's what they like to _____ (eat).
Sometimes God sends rainy weather,
So they can wash each pretty _____ (feather).
God gives them for their families
Cozy nests in tall green _____ (trees).
All things are from God above,
Who cares for birds, and us, with _____ (love).

Pam Bernstein

7 Teach the children this poem:

I saw a little bird go hop, hop, hop.
I told the little bird to stop, stop, stop.
I went to the window to say "How do you do?"
He wagged his little tail and away he flew.

8 Play "Bird Catcher." Have the children form three or four groups and give each group the name of a bird. Tell the "birds" to flap their wings at one end of the room. Appoint one child bird catcher. The bird catcher stands in the middle of the room and calls out the name of one kind of bird. The birds who have that name run to their "nest in the forest" at the other end of the room while the bird catcher tries to tag them.

PREPARING THE FAITH EXPERIENCE

LISTENING

Then God said, "Let the water teem with an abundance of living creatures, and on the earth let birds fly beneath the dome of the sky." And so it happened: God created the great sea monsters and all kinds of swimming creatures with which the water teems, and all kinds of winged birds. God saw how good it was, and God blessed them, saying, "Be fertile, multiply, and fill the water of the seas; and let the birds multiply on the earth."

Genesis 1:20–22

REFLECTING

We are still discovering new life-forms in the water, the source of the very first forms of life. God has stocked the earth's bodies of water with many wonderful creatures: the starfish, which can regenerate its arms; the octopus, which fools its enemies by ejecting an ink-like substance; the flowerlike anemone; the winsome dolphin; the phosphorescent fish; the gigantic whale, which glides through the ocean depths. Sea creatures are not only sources of fascination and study but also sources of food. Lobsters, clams, oysters, shark, shrimp, and a multitude of fish are delicacies that God has given us to enjoy.

The Book of Sirach describes our reactions to the creatures of the sea:

*Those who go down to the sea tell part of
   its story,
 and when we hear them we are thunderstruck;
In it are his creatures, stupendous, amazing,
 all kinds of life, and the monsters of the deep.*

Sirach 43:25–26

Fish played an important role in the life of Jesus, who lived near the Sea of Galilee. Some of his best friends were fishermen. Several of the miracles of Jesus involved fish (the large catch of fish, the multiplication of loaves and fish). After Jesus rose from the dead, fish was the food he ate in front of his apostles to prove that he was alive. Later he prepared a breakfast of grilled fish for them on the shore.

Furthermore, a fish was the secret sign that the early Christians used to identify themselves in times of persecution. The letters of the Greek word for *fish,* ICHTHYS, are the first letters of the Greek words for *Jesus Christ, Son of God, Savior.*

Jesus told his apostles that they were to be fishers of people. Today his followers continue to "catch" others for Christ. Our words and our example should have the power to lure others to share the Christian life with us.

RESPONDING

God's Word moves us to respond in word and action. Let God's Spirit work within you as you prayerfully consider how you are being called to respond to God's message to you today. Responding through your journal may help to strengthen your response.

- To what extent do I work to bring others to Christ?

Father, may the children have the freedom and opportunities to delight in your world.

Catechism of the Catholic Church

The themes of this chapter correspond to the following paragraphs: 293–294.

THE FAITH EXPERIENCE

Child's Book pages 87–90

SCRIPTURE IN THIS CHAPTER
- *Genesis 1:21*
- *Luke 5:1–10*

MATERIALS
- Chapter 20 Scripture card
- Bible
- Cutouts: #41–50, fish
- Option: 10 paper clips; stick; magnet; string; blue material, tub, or plastic swimming pool
- Crayons or markers
- Option: goldfish in a bowl or a toy fishing pole
- Recording of music for ACTING #1
- Box, at least 11 by 12 inches
- Marble
- White tempera paint

PREPARATION
- Write the children's names on pages 87 and 90.
- Place the Chapter 20 Scripture card for SHARING #2 in the Bible.
- Cover the painting area with newspapers.

MUSIC 'N MOTION

Use *Music 'n Motion* page T274 and CD Track 9 "Praise and Glorify" for this chapter. For a list of additional music, see page T320.

ENRICHING THE FAITH EXPERIENCE
Use the activities at the end of the chapter to enrich the lesson or to replace an activity with one that better meets the needs of your group.

BOOKS TO SHARE
The Rainbow Fish by Marcus Pfister
  (North-South Books, 1992)

Fish Is Fish by Leo Lionni
  (Knopf Books for Young Readers, 2005)

Swimmy by Leo Lionni (Dragonfly Books, 1973)

Row the Boat: Jesus Fills the Nets by Mary Manz Simon
  (Concordia Publishing House, 1990)

SNACK
Suggestion: small fish-shaped crackers

ALTERNATIVE PROGRAMS

DAILY PROGRAM
Day 1: Centering, Sharing A
Day 2: Enriching the Faith Experience choice
Day 3: Sharing B, Acting #1
Day 4: Enriching the Faith Experience choice
Day 5: Acting #2 and #3

THREE-DAY PROGRAM
Day 1: Centering, Sharing A
Day 2: Sharing B, Acting #1
Day 3: Acting #2 and #3

LEARNING OUTCOMES

The children will

• know that God made the sea creatures.

• enjoy the story of the large catch of fish.

• be grateful to God for fish.

COMMENTS

1. This lesson deepens the children's awareness of the wonderful beneficence of God in filling the earth with creatures. As they learn about the variety of sea creatures, children praise God, the Creator of all. Jesus liked to compare us to fish. In a parable, he said that the Kingdom of Heaven is like a dragnet that takes in all kinds of things. Tertullian echoed this comparison in his work *On Baptism.* He wrote: "We are little fish and like the Ichthys Jesus Christ, we are born in the water; we are not safe in any other way than by remaining in the water." Water here is presumably God, the great Ocean.

2. The story about the large catch of fish introduces Jesus as someone who has powers that are more than human.

CENTERING

❶ Gather the children in a circle for *Music 'n Motion* time. Play the Unit 4 song (Track 9). Invite the children to do motions to the song along with you, using *Music 'n Motion* page T274.

❷ Have the children go "fishing." Hide the fish from Cutouts #41–50, fish, and let the children find them. Or attach a paper clip to each fish. Put the fish on a piece of blue material or in a tub or plastic swimming pool and let the children catch the fish with a magnet tied to a stick. Show them how to hold the stick and caution them not to swing it or poke other children with it.

SHARING [A]

❶ Talk about fish. [Option: Show the fish or fishing pole.]

• *Do you like to eat fish?*

• *Does anyone have a fish for a pet?*

• *God made many things that live in the water.*

Name_____

2 **SCRIPTURE** Read the adaptation of Genesis 1:21 from the Scripture card in the Bible.

• *God created huge creatures and all kinds of swimming creatures to fill the water.*

3 **PRAYER** Distribute page 87 and have the children identify as many sea creatures as they can. (Dolphin, anemones, seal, starfish, jellyfish, fish, octopus, sea horse, eel, turtle, whale, coral, crab, clam, lobster) Invite the children to praise God for each of these sea creatures.

• *What are some other things that live in the water besides fish? As one of you names something, let's jump up, raise our hands, and say "Praise the Lord!"*

SHARING [B]

4 **SCRIPTURE** Tell the story "Jesus and the Fishermen," adapted from Luke 5:1–10 (above right), as the children look at page 88.

• *I will tell you a good story from the Bible about Jesus and fish. When you hear me say "fish," make your mouth look like a fish's mouth and say "glub, glub, glub."*

• *Jesus wants everyone to be in his Church. You are in the Church. Jesus caught you.*

Jesus and the Fishermen

Jesus lived near a sea. He ate fish *[glubs]* often. His friends were fishermen.

One day Jesus was in the boat of his friend Peter. He said to Peter, "Go out into deep water and lower your nets to catch fish." *[glubs]* Peter said, "We have worked hard all night and haven't caught one fish. *[glubs]* But we'll do as you say."

Peter and the other fishermen went out on the lake and lowered their nets. So many fish *[glubs]* swam into their nets that the nets were breaking. Peter and the other fishermen called to their partners in the other boat to help. The men filled both boats with fish. *[glubs]* The boats were so full of fish *[glubs]* that they almost sank. Jesus said, "You will catch people for me." He meant that he wanted his friends to bring other people to him and to help them follow his teachings.

Connect the dots that are the same color to make the net.

Family Time

Chapter 20:
God Made Fish

In this lesson the children learned about fish and other sea creatures. They praised God for these creatures. They heard the story of Jesus helping his friends catch an enormous quantity of fish. (Luke 5:1–11) Ask your child to tell you the story, using the picture on this page. Be sure to admire the picture of the fish your child made.

Your Child
The children belong to Jesus through Baptism. One spiritual writer said we are like fish in the great ocean that is God.

Reflect
Simon said in reply, "Master, . . . at your command I will lower the nets." When the fishermen had done this, they caught a great number of fish, and their nets were tearing. (adapted from Luke 5:5–6)

Pray
Jesus, help us bring others to follow you.

Do
• Enjoy a fish dinner with your child.
• Visit an aquarium or tropical fish store with your child.
• Tell your child about the day he or she was baptized and became a member of the Church. Show pictures of the event.
• Read to your child *Fish Is Fish* or *Swimmy* by Leo Lionni. Discuss the unique qualities of fish and other creatures that live in water. Praise God for the variety and beauty of fish and all the creatures of the sea.

For more family resources, refer to the Family Activity Booklet and visit **www.loyolapress.com/preschool.**

© LOYOLAPRESS.

88 God Made the World

5 Have the children draw the net on page 88 by connecting the dots that are the same color.

ACTING

1 Have the children put their palms together and cross their thumbs to make a fish shape. Play music and have them move their "fish" from side to side as if they were swimming. Teach them the following poem to recite as they move their hands:

> I am a fish in the great
>   blue sea.
> God made me as happy
>   as can be.
> I swim all day and sleep
>   all night.
> To be God's fish is my
>   delight.
>
> *Mary Kathleen Glavich,*
> *S.N.D.*

2 Have the children decorate the large fish on page 89 with crayons or markers. Then have them place their picture in a box. Give them a marble dipped in white tempera paint and have them tilt the box from side to side so that the marble leaves tracks that make a net. Tell the children that their fish should remind them that they belong to Jesus.

Here are alternative activities for page 89:

- Have the children paint the large fish, or glue on sequins, glitter, or bits of colored paper.

- Give the children triangles of corrugated cardboard that has been peeled to reveal the ridges. Have the children paint the ridges and glue the triangles on the big fish to represent fins.

- The children may make a picture to hang in the window. Have them cut out the three fish and place them on wax paper. Iron another sheet of wax paper over the top to seal the picture for the children.

- Have the children cut out the fish and glue them onto plastic-foam plates or pans. Then cover the plates or pans with clear plastic.

89 God Made the World

Page 90 is blank.

3 Gather the children in a circle for *Music 'n Motion* time. Play the Unit 4 song (Track 9). Invite the children to do motions to the song along with you, using *Music 'n Motion* page T274.

Have the children take home their pages and show their family the Family Time section.

CHECKPOINT

- *Were the learning outcomes achieved?*
- *What did the children's reactions to the story of the large catch of fish tell you about their concepts of Jesus?*

ENRICHING THE FAITH EXPERIENCE

Use the following activities to enrich the lesson or to replace an activity with one that better meets the needs of your group.

1 Read to the children *Swimmy* by Leo Lionni (Dragonfly Books, 1973). Then cut sponges in the shape of fish and let the children play with the sponges in water. You might have the children dip the fish-shaped sponges in tempera paint and stamp them on a large sheet of butcher paper or poster board.

2 Have the children play tug-of-war with a rope. Call one side the fish and the other side the fishers.

3 Make fish mobiles for the classroom. Give the children strips of paper notched two inches from the top at one end and two inches from the bottom at the other end. Let the children decorate the strips. Then have them slip the notched ends into each other to create a fish shape. With a hole punch, string yarn of various lengths through the fish and attach them to hangers or to two cardboard tubes from dry-cleaning hangers fastened in the shape of an X.

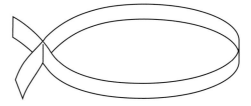

4 Let the children act out the story of the apostles' large catch of fish.

5 Mark off the shape of a boat on the floor, using yarn, string, or tape. Let the children take turns sitting in the "boat," rowing and commenting on the fish they see in the water.

God Made Surprises

The children will experience the world as a surprising place of joy.
They will be prepared to look forward to eternal life.

21 GOD MADE BUTTERFLIES

The children learn that a butterfly comes from a caterpillar.
They talk about other surprises in our world, such as
seeds that become flowers. They thank God in song.
They make a three-dimensional picture of butterflies
and flowers.

22 GOD MADE BIG THINGS

The children talk and think about enormous creations. They
praise God, who is all-powerful. They make a book about
the greatness of God's love. Each child contributes to a class
thank-you card to God.

23　GOD MADE LITTLE THINGS

The children talk about small things, including babies. They are led to value small things as important. They make a pet pocket for five small creatures.

24　GOD MADE COUNTRIES

The children become aware of the many countries in the world. They learn that although people may look different, all are equal and precious in God's sight. They practice saying nice things to others. They make a flag from another nation and have a parade.

25　GOD MADE LAUGHTER

The children learn that God wants us to be happy. Together in class they experience happiness through various activities. Then they think of ways they can make others happy. They make a party hat.

FAITH FOCUS

God surprises us with changes in life.

John 10:10; Romans 6:4; 1 Corinthians 15:36–49

PREPARING THE FAITH EXPERIENCE

LISTENING

We were indeed buried with him through baptism into death, so that, just as Christ was raised from the dead by the glory of the Father, we too might live in newness of life.

Romans 6:4

REFLECTING

Our world is full of marvelous things. Children are in awe of its wonders—snow and hail, ladybugs, a smooth stone, a daisy. They realize how wonderful life on earth is. To realize something is to see it with "real eyes." As we age, we lose some of our early perceptions and sensitivity and take for granted the natural miracles in our lives. It is good now and then to pause and take a fresh look at the world. Through the gifts of the earth, we will hear God saying "I love you." We will also come to know that there is more to life than this world.

At the end of our journey on earth, life is not taken away but changed. Certain phenomena in life remind us of this transformation and renew our hope. Who would ever think that the caterpillar crawling on the ground would one day become a beautiful butterfly? Who would ever think that a tiny seed would become a flowering plant or even a gigantic tree? Who would ever think that a bald, wailing baby—who cannot even crawl and is dependent on others for everything—would someday be a strong person with the ability to think and to influence the world?

From Jesus' Death and Resurrection comes the great assurance that we too will live forever, but in a different form.

After a horrible death, Jesus was raised from the dead and seen by many people. He was so different from his former self, however, that Mary Magdalene failed to recognize him. He passed through locked doors. He could appear and disappear. He was the same person, but he was different. Jesus was the risen Lord, the Christ. And his Resurrection was the promise of our own.

God is a source of continual surprises. The ingenious Creator of butterflies, rainbows, and zebras undoubtedly has a wonderful plan for us in the next life.

RESPONDING

Having reflected upon God's Word, take some time now to continue to respond to God in prayer. You might wish to record your responses in your journal.

- When can I take time to focus on the earth's gifts?

  Risen Lord, give the children eyes to see you.

Catechism of the Catholic Church

The themes of this chapter correspond to the following paragraphs: 279–281.

THE FAITH EXPERIENCE

Child's Book pages 91–94

SCRIPTURE IN THIS CHAPTER
- *2 Corinthians 5:1*

MATERIALS
- Chapter 21 Scripture card
- Bible
- Cutouts: #51, monarch butterfly; #52–59, butterflies
- Option: butterfly, caterpillar, or chrysalis
- Bedsheet or large piece of material
- Craft stick or pencil
- Transparent tape
- Crayons or markers
- Scissors
- Glue

PREPARATION
- Write the children's names on page 91.
- Place the Chapter 21 Scripture card for SHARING #3 in the Bible.
- If you wish, use a paper cutter to cut off the strip with the butterflies on page 93 for the children.

MUSIC 'N MOTION
Use *Music 'n Motion* page T276 and CD Track 10 "Care for Life" for this chapter. For a list of additional music, see page T320.

ENRICHING THE FAITH EXPERIENCE
Use the activities at the end of the chapter to enrich the lesson or to replace an activity with one that better meets the needs of your group.

BOOKS TO SHARE
The Very Hungry Caterpillar by Eric Carle
   (Philomel, 1981)

I Wish I Were a Butterfly by James Howe
   (Voyager Books, 1994)

The Carrot Seed by Ruth Krauss (HarperFestival, 1993)

SNACK
Suggestion: Cut slices of bread diagonally into four parts. Using two parts at a time, make the points touch to create butterfly shapes. Place a carrot or celery stick down the center. Give a butterfly to each child and have the child spread butter, cream cheese, or jelly on the "wings" and then decorate them with raisins.

ALTERNATIVE PROGRAMS

DAILY PROGRAM
Day 1: Centering, Sharing A
Day 2: Enriching the Faith Experience choice
Day 3: Sharing B
Day 4: Acting #1, Enriching the Faith
   Experience choice
Day 5: Acting #2 and #3

THREE-DAY PROGRAM
Day 1: Centering, Sharing A
Day 2: Sharing B, Acting #1
Day 3: Acting #2 and #3

LEARNING OUTCOMES

The children will

• marvel at the special wonders of the earth.

• praise and thank God.

• know that forms of life change.

COMMENT

This lesson lays the foundation for a child's hope and belief in eternal life. By reflecting on the phenomenon of a caterpillar's transformation into a butterfly, the child is being prepared to accept our transformation into a new life after death. Jesus' Resurrection is the basis of our faith. His victory over sin and death proves he is both God and man. His triumph is ours as well. By reestablishing for us a loving relationship with the Father, Jesus makes it possible for us to have the fullness of life for which we yearn.

CENTERING

❶ Gather the children in a circle for *Music 'n Motion* time. Play the Unit 5 song (Track 10). Invite the children to do motions to the song along with you, using *Music 'n Motion* page T276.

❷ Play "Butterfly—Fly." Place Cutout #51, monarch butterfly, and #52–59, butterflies, on a bedsheet (or a large piece of material or paper) spread on the floor. Have the children sit around the sheet and hold the edges. Say "One, two, three, butterflies—fly, and on the word *fly,* have the children quickly raise and then lower the sheet, continuing to hold on to it. Then have them release the sheet and gather as many butterflies as they can. The child who captures the monarch butterfly says the words for the next game.

SHARING [A]

❶ Tell the children the story of a butterfly's life, using the hand movements described on page T159. [Option: Show the butterfly, caterpillar, or chrysalis.]

Name_____

91 God Made the World

- *Butterflies are very pretty, aren't they? They weren't always able to fly. They didn't always have such pretty wings. Does anyone know what a butterfly was before it was a butterfly?* (Caterpillar)

- *I'll tell you what happens. Here is a caterpillar.* [Hold up your index finger and wiggle it. Set it on your arm.]

- *A caterpillar crawls around and eats leaves.* [Make your index finger crawl down your arm toward your fist.]

- *One day the caterpillar spins a house around itself.* [Put your finger into your fist.]

- *Inside, the caterpillar changes. When it comes out, it is a butterfly.* [Remove your index finger from your fist and tap it against your thumb on the same hand over and over, moving your hand to represent a butterfly flying.]

2 Repeat the story and have the children mimic your hand movements.

SHARING [B]

3 **SCRIPTURE** Distribute page 91 and have the children talk about the surprises in the picture. Read the adaptation of 2 Corinthians 5:1 from the Scripture card in the Bible.

- *God has put a lot of surprises in our world. What surprises do you see in the picture?*

- *God is very good to make the world so wonderful for us.*

- *Surely God will make our home in heaven wonderful too.*

- *Listen to what we read in the Bible:*

  "God has made a home for us in heaven."

4 **PRAYER** Teach the children to sing the following prayer to the tune of "Happy Birthday."

> God our Father, thank you
> For all that you do.
> You're full of surprises.
> How much we love you!
> *Mary Kathleen Glavich, S.N.D.*

5 Have the children do the activity on page 92. Tell them to circle the butterfly that is different in each row.

Draw a circle around the butterfly that is different.

Family Time

Chapter 21:
God Made Butterflies
In this lesson the children talked about surprises God put in our world—in particular, lovely butterflies that come from caterpillars. This prepares the children for the dramatic change we make at death when we enter into new eternal life. Have your child talk about the surprises pictured on page 91 and tell you the story of a butterfly's life. Display the picture your child made.

Your Child
The life cycle of a butterfly and the death of a seed that is born again as a flower are symbols and promises of our new life. As Jesus rose from the dead, so will we. This mystery is beyond the scope of our understanding. Answer your child's questions about death simply and honestly. Because of Jesus' Resurrection, we can rejoice in this life in preparation for the next.

Reflect
God has made a home for us in heaven.
(adapted from 2 Corinthians 5:1)

Pray
Praise the LORD, who is so good . . .
(Psalm 136:1)

Do
- Point out natural wonders, such as rainbows, to your child.
- Take your child to a natural history museum. Convey wonder over the world's marvels.
- Take a nature walk with your child and admire God's gifts.
- Plant seeds with your child and watch them grow.
- Read to your child *The Very Hungry Caterpillar* by Eric Carle. Consider the wonder of the caterpillar's transformation into a butterfly. Thank God for all the surprises in the world.

For more family resources, refer to the Family Activity Booklet and visit www.loyolapress.com/preschool.

92 God Made the World

© LOYOLA PRESS.

ACTING

1 Have the children act out the life of a caterpillar. Hand one child a butterfly wand—a butterfly cutout taped to a craft stick. Give these directions:

• *Let's pretend you are caterpillars. You crawl on the ground and eat leaves.*

• *Now you make a house around yourself and curl up in it. You are very quiet and still.*

• *While you're in the house, you change into a butterfly. When* [name] *touches you with the butterfly wand, you may come out and fly around like a butterfly.*

2 Have the children use page 93 to make a three-dimensional picture of butterflies. Help them follow these directions:

• Cut out the two butterflies and fold them on the dotted lines.

• Color the flower.

• Put glue on the white part of the wings of the two butterflies and place the butterflies on the picture.

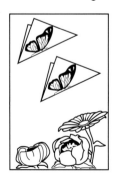

3 Gather the children in a circle for *Music 'n Motion* time. Play the Unit 5 song (Track 10). Invite the children to do motions to the song along with you, using *Music 'n Motion* page T276.

Have the children take home their pages and show their family the Family Time section.

93

ENRICHING THE FAITH EXPERIENCE

Use the following activities to enrich the lesson or to replace an activity with one that better meets the needs of your group.

1 Teach the children this poem:

Little Arabella Miller

Little Arabella Miller
Found a woolly caterpillar.
First it crawled upon her
    mother,
Then upon her baby brother.
All said, "Arabella Miller,
Take away that caterpillar!"

2 Precut butterfly wings from construction paper (one set for each child). Punch a hole at the top and bottom of each set. Distribute the wings and invite the children to decorate them. Then have the children bend in half craft stems. Show them how to thread the craft stems through the holes to make the butterfly body. Help them twist the ends of the craft stems at the top to make antennae.

3 Have the children bring a baby picture to class. Talk about how much the children have changed. Measure each child's height.

4 Take the children on a nature walk to find God's surprises. Let them bring small treasures from nature back to the room and display them.

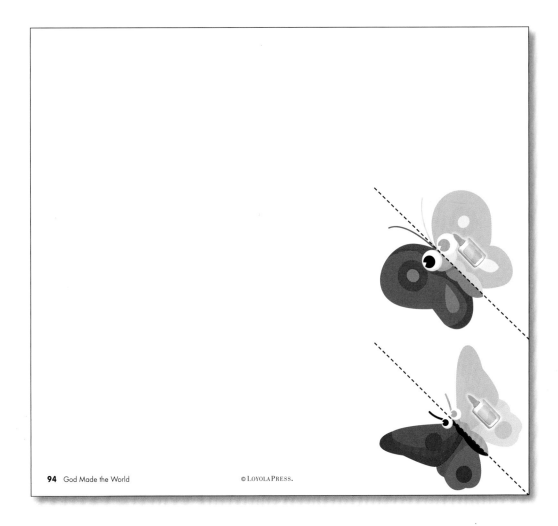

Chapter 22

God Made Big Things

God is great and powerful.

Job 40:15—41:26; Psalm 104:24–32; Sirach 43:29–31,35

PREPARING THE FAITH EXPERIENCE

LISTENING

*Let us praise him the more, since we cannot
    fathom him,
 for greater is he than all his works;
Awful indeed is the LORD's majesty,
 and wonderful is his power.
Lift up your voices to glorify the LORD,
 though he is still beyond your
    power to praise. . . .
It is the LORD who has made all things,
 and to those who fear him he gives wisdom.*

Sirach 43:29–31,35

REFLECTING

Consider some of the grandiose achievements of God—the oceans, whose depths we have yet to fathom; the sun, which is more than a million times larger than the earth; the magnificent display of a thunderstorm; a starry night sky; the Andes; Victoria Falls; the Grand Canyon. In awe of these works of God's hands, we acknowledge God's supreme might and wisdom. With the psalmist we cry out,

*What are humans that you are mindful of them,
 mere mortals that you care for them?*

Psalm 8:5

Ancient people lived in fear of the gods they conjured up to explain the universe. These people offered sacrifices to placate or please the gods. The one true God is beyond our imagination and hopes. God is not only all-powerful, all-knowing, and all-wise but also all-loving. Scripture assures us that we are precious to God, the apple of God's eye.

Yes, we raise our hands in adoration of God, which is our foremost duty. As Saint Ignatius taught, we are made to praise and reverence God. We believe, however, that God is not only transcendent but also close to us. God watches over us with loving care, loving us so much that he became one of us, enduring suffering and death so that we might live forever. Therefore, despite the immense disparity between us, we are able to love God.

We have been made in God's image and likeness. God regards us as sons and daughters. The tremendous creations such as the mountains and seas are for our benefit. They are tokens of God's love. May we always use them in such a way that we express love in return.

RESPONDING

God's Word calls us to respond in love. Respond to God now in the quiet of your heart and perhaps through your journal.

• What is my favorite large creation of God's?

Holy Spirit, fill the children with your gifts, especially wonder and awe (fear of the Lord).

Catechism of the Catholic Church

The themes of this chapter correspond to the following paragraphs: 268, 278, 299.

THE FAITH EXPERIENCE

Child's Book pages 95–100

SCRIPTURE IN THIS CHAPTER
• *Sirach 43:29*

MATERIALS
• Chapter 22 Scripture card
• Bible
• Building blocks
• Option: yardstick
• White paper
• Construction paper
• Crayons or markers
• Tape

PREPARATION
• Write the children's names on pages 95 and 97.
• Place the Chapter 22 Scripture card for SHARING #3 in the Bible.

MUSIC 'N MOTION
Use *Music 'n Motion* page T276 and CD Track 10 "Care for Life" for this chapter. For a list of additional music, see page T320.

ENRICHING THE FAITH EXPERIENCE
Use the activities at the end of the chapter to enrich the lesson or to replace an activity with one that better meets the needs of your group.

BOOKS TO SHARE
The Snail and the Whale by Julia Donaldson
    (Puffin, 2006)

Bones, Bones, Dinosaur Bones by Byron Barton
    (HarperCollins, 1990)

A Giraffe and a Half by Shel Silverstein
    (HarperCollins, 1964

Patrick's Dinosaurs by Carol Carrick (Clarion Books, 2003)

The Story of Babar by Jean de Brunhoff
    (Egmont Books Ltd, 2008)

SNACK
Suggestion: giant cookie to be broken and shared by all, or a sandwich made on a long loaf of french bread for everyone to share

ALTERNATIVE PROGRAMS

DAILY PROGRAM
Day 1: Centering, Sharing A
Day 2: Enriching the Faith Experience choice
Day 3: Sharing B, Acting #1
Day 4: Enriching the Faith Experience choice
Day 5: Acting #2 and #3

THREE-DAY PROGRAM
Day 1: Centering, Sharing A
Day 2: Sharing B
Day 3: Acting

LEARNING OUTCOMES

The children will

• be impressed with some big things made by God.

• realize that God is great and powerful.

• praise and thank God.

COMMENTS

1. In this lesson the children are motivated to praise God as a response to reflecting on the immense creatures God has made. The children come to an understanding of God's power and majesty. In addition they learn the joy and advantages of cooperation as they work together to make a giant card.

2. Children are surrounded by powerful people and sometimes feel quite powerless themselves. For them to know that God, who is very great, loves them and is their friend is comforting. In speaking about God to the children, stress God's kind and loving ways.

CENTERING

❶ Gather the children in a circle for *Music 'n Motion* time. Play the Unit 5 song (Track 10). Invite the children to do motions to the song along with you, using *Music 'n Motion* page T276.

❷ Have the children use blocks to build the biggest building they can.

SHARING [A]

❶ Distribute page 95. Have the children look at the picture. Ask:

• *What large animals do you see in the picture?* (Elephant, ostrich, lion, gorilla, giraffe, hippopotamus) [Option: Show the yardstick and tell the children that the footprint of a dinosaur found in New Mexico was as long as the yardstick.]

• *God made all these large creatures. Of all the creatures in the picture, which does God show the most love for?* (Children)

Name_____

95 God Made the World

2 Invite the children to draw a picture on page 96 of something very large that they like or have seen.

3 SCRIPTURE Invite the children to talk about what they drew on their pages. Comment and read the adaptation of Sirach 43:29 from the Scripture card in the Bible:

• *Have you ever seen the ocean? It is so big you can't see across it.*

• *Have you ever seen a mountain? Some mountains are so high that on some days you can't see their tops. They are hidden in the clouds.*

• *God made huge things like this. God is very strong and powerful to be able to do that.*

• *Listen to what we read in the Bible:*

  "God is greater than all his works."

SHARING [B]

4 Play "Bigger Than, Stronger Than." Have the children stand. Guide them in the following imaginative exercises:

• *In your mind, picture the highest mountain in the world. Let's climb it together.* [Make climbing movements.]

• *Now picture the widest ocean in the world. Let's swim it.* [Make swimming movements.]

• *Picture the largest rock in the world. Let's lift it.* [Make lifting movements.]

• *Picture the largest tree in the world. Let's put our arms around it.* [Extend arms.]

• *Think of the loudest clap of thunder in the world. Let's protect our ears.* [Cover ears.]

• *Think of the strongest wind in the world. Let's fight against it.* [Struggle against wind.]

• *Think of the largest animal that ever walked the earth, a dinosaur. Let's pet it.* [Stretch and pet the dinosaur.]

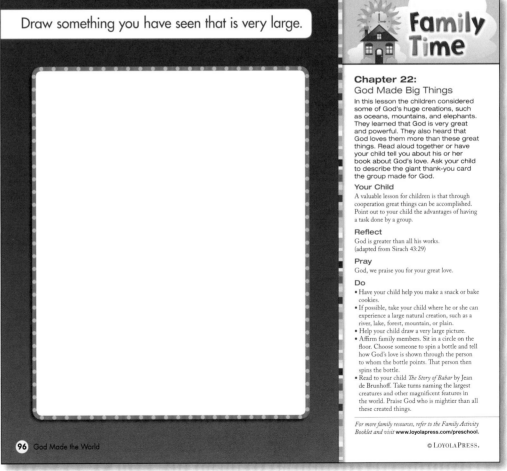

Draw something you have seen that is very large.

96 God Made the World

Family Time

Chapter 22:
God Made Big Things

In this lesson the children considered some of God's huge creations, such as oceans, mountains, and elephants. They learned that God is very great and powerful. They also heard that God loves them more than these great things. Read aloud together or have your child tell you about his or her book about God's love. Ask your child to describe the giant thank-you card the group made for God.

Your Child
A valuable lesson for children is that through cooperation great things can be accomplished. Point out to your child the advantages of having a task done by a group.

Reflect
God is greater than all his works.
(adapted from Sirach 43:29)

Pray
God, we praise you for your great love.

Do
• Have your child help you make a snack or bake cookies.
• If possible, take your child where he or she can experience a large natural creation, such as a river, lake, forest, mountain, or plain.
• Help your child draw a very large picture.
• Affirm family members. Sit in a circle on the floor. Choose someone to spin a bottle and tell how God's love is shown through the person to whom the bottle points. That person then spins the bottle.
• Read to your child *The Story of Babar* by Jean de Brunhoff. Take turns naming the largest creatures and other magnificent features in the world. Praise God who is mightier than all these created things.

For more family resources, refer to the Family Activity Booklet and visit www.loyolapress.com/preschool.

© LOYOLAPRESS.

My God Is So Great

My God is so great, so strong, and so might-y! There's noth-ing my God can-not do! (clap, clap) My God is so great, so strong, and so might-y! There's noth-ing my God can-not do! (clap, clap) The

moun-tains are his, the riv-ers are his, the stars are his hand-i-work too. _____ My God is so great, so strong, and so might-y! There's noth-ing my God can-not do! For you!

5 **PRAYER** Sing with the children "My God Is So Great" or another song praising God. Let them sway in time to the music as you sing and pray together. Introduce the song:

• *Let us praise God who made all these things. We'll sing about God's might and power. We'll sing about how wonderful God is.*

stronger than a lion.

And God loves me!

My Book About God's Great Love

God's love is higher than a mountain,

Name _____

④

①

97 God Made the World

ACTING

1 Distribute page 97. Have the children fold it in half. Invite the children to follow along as you read "My Book About God's Great Love."

2 Make a huge thank-you card for God. Have each child draw on or decorate page 99 with things that God made. Write "Thank you, God" on a separate sheet of construction paper. Guide the children in taping their pages together one-by-one to form one large card, with "Thank you, God" (written on white paper) in the center. The card may be displayed on a wall, in church, or in a hallway.

3 Gather the children in a circle for *Music 'n Motion* time. Play the Unit 5 song (Track 10). Invite the children to do motions to the song along with you, using *Music 'n Motion* page T276.

Have the children take home their pages and show their family the Family Time section.

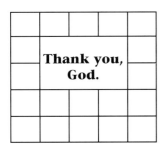

Thank you,
God.

wider than the sky,

deeper than the ocean,

bigger than a whale,

98 God Made the World

© LOYOLAPRESS.

ENRICHING THE FAITH EXPERIENCE

Use the following activities to enrich the lesson or to replace an activity with one that better meets the needs of your group.

1 Let the children have a dress-up day on which they wear clothes that grownups might wear.

2 Lead the children in a big cheer for God. Teach them the following cheer or another one. Let them holler, blow horns, jump, and clap for God.

> Two, four, six, eight.
> Who do we appreciate?
> Yea, God!

3 Teach the children the big names of some big creatures: hippopotamus, rhinoceros, tyrannosaurus.

4 Show the children slides of large things in nature: a sunset, a mountain, a waterfall, a river, an ocean. After each slide, lead the children in praying "O God, how great and wonderful you are!"

God made . . .

Name_____

99 God Made the World

Page 100 is blank.

5 Read this poem to the children:

Way down south where
   bananas grow,
A grasshopper stepped on
   an elephant's toe.
The elephant said, with tears
   in his eyes,
"Pick on somebody your
   own size."

6 Teach this finger play:

The elephant goes like this and that.
[Hold one hand over the other and sway
arms from side to side.]
He's oh, so big, and he's oh, so fat.
[Curve arms outward.]
He has no fingers, and he has no toes.
[Hold hand in front with fingers closed.]
But goodness gracious, what a nose!
[Extend arms up with fingers intertwined.]

God Made Little Things

FAITH FOCUS

Small things that God made are important.

Luke 13:18–21

PREPARING THE FAITH EXPERIENCE

LISTENING

Then he said, "What is the kingdom of God like? To what can I compare it? It is like a mustard seed that a person took and planted in the garden. When it was fully grown, it became a large bush and 'the birds of the sky dwelt in its branches.'"

Luke 13:18–19

REFLECTING

God has a heart for small things. The world is filled with tiny creatures, including more than two million kinds of insects—some too small to be seen with the unaided eye. Some insects have incredible powers. An ant can carry a load 27 times bigger than itself. A bee can fly with cargo twice its weight.

Although a seed is tiny, it can grow into a tall tree with a thick trunk and wide-spreading branches. Jesus used a seed to teach how the Kingdom of God can grow and spread throughout the world. A seed is a wonderful symbol for showing that a small thing may have the potential to become a powerful influence, and it reminds us that even one person can make a difference.

In God's divine plan, every living creature begins as something small. God has provided animals with instinct, enabling them to care for their young. By feeding and protecting them, adult animals prepare their offspring for life. Similarly, human beings care for and raise their children.

As catechists, we have the privilege to share responsibility for passing on the truths of our faith and Christian values to the children. As we teach young Christians, we also learn from them, for Jesus said that only the childlike will enter heaven.

RESPONDING

Having been nourished by God's Word, we are able to respond to God's great love for us. In prayer, respond to God's call to you to share his Word with others. You may also wish to respond in your prayer journal.

- What have the children taught me?

God, watch over the children so that they may grow into people of integrity and Christian love.

Catechism of the Catholic Church

The themes of this chapter correspond to the following paragraph: 2416.

THE FAITH EXPERIENCE

Child's Book pages 101–104

SCRIPTURE IN THIS CHAPTER
• *Genesis 1:31*

MATERIALS
• Chapter 23 Scripture card
• Bible
• Cutouts: #18, baby; #60, acorn/oak tree
• Option: baby doll
• Recording of quiet music for SHARING #6
• Crayons or markers
• 4-inch piece of yarn for each child
• Scissors
• Stapler or glue

PREPARATION
• Write the children's names on page 101.
• Place the Chapter 23 Scripture card for SHARING #2 in the Bible.
• If you wish, use a paper cutter to cut off the light blue strip on page 103 for the children.

MUSIC'N MOTION
Use *Music 'n Motion* page T276 and CD Track 10 "Care for Life" for this chapter. For a list of additional music, see page T320.

ENRICHING THE FAITH EXPERIENCE
Use the activities at the end of the chapter to enrich the lesson or to replace an activity with one that better meets the needs of your group.

BOOKS TO SHARE
The Very Quiet Cricket by Eric Carle (Philomel, 1990)

Be Nice to Spiders by Margaret Bloy Graham (HarperCollins, 1967)

Whose Mouse Are You? by Robert Kraus (Aladdin, 2005)

I Like to Be Little by Charlotte Zolotow (HarperTrophy, 1990)

SNACK
Suggestion: graham crackers and miniature marshmallows, which the children can pretend are insects

ALTERNATIVE PROGRAMS

DAILY PROGRAM
Day 1: Centering, Sharing A
Day 2: Enriching the Faith Experience choice
Day 3: Sharing B
Day 4: Enriching the Faith Experience choice
Day 5: Acting

THREE-DAY PROGRAM
Day 1: Centering, Sharing A
Day 2: Sharing B, Acting #1
Day 3: Acting #2 and #3

LEARNING OUTCOMES

The children will
- know that God made small things.
- realize that small things are important.
- praise and thank God for small things.

COMMENTS

1. This lesson teaches the children to have regard for small things and to care for them. It reinforces the truth that all life is precious.

2. Children are quick to distinguish between little and big, and to them bigger means better. If offered a choice of a dime or a nickel, they will choose the nickel. Similarly, children consider themselves less worthwhile than grownups, who tower over them. Children can be taught to understand that God's goodness is revealed as much in little things as in large ones. Small things are signs of God's love for us too. As the children come to value little things, their self-worth will increase.

CENTERING

❶ Gather the children in a circle for *Music 'n Motion* time. Play the Unit 5 song (Track 10). Invite the children to do motions to the song along with you, using *Music 'n Motion* page T276.

❷ Teach the children this finger play:

The Itsy, Bitsy Spider

The itsy, bitsy spider went up the water spout.
[Place thumbs against forefingers of the other hand and swivel the fingers so that one pair and then the other goes above to represent climbing.]
Down came the rain and washed the spider out.
[Wiggle fingers in downward motion; Sweep arms out and drop to sides.]
Out came the sun and dried up all the rain.
[Make large circle with arms over head.]
So the itsy bitsy spider went up the spout again.
[Repeat climbing motion.]

101 God Made the World

Name_____

SHARING [A]

1 Show the children the acorn on Cutout #60 and ask what an acorn can become. (Oak tree) Turn over the cutout to reveal the tree on the other side.

2 **SCRIPTURE** Talk about small things. Read the adaptation of Genesis 1:31 from the Scripture card in the Bible.

• *God made many things that are very small, such as spiders and acorns. Small things are just as important as big things. What are other small things that God made?*

• *God must be kind and gentle to make so many little things.*

• *Saint Francis of Assisi cared for small things. When he saw a worm on the road, he carried it to the side so that it wouldn't be stepped on.*

• *God wants us to care for all living creatures, big and small. They are all precious because God made them. Listen to what we read in the Bible: "God looked at everything he had made and called it very good."*

3 Show Cutout #18, baby, or a baby doll. Ask:

• *Here is another small creature. What will the baby become?* (Man or woman)

• *What are some things that others must do for a baby?* (Feed, clothe, and carry the baby, change the baby's diapers, teach the baby to walk and talk)

SHARING [B]

4 Distribute page 101 and have the children look at the picture. Ask:

• *What is the girl doing?* (Looking at something through a magnifying glass)

• *A glass like that makes things look larger so that we can see them better.*

• *What is the girl looking at?* (A leaf)

• *Have you ever watched an ant? What was it doing?*

5 Have the children find and circle the seven little creatures that are hidden in the picture on page 102.

Circle the seven little creatures hidden in the picture.

Family Time

Chapter 23:
God Made Little Things

In this lesson the children focused on small things that God made. They learned to value small living things and praised God for them. They saw the potential of small things, such as acorns and babies. Ask your child to show you the pet pocket he or she made.

Your Child
Children can appreciate the ingenuity of the Creator by examining the intricacies of small, delicate creations. Often during walks children will stop abruptly, absorbed by some small thing.

Reflect
God looked at everything he had made and called it very good.
(adapted from Genesis 1:31)

Pray
God, help us care for all living creatures, great and small.

Do
• Study an ant or another small thing with your child. Point out its features and unique powers.
• Show your child his or her baby pictures. Call attention to the tiny fingernails and toes.
• Look at several small things through a magnifying glass with your child.
• Provide your child with a special box for collecting small treasures.
• Read to your child *The Very Quiet Cricket* by Eric Carle. Count how many small creatures your child can name. Ask God to show you ways to appreciate and care for little things.

For more family resources, refer to the Family Activity Booklet and visit **www.loyolapress.com/preschool.**

© LOYOLAPRESS.

102 God Made the World

6 PRAYER Invite the children to find a spot where they can be alone to thank God in their hearts for small things. Play quiet music as they pray.

ACTING

1 Read to the children "The Teeny Tiny Family" on page T175. Talk about how there are advantages to being small.

2 Have the children make pet pockets, using page 103. Tell the children that they will make a pocket for carrying five little pets. Have the children identify the four creatures on page 104. (Ant, bee, fly, ladybug) Give each child a four-inch piece of yarn as the fifth pet—a worm. Help them follow these directions:

- Cut apart the four pet cards on page 104.

- Fold each card so that it stands.

- Follow the diagrams below for cutting and folding the pocket.

- Staple or glue the sides of the pocket.

- Put the five pets inside the pocket.

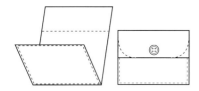

3 Gather the children in a circle for *Music 'n Motion* time. Play the Unit 5 song (Track 10). Invite the children to do motions to the song along with you, using *Music 'n Motion* page T276.

Have the children take home their pages and show their family the Family Time section.

CHECKPOINT

- *Were the learning outcomes achieved?*

- *What signs are there that the children are delighting in God's world?*

103 God Made the World

The Teeny Tiny Family

Once upon a time there was a teeny tiny family. The mother, the father, and the two children, Tina and Tommy, were no bigger than mice. They lived in a teeny tiny house with a teeny tiny yard. They had a teeny tiny cat named Tuggle and a teeny tiny dog named Tinky.

One day when the teeny tiny family was eating dinner at its teeny tiny table, the doorbell rang. A strange man was at the family's teeny tiny door. He said to the teeny tiny father, "I am selling a special drink that will make you as big as other people. Would you like some?"

The teeny tiny father said, "Come back tomorrow." He sat down at the teeny tiny table and asked his teeny tiny family, "What do you think? Would you like to be big?"

"Well," said the teeny tiny mother, "if we were big, we would have to cook more food and wash more clothes."

"If we were big," said tiny Tommy, "we couldn't ride on the backs of frogs or hide in rabbit holes."

"If we were big," said tiny Tina, "then we couldn't sit under the shade of a flower or wear dresses made of spiderweb lace."

"And," said the teeny tiny father, "if we were big, we would have more grass to cut and a bigger house to care for. Who wants to stay as we are?"

"I do," said the teeny tiny mother.

"I do," said tiny Tommy.

"I do," said tiny Tina.

"I do too," said the teeny tiny father.

So everyone in the teeny tiny family stayed teeny tiny. They lived in their teeny tiny house with the teeny tiny yard. They played with their teeny tiny cat named Tuggle and their teeny tiny dog named Tinky and lived happily ever after.

104

ENRICHING THE FAITH EXPERIENCE

Use the following activities to enrich the lesson or to replace an activity with one that better meets the needs of your group.

1 Have the children make a tiny-things collage. Bring in tiny things from nature: small, pressed flowers; shells; pebbles; leaves; seeds. Give each child a wide strip of two-sided tape placed on a long piece of tagboard or poster board. Let the children choose items and arrange them on their strips of tape. Instead of tape, you may want to have the children glue their items to the shallow lid of a box.

2 Tell the Aesop fable about the lion and the mouse.

3 Make a class book called "Thank You, God, for Small Things." Let each child contribute a page on which he or she has drawn a small thing. Use a hole punch and yarn to bind the pages or put each child's page in a plastic zipper bag with holes punched in the side.

4 Have the children bring in their baby pictures and show them to the other children.

5 Teach this finger play:

> This is my turtle.
> [Have thumb tucked into fist.]
> He lives in a shell.
> He likes his home very well.
> He pokes his head out
> [Stick out thumb from fist.]
> when he wants to eat.
> And he pulls it back
> [Put thumb back into fist.]
> when he wants to sleep.

6 Purchase or make an ant farm for the children so they can observe ants making tunnels. Set a small plastic container or glass inside a larger plastic container and fill the area between them (about half an inch) with dirt. Add some ants and place a screen over the top. Every few days supply the ants with jam, sweet cereal, or candy. Release the ants after the children have seen them.

7 Teach this song to the tune of "When Johnny Comes Marching Home Again."

2. The ants go marching two by two . . .
   The little one stops to tie his shoe . . .

3. The ants go marching three by three . . .
   The little one stops to climb a tree . . .

4. The ants go marching four by four . . .
   The little one stops to shut the door . . .

5. The ants go marching five by five . . .
   The little one stops to kick a hive . . .

6. The ants go marching six by six . . .
   The little one stops to pick up sticks . . .

7. The ants go marching seven by seven . . .
   The little one stops to go to heaven . . .

8. The ants go marching eight by eight . . .
   The little one stops to shut the gate . . .

9. The ants go marching nine by nine . . .
   The little one stops to pick up a dime . . .

10. The ants go marching ten by ten . . .
    The little one stops to shout THE END!

FAITH FOCUS

All people are God's children.

Galatians 3:26–29

PREPARING THE FAITH EXPERIENCE

LISTENING

For through faith you are all children of God in Christ Jesus. For all of you who were baptized into Christ have clothed yourselves with Christ. There is neither Jew nor Greek, there is neither slave nor free person, there is not male and female; for you are all one in Christ Jesus.

Galatians 3:26–28

REFLECTING

Modern technology has produced instant communication and rapid transportation, transforming our world into a global village. We therefore are well aware of the variety of people who inhabit our planet—Europeans, Native Americans, North Americans, South Americans, Asians, Africans, Australians, and many others. God's creativity is amply reflected by humankind.

Cultural diversity enriches our lives. Through contact with the literature, music, dances, and foods of various countries, we learn to celebrate differences as well as similarities and come to enjoy life more fully. When a particular culture is lost, it is a loss for all humanity.

In God's plan no one country or race is greater than another. Ideally we must all live as a family, helping one another not only survive but thrive. Just as sin mars individual families, it also mars our global family. Greed and thirst for power have caused countries to plunder and pillage. Prejudice, racism, and fear have led to wars and genocide.

Christ calls us to the peace that is the result of justice. His final prayer before he died was that we all may be one. To know one another and to respect one another's cultures and traditions is a way for the world community to become a smoothly running interdependent system. This awareness of other cultures should begin at an early age and should last a lifetime.

A tale teaches the interconnectedness of all people. A sage once asked his disciples when the first moment of daybreak occurs. One disciple inquired, "Is it when you can see the trees in the distance?" "No," said the sage. "Is it when you can discern whether an animal is a sheep or a wolf?" asked another. "No," replied the sage. "The first moment of daybreak occurs when you can see in your neighbor the face of your brother or sister."

RESPONDING

God's Word moves us to respond in word and action. Let God's Spirit work within you as you prayerfully consider how you are being called to respond to God's message to you today. Responding through your journal may help to strengthen your response.

- How can I learn more about other cultures?

  Jesus, help the children accept all people as their brothers and sisters.

Catechism of the Catholic Church

The themes of this chapter correspond to the following paragraphs:1934–1938, 2304, 2319.

THE FAITH EXPERIENCE

Child's Book pages 105–108

SCRIPTURE IN THIS CHAPTER
• *Galatians 3:26*

MATERIALS
• Option: globe
• Bible
• Cutouts: #61, Veena, girl from India; #62, Ali, boy from Kenya
• Scissors
• Crayons or markers
• Tape or stapler
• Straw or craft stick
• Recording of marching music for ACTING #3

PREPARATION
• Write the children's names on pages 105 and 108.
• Before class, ask any children from other countries whether they would like to talk to the class about where they came from.
• If you wish, cut out the flag samples on page 107 for the children.

MUSIC 'N MOTION

Use *Music 'n Motion* page T276 and CD Track 10 "Care for Life" for this chapter. For a list of additional music, see page T320.

ENRICHING THE FAITH EXPERIENCE
Use the activities at the end of the chapter to enrich the lesson or to replace an activity with one that better meets the needs of your group.

BOOKS TO SHARE
Whoever You Are by Mem Fox (Voyager Books, 2001)

Why Mosquitoes Buzz in People's Ears: A West African Tale by Verna Aardema (Puffin/Dial, 2004)

Anansi the Spider: A Tale from the Ashanti by Gerald McDermott (Henry Holt an Co., 1987)

Nursery Tales Around the World by Judy Sierra (Clarion Books, 1996)

Madeline by Ludwig Bemelmans (Puffin, 1993)

SNACK
Suggestion: a party snack mix (without nuts)

ALTERNATIVE PROGRAMS

DAILY PROGRAM
Day 1: Centering, Sharing A
Day 2: Sharing B, Acting #1
Day 3: Enriching the Faith Experience choice
Day 4: Enriching the Faith Experience choice
Day 5: Acting #2–4

THREE-DAY PROGRAM
Day 1: Centering, Sharing A
Day 2: Sharing B, Acting #1
Day 3: Acting #2–4

LEARNING OUTCOMES

The children will
- know that God made and loves all people.
- respect people from other countries.
- appreciate the variety among people.

COMMENTS

1. If a child in your class has recently arrived from another country, ask the child whether he or she would like to talk about his or her country or have a relative do so. (Some children do not want to be singled out as being different.) If the child agrees, you might ask the child's parents to share their culture by bringing to the class some pictures, clothing, or foods from their country.

2. Children frequently learn prejudice at a young age. It can be counteracted by teaching children to love and respect others as their brothers and sisters.

CENTERING

❶ Gather the children in a circle for *Music 'n Motion* time. Play the Unit 5 song (Track 10). Invite the children to do motions to the song along with you, using *Music 'n Motion* page T276.

❷ Teach the children "Frère Jacques." Introduce it:

• *France is a country that is far away across the ocean. People who live in France speak a language called French. Today I'll teach you a French song.*

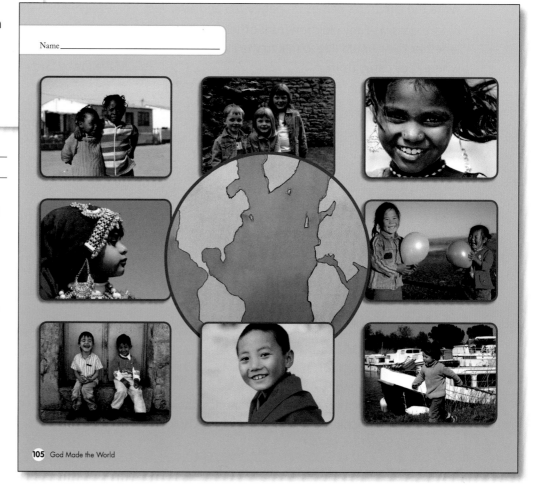

SHARING [A]

1 Talk about the children's experiences with other countries. You might begin by telling about your own experiences.

• *Are any of you from another country?*

• *Has anyone ever visited another country?*

• *Does anyone have relatives that live in another country?*

2 Distribute page 105. Discuss:

• *This is a picture of the world. The world is like a big ball.* [Option: Show a globe.] *There are countries all over the world. The people who live in other countries are different from us in some ways. They have their own languages. They eat different kinds of food. Sometimes they wear different sorts of clothing.*

• *Where do you think the children in the picture are from?* (Note: clockwise from top left: Namibia, Africa; England; India; Mongolia; France; China; Mexico; India)

• *Having different kinds of people in the world is more interesting than having people who are all the same.*

3 **SCRIPTURE** Talk about God's love for all and about being children of God. (based on Galatians 3:26) Show the Bible.

• *Who do you think made all these different people?* (God)

• *God loves everyone. In the Bible we read that we are all God's children. We are like brothers and sisters in the family of God.*

SHARING [B]

4 Play "Love Around the World." Have the children form a circle and hold hands. Tell them to pretend that they are the children in the picture on page 105, who are in different places around the world. Tell them to send love around the world by giving their neighbor's hand a love squeeze when they receive one. Squeeze the hand of the child on your right. Let the love squeeze travel around the circle several times.

Draw a line from each child to the heart.

106 God Made the World

Family Time

Chapter 24:
God Made Countries

In this lesson the children were made aware of the many different countries that make up the world. They learned that although people in these countries may look different, eat different things, and have different customs, they are all human beings. They were led to regard others as their brothers and sisters in the family of God. Find out about the country whose flag your child made. Tell your child about it.

Your Child
Prejudice is learned quickly by children. Help your child respect other people by introducing him or her to people of different races and nationalities.

Reflect
For through faith you are all children of God in Christ Jesus. (Galatians 3:26)

Pray
Jesus, help us grow in love as brothers and sisters in God's family.

Do
• Try recipes from other countries.
• Point out to your child some accomplishments of people from other nations.
• Pray together for people in other countries who need our prayers.
• Read to your child *Whoever You Are* by Mem Fox. Ask your child to tell you what he or she knows about people who live in other countries. Ask God to bless all the people in the world.

For more family resources, refer to the Family Activity Booklet and visit www.loyolapress.com/preschool.

© LOYOLAPRESS.

❺ Show Cutouts #61 and #62, Veena, girl from India, and Ali, boy from Kenya. Explain:

• *This girl is named Veena. She is from India. She is wearing a sari. A sari is a long piece of material that the women of India wrap around themselves.*

• *This boy is from Kenya in Africa. His name is Ali.*

❻ Let the children practice saying kind things to the cutout children. Have them come up and hold the cutout as they speak to it. Alternatively, show the cutout and invite a volunteer to offer something kind to say. Introduce the activity:

• *God wants all children to love one another. We show love by what we say and do. Let's practice saying nice things to these children.*

• *What can you say to Veena when you see her in school?*

• *What can you say to Ali when you are playing and he is sitting by himself?*

• *What can you say to Veena when she sneezes?*

• *What can you say to Ali when he suddenly drops something?*

• *What can you say to Veena when she's crying?*

• *What can you say to Ali when he gets a high score on a game you are playing?*

• *What can you say to Veena when you accidentally bump into her?*

ACTING

❶ Have the children draw a line from each child to the heart on page 106. Introduce the activity:

• *Even though people look different, we all are human beings. Each of us has a heart.*

• *We are all God's special children. We care for all people as brothers and sisters in the family of God.*

❷ Have the children make a country's flag from page 107. Tell them that every country in the world has a flag. Then help them follow these directions:

• Choose a flag from those shown.
• Draw the flag above the pictures in the empty space. [Tell each child which country's flag he or she has chosen.]
• Cut off the section with the many flags.

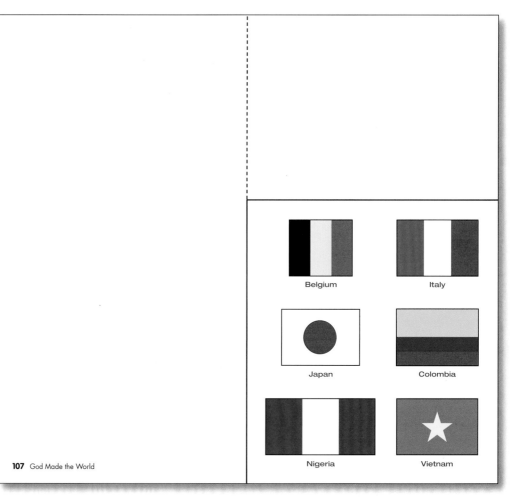

107 God Made the World

Belgium   Italy

Japan   Colombia

Nigeria   Vietnam

Page 108 is blank.

- Roll the long piece of paper up to the flag and tape or staple it to form a stick. [You might prefer to have the children draw the flag on the longer piece and tape it to a straw or craft stick.]

❸ PRAYER Hold a parade of countries. Play lively music as the children march and wave the flags they made. End with a prayer that the children repeat after you line by line.

Father in heaven, thank you for your love and care. Please bless all children in the whole world—wherever they may live.

❹ Gather the children in a circle for *Music 'n Motion* time. Play the Unit 5 song (Track 10). Invite the children to do motions to the song along with you, using *Music 'n Motion* page T276.

Have the children take home their pages and show their family the Family Time section.

CHECKPOINT

- *Were the learning outcomes achieved?*
- *Do all the children exhibit tolerance for people who are different from themselves?*

ENRICHING THE FAITH EXPERIENCE

Use the following activities to enrich the lesson or to replace an activity with one that better meets the needs of your group.

❶ Take the children on a pretend ride on a magic carpet. Fly over various countries and make comments about them.

❷ Teach the children to say "thank you" in other languages: merci [mair-SEE] (French); danke shoen [DON-ka shone] (German); gracias [GRAH-see-us] (Spanish).

❸ Read the children a fairy tale from another country.

❹ Bring food to share with the group made by people of various nationalities or food you have made that is associated with a foreign country. Be aware of food allergies.

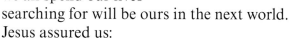

PREPARING THE FAITH EXPERIENCE

LISTENING

Rejoice in the Lord always. I shall say it again: rejoice!

Philippians 4:4

REFLECTING

Joyfulness is one of the characteristics of a Christian. Because we know Jesus, and Jesus has risen from the dead, we can afford to laugh. We know that death has been conquered once and for all.

Convinced that God is our loving Father, that we are redeemed by Jesus and empowered by the Holy Spirit, we can manifest freedom and joy. Our faith gives us hope, and hope gives us joy. Christians are not exempt from difficulties in life. No matter what trials assail us, however, Jesus is with us as we weather the storm. Jesus has given even suffering a meaning. United with his suffering and death, our suffering leads to glory.

Joy is one of the Fruits of the Holy Spirit, which first filled us at Baptism. The joy and peace radiating from our faces ought to be a strong argument for becoming a Christian.

We were created for God and, as Saint Augustine realized, our hearts are restless until they rest in God. Scripture also acknowledges that God is the wellspring of perfect happiness:

My joy lies in being close to God.

Psalm 73:28
Jerusalem Bible (© 1966)

Someone has pointed out that JOY is the result of putting nothing (0) between Jesus (J) and you (Y).

If we live with faith in God and follow Jesus, we can hope that the happiness we all spend our lives searching for will be ours in the next world. Jesus assured us:

I will see you again, and your hearts will rejoice, and no one will take your joy away from you.

John 16:22

RESPONDING

Having reflected upon God's Word, take some time now to continue to respond to God in prayer. You might wish to record your responses in your journal.

- When am I the happiest?

   Jesus, fill the children with true joy.

Catechism of the Catholic Church

The themes of this chapter correspond to the following paragraphs: 1718–1719.

THE FAITH EXPERIENCE

Child's Book pages 109–112

SCRIPTURE IN THIS CHAPTER
• *John 16:22*

MATERIALS
• Chapter 25 Scripture card
• Bible
• Option: unbreakable mirror
• Cutout #63, smile/frown
• Scissors
• Tape or stapler
• Two 12-inch pieces of yarn as ties for the hats
• Round sticker for each child
• Option: paints for faces (See Homemade Materials at the back of this manual for the recipe.)

PREPARATION
• Write the children's names on pages 109 and 112.
• Place the Chapter 25 Scripture card for SHARING #1 in the Bible.
• If you wish, cut out the party hats for the children.
• You may wish to buy or make pom-poms for the party hats. To make four at once:

Wrap yarn at least 30 times around an 8½-inch piece of cardboard.

Tie a 4½-inch piece of yarn in a knot around the  wrapped yarn in four places: at either end of the cardboard and in the middle of both sides.

Cut the yarn halfway between each knot.

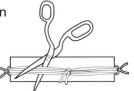

MUSIC 'N MOTION
Use *Music 'n Motion* page T276 and CD Track 10 "Care for Life" for this chapter. For a list of additional music, see page T320.

BOOKS TO SHARE
The Stupids Step Out by Harry G. Allard (Houghton Mifflin, 1977)

What Do You Do, Dear? by Sesyle Joslin (HarperTrophy, 1986)

The Seven Chinese Brothers by Margaret Mahy (Scholastic Paperbacks, 1992)

The Little Old Lady Who Was Not Afraid of Anything by Linda Williams (HarperTrophy, 1988)

Silly Sally by Audrey Wood (Red Wagon Books, 1999)

SNACK
Suggestion: orange segments or apple slices (smiles)

ALTERNATIVE PROGRAMS

DAILY PROGRAM
Day 1: Centering, Sharing A
Day 2: Enriching the Faith Experience choice
Day 3: Sharing B, Acting #1
Day 4: Enriching the Faith Experience choice
Day 5: Acting #2–5

THREE-DAY PROGRAM
Day 1: Centering, Sharing A
Day 2: Sharing B, Acting #1
Day 3: Acting #2–5

LEARNING OUTCOMES

The children will
- know that God wants them to be happy.
- desire to give joy to others.
- thank God for the gift of laughter.

COMMENTS

1. Human beings were made for happiness. Eden must have rung with joy and laughter until sin came on the scene, along with worry, fear, guilt, and depression. When Jesus appeared, he brought smiles and laughter back to us. He taught us to laugh at our own self-importance and to bring joy to others. Jesus promises us an eternity of joy.

2. Four-year-old children have a good sense of humor. They should enjoy this lesson.

3. If this is the last lesson of the year, you may wish to invite parents to a special class program and let the children share some of the things they have made and learned. Note: Special Lesson Last Class/ Summer discusses the last day of class.

CENTERING

Gather the children in a circle for *Music 'n Motion* time. Play the Unit 5 song (Track 10). Invite the children to do motions to the song along with you, using *Music 'n Motion* page T276.

SHARING [A]

1 Distribute page 109. Talk about the picture. Read the adaptation of John 16:22 from the Scripture card in the Bible.

- *How do you know that the children and Jesus are happy?* (They are smiling.)

- *Why do you think they are happy?*

- *God wants us to be happy. Everything God does is to make us happy. God likes to see us smiling and hear us laughing.*

- *Can any animals really laugh?* (No.) *We are special. God gave us the gift of laughter.*

- *When are you happy?*

- *We are happy when we act like Jesus, when we do nice things for people, and when we are kind and loving.*

- *In heaven our happiness will never stop. Listen to what Jesus says: "Your hearts will be happy and your joy will last forever."*

109 God Made the World

If You're Happy and You Know It

Verse 2. If you're happy and you know it, stamp your feet . . .

Verse 3. If you're happy and you know it, nod your head . . .

2 Teach the children verses one and two of the song "If You're Happy and You Know It."

3 Have the children make grumpy faces. Then have them make happy faces. Tell them that they look much friendlier when they are happy. [Option: have them look in a mirror to see the

difference between a grumpy face and a happy face.]

4 Ask the children to tell what things in the picture on page 110 make them laugh.

SHARING [B]

5 Show Cutout #63, smile/frown, and ask the children to tell or act out how they can make others happy. Have each child who answers turn the frown upside down to make a smile.

• *How can you make your father happy?*

• *How can you make your mother happy?*

• *How can you make your brother or sister happy?*

• *How can you make your friend happy?*

6 Teach verse three of the song "If You're Happy and You Know It."

ACTING

1 PRAYER Lead the children in a prayer. Have them close their eyes and repeat the words silently in their heart.

Dear God, thank you for making us to be happy. Thank you for the gift of laughter. I love you. Help me to make others happy.

2 Talk about parties and their role in making people laugh.

• *Are parties fun?*

• *What do you do at parties?*

• *When you are having fun, what do you do?* (Smile; laugh)

• *What do you sometimes wear at a party?* (Party hat)

3 Distribute page 111 and have the children cut out the party hat. Help them bend and staple it together. Then help them tape or staple yarn to the hat where the squares appear (for ties). If you have pom-poms, help the children staple or tape them to the tops of the hats.

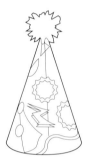

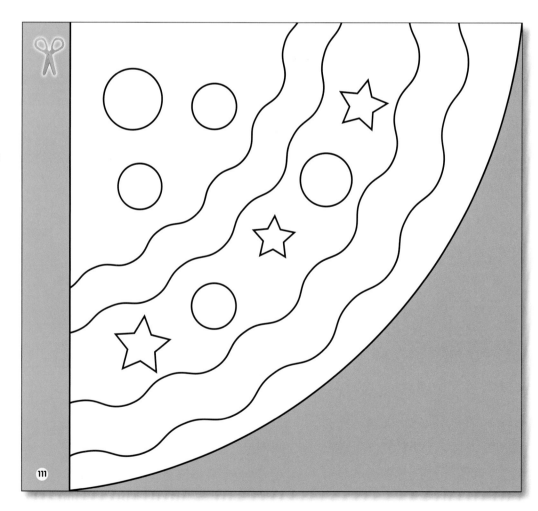

4 Let the children wear the party hats. Help them tie the yarn under their chins. Put a round sticker on each child's cheek. Paint flowers on the children's faces if possible.

5 Gather the children in a circle for *Music 'n Motion* time. Play the Unit 5 song (Track 10). Invite the children to do motions to the song along with you, using *Music 'n Motion* page T276.

Have the children take home their pages and show their family the Family Time section.

ENRICHING THE FAITH EXPERIENCE

Use the following activities to enrich the lesson or to replace an activity with one that better meets the needs of your group.

1 Invite the children to experience the joy that comes from play. Let them play "Hot Potato." Direct them to sit in a circle. Give them a beanbag or ball to pass around the circle as long as the music plays. When the music stops, the child holding the beanbag or ball is "burned" but continues to play the game.

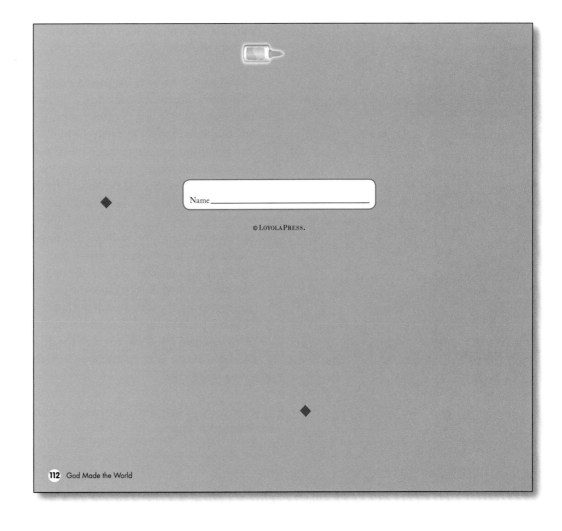

Name _____

© LOYOLA PRESS.

112 God Made the World

2 Play "I Can Make You Smile." Have a child sit in the "sad seat" and try not to smile. Let other children come up one by one and try, without touching the sad child, to make him or her smile. Whoever succeeds becomes the next sad child in the seat.

3 Invite the children to finger paint or draw a picture of joy.

4 Read the children this nonsense poem:

I know an old lady who swallowed a fly,
I don't know why she swallowed a fly,
Perhaps she'll die.

I know an old lady who swallowed a spider
That wriggled and wriggled and tickled inside her;
She swallowed the spider to catch the fly,
But I don't know why she swallowed the fly,
Perhaps she'll die.

I know an old lady who swallowed a bird,
Now, ain't it absurd to swallow a bird?
She swallowed the bird to catch the spider,
She swallowed the spider to catch the fly,
But I don't know why she swallowed the fly,
Perhaps she'll die.

I know an old lady who swallowed a cat,
Now fancy that, to swallow a cat!
She swallowed the cat to catch the bird,
She swallowed the bird to catch the spider,
She swallowed the spider to catch the fly,
But I don't know why she swallowed the fly,
Perhaps she'll die.

I know an old lady who swallowed a dog,
Oh, what a hog to swallow a dog!
She swallowed the dog to catch the cat,
She swallowed the cat to catch the bird,
She swallowed the bird to catch the spider,
She swallowed the spider to catch the fly,
But I don't know why she swallowed the fly,
Perhaps she'll die.

I know an old lady who swallowed a cow,
I don't know how she swallowed a cow.
She swallowed the cow to catch the dog,
She swallowed the dog to catch the cat,
She swallowed the cat to catch the bird,
She swallowed the bird to catch the spider,
She swallowed the spider to catch the fly,
But I don't know why she swallowed the fly,
Perhaps she'll die.

I know an old lady who swallowed a horse,
She died, of course!

5 Teach the children the song "Rejoice in the Lord Always."

Rejoice in the Lord Always
(Round)

Philippians 4:4

Re - joice in the Lord __ al - ways, and a -
gain I say re - joice! (clap, clap) Re -
joice in the Lord __ al - ways, and a - gain I say re -
joice! (clap, clap) Re - joice, __ re - joice, __ and a -
gain I say re - joice! (clap, clap) Re - joice, __ re -
joice, __ and a - gain I say re - joice! (clap, clap)

Special Seasons and Days

In these lessons the children will learn about seasons and feast days of the Church year as well as other special days. They will be encouraged to participate more fully in celebrations that are part of Church and family life.

Special Seasons

1 Halloween/Feast of All Saints
The children learn that Halloween is the night before the feast of All Saints. They are encouraged to let their light shine by smiling. They make a crown and hold a saint celebration.

2 Advent
The children prepare for Jesus' birthday by doing kind acts. They make a manger to fill with a piece of "straw" whenever they do a kind act.

3 Christmas
The children talk about Christmas as Jesus' birthday. They decorate a tree and hear the Christmas story. Then they have a procession to the manger.

4 Lent
The children identify actions that show love. They learn about Lent and are reminded to follow Jesus and show love for God in words and deeds.

5 Easter
The children hear that Jesus rose from the dead. They hear the Good News that we share the life of Jesus. They make a reversible Easter card.

6 Pentecost
The children talk about helpers. They learn that Jesus gave us a helper, the Holy Spirit, who is with us always and brings us peace. The children practice sharing the sign of peace. They make a wind sock as a reminder to be peacemakers.

Special Days

7 Thanksgiving
The children practice saying thank you. They talk about Thanksgiving Day and make thank-you cards for God. They make stand-up turkeys.

8 Valentine's Day
The children learn that Valentine's Day is a day to love people. They hear Jesus' command to love one another and talk about how to do this. They make a valentine.

9 Mother's Day
The children consider what their mothers do for them and recall that Mary is their mother. They make a scroll for their mothers.

10 Father's Day
They learn that Jesus told us that God is our Father in heaven and recall that Saint Joseph was Jesus' father on earth. They make a Father's Day card.

11 Birthdays
The children talk about birthdays—days when we celebrate the gift of life. They have a mini-birthday party and make a book celebrating their lives.

12 Last Class/Summer
The children anticipate summer and thank God for it. They receive a certificate for having participated in the preschool program.

The Year in Our Church

- Ordinary Time
- Lent
- Holy Week
- Ash Wednesday
- Epiphany
- Christmas
- Easter Sunday
- Easter
- Advent
- First Sunday of Advent
- Feast of All Saints
- Winter
- Spring
- Summer
- Fall
- Pentecost
- Ordinary Time

Special Lesson 1
Halloween/ Feast of All Saints

PREPARING THE FAITH EXPERIENCE

LISTENING

After this I had a vision of a great multitude, which no one could count, from every nation, race, people, and tongue. They stood before the throne and before the Lamb, wearing white robes and holding palm branches in their hands. They cried out in a loud voice:

*"Salvation comes from our
     God, who is seated on the throne,
   and from the Lamb."*

Revelation 7:9–10

REFLECTING

Some of the delightful customs of Halloween (trick-or-treating, making jack-o'-lanterns, wearing costumes) originated with the Celts in pre-Christian times. For Christians, however, Halloween marks the beginning of a religious celebration. The word *halloween* is derived from *hallows' eve,* the night before the feast of the hallowed (or holy) ones—the feast of All Saints.

The canonized saints assure us that sanctity is possible and show us how to acquire it. They are of all ages, of all nationalities, and from all walks of life. The common denominator is that they loved as Christ loved. On the feast of All Saints, we celebrate all the saints, those who are canonized and the countless others who are not officially recognized. The latter include our family members and friends who are in heaven with God.

Someone once said, "The greatest tragedy in life is not to be a saint." God is calling all of us to be holy. We are redeemed by Christ and given a share in divine life through Baptism. For this reason Saint Paul, in his letters, refers to Church members as "holy ones" or "saints." We are all saints in the making.

When a teacher asked her class, "What is a saint?" one child thought of the stained-glass

windows in church and answered, "Someone the light shines through." This answer is true in more ways than one. Saints let the light of Christ shine through them. The joy, love, and goodness that radiated from Jesus radiate from the saints. While on the earth, they loved God and others well; in heaven they show love for us by their intercession. The patron saint whose name we bear or the favorite saints whom we adopt befriend us in a special way.

We pray to the saints, who are united with us in the Communion of Saints, and we ask them to pray for us. We honor them for their holiness and strive to imitate their outstanding love. At Mass on the feast of All Saints, we pray,

> **God our Father
> source of all holiness,
> the work of your hands is manifest in your
> saints, the beauty of your truth is reflected in
> their faith.**
>
> **May we who aspire to have part in their joy
> be filled with the Spirit that blessed their lives,
> so that having shared their faith on earth we
> may also know their peace in your kingdom.**

Alternative Opening Prayer

RESPONDING

God's Word calls us to respond in love. Respond to God now in the quiet of your heart and perhaps through your journal.

- Who are some saints, living and dead, in my life?

Holy Spirit, make the children holy.

Catechism of the Catholic Church

The themes of this lesson correspond to the following paragraph: 2683.

THE FAITH EXPERIENCE

Child's Book pages 113–116

SCRIPTURE IN THIS LESSON
• *Matthew 5:14,16*

MATERIALS
• Halloween/Feast of All Saints Scripture card
• Bible
• Cutout #64, pumpkin
• Option: mask
• Orange crayons or markers
• Scissors
• Stapler
• Pumpkin
• Newspapers
• Knife or black marker
• Music for marching for ACTING #2

PREPARATION
• Write the children's names on page 113.
• Place the Halloween/Feast of All Saints Scripture card for SHARING #3 in the Bible.
• If you wish, use a paper cutter to cut off the strip on page 115 for the children.
• Before carving the pumpkin, cover your work area with newspapers.

MUSIC 'N MOTION
Use *Music 'n Motion* page T280 and CD Track 11 "When the Saints Go Marching In" for this lesson. For a list of additional music, see page T320.

ENRICHING THE FAITH EXPERIENCE
Use the activities at the end of the lesson to enrich the lesson or to replace an activity with one that better meets the needs of your group.

BOOKS TO SHARE
The Pumpkin Book by Gail Gibbons
(Holiday House, 2000)

Harriet's Halloween Candy by Nancy Carlson
(First Avenue Editions, 2003)

Strega Nona's Magic Lessons by Tomie dePaola
(Voyager Books, 1984)

The Perky Little Pumpkin by Margaret Friskey
(Children's Press, 1990)

Which Witch Is Which? by Pat Hutchins
(Greenwillow, 1989)

SNACK
Suggestion: doughnuts

ALTERNATIVE PROGRAMS

DAILY PROGRAM
Day 1: Centering, Sharing A
Day 2: Enriching the Faith Experience choice
Day 3: Sharing #3 and #4
Day 4: Sharing #5, Acting #1
Day 5: Acting #2 and #3

THREE-DAY PROGRAM
Day 1: Centering, Sharing A
Day 2: Sharing #3 and #4
Day 3: Sharing #5, Acting

LEARNING OUTCOMES

The children will

- know that Halloween is related to a celebration of all the saints.
- become acquainted with Saint Elizabeth of Hungary.
- realize that they are to be saints.

COMMENT

This lesson focuses on the religious meaning of Halloween as the eve of the feast of All Saints. Each saint had an individual perception of God and God's love, and reflects particular qualities of Christ in his or her own expression of love. Some saints appeal to us more than others. Preschool children are not too young to be introduced to some of the saints, the friends of God.

CENTERING

❶ Gather the children in a circle for *Music 'n Motion* time. Play Track 11. Invite the children to do motions to the song along with you, using *Music 'n Motion* page T280.

❷ Show Cutout #64, pumpkin. Talk about Halloween.

- *When do we make faces on pumpkins and wear masks?* [Option: Show mask.] (On Halloween)

- *Halloween is the night before a day for celebrating the saints, the people who are with God. November 1, the day after Halloween, is the feast of All Saints.*

- *Saints are people who followed Jesus and acted like him. When they did this, they were like lights shining with God's love.*

- *Do you know the names of any saints?*

Name_____

SHARING [A]

1 Distribute page 113 and tell the story of Saint Elizabeth of Hungary.

• *One saint who let God's light shine through her was Elizabeth. She married a ruler in the country of Hungary and became like a queen. Even though she was rich, she remembered the poor people. She went out to take care of sick people. She fed hungry people too.*

• *There is a story about Saint Elizabeth. One day she was carrying bread in her cloak to hungry people. Her husband stopped her and asked what she was doing. When Elizabeth opened her cloak, roses fell out instead of bread.*

• *Saint Elizabeth loved God. She loved other people. She made them happy. She was like Jesus.*

• *Do you know anyone like Saint Elizabeth?*

• *We celebrate Saint Elizabeth and other saints on the feast of All Saints.*

2 On page 114 invite the children to color the dotted pieces orange to see something that has light shining from it.

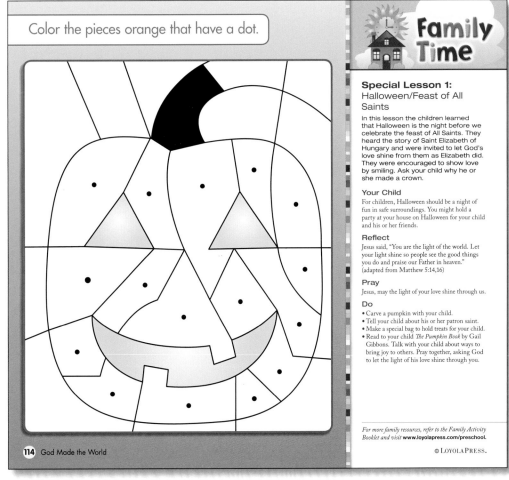

Color the pieces orange that have a dot.

114 God Made the World

Family Time

Special Lesson 1:
Halloween/Feast of All Saints

In this lesson the children learned that Halloween is the night before we celebrate the feast of All Saints. They heard the story of Saint Elizabeth of Hungary and were invited to let God's love shine from them as Elizabeth did. They were encouraged to show love by smiling. Ask your child why he or she made a crown.

Your Child

For children, Halloween should be a night of fun in safe surroundings. You might hold a party at your house on Halloween for your child and his or her friends.

Reflect

Jesus said, "You are the light of the world. Let your light shine so people see the good things you do and praise our Father in heaven." (adapted from Matthew 5:14,16)

Pray

Jesus, may the light of your love shine through us.

Do

• Carve a pumpkin with your child.
• Tell your child about his or her patron saint.
• Make a special bag to hold treats for your child.
• Read to your child *The Pumpkin Book* by Gail Gibbons. Talk with your child about ways to bring joy to others. Pray together, asking God to let the light of his love shine through you.

For more family resources, refer to the Family Activity Booklet and visit www.loyolapress.com/preschool.

© LOYOLAPRESS.

SHARING [B]

3 **SCRIPTURE** Tell the children about their call to be saints. Read the adaptation of Matthew 5:14,16 from the Scripture card in the Bible.

• *All of us are to be saints. We are all to let the light of God's love shine from us. We are to bring joy to others.*

• *Listen to what Jesus says:*

"You are the light of the world. Let your light shine so people see the good things you do and praise our Father in heaven."

• *Then someday we will be with all the other saints in heaven. We say that the saints wear crowns because they are wonderful people.*

4 Have the children make the crown on page 115. You might have them add glitter or sequins. Help them follow these directions:

• Write your name on the line.

• Color the jewels on the crown.

• Cut out the crown and the strip of paper.

• Staple the strip to one end of the crown.

• Put on the crown and staple the other end of the strip to it so that the crown fits.

5 Talk about sharing joy.

• *One way you can bring joy to others is by smiling. It makes other people happy to see you happy and smiling.*

• *If you see a person without a smile, give that person one of yours. Let's see your smile now.*

ACTING

1 Carve a pumpkin or use a black marker to draw a face on it. Remind the children:

• *When you see a pumpkin smiling, think of God's light shining from you.*

• *See how many people you can smile at today.*

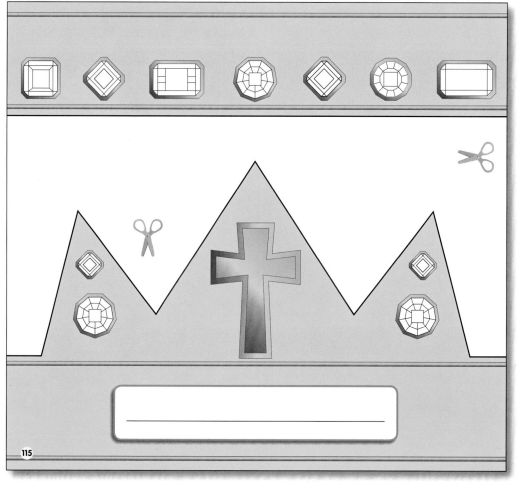

Page 116 is blank.

2 PRAYER Hold a saint celebration. Let the children march to music, wearing their crowns. At the end invite the children to raise their arms and pray with you:

• *Dear God, we love you. Help us let the light of your love shine through us to other people. Help us be saints.*

3 Gather the children in a circle for *Music 'n Motion* time. Play Track 11. Invite the children to do motions to the song along with you, using *Music 'n Motion* page T280.

Have the children take home their pages and show their family the Family Time section.

CHECKPOINT

- *Were the learning outcomes achieved?*
- *How familiar were the children with saints?*

ENRICHING THE FAITH EXPERIENCE

Use the following activities to enrich the lesson or to replace an activity with one that better meets the needs of your group.

1 Have the children act out the story of Saint Elizabeth and the roses.

2 Tell or have the children tell about some other saints, especially their patron saints and the patron saint of their parish church.

3 Put a flashlight in a carved pumpkin and set it in a dark place so that the children can see the light shining from it.

4 Prepare a hidden picture for each child. On white paper draw Halloween pictures with a white crayon: ghosts, pumpkins, and witches. Have the children paint over the hidden picture so that it is revealed.

5 Play "Put a Smile on the Pumpkin." Draw a large pumpkin without a smile on a large sheet of paper. Cut out a black pumpkin smile and put a piece of rolled tape on the back. One by one, blindfold the children and let them take turns trying to put the smile on the pumpkin. The child who puts the smile closest to the right place wins.

PREPARING THE FAITH EXPERIENCE

LISTENING

Therefore the Lord himself will give you this sign: the virgin shall be with child, and bear a son, and shall name him Immanuel.

Isaiah 7:14

REFLECTING

Advent is the special season when we often ponder the Incarnation, the mystery of Emmanuel, God among us. The word *advent* means "coming." During the four weeks of Advent as we wait, preparing to have Christ born in us anew, the Church invites us to let Mary be our model of joyful anticipation.

Mary was humble and trusting enough to let God's Son come into the world through her. Like all mothers Mary spent much of her life waiting. After the angel's visit, she waited for Joseph to understand what had happened to her. Then in quiet awe she waited for her child's birth. As her Son grew, she waited and wondered what his destiny would be. She waited a long, painful time at the foot of the cross for Jesus' death. Then she waited in hope for his Resurrection. Mary, Mother of the Church, waited for the Holy Spirit to give birth to the Church in wind and flame. Finally she waited for her own death when she would once again be united with her Son. Through all these periods of waiting, Mary was patient, loving, and faithful.

Mary can help us prepare our hearts for Jesus. Mary's Son comes to us mysteriously in the surprises and routines of daily life. He comes to us in the sacraments, most clearly

and wondrously in the Eucharist. He appears in the people we encounter—the familiar face, the occasional visitor, and the stranger. He will come in glory and majesty at the world's end and will call his faithful followers into his kingdom, a kingdom of justice and peace. We wait in joyful hope.

During Advent we pray the seven O Antiphons, singing them in the song "O Come, O Come, Emmanuel." Our cry for the Savior culminates in the final antiphon in a joyful outburst:

O Emmanuel, God-with-us,
our King and Lawgiver,
the awaited of the people
and their Savior,
Come to save us, O Lord our God!

RESPONDING

Having been nourished by God's Word, we are able to respond to God's great love for us. In prayer, respond to God's call to you to share his Word with others. You may also wish to respond in your prayer journal.

- Am I open to Christ's coming? Am I ready?

Mary, pray that the children may be prepared to welcome Christ.

Catechism of the Catholic Church

The themes of this lesson correspond to the following paragraphs: 524, 1171.

THE FAITH EXPERIENCE

Child's Book pages 117–120

SCRIPTURE IN THIS LESSON
• *Luke 2:1–7*

MATERIALS
• Option: manger
• Option: Cutouts #1–4, the Riley family
• Gift-wrapped box
• Red and green crayons or markers
• Scissors
• Transparent tape
• About 25 pieces of three-inch yellow yarn or strips of yellow paper for each child
• Envelopes

PREPARATION
• Write the children's names on pages 117 and 120.
• If you wish, make the necessary cuts on page 119 for the children.

ENRICHING THE FAITH EXPERIENCE
Use the activities at the end of the lesson to enrich the lesson or to replace an activity with one that better meets the needs of your group.

BOOKS TO SHARE
The Christmas Story by Jane Werner Watson
(Golden Books, 2000)

My Catholic Advent and Christmas Book by Jennifer Galvin (Paulist Press, 2004)

Waiting for Christmas: A Story about the Advent Calendar by Kathleen Long Bostrom
(Zonderkidz, 2006)

SNACK
Suggestion: candy canes that take a long time to eat (We wait a long time for Jesus to come.)

ALTERNATIVE PROGRAMS

DAILY PROGRAM
Day 1: Centering, Sharing A
Day 2: Enriching the Faith Experience choice
Day 3: Sharing B
Day 4: Enriching the Faith Experience choice
Day 5: Acting

THREE-DAY PROGRAM
Day 1: Centering, Sharing A
Day 2: Sharing B
Day 3: Acting

LEARNING OUTCOMES

The children will

• know that at Christmas we celebrate the birth of Jesus.

• desire to prepare for Jesus' birthday.

• think of several kind acts they might perform as a gift for Jesus.

COMMENT

The children will be excited about preparing for the birth of Baby Jesus. Many of them will already be familiar with the story of Christmas. Advent, the beginning of a new liturgical year, is the season of spiritual preparation for Christmas. During Advent we prepare for the three comings of Christ—in history, in grace, and in glory. This lesson helps focus the children's Christmas activities on Jesus.

CENTERING

Show the gift-wrapped box and ask the children on what occasions they receive gifts.

SHARING [A]

❶ Talk about Christmas.

• *People give gifts at Christmas to celebrate a birthday. Whose birthday is it?* (Jesus')

• *Every year we celebrate Jesus' birthday because we love Jesus.*

• *God's family, the Church, prepares for this day long before it comes.*

• *How would you like to do something to prepare for Jesus' birthday?*

❷ **SCRIPTURE** Explain how the children can give gifts to Jesus. Show the Bible as you tell the story of Jesus' birth (adapted from Luke 2:1–7).

• *Let's prepare a gift for Jesus. Jesus likes us to be kind and loving. We can give Jesus kind acts. When we do them, we make Jesus happy.*

• *When Baby Jesus was born, his parents were away from home in a strange place. He had no crib as you did. His mother, Mary, placed him in a box where people put food for*

Name_____

117 God Made the World

animals. This box that holds food is called a manger. Mary and Joseph lined it with straw to make it soft. This manger was Jesus' crib. [Option: Show the manger.]

• *Today you will make a manger for Jesus. Every day you can try to do kind acts. Whenever you do a kind act, you can put a piece of yellow yarn or paper in the manger.*

3 Have the children act out kind actions they might perform. They might use Cutouts #1–4, the Riley family, as they demonstrate. Pose these situations:

• The baby is crying at home.

• The children are playing outside, and Mom calls them to come in.

• There are toys all over the floor.

• Dad is raking leaves and asks you to help him.

• A woman in a store drops something.

• The family dog needs some water.

• The phone is ringing.

• You have some candy, and your little brother or sister sees it.

• Your little sister or brother wants to watch something on TV that you don't want to watch.

SHARING [B]

4 Distribute page 117 and talk about preparing for the birth of Jesus.

• *Mary and Joseph waited many months for Jesus to come. They got ready for him. What do you think they did to prepare for Baby Jesus?* (Mary probably made clothes for him; Joseph probably made him a crib and some toys.)

• *What are you going to do to prepare for Jesus' birthday?* (Kind acts) *Your kind acts will be like a gift for Jesus.*

5 On page 118 have the children color red the pieces that have a star in them and color green those that have a dot in them.

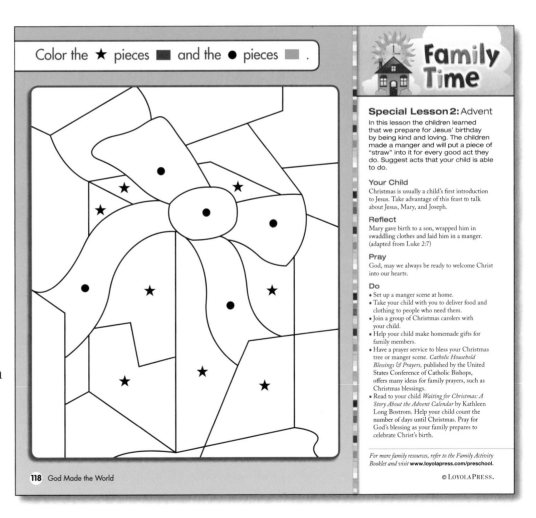

Color the ★ pieces ■ and the ● pieces ■ .

Family Time

Special Lesson 2: Advent
In this lesson the children learned that we prepare for Jesus' birthday by being kind and loving. The children made a manger and will put a piece of "straw" into it for every good act they do. Suggest acts that your child is able to do.

Your Child
Christmas is usually a child's first introduction to Jesus. Take advantage of this feast to talk about Jesus, Mary, and Joseph.

Reflect
Mary gave birth to a son, wrapped him in swaddling clothes and laid him in a manger. (adapted from Luke 2:7)

Pray
God, may we always be ready to welcome Christ into our hearts.

Do
• Set up a manger scene at home.
• Take your child with you to deliver food and clothing to people who need them.
• Join a group of Christmas carolers with your child.
• Help your child make homemade gifts for family members.
• Have a prayer service to bless your Christmas tree or manger scene. *Catholic Household Blessings & Prayers,* published by the United States Conference of Catholic Bishops, offers many ideas for family prayers, such as Christmas blessings.
• Read to your child *Waiting for Christmas: A Story About the Advent Calendar* by Kathleen Long Bostrom. Help your child count the number of days until Christmas. Pray for God's blessing as your family prepares to celebrate Christ's birth.

For more family resources, refer to the Family Activity Booklet and visit **www.loyolapress.com/preschool.**

118 God Made the World

© LOYOLAPRESS.

ACTING

1 **PRAYER** Lead the children in a prayer. Tell them to repeat the words after you.

Thank you, Jesus, for coming to us. [Pause.]

We will prepare for your birthday. [Pause.]

We will give you kind acts. [Pause.]

2 Give the children time to plan some kind acts they will do as gifts for Jesus before Christmas.

3 Have the children make a manger from page 119. Help them follow these directions:

- Cut in on the four solid black lines.
- Fold down the edge with the star to meet the other star.
- Fold down the edge with the flower to meet the other flower.
- Fold the four sides so that they stand.
- Overlap the ends and tape them together.

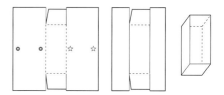

4 Give each child a supply of yellow yarn or paper in an envelope. Remind the children to put a piece of "straw" in their manger each time they do a kind act.

Have the children take home their pages and show their family the Family Time section.

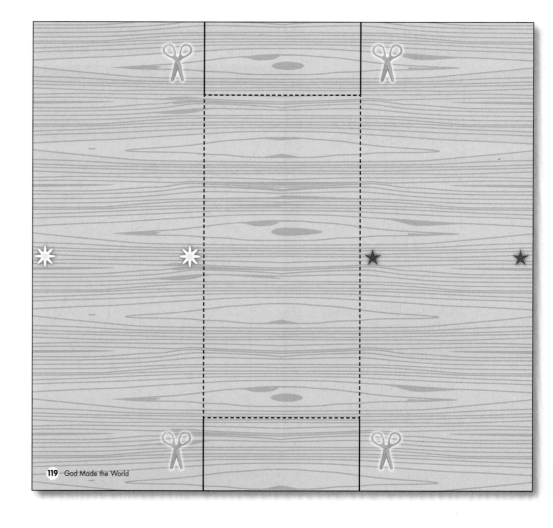

119 · God Made the World

- *Were the learning outcomes achieved?*
- *How readily can the children act out good deeds?*

ENRICHING THE FAITH EXPERIENCE

Use the following activities to enrich the lesson or to replace an activity with one that better meets the needs of your group.

1 Have the children do an echo pantomime for Advent and repeat each line and gesture after you.

Hush! The world is waiting—
[Raise finger to lips.]
Waiting for Baby Jesus.
[Rock arms.]
Mary and Joseph are waiting—
[Extend one arm, then the other.]
Waiting for Mary's Son.
[Rock arms.]
Shepherds and kings are
     waiting—
[Extend one arm, then the other.]
Waiting for the newborn king.
[Rock arms.]
I am waiting—
[Point to self.]
Waiting for my Savior.
[Extend arms up.]
Mary Kathleen Glavich, S.N.D.

2 Help the children make gifts for their parents.

3 Have the children make a Christmas card for someone special.

4 Invite the children to bring in toys for those who are poor.

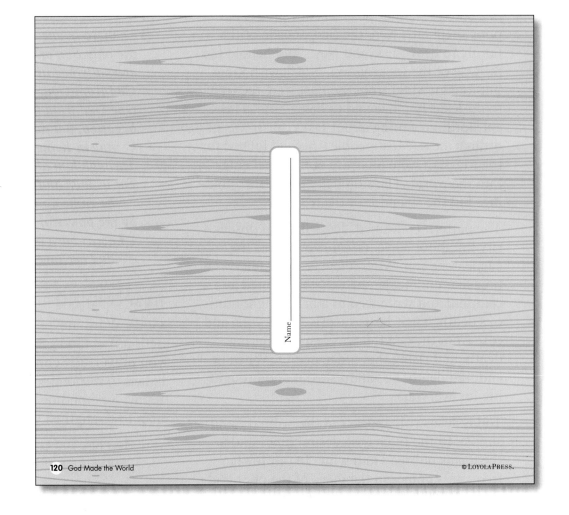

Name

PREPARING THE FAITH EXPERIENCE

LISTENING

"For today in the city of David a savior has been born for you who is Messiah and Lord."

Luke 2:11

"God has visited his people."

Luke 7:16

REFLECTING

God does the most amazing, unexpected things. God sent his Son to save us. Jesus, the Son of God, came as a baby born of a virgin and was laid in a straw-filled manger in a stable. Neither prophets nor priests but poor shepherds were the first outside of the family to hear the Good News and behold the miracle of the Incarnation. Not Jewish kings but foreign Magi from the East were the first to do Jesus homage and to bring gifts. The extraordinary thing about Jesus' birth was its ordinariness. Most people who had longed for the Messiah were unaware of his quiet entry into the world. The simplicity of his surroundings hid the splendor of the reality.

The pattern continued. Jesus lived in obscurity for about 30 years, known only as the carpenter's son. After a few years of fame as a preacher and healer, he was condemned as a criminal and sentenced to a brutal, ignominious death. Then Jesus surprised everyone and rose from the dead. It was Jesus' suffering, death, and rising that redeemed us. When he endured death, he vanquished it and brought life for everyone.

Today Jesus still appears in the ordinary and simple. In the Eucharist, Jesus comes under the forms of bread and wine. In our life he frequently comes in the guise of the poor and weak. Over and over God's strength is manifested in weakness. And sometimes God still

surprises us, working in ways we least expect.

Let the Nativity scenes we see at Christmas remind us that God's ways are not our ways, that we must be ready for divine surprises and, most of all, that God loves us with a love beyond human understanding.

With awe and gratitude at our Eucharistic celebrations, we declare in the Nicene Creed:

> *We believe in one Lord, Jesus Christ,*
> *the only Son of God,*
> *eternally begotten of the Father,*
> *God from God, Light from Light,*
> *true God from true God,*
> *begotten, not made,*
> *one in Being with the Father.*
> *Through him all things were made.*
> *For us men and for our salvation*
> *he came down from heaven:*
> *by the power of the Holy Spirit,*
> *he was born of the Virgin Mary,*
> *and became man.*

RESPONDING

God's Word moves us to respond in word and action. Let God's Spirit work within you as you prayerfully consider how you are being called to respond to God's message to you today. Responding through your journal may help to strengthen your response.

- How has God entered my life in an extraordinary way recently?

  God, help the children and me become more aware of your presence.

Catechism of the Catholic Church

The themes of this lesson correspond to the following paragraphs: 437, 525.

THE FAITH EXPERIENCE

Child's Book pages 121–124

SCRIPTURE IN THIS LESSON
• *Luke 2:1–20*
• *Matthew 2:1–12*

MATERIALS
• Recording of a Christmas song
• Cutouts: #65, Baby Jesus; #66, star
• Option: Nativity set displayed
• Option: small artificial tree or Christmas tree drawn on a large sheet of paper or on the board
• Bible
• One manger from page 119, possibly placed under a tree
• Soft music
• Crayons or markers
• Scissors
• Circle stickers or star stickers
• Option: glitter, sequins
• Transparent tape or stapler

PREPARATION
• Write the children's names on pages 121 and 124.
• If you wish, cut out the trees and stars on page 123 for the children.

MUSIC'N MOTION

Use *Music 'n Motion* page T282 and CD Track 12 "No Place to Stay" for this lesson. For a list of additional music, see page T320.

ENRICHING THE FAITH EXPERIENCE
Use the activities at the end of the lesson to enrich the lesson or to replace an activity with one that better meets the needs of your group.

BOOKS TO SHARE
The Friendly Beasts by Tomie dePaola
  (Putnam Juvenile, 1998)

The Night Before Christmas by Clement C. Moore
  (HarperCollins, 2004)

Mr. Willowby's Christmas Tree by Robert Barry
  (Doubleday Books for Young Readers, 2000)

Madeline's Christmas by Ludwig Bemelmans
  (Puffin, 2007)

SNACK
Suggestion: Christmas cookies

ALTERNATIVE PROGRAMS

DAILY PROGRAM
Day 1: Centering, Sharing A
Day 2: Enriching the Faith Experience choice
Day 3: Sharing B
Day 4: Enriching the Faith Experience #3, Acting #1
Day 5: Acting #2–4

THREE-DAY PROGRAM
Day 1: Centering, Sharing A
Day 2: Sharing B, Acting #1
Day 3: Acting #2–4

LEARNING OUTCOMES

The children will
- know the Christmas story.
- be grateful that Jesus came to earth.
- enjoy making a Christmas decoration.

COMMENT

Caesar Augustus, ruler of the Roman Empire, decreed that all must go to their ancestral towns for a census. Complying with this decree, Mary and Joseph left Nazareth and journeyed to Bethlehem, the city of David. There Mary gave birth to Jesus, who was not a mere statistic but "the image of the invisible God, /the firstborn of all creation." (Colossians 1:15) Through music and celebration, this lesson awakens in children the awe and wonder that the birth of Jesus evokes.

CENTERING

❶ Gather the children in a circle for *Music 'n Motion* time. Play Track 12. Invite the children to do motions to the song along with you, using *Music 'n Motion* page T282.

❷ Talk about family celebrations of Christmas. Play a recording of a Christmas song during the discussion.

• *What is your family doing to get ready for Christmas?* (Sending cards, making cookies, decorating the house, putting up a tree, buying or making gifts)

• *What will your family do on Christmas Day?* (Go to church, give gifts, sing Christmas carols)

SHARING [A]

❶ Show Cutout #65, Baby Jesus. Talk about it.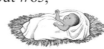

• *Jesus was born on Christmas Day. We are happy that God the Father sent Jesus to us. We celebrate his birthday every year.*

• *God the Father showed love for us by sending Jesus. At Christmas we show that we love others.*

• *One thing we do to celebrate Jesus' birthday is to put up Christmas trees. We also set up scenes of the first Christmas with statues of Mary, Joseph, and Baby Jesus.*

❷ Have the children pretend to decorate a Christmas tree together through pantomime. Model each action for them to follow.

- Wrap the lights around.
- Put on ornaments carefully.
- Drape tinsel.
- Put a star on top.
- Instead of pantomiming, you might have a small artificial tree and a nativity scene for the children to set

Name_____

121 God Made the World

up. Or you might draw a Christmas tree on a large sheet of paper or on the board and have the children draw the decorations.

SHARING [B]

3 **SCRIPTURE** Distribute page 121 and have the children look at the picture as you tell the Christmas story (adapted from Luke 2:1–20 and Matthew 2:1–12). [Show the Bible.]

Mary and Joseph had to go to another town. When they got to the town, there was no place for them to stay. Finally a man let them stay in his stable with the animals. That night Jesus was born. Mary laid him in a manger filled with straw.

Out in the fields, there were shepherds guarding their sheep. Suddenly angels appeared to them. The angels told the shepherds that Jesus was born and lying in a manger. The shepherds went to the stable and saw Jesus. They praised God.

In a faraway land, some Wise Men heard that Jesus was born. They followed a moving star until it stopped above the place where Jesus was. The Wise Men found Jesus there and gave him precious gifts.

4 Have the children sing "Away in a Manger" or play it for them. Have one child place Cutout #65, Baby Jesus, in a manger.

Away in a Manger
Martin Luther

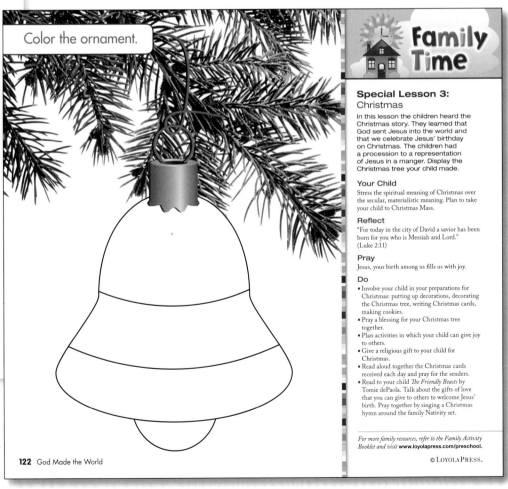

Color the ornament.

122 God Made the World

Family Time

Special Lesson 3:
Christmas

In this lesson the children heard the Christmas story. They learned that God sent Jesus into the world and that we celebrate Jesus' birthday on Christmas. The children had a procession to a representation of Jesus in a manger. Display the Christmas tree your child made.

Your Child
Stress the spiritual meaning of Christmas over the secular, materialistic meaning. Plan to take your child to Christmas Mass.

Reflect
"For today in the city of David a savior has been born for you who is Messiah and Lord." (Luke 2:11)

Pray
Jesus, your birth among us fills us with joy.

Do
• Involve your child in your preparations for Christmas: putting up decorations, decorating the Christmas tree, writing Christmas cards, making cookies.
• Pray a blessing for your Christmas tree together.
• Plan activities in which your child can give joy to others.
• Give a religious gift to your child for Christmas.
• Read aloud together the Christmas cards received each day and pray for the senders.
• Read to your child *The Friendly Beasts* by Tomie dePaola. Talk about the gifts of love that you can give to others to welcome Jesus' birth. Pray together by singing a Christmas hymn around the family Nativity set.

For more family resources, refer to the Family Activity Booklet and visit **www.loyolapress.com/preschool.**

© LOYOLAPRESS.

5 Invite the children to color the ornament on page 122. Suggest that they do their best work as a gift for Jesus.

ACTING

1 **PRAYER** Hold a Christmas procession. Lead the children around the room, holding the star, Cutout #66. Play soft music and walk on tiptoe. End up around the image of baby Jesus in the manger. Invite the children to go to the manger one by one and whisper "I love you, Jesus."

2 Have the children make the tree on page 123 as a table decoration for their homes. If you do not have stickers, decorations could be painted or colored. Help the children follow these directions:

- Put round stickers or star stickers on the tree, being careful not to put them on the lines. (Glitter and sequins might be added.)

- Write your name on the line.

- Cut out the tree and the square with the star.

- Cut a slit on the heavy black line at the top of the tree.

- Fold the tree on the dotted lines and tape or staple it together.

- Insert the star into the slit at the top.

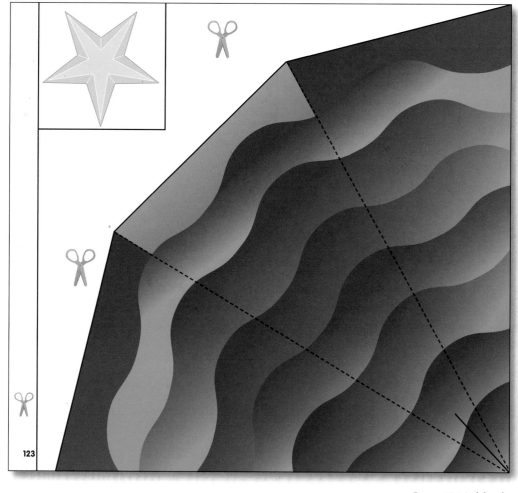

Page 124 is blank.

3 Suggest to the children that they set their tree on the table or under their Christmas tree along with the manger, made in Special Lesson Advent, which should now be full of "straw."

4 Gather the children in a circle for *Music 'n Motion* time. Play Track 12. Invite the children to do motions to the song along with you, using *Music 'n Motion* page T282.

Have the children take home their pages and show their family the Family Time section.

CHECKPOINT

- *Were the learning outcomes achieved?*
- *What signs are there that the children are focused on the real meaning of Christmas and not caught up in materialism?*

ENRICHING THE FAITH EXPERIENCE

Use the following activities to enrich the lesson or to replace an activity with one that better meets the needs of your group.

1 Have the children sing "Silent Night" or play it for them. Teach them the following motions:

> Silent night,
> [Make a wide arc with right arm.]
> Holy night,
> [Make a wide arc with left arm.]
> All is calm,
> [Move hands palms down, apart, and together again.]
> All is bright,
> [Move hands upward and out as if in explosion.]
> 'Round yon Virgin mother and child.
> [Fold hands palm to palm.]
> Holy infant so tender and mild,
> [Rock arms together.]
> Sleep in heavenly peace.
> [Fold hands to side of head.]
> Sleep in heavenly peace.

2 Teach the children to sing "We Wish You a Merry Christmas."

3 Help the children make a wreath by shaping a wire hanger into a circle and then tying one-by four-inch pieces of cloth all around it. All the children can work on one wreath for the classroom, or each child can make one.

4 Have the children paint Christmas cards for their family. Use a large sheet of paper folded in half. Give the children stencils of Christmas shapes to use: bells, holly, Christmas tree, wreath, angel, star. Let them glue on ribbon, glitter, or sequins. Write "Merry Christmas!" inside each child's card. Help the children sign their names.

5 Help the children make ornaments out of inedible dough. Caution the children not to eat the dough. Mix 4 cups flour with 1 cup salt. Add 1½ cups water. Mix until dough holds together, adding water as necessary. Roll and cut dough into shapes. Insert a paper clip at the top of each ornament for hanging. Bake at 350°F for one hour.

PREPARING THE FAITH EXPERIENCE

LISTENING

"Amen, amen, I say to you, unless a grain of wheat falls to the ground and dies, it remains just a grain of wheat; but if it dies, it produces much fruit. Whoever serves me must follow me, and where I am, there also will my servant be."
John 12:24,26

REFLECTING

Each spring we begin to observe signs of new life awakening around us. Daffodils, tulips, hyacinths, and a myriad of other flowers emerge from bulbs planted in the fall. Caterpillars appear and enter their cocoons to be transformed into beautiful butterflies. Seeds we plant in the ground now will sprout and bear fruit in the weeks and months ahead. These natural signs can serve as reminders to us of the mystery of new life that we receive through Christ.

Through the Paschal Mystery of his Passion, Death, Resurrection, and Ascension, Christ transformed suffering, death, and evil into glorious new life. Strengthened by prayerful union with his Father, Jesus freely accepted the consequences of humanity's sin. He countered hatred with love, arrogant pride with humble docility, death with life. His victory over sin and death gained for us a share of divine life and eternal glory.

In Baptism we died with Christ and rose with him to new life. Through all the sacraments, and especially in the Eucharist, we participate in the Paschal Mystery. We receive God's grace so that we may be more like Christ. We journey in the footsteps of Jesus, who told his disciples: "Whoever wishes to come after me must deny himself, take up his cross, and

follow me." (Matthew 16:24) We strive to keep the new commandment: "[l]ove one another as I love you. No one has greater love than this, to lay down one's life for one's friends. You are my friends if you do what I command you." (John 15:12–14) Imitation of Christ—even unto death—is the standard of perfection for the Christian. It is our response to Jesus' words "Do this in remembrance of me." (1 Corinthians 11:24)

During the Lenten season, the Church community as a whole looks at the new life that Jesus offers to all who commit themselves to share in his Paschal Mystery. We devote ourselves to acts of Christian living that increase our participation in Christ's saving Death and Resurrection. The Lenten practices of prayer, fasting, and almsgiving are signs of our repentance and renewed commitment to living as Christ's disciples. Together with the community of faith, we journey with Christ, looking forward to sharing in the joy of the Resurrection.

RESPONDING

Having reflected upon God's Word, take some time now to continue to respond to God in prayer. You might wish to record your responses in your journal.

- What acts of Christian living will I make a priority during this Lenten season?

  Holy Spirit, strengthen us to live as Christ's disciples.

Catechism of the Catholic Church

The themes of this lesson correspond to the following paragraphs: 1168, 1438, 2014–2015.

THE FAITH EXPERIENCE

Child's Book pages 125–128

SCRIPTURE IN THIS LESSON
• *1 John 3:16–18*

MATERIALS
• Lent Scripture card
• Bible
• Blocks
• Crayons or markers

PREPARATION
• Place the Lent Scripture card for SHARING #2 in the Bible.
• Write the children's names on pages 125 and 127.

ENRICHING THE FAITH EXPERIENCE
Use the activities at the end of the lesson to enrich the lesson or to replace an activity with one that better meets the needs of your group.

BOOKS TO SHARE
Coloring Book About Lent by Paul T. Bianca
(Catholic Book Publishing Company, 2002)

Family Countdown to Easter: A Day-by-Day Celebration by Debbie Trafton O'Neal
(Augsburg Fortress Publishers, 1999)

A Family Journey with Jesus Through Lent: Prayers and Activities for Each Day by Angela M. Burrin
(Word Among Us Press, 2004)

My Day with Jesus by Alice Joyce Davidson
(Zonderkidz, 2005)

SNACK
Suggestion: pretzels

ALTERNATIVE PROGRAMS

DAILY PROGRAM
Day 1: Centering, Sharing A
Day 2: Enriching the Faith Experience choice
Day 3: Sharing B, Acting #1
Day 4: Enriching the Faith Experience choice
Day 5: Acting #2

THREE-DAY PROGRAM
Day 1: Centering, Sharing A
Day 2: Sharing B, Acting #1
Day 3: Acting #2

LEARNING OUTCOMES

The children will
- identify ways we show love to others.
- know that we show our love for God in our deeds.
- know that we follow Jesus when we show love to others.

COMMENT

The Church season of Lent often corresponds to the change of seasons from winter to spring. The word *Lent* is derived from an Old English word meaning "springtime" and may be a reference to the lengthening of the daylight hours that occurs during this time of year. During the weeks of Lent, we let the warmth of God's love permeate our hearts and transform our lives.

CENTERING

Let the children engage in free-play activity with blocks. Encourage the children to work together and share the blocks with one another.

SHARING [A]

❶ Distribute page 125 and talk about the loving action shown in the picture.

- *What is happening in this picture?*

- *Who is showing love in this picture?*

- *Who are people who show love to you? How do you show love to others?* (If the children succeeded in working together building with blocks, observe and acknowledge that sharing and working together are ways we show love.)

❷ **SCRIPTURE** Read the adaptation of 1 John 3:16–18 from the Scripture card in the Bible.

- *When we show our love to others, we also show our love for God.*

- *Listen to what we read in the Bible:*

   "Our love for God is shown in our deeds."

❸ On page 126 have the children circle the pictures of people showing love to others.

Name

SHARING [B]

4 Play a game of "Follow the Leader."

5 Talk about Lent.

• *During Lent we get ready for Easter. We follow Jesus.*

• *We show our love for God in our deeds. We show our love for God when we pray. We show our love for God when we do good things for other people.*

• *Name good things to do to prepare for Easter.*

6 Teach the children the song "Love, Love."

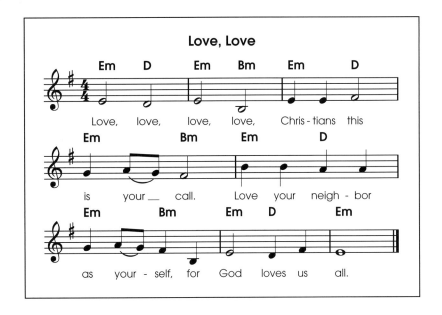

Circle the pictures of people showing love to others.

Family Time

Special Lesson 4: Lent

During the season of Lent, the Church community prepares to celebrate Easter by renewing our commitment to live as Christ's disciples. In this lesson the children identified ways that we can show love to others and learned that these actions also show our love for God. They learned that we follow Jesus when we show our love for God in our words and deeds.

Your Child

Through the example of those who love and care for them, children learn the importance of showing love to others in word and action. Encourage your child's efforts to demonstrate care for others. Invite your child to participate with you in activities that show care and concern for others.

Reflect

Children, let us love not in word or speech but in deed and truth. (1 John 3:18)

Pray

Jesus, help us follow you by showing love to others.

Do

• Invite your child to draw a picture for a family member or neighbor who is ill or needs cheering up.
• Take your child grocery shopping to select food items to donate to the local food pantry.
• Choose a special prayer to say each day during Lent, such as the prayer above.
• Read to your child *My Day with Jesus* by Alice Joyce Davidson. Together choose an action to do during Lent to demonstrate your love for God and for others. Pray for God's blessing during this season of Lent.

For more family resources, refer to the Family Activity Booklet and visit www.loyolapress.com/preschool.

126 God Made the World

© LOYOLAPRESS.

ACTING

1 **PRAYER** Invite the children to pray together:

God, help us love you always.

Help us show our love for you in our deeds.

2 Have the children prepare to take home page 127. Give instructions to color part of the footprints each day the children say a prayer or do a good deed during Lent.

Have the children take home their pages and show their family the Family Time section.

CHECKPOINT

• Were the learning outcomes achieved?

• Were the children able to name ways we show our love for God?

ENRICHING THE FAITH EXPERIENCE

Use the following activities to enrich the lesson or to replace an activity with one that better meets the needs of your group.

1 Have the children plant seeds. After they have sprouted, observe together how the plants grow.

2 Teach a song to the tune of "God Is So Good."

• *Growing is good.* [3 times]

• *I grow as God's child.*

• *Christians are good.* [3 times]

• *They love like Jesus.*

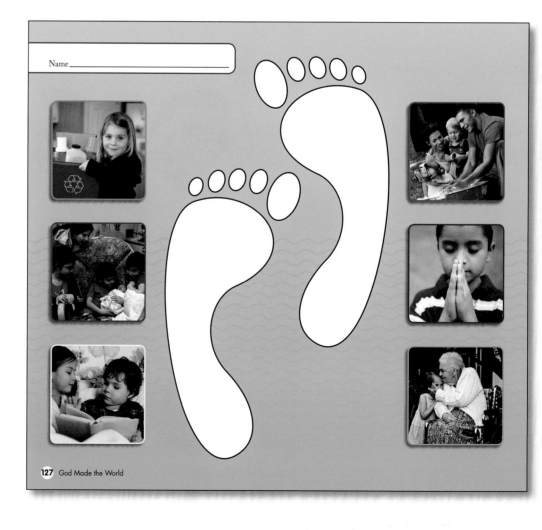

Name_____

127 God Made the World

3 Teach the children the song "Oh, How I Love Jesus." (See page T27.)

4 Explain that the pretzel shape looks like arms crossed in prayer. Give each child a twisted pretzel as a reminder that Lent is a time for special prayer.

5 Teach the children "Sharing Poem." Direct them to say "We share" twice at the right times, patting their thighs on each word and clapping twice afterward.

Sharing Poem

When we're munching on a treat,
And our friend has none to eat,
What do we do?
We [Pat] share. [Pat] [Clap, clap]
We [Pat] share. [Pat] [Clap, clap]
When we're paging through a
    book,
And our sister wants a look,
What do we do?
We [Pat] share. [Pat] [Clap, clap]
We [Pat] share. [Pat] [Clap, clap]
When we're watching the TV,
And there's a show Dad wants
    to see,

What do we do?
We [Pat] share. [Pat] [Clap, clap]
We [Pat] share. [Pat] [Clap, clap]
When we're bouncing a new ball,
And someone's playing not at all,
What do we do?
We [Pat] share. [Pat] [Clap, clap]
We [Pat] share. [Pat] [Clap, clap]
When we're playing with a toy,
And here comes a girl or boy,
What do we do?
We [Pat] share. [Pat] [Clap, clap]
We [Pat] share. [Pat] [Clap, clap]

Mary Kathleen Glavich, S.N.D.

© LOYOLA PRESS.

PREPARING THE FAITH EXPERIENCE

LISTENING

For his sake I have accepted the loss of all things . . . that I may gain Christ and be found in him . . . depending on faith to know him and the power of his resurrection . . .

Philippians 3:8–10

REFLECTING

Life in Christ calls us to walk daily in newness of life, a life no longer enslaved to sin. Through his Resurrection, Jesus won for us new life and new hope; we no longer need to fear suffering and death. Belief in the Resurrection moves us from a limited, earthbound outlook to a radically different, eternity-oriented view of life. We can see the suffering that marks segments of our journey as part of the Paschal Mystery:

For this momentary light affliction is producing for us an eternal weight of glory beyond all comparison . . .

2 Corinthians 4:17

The frightened disciples experienced the risen Christ and were radically changed. Christ, raised and glorified, had broken the power of death. The disciples could share his power; through Baptism they would one day share eternal life with him. Jesus fulfills forever the deepest of all desires—the desire of life.

The same risen Jesus is the companion of every Christian, giving each of us courage to accept the Christian mission. Jesus enables Christians to risk their lives, jobs, and reputations for his kingdom of peace and justice. Today some Christians practice their faith where it is forbidden. They bring the Gospel to those who have nothing. Contemplatives embrace a life of prayer and penance that makes no sense to this world but brings strength and hope to many.

Christians everywhere make the risen Christ visible. They endure suffering patiently, give themselves to thankless tasks, and speak the truth in love. They are signs of hope. Through their witness, others see how powerful Jesus is and entrust their lives to him.

At each Eucharist we celebrate the dying and rising of Christ. During the Easter season, we remember this great mystery in a special way, proclaiming:

This is the night when Jesus Christ
broke the chains of death
and rose triumphant from the grave.

What good would life have been to us
had Christ not come as our Redeemer?

Father, how wonderful your care for us!
How boundless your merciful love!

The power of this holy night
dispels all evil, washes guilt away,
restores lost innocence, brings mourners
joy;
it casts out hatred, brings us peace,
and humbles earthly pride.

*From the Easter Proclamation
The Easter Vigil*

RESPONDING

God's Word calls us to respond in love. Respond to God now in the quiet of your heart, and perhaps through your journal.

- How do I show my belief in the Resurrection?

Risen Lord, fill the children and me with an abiding hope in you.

Catechism of the Catholic Church

The themes of this lesson correspond to the following paragraphs: 638, 654–655, 1168–1171.

THE FAITH EXPERIENCE

Child's Book pages 129–132

SCRIPTURE IN THIS LESSON
• *John 11:25*

MATERIALS
• Easter Scripture card
• Bible
• Cutouts: #8, Jesus; #20, sun
• Option: Easter egg
• Crayons or markers
• Option: gold contact-paper circle or yellow paper circle and glue for each child

PREPARATION
• Write the children's names on pages 129 and 131.
• Place the Easter Scripture card for SHARING #2 in the Bible.

MUSIC 'N MOTION
Use *Music 'n Motion* page T284 and CD Track 13 "Easter Alleluia" for this lesson. For a list of additional music, see page T320.

ENRICHING THE FAITH EXPERIENCE
Use the activities at the end of the lesson to enrich the lesson or to replace an activity with one that better meets the needs of your group.

BOOKS TO SHARE
Silly Tilly and the Easter Bunny by Lillian Hoban
(HarperTrophy, 1989)

The Bunny Who Found Easter by Charlotte Zolotow
(Houghton Mifflin, 2001)

Clifford's Happy Easter by Norman Bridwell
(Cartwheel Books, 1994)

My First Story of Easter by Tim Dowley
(Moody Publishers, 2005)

SNACK
Suggestion: carrots and celery (rabbit food), candy eggs, or jelly beans

---

ALTERNATIVE PROGRAMS

DAILY PROGRAM
Day 1: Centering, Sharing A
Day 2: Enriching the Faith Experience choice
Day 3: Sharing B
Day 4: Enriching the Faith Experience choice, Acting #1
Day 5: Acting #2 and #3

THREE-DAY PROGRAM
Day 1: Centering, Sharing A
Day 2: Sharing B, Acting #1
Day 3: Acting #2 and #3

LEARNING OUTCOMES

The children will
- identify Easter as a feast of life.
- know that Jesus gives us new life.
- thank God for life.

COMMENTS

1. Peter Marshall, once the chaplain of the U.S. Senate, compared our dying to a child falling asleep before going to bed. Just as the child goes to sleep in one place and awakens in another, having been carried to his or her room by a parent, so too, when we die, we hope to awaken to find ourselves in our heavenly home where we will enjoy eternal life. This lesson stirs in us an appreciation for this great gift of life, which lasts forever. Through the Resurrection of Jesus, all things are made new. Because we died and rose with Jesus in Baptism, we can overcome sin and live Jesus' new life. Our daily sufferings and dyings will someday give way to a life of glory. The Eucharist continues the process of dying and rising.

2. The Easter Mystery is just that, a great mystery. The children's understanding of it, as well as our own, will deepen with time. Logically, Easter has come to be associated with the sun's rising in the east—a glorious and reliable event. For the day that the Son of God rose from the dead marked a new dawn for us all.

CENTERING

1 Gather the children in a circle for *Music 'n Motion* time. Play Track 13. Invite the children to do motions to the song along with you, using *Music 'n Motion* page T284.

2 Ask several children to tell how they are awakened each morning.

SHARING [A]

1 Distribute page 129 and talk about the sunrise. Show Cutout #20, sun.

- *Every day the sun comes up. We wake up and have a new day of life.*

- *Every night the sun disappears, and we go to sleep.*

- *The same thing happens over and over. Year after year the sun comes up every morning.*

- *If you can't see the sun during the day, where is it?* (Behind clouds)

2 SCRIPTURE Present Easter as a celebration of life. Read the adaptation of John 11:25 from the Scripture card in the Bible.

- *Just as the sun comes up each day, we will always live. Jesus promised that we will live forever.*

Name_____

129 God Made the World

• *Listen to what Jesus tells us in the Bible: "I am the resurrection and the life; whoever believes in me will live forever."*

• *We believe Jesus because after he died and was buried, he came back to life.* [Put Cutout #8, Jesus, next to Cutout #20, sun.]

• *This makes us happy, so we celebrate. Each Easter we celebrate that Jesus is still alive. We celebrate that our life lasts forever.*

3 Lead the children in a cheer for Jesus and new life.

> I live.
> [Point to self.]
> You live.
> [Point out.]
> We'll all live forever.
> [Sweep arm across front.]
> Jesus died and rose
>   to life.
> [Stoop and rise.]
> We'll live with him
>   forever.
> Yeah, Jesus!
> [Jump and wave arms in
>   the air.]
>
> *Mary Kathleen Glavich,*
>   *S.N.D.*

SHARING [B]

4 Explain the Easter story.

• *We love Jesus and we tell the story about him year after year. We tell what he did and what he said. We tell how he died and how he rose again.*

• *We celebrate Easter with eggs.* [Option: Show an Easter egg.] *What comes out of an egg?* (Chick) *New life comes out of eggs, just as Jesus came out of the tomb after he was buried.*

5 PRAYER Have the children color the egg on page 130. When all have finished, invite the children to pray as they look at the decorated Easter egg. Suggest that they pray to Jesus, "Thank you for life."

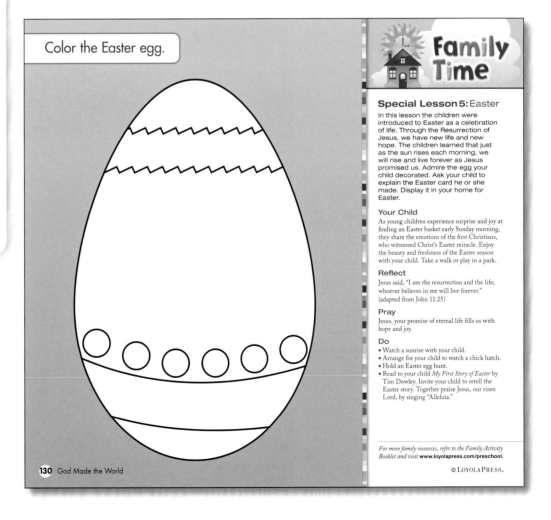

Color the Easter egg.

130 God Made the World

Family Time

Special Lesson 5: Easter
In this lesson the children were introduced to Easter as a celebration of life. Through the Resurrection of Jesus, we have new life and new hope. The children learned that just as the sun rises each morning, we will rise and live forever as Jesus promised us. Admire the egg your child decorated. Ask your child to explain the Easter card he or she made. Display it in your home for Easter.

Your Child
As young children experience surprise and joy at finding an Easter basket early Sunday morning, they share the emotions of the first Christians, who witnessed Christ's Easter miracle. Enjoy the beauty and freshness of the Easter season with your child. Take a walk or play in a park.

Reflect
Jesus said, "I am the resurrection and the life; whoever believes in me will live forever." (adapted from John 11:25)

Pray
Jesus, your promise of eternal life fills us with hope and joy.

Do
• Watch a sunrise with your child.
• Arrange for your child to watch a chick hatch.
• Hold an Easter egg hunt.
• Read to your child *My First Story of Easter* by Tim Dowley. Invite your child to retell the Easter story. Together praise Jesus, our risen Lord, by singing "Alleluia."

For more family resources, refer to the Family Activity Booklet and visit www.loyolapress.com/preschool.

© LOYOLAPRESS.

ACTING

1 Let the children suggest a game they can play because they are full of life. Then play it. If the children do not offer ideas for games, you might suggest "Follow the Leader" or teach them to play "Drop the Handkerchief." For this game, choose one child to be "It" and give him or her a handkerchief. Have the other children sit in a circle. "It" walks around the circle and drops the handkerchief behind a child. This seated child picks up the handkerchief and chases "It" around the circle. If "It" reaches the empty space without being tagged, the chaser becomes the next one to drop the handkerchief. If "It" is tagged, this child continues to be "It."

2 Have the children make the reversible Easter card on page 131. (Instead of having them color the sun, you might give them paper circles to glue on.) Help them follow these directions:

- Color the sun yellow.

- Fold the sides forward to cover the sun.

Show the children how to open the card to show darkness giving way to the sun.

Then show them how to fold the sides the other way so that the card shows an egg and when the sides are opened, a chick.

3 Gather the children in a circle for *Music 'n Motion* time. Play Track 13. Invite the children to do motions to the song along with you, using *Music 'n Motion* page T284.

Have the children take home their pages and show their family the Family Time section.

Name

131 God Made the World

CHECKPOINT

• *Were the learning outcomes achieved?*

ENRICHING THE FAITH EXPERIENCE

Use the following activities to enrich the lesson or to replace an activity with one that better meets the needs of your group.

1 Hide paper eggs, plastic eggs, or wrapped candy eggs and let the children hunt for them. Tell the children that they may keep what they find.

2 Color Easter eggs with the children.

3 Give the children an outline of a rabbit and have them color it. Have them glue on cotton for a tail.

132 God Made the World

Special Lesson 6
Pentecost

FAITH FOCUS
The Holy Spirit brings peace.

John 15:26–27; Galatians 5:22–23

PREPARING THE FAITH EXPERIENCE

LISTENING

When the time for Pentecost was fulfilled, they were all in one place together. And suddenly there came from the sky a noise like a strong driving wind, and it filled the entire house in which they were. Then there appeared to them tongues as of fire, which parted and came to rest on each one of them. And they were all filled with the holy Spirit and began to speak in different tongues, as the Spirit enabled them to proclaim.

Acts of the Apostles 2:1–4

REFLECTING

Wind and air are metaphors often used to describe the action of the Holy Spirit in our lives. We do not see the air that is always around us, yet we feel its effects, especially in its movement as wind, and know its presence. So it is with the life of the Holy Spirit whose effects we can see in our lives. Like wind that can fan a fire's flame, the Holy Spirit can enkindle in us the fire of God's love.

Wind cannot be perceived as any definite shape or form. Rather, it fills out and then is limited only by the size of its container. Similarly, the Holy Spirit has no definite shape or form. The Holy Spirit's presence in our lives, though, is surely discernible as God brings us to completion, limited only by our finite capacity. Our spiritual life is sustained and renewed by the Holy Spirit, who is always working within us to make us holy.

Jesus promised to send his disciples the Holy Spirit, the Advocate who would help them testify on his behalf. This promise was fulfilled on Pentecost. The gift of the Holy Spirit transformed the fearful disciples into a community

of believers, making them bold witnesses to the Good News. Jesus, the Crucified One, had been raised from the dead and was revealed as Lord and Savior.

Pentecost is the Greek word for the Jewish Festival of Weeks celebrated 50 days after Passover. It was originally a celebration of thanksgiving for the grain harvest. It later became a celebration of God's gift of the Law given at Mount Sinai. Pentecost is also the name given to the day Christians celebrate the first outpouring of the Holy Spirit on Jesus' disciples because it happened on the Jewish feast of Pentecost. The Christian feast of Pentecost is celebrated at the conclusion of the Easter season.

On Pentecost we celebrate the gift of the Holy Spirit and his importance in our lives. We are strengthened and renewed by the Gifts of the Holy Spirit. With the Church we pray that the Holy Spirit will direct our use of every gift and that our lives may bring Christ to others. We seek to know peace and joy and all the Fruits of the Holy Spirit's actions in our lives.

RESPONDING

Having been nourished by God's Word, we are able to respond to God's great love for us. In prayer, respond to God's call to you to share his Word with others. You may also wish to respond in your prayer journal.

- In what ways am I aware of the action of the Holy Spirit in my life?

Holy Spirit, fill the children with your peace and joy.

Catechism of the Catholic Church

The themes of this lesson correspond to the following paragraphs: 731–732, 733–736, 739, 1287, 2623.

THE FAITH EXPERIENCE

Child's Book pages 133–134

SCRIPTURE IN THIS LESSON
• *John 20:19,22*

MATERIALS
• Pentecost Scripture card
• Bible
• Crayons or markers
• Paper streamers, one for each child
• Paper plate
• Stapler
• Yarn
• Hole punch

PREPARATION
• Place the Pentecost Scripture card for SHARING #2 in the Bible.
• Write the children's names on page 133.
• Punch a hole at the top of the paper plate to thread yarn through.

ENRICHING THE FAITH EXPERIENCE
Use the activities at the end of the lesson to enrich the lesson or to replace an activity with one that better meets the needs of your group.

BOOKS TO SHARE
The Fruit of the Spirit Is Jesus in Me by Dandi Daley Mackall
(Standard Publishing Company, 2005)

The Very First Christians by Paul L. Maier
(Concordia Publishing House, 2001)

SNACK
Suggestion: popcorn

ALTERNATIVE PROGRAMS

DAILY PROGRAM
Day 1: Centering, Sharing A
Day 2: Enriching the Faith Experience choice
Day 3: Sharing B, Acting #1
Day 4: Enriching the Faith Experience choice
Day 5: Acting #2

THREE-DAY PROGRAM
Day 1: Centering, Sharing A
Day 2: Sharing B, Acting #1
Day 3: Acting #2

LEARNING OUTCOMES

The children will

- identify ways that people are helpers.
- learn that Jesus sent the Holy Spirit to be our helper.
- discuss how to bring peace to others.

COMMENT

The Holy Spirit is given to us to strengthen our witness to Christ and to make us holy. The Holy Spirit also fills us with peace, joy, and love. Young children find comfort in knowing that God is with us always in the Person of the Holy Spirit.

CENTERING

Have the children stand and sing the following verses to the tune of "Here We Go 'Round the Mulberry Bush" and act out the ways to help:

> This is the way we set the table . . .
> so early in the morning.
>
> This is the way we carry the package . . .
>
> This is the way we share our toys . . .
>
> This is the way we show we care . . .

SHARING [A]

❶ Distribute page 133 and talk about the helpers shown in the picture.

- *Who is being a helper in these pictures? How are they helping? What are some things you can do to be a helper?*

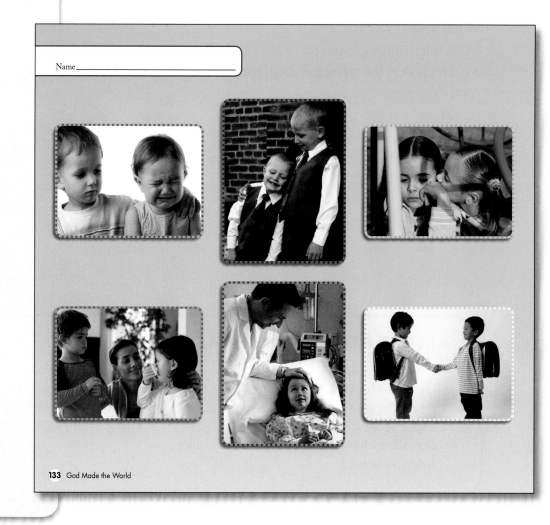

Name_____

133 God Made the World

2 **SCRIPTURE** Read the adaptation of John 20:19,22 from the Scripture card in the Bible.

• *Jesus gave his friends a helper who would be with them always.*

• *Listen to these words of Jesus from the Bible: "Peace be with you. Receive the holy Spirit."*

• *The Holy Spirit is with us always. The Holy Spirit brings us peace.*

3 Invite the children to match the pictures on page 134, showing ways we can bring peace to others.

SHARING [B]

4 Play this variation of "Simon Says." Direct the children to perform the action only if the example offered is an action that could bring peace. Use the following examples and create your own:

• *"Simon says touch your toes if sharing toys brings peace."*

• *"Simon says clap your hands if taking all the crayons brings peace."*

• *"Simon says jump up and down if speaking kind words brings peace."*

5 Demonstrate and practice exchanging a sign of peace as we do at Mass.

• *When we go to church, we share a sign of peace with one another. People shake hands and say "Peace be with you." Let's learn and practice this now.*

• (Demonstrate exchanging a sign of peace. Have each child find a partner to practice.)

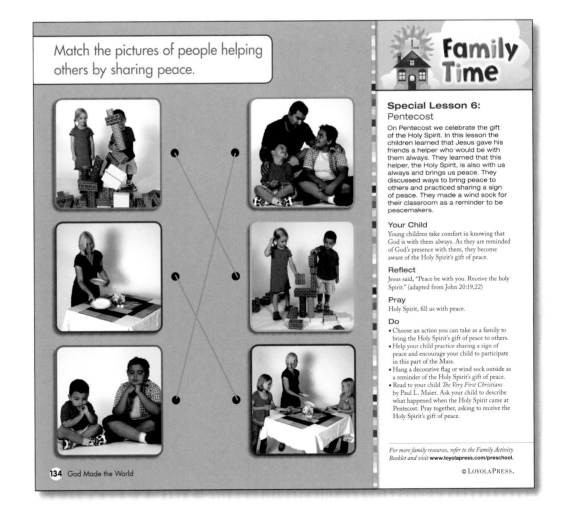

Match the pictures of people helping others by sharing peace.

Family Time

Special Lesson 6:
Pentecost

On Pentecost we celebrate the gift of the Holy Spirit. In this lesson the children learned that Jesus gave his friends a helper who would be with them always. They learned that this helper, the Holy Spirit, is also with us always and brings us peace. They discussed ways to bring peace to others and practiced sharing a sign of peace. They made a wind sock for their classroom as a reminder to be peacemakers.

Your Child
Young children take comfort in knowing that God is with them always. As they are reminded of God's presence with them, they become aware of the Holy Spirit's gift of peace.

Reflect
Jesus said, "Peace be with you. Receive the holy Spirit." (adapted from John 20:19,22)

Pray
Holy Spirit, fill us with peace.

Do
• Choose an action you can take as a family to bring the Holy Spirit's gift of peace to others.
• Help your child practice sharing a sign of peace and encourage your child to participate in this part of the Mass.
• Hang a decorative flag or wind sock outside as a reminder of the Holy Spirit's gift of peace.
• Read to your child *The Very First Christians* by Paul L. Maier. Ask your child to describe what happened when the Holy Spirit came at Pentecost. Pray together, asking to receive the Holy Spirit's gift of peace.

For more family resources, refer to the Family Activity Booklet and visit **www.loyolapress.com/preschool.**

134 God Made the World

© LOYOLAPRESS.

6 Teach the children the song "I'm Gonna Sing When the Spirit Says Sing." Add verses by substituting words for *sing,* such as *dance, hope, jump, spin,* and *clap.*

I'm Gonna Sing When the Spirit Says Sing

I'm gon-na sing when the spi-rit says sing;___ I'm gon-na sing when the spi-rit says sing;___ I'm gon-na sing when the spi-rit says sing, and o-bey the spi-rit of the Lord.___

ACTING

1 **PRAYER** Invite the children to pray:

Come, Holy Spirit, fill our hearts with your love and peace.

2 Make a class wind sock by stapling colored streamers to a paper plate. Help each child name an action he or she can take to be a peacemaker and then give the children a piece of colored streamer. Help them add their streamers to the paper plate. When finished, thread yarn through the paper plate to display the wind sock in the classroom as a reminder to be peacemakers.

Have the children take home their pages and show their family the Family Time section.

CHECKPOINT

- *Were the learning outcomes achieved?*
- *How familiar were the children with the sign of peace?*

ENRICHING THE FAITH EXPERIENCE

Use the following activities to enrich the lesson or to replace an activity with one that better meets the needs of your group.

1 Celebrate the feast of Pentecost with a parade. Give the children colored streamers to wave as they march and sing "I'm Going to Sing When the Spirit Says Sing."

2 Read aloud this poem:

God Is There

When I run in the sun,
God is there, God is there.
When I fall playing ball,
God cares, God cares.
When I'm sad or I'm glad,
God knows, God knows.
When I mind or I'm kind,
God sees, God sees.
God is with me day and night,
Help me to do what's right.
I love you, God!

Mary Kathleen Glavich, S.N.D.

PREPARING THE FAITH EXPERIENCE

LISTENING

[B]e filled with the Spirit, addressing one another [in] psalms and hymns and spiritual songs, singing and playing to the Lord in your hearts, giving thanks always and for everything in the name of our Lord Jesus Christ to God the Father.

Ephesians 5:18–20

REFLECTING

The primary attitudes of human beings toward God are adoration and thanksgiving. We respond to God with adoration because God is infinite and transcendent. We respond with thanksgiving because God is good and loving. Everything we have has been given to us by God—our homes, family, friends, food, our very lives. God has also given us a remarkable gift: the life of Jesus, the Son of God, sacrificed on the cross for our redemption after we showed base ingratitude by sinning. God is probably the only one for whom the expression "Thanks a million" is not an overstatement.

Interestingly, the word *thank* has its origin in the word *think*. To thank is to realize and to acknowledge that someone has bestowed a favor on us. We don't always remember to express gratitude for God's gifts. And yet, God is pleased when we do so, as the story of the ten lepers reveals (Luke 17:11–19). After Jesus had cured the ten seriously ill people and only one came back to thank him, Jesus asked, "Where are the other nine?" No doubt he was disappointed by their thoughtlessness and lack of manners.

Although every day is really a day for thanksgiving, once a year in the United States a special day—Thanksgiving Day—is set aside to give God thanks and celebrate. There is no better way to observe this day than to include the Eucharist. The word *eucharist* itself comes

from the Greek for "thanksgiving." In the celebration of the Eucharist, we give God thanks in the most effective way possible—through song, prayer, the sacrifice of Jesus, the sacrifice of ourselves, and sharing the sacred meal. During the Mass sometimes we pray:

Father, it is our duty and our salvation, always and everywhere to give thanks through your beloved Son, Jesus Christ.

Eucharistic Prayer II

We also show thanks by using the gifts we have received in ways that show our gratitude for them. As someone put it, "Thanksgiving is thanksliving." If we appreciate life, we respect it. If we are grateful for the earth, we care for it. If we appreciate other people, we show love and concern for them. Above all, we share our gifts, especially with those in need. This is what God, the Giver, intends that we do.

The words of Dag Hammarskjöld offer us a good motto for life: "For all that has been—Thanks! To all that will be—Yes!"

RESPONDING

God's Word moves us to respond in word and action. Let God's Spirit work within you as you prayerfully consider how you are being called to respond to God's message to you today. Responding through your journal may help to strengthen your response.

- What are some things I have never thought to thank God for?

God, give the children thankful hearts.

Catechism of the Catholic Church

The themes of this lesson correspond to the following paragraphs: 224, 2637–2638.

THE FAITH EXPERIENCE

Child's Book pages 135–138

SCRIPTURE IN THIS LESSON
• *Psalm 118:29*

MATERIALS
• Thanksgiving Scripture card
• Bible
• Small gift for each child, such as a piece of candy or a picture
• Beanbag or ball
• Option: stand-up turkey
• Cutout #64, pumpkin
• Crayons, markers, or paints
• Option: feathers

PREPARATION
• Write the children's names on pages 135 and 138.
• Place the Thanksgiving Scripture card for SHARING #2 in the Bible.

MUSIC'N MOTION
Use *Music 'n Motion* page T286 and CD Track 14 "Thank You, Jesus" for this lesson. For a list of additional music, see page T320.

ENRICHING THE FAITH EXPERIENCE
Use the activities at the end of the lesson to enrich the lesson or to replace an activity with one that better meets the needs of your group.

BOOKS TO SHARE
Sometimes It's Turkey, Sometimes It's Feathers by Lorna Balian (Star Bright Books, 2004)

Silly Tilly's Thanksgiving Dinner by Lillian Hoban (HarperTrophy, 2005)

Thanksgiving Is . . . by Gail Gibbons (Holiday House, 2005)

Thanksgiving at the Tappletons' by Eileen Spinelli (HarperTrophy, 2004)

SNACK
Suggestion: candy corn or turkey-shaped cookies

ALTERNATIVE PROGRAMS

DAILY PROGRAM
Day 1: Centering, Sharing A
Day 2: Enriching the Faith Experience choice
Day 3: Sharing B, Acting #1
Day 4: Enriching the Faith Experience choice
Day 5: Acting #2 and #3

THREE-DAY PROGRAM
Day 1: Centering, Sharing A
Day 2: Sharing B, Acting #1
Day 3: Acting #2 and #3

LEARNING OUTCOMES

The children will
• know that everything we have is a gift from God.
• say "thank you" for gifts and services.
• express thanks to God.

COMMENTS

1. Thanksgiving is the primary attitude of a Christian. Our great celebration, the Eucharist, is basically an act of thanksgiving. Prayers of thanksgiving are the easiest prayers for a child to understand.

2. The Pilgrims' first feast in America in 1621 may have been like a harvest festival celebrated in England. Despite a year of hardship and a meager harvest, the Pilgrims held a three-day Thanksgiving. About 90 Native Americans contributed to and shared the banquet and participated in the games that were played. In 1623, when the Pilgrims were threatened by drought and starvation, they held a day of fasting and prayer. The following day brought not only rain but also news of the arrival of a ship with supplies. This led Governor Bradford to proclaim a day of thanksgiving and prayer. Later, in 1863, President Lincoln proclaimed the last Thursday of November as Thanksgiving Day. Now it is a national holiday.

CENTERING

❶ Gather the children in a circle for *Music 'n Motion* time. Play Track 14. Invite the children to do motions to the song along with you, using *Music 'n Motion* page T286.

❷ Give small gifts to the children. If any child does not say thank you, remind him or her. Comment:

• *Saying thank you tells the other person we are happy for the gift. We are glad that person thought of us and likes us.*

• *Sometimes we even write thank-you notes to people who have given us gifts. We let them know we liked their gifts.*

SHARING [A]

❶ Play "Thank-You Relay." Have the children form one or two lines. Give the first child in the row a beanbag or ball. The first child hands it to the child who is next in line. The second child says "Thank you," and the first child responds "You're welcome." The second child hands the object to the next child in line.

Name_____

2 **SCRIPTURE** Introduce Thanksgiving Day. Read the adaptation of Psalm 118:29 from the Scripture card in the Bible.

• *Who gave us everything in the world?* (God)

• *We should thank God every day for being so good to us, shouldn't we?*

• *Listen to this prayer from the Bible: "Give thanks to the Lord, who is good, whose love lasts forever."*

• *Once a year, though, we take a special day to thank God for everything. What is this day?* (Thanksgiving Day)

3 Talk about what we do on Thanksgiving Day.

• *How do we celebrate Thanksgiving Day?* (We go to church, visit relatives and friends, have a big dinner with turkey.) [Option: Show the stand-up turkey.]

• *On Thanksgiving we thank God especially for giving us food, such as meat, vegetables, and fruit, and letting us enjoy such good things as pie.* [Show Cutout #64, pumpkin.]

SHARING [B]

4 Distribute page 135 and ask the children to name the foods pictured on the table. Ask them whether they eat these foods on Thanksgiving.

5 Have the children make a thank-you card for God on page 136 by drawing a picture of something for which they are grateful. Tell them that the words on the card say "Thank you, God." Encourage them to try to do their best work as a gift to God.

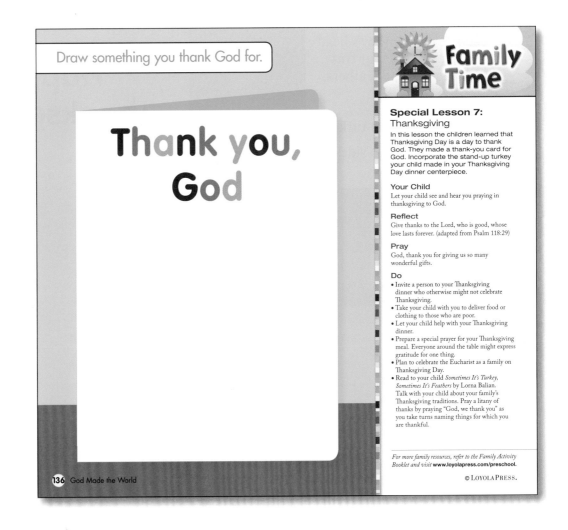

Draw something you thank God for.

Thank you, God

136 God Made the World

Family Time

Special Lesson 7:
Thanksgiving

In this lesson the children learned that Thanksgiving Day is a day to thank God. They made a thank-you card for God. Incorporate the stand-up turkey your child made in your Thanksgiving Day dinner centerpiece.

Your Child
Let your child see and hear you praying in thanksgiving to God.

Reflect
Give thanks to the Lord, who is good, whose love lasts forever. (adapted from Psalm 118:29)

Pray
God, thank you for giving us so many wonderful gifts.

Do
• Invite a person to your Thanksgiving dinner who otherwise might not celebrate Thanksgiving.
• Take your child with you to deliver food or clothing to those who are poor.
• Let your child help with your Thanksgiving dinner.
• Prepare a special prayer for your Thanksgiving meal. Everyone around the table might express gratitude for one thing.
• Plan to celebrate the Eucharist as a family on Thanksgiving Day.
• Read to your child *Sometimes It's Turkey, Sometimes It's Feathers* by Lorna Balian. Talk with your child about your family's Thanksgiving traditions. Pray a litany of thanks by praying "God, we thank you" as you take turns naming things for which you are thankful.

For more family resources, refer to the Family Activity Booklet and visit **www.loyolapress.com/preschool.**

© LOYOLAPRESS.

ACTING

1 **PRAYER** Invite the children to show their thank-you cards one by one and to tell what is on them. After each child speaks, have the class respond with Psalm 118:29:

> **Give thanks to the Lord, who is good,**
> **whose love lasts forever.**

2 Have the children make the stand-up turkey on page 137, which might be used as part of a Thanksgiving Day centerpiece at home. You might purchase feathers at a craft store to tape on for the tail. Help the children follow these directions:

- Trace your hand in the center section. Your thumb becomes the turkey's head and neck; your four fingers become tail feathers.

- Add legs.

- Color or paint the turkey.

- Fold back the two sides on the dotted lines.

3 Gather the children in a circle for *Music 'n Motion* time. Play Track 14. Invite the children to do motions to the song along with you, using *Music 'n Motion* page T286.

Have the children take home their pages and show their family the Family Time section.

CHECKPOINT

- *Were the learning outcomes achieved?*
- *What indication was there that the children are sincerely grateful to God?*

137 God Made the World

Page 138 is blank.

ENRICHING THE FAITH EXPERIENCE

Use the following activities to enrich the lesson or to replace an activity with one that better meets the needs of your group.

1 Invite the children to sing the following words to the tune of "Happy Birthday":

> Oh, we thank you, we do.
> Oh, we thank you, we do.
> Oh, we thank you, dear God.
> Oh, we thank you, we do.

2 Read the following poem to the children:

> ### Turkey Time
>
> Thanksgiving Day will soon be here;
> It comes around but once a year.
> If I could only have my way,
> We'd have Thanksgiving every day!

3 Play "Pin the Tail on the Turkey." Draw a large turkey and post it on the wall. Make a feather for each child to pin on the turkey and put a piece of rolled tape on the back of each. Blindfold the children one by one, turn them around once, and let them try to make a tail by placing their feather on the turkey.

4 Explain to the children that the celebration of Thanksgiving includes sharing the gifts we have with others. Plan special snacks and invite people the children know. Have each child bring in a can or box of food that will be given to those who are poor.

Valentine's Day

FAITH FOCUS

On Valentine's Day we express love.

1 John 4:7–11

PREPARING THE FAITH EXPERIENCE

LISTENING

Beloved, let us love one another, because love is of God; everyone who loves is begotten by God and knows God. Whoever is without love does not know God, for God is love. In this way the love of God was revealed to us: God sent his only Son into the world so that we might have life through him. In this is love: not that we have loved God, but that he loved us and sent his Son as expiation for our sins. Beloved, if God so loved us, we also must love one another.

1 John 4:7–11

REFLECTING

Love is the most wonderful and most important thing in the world. Jesus told us that the greatest commandment is to love. Saint John of the Cross wrote that in the end we will all be judged on love. In Scripture we find that love defines God: "God is love." (1 John 4:8)

Love is ennobling and demanding. Jesus became one of us and showed us how to love. He challenged us to love as he loved—with a love that is universal. Jesus loved the wealthy and the poor, the popular and the outcasts, the educated and the illiterate, the Galileans and the Samaritans. His love encompassed his family and friends as well as his enemies. His heart was large enough to embrace us all. Jesus loved by showing concern for the daughter of Jairus and for the adulterous woman, and by showing compassion for widows and for crowds hungry for truth and bread. He loved by teaching people, by healing lepers and those possessed by evil spirits, and by forgiving his executioners and his fair-weather friend, Peter. He loved us to death—death on a cross. With arms outstretched, Jesus shed his blood for us.

Our heart, that marvelous organ that pumps our lifeblood, is a fitting symbol for love. Saying we love someone with all our heart means that we love with our entire being. When Jesus appeared to Saint Margaret Mary, he used a vision of his heart to express how much he loved us, giving impetus to devotion to the Sacred Heart of Jesus. Someone has called the Bible a book drenched in love. The heartbeat of God can be heard in these verses: Isaiah 42:6, 43:1, 49:15–16, 54:10; Hosea 2:21; Matthew 28:20; John 14:23.

We look to many people and in many places for love. Saint Augustine pointed out the goal of our quest. Addressing God, he wrote, "Our hearts are restless until they rest in you." We pray to be better at loving:

Father, we honor the heart of your Son broken by man's cruelty, yet symbol of love's triumph, pledge of all that man is called to be. Teach us to see Christ in the lives we touch, to offer him living worship by love-filled service to our brothers and sisters.

Solemnity of the Sacred Heart Alternative Opening Prayer

RESPONDING

Having reflected upon God's Word, take some time now to continue to respond to God in prayer. You might wish to record your responses in your journal.

- Who in my life needs to be loved?

Jesus, help the children and me love like you.

Catechism of the Catholic Church

The themes of this lesson correspond to the following paragraphs: 214, 368, 478, 2055, 2563, 2842–2844.

THE FAITH EXPERIENCE

Child's Book pages 139–142

SCRIPTURE IN THIS LESSON
• *John 13:34*

MATERIALS
• Valentine's Day Scripture card
• Bible
• Paper hearts, three per child, hidden in the room
• Cutout #67, heart
• Option: valentine card
• Crayons or markers
• Option: hole punch
• Option: red yarn or ribbon
• Scissors
• Glue

PREPARATION
• Write the children's names on pages 139 and 142.
• Place the Valentine's Day Scripture card for SHARING #2 in the Bible.
• Hide the paper hearts around the room.
• Cut out the hearts on page 141 for the children.

MUSIC'N MOTION
Use *Music 'n Motion* page T288 and CD Track 15 "God Is Love" for this lesson. For a list of additional music, see page T320.

ENRICHING THE FAITH EXPERIENCE
Use the activities at the end of the lesson to enrich the lesson or to replace an activity with one that better meets the needs of your group.

BOOKS TO SHARE
Louanne Pig in the Mysterious Valentine by Nancy Carlson (Carolrhoda Books, 2004)

Valentine Friends by April Jones Prince (Cartwheel Books, 2004)

The Night Before Valentine's Day by Natasha Wing (Grosset & Dunlap, 2001)

Fluffy's Valentine's Day by Kate McMullan (Cartwheel Books, 2000)

SNACK
Suggestion: heart-shaped cookies

ALTERNATIVE PROGRAMS

DAILY PROGRAM
Day 1: Centering, Sharing A
Day 2: Enriching the Faith Experience choice
Day 3: Sharing B, Acting #1
Day 4: Enriching the Faith Experience choice
Day 5: Acting #2 and #3

THREE-DAY PROGRAM
Day 1: Centering, Sharing A
Day 2: Sharing B, Acting #1
Day 3: Acting #2 and #3

LEARNING OUTCOMES

The children will
- know that on Valentine's Day we show love.
- be grateful for God's love.
- show love for someone.

COMMENTS

1. Two Saint Valentines are listed in the Roman Martyrology for February 14—one a priest, the other a bishop. No one knows how our Valentine's Day, a day for showing love, is related to these saints, and very little is known about their lives. If, as it is believed, they were martyrs, their lives ended with the supreme sign of love.

2. Children respond easily to love and are eager to show it. This day offers a good opportunity to plant the seeds for understanding Christ's Great Commandment.

CENTERING

❶ Gather the children in a circle for *Music 'n Motion* time. Play Track 15. Invite the children to do motions to the song along with you, using *Music 'n Motion* page T288.

❷ Invite the children to search for the paper hearts you have hidden around the room. Tell them they may keep what they find, but encourage those who gather many hearts to share with those who have only one or none.

SHARING [A]

❶ Talk about Valentine's Day.

• [Show Cutout #67, heart.] *What is this?* (Heart) *Many times we use a picture of a heart to talk about love, or to show that we love someone.*

• *Once a year we celebrate a special day on which we tell people we love them. We call it Valentine's Day for Saint Valentine, who was a very loving man. We give valentines with hearts on them to the people we love.* [Option: Show a valentine card.]

Name _____

• *We don't need to wait for Valentine's Day to show people we love them. Every day is a day to love others.*

• *Guess who loves you more than anyone else in the world loves you.* (Jesus)

2 SCRIPTURE Read John 13:34 from the Scripture card in the Bible.

• *Jesus wants us to love others. The Bible tells us that Jesus said,*

   "As I have loved you, so you also should love one another."

3 Talk about forgiveness.

• *If we love someone and we hurt that person, we say "I'm sorry."*

• *Sometimes people hurt us, and they say "I'm sorry." If we love them, what do we say when people tell us they are sorry?* (I forgive you.)

SHARING [B]

4 Distribute page 139. Have the children tell how the people in the pictures need love. Ask what they could do to show love for those people.

5 Have the class give a group hug. Help each child find a partner. Tell the partners to give each other a hug. Then have the pairs find another pair and give a hug. Have the foursomes join with another group and give a hug. Continue until the entire class is joined in a group hug.

6 Have the children find and circle the five hearts hidden in the picture on page 140. Introduce the activity:

• *God loves us very much. Everything good in the world is like a valentine from God that says "I love you."*

ACTING

1 PRAYER Help the children find their heartbeat by pressing their hands against their chests. Invite them to put their hands over their hearts and pray a prayer of love.

Dear God, you love me very much. I love you too. Help me love you with all my heart.

Find and circle the five hearts.

140 God Made the World

Family Time

Special Lesson 8: Valentine's Day

In this lesson the children learned that Valentine's Day is a day to show love. They talked about how to show love for other people. They made a special valentine for someone. Give your child a big hug on Valentine's Day.

Your Child

Children learn how to love in the home. God's love is usually first communicated to them through their parents. Surprise your child sometimes with hugs, kisses, and little gifts. Show appreciation for signs of love from your child.

Reflect

[Jesus said,] "As I have loved you, so you also should love one another." (John 13:34)

Pray

Jesus, help us love others as you have loved us.

Do

• Bake heart-shaped cookies with your child. Decorate them, if you wish, and take some to a neighbor.
• Help your child address and send valentine cards to friends, relatives, and helpers.
• Read to your child *Louanne Pig in the Mysterious Valentine* by Nancy Carlson. Ask your child to name ways we show love to others, on Valentine's Day and every day. Thank God for loving us always.

For more family resources, refer to the Family Activity Booklet and visit www.loyolapress.com/preschool.

© LOYOLAPRESS.

2 Have the children make the valentine on page 141 as a gift to show their love for someone special. (If you wish, punching the holes and sewing the cards can be omitted.) Help the children follow these directions:

- Cut out the two hearts.

- Write your name on the line.

- Punch holes in the small hearts around the white heart.

- Go into the first hole under the flower with red yarn or ribbon, leaving a tail of about five inches. Sew around the heart.

- Tie the ends of the yarn or ribbon to make a bow.

- Glue the small red heart in the middle of the white heart.

3 Gather the children in a circle for *Music 'n Motion* time. Play Track 15. Invite the children to do motions to the song along with you, using *Music 'n Motion* page T288.

Have the children take home their pages and show their family the Family Time section.

CHECKPOINT

- *Were the learning outcomes achieved?*

ENRICHING THE FAITH EXPERIENCE

Use the following activities to enrich the lesson or to replace an activity with one that better meets the needs of your group.

1 Give each child a valentine from you.

2 Have the children glue red paper hearts on paper doilies.

141 God Made the World

❸ Teach the children the song "Love, Love."

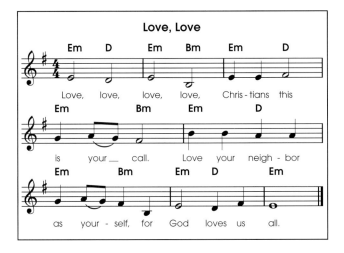

❹ Teach the children the following words to the tune of "Clementine."

Oh, my darling, oh, my darling,
Will you be my Valentine?
I will love you now and always.
Won't you say that you'll be mine?

Mary Kathleen Glavich, S.N.D.

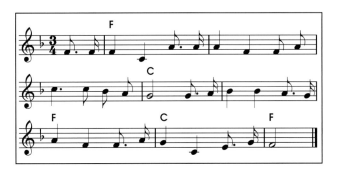

PREPARING THE FAITH EXPERIENCE

LISTENING

*Can a mother forget her infant,
  be without tenderness for the child of her womb?
Even should she forget,
  I will never forget you.*

Isaiah 49:15

REFLECTING

The feminist movement has heightened our awareness of the feminine aspects of God, who, being pure spirit, is really neither male nor female. Even without the benefit of this movement, it is easy to see why the concept of mother is an apt image for God.

A unique bond exists between a child and his or her mother. The mother brings the child into the world and nurtures the child, providing for the child's needs, teaching skills for living, and guiding her child in acquiring knowledge. Most importantly, a mother loves her child and willingly sacrifices for her child's well-being. The child is dependent on his or her mother and looks to her for help, understanding, and advice. The child trusts in the mother's love and feels secure when she is near. With the passing of years, the love and appreciation the child feels for his or her mother usually grow. These descriptions also apply to our relationship with God.

The bond between mother and child united Jesus, the Son of God, and the Blessed Virgin Mary. Mary's body gave flesh and blood to Jesus. Her milk nourished him, and her arms cradled him. Mary was the first teacher of the master teacher. She helped him take his first steps, speak his first words, and pray. She cooked his meals and made his clothes. And she loved him.

Because Mary gave birth to Christ and because we are the members of his mystical body, it follows that she is also our mother. Tradition holds that from the cross Jesus officially gave us the gift of Mary, his mother, when he said to John, our representative, "Behold your mother" and to Mary, "Behold your son." Mary loves and cares for us and prays for us. May each of us reflect something of the way she lived. May we heed her advice, her last recorded words in Scripture: "Do whatever he tells you." (John 2:5)

Certainly we owe our mothers on earth thanks. We also ought to thank and honor our heavenly mother, especially by trying to be as faithful and open to God as she was.

Let us pray a prayer attributed to Saint Bernard:

Remember, O most gracious Virgin Mary, that never was it known that anyone who fled to your protection, implored your help, or sought your intercession was left unaided.

Inspired by this confidence, I fly unto you, O Virgin of virgins, my Mother. To you do I come, before you I stand, sinful and sorrowful. O Mother of the Word incarnate, despise not my petitions, but in your mercy hear and answer me. Amen.

RESPONDING

God's Word calls us to respond in love. Respond to God now in the quiet of your heart, and perhaps through your journal.

- How can I show motherly care for others?

  Mary, pray for the children.

Catechism of the Catholic Church

The themes of this lesson correspond to the following paragraphs: 507, 2215, 2618, 2679.

THE FAITH EXPERIENCE

Child's Book pages 143–146

SCRIPTURE IN THIS LESSON
• *Colossians 3:20*

MATERIALS
• Mother's Day Scripture card
• Bible
• Dolls, women's clothing, items mothers use
• Option: Cutout #2, mother
• Cutout #10, Mary
• Crayons, paints, or markers
• 15-inch piece of yarn or ribbon for each child

PREPARATION
• Write the children's names on page 143.
• Place the Mother's Day Scripture card for SHARING #4 in the Bible.
• If you wish, post Cutout #2.

ENRICHING THE FAITH EXPERIENCE
Use the activities at the end of the lesson to enrich the lesson or to replace an activity with one that better meets the needs of your group.

BOOKS TO SHARE
The Mother's Day Mice by Eve Bunting
  (Clarion Books, 1988)

Mama, Do You Love Me? by Barbara M. Joosse
  (Chronicle Books, 1991)

Hazel's Amazing Mother by Rosemary Wells
  (Puffin, 1992)

SNACK
Suggestion: cookies

ALTERNATIVE PROGRAMS

DAILY PROGRAM
Day 1: Centering, Sharing A
Day 2: Enriching the Faith Experience choice
Day 3: Sharing B
Day 4: Enriching the Faith Experience choice
Day 5: Acting

THREE-DAY PROGRAM
Day 1: Centering, Sharing A
Day 2: Sharing B
Day 3: Acting

LEARNING OUTCOMES

The children will

• know that God gave them mothers.

• be grateful for their mothers.

• show love for their mothers.

COMMENTS

1. A mother is often the one who is there in time of sickness or when a child has nightmares. She calms fears and soothes hurt feelings. A mother cheers on her children as they master new skills. Understanding the devotion and services of a mother helps children understand the maternal qualities of God. For children who lack a mother's presence, the catechist can provide love and concern to a certain degree.

2. Be sensitive to children who do not live with their mothers. Children whose fathers are single parents can present the scroll to someone who is like a mother to them—they might even choose to present it to their father if he is like a father and mother to them.

CENTERING

Have the children play house in small groups, allowing them to choose their own roles.

SHARING [A]

❶ Distribute page 143 and talk about the picture of the mother.

• *The mother in the picture loves her child. God gave each of us a mother. Mothers love us and do a lot for us to show their love. What does your mother do for you?*

• *Isn't God good to give us mothers and people who are like mothers to us?*

❷ Have the children circle what their mother does for them on page 144.

❸ Introduce Mother's Day.

• *Once a year we celebrate our mothers on Mother's Day. On this day we do special things for our mothers to show our love. What can you do for your mother on this day?*

Name _____

SHARING [B]

4 **SCRIPTURE** Read what God says about parents from the Scripture card in the Bible. (Colossians 3:20)

• *In the Bible, God says "Children, obey your parents in everything."*

• *Your mother tells you to do certain things because she wants what is good for you. She wants you to be healthy and happy.*

• *What are some of the things your mother tells you to do?*

5 Have the children play "Mother May I?" Appoint one child to be the mother. (The child may hold Cutout #2, mother.) Have the other children line up about 10 feet away facing that child. Beginning with the first child in the row, the "mother" says the child's name and tells the child that he or she may take a number of giant steps or baby steps. For example, "Sarah may take two giant steps." The child must ask "Mother, may I?" before taking the steps. The first child to reach the "mother" wins and becomes the next "mother."

6 Recall that Mary is our mother.

• *We have a mother in heaven too. Who is she?* (Mary) [Show Cutout #10, Mary.]

• *Mary was a good mother to Jesus. He gave you Mary to be your mother too.*

• *What does Mary do for you?* (Watches over us, prays for us)

• *On Mother's Day you can thank Mary for being your mother.*

7 **PRAYER** Invite the children to thank God in their hearts for giving them mothers.

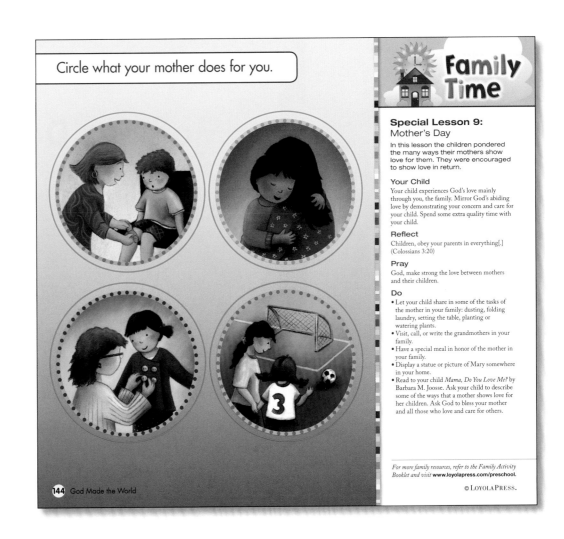

Circle what your mother does for you.

144 God Made the World

Family Time

Special Lesson 9:
Mother's Day

In this lesson the children pondered the many ways their mothers show love for them. They were encouraged to show love in return.

Your Child
Your child experiences God's love mainly through you, the family. Mirror God's abiding love by demonstrating your concern and care for your child. Spend some extra quality time with your child.

Reflect
Children, obey your parents in everything[.] (Colossians 3:20)

Pray
God, make strong the love between mothers and their children.

Do
• Let your child share in some of the tasks of the mother in your family: dusting, folding laundry, setting the table, planting or watering plants.
• Visit, call, or write the grandmothers in your family.
• Have a special meal in honor of the mother in your family.
• Display a statue or picture of Mary somewhere in your home.
• Read to your child *Mama, Do You Love Me?* by Barbara M. Joosse. Ask your child to describe some of the ways that a mother shows love for her children. Ask God to bless your mother and all those who love and care for others.

For more family resources, refer to the Family Activity Booklet and visit **www.loyolapress.com/preschool.**

© LOYOLAPRESS.

ACTING

1 Teach the children one of the following verses to recite to their mothers on Mother's Day:

> Roses are red, violets are blue.
> Sugar is sweet, and so are you.

> Do you love me,
> Or do you not?
> You told me once,
> But I forgot.

2 Have the children make a scroll from page 145 to present to their mothers on Mother's Day. Read the scroll to them and then help them follow these directions:

- Write your name on the line.
- Color or paint the flowers.
- Roll up the scroll.
- Tie yarn or ribbon around the scroll to hold it together.

Have the children take home their pages and show their family the Family Time section.

CHECKPOINT

- *Were the learning outcomes achieved?*

Page 146 is blank.

ENRICHING THE FAITH EXPERIENCE

Use the following activities to enrich the lesson or to replace an activity with one that better meets the needs of your group.

1 Have the children make a gift for their mothers. Here are some suggestions:

- *Cutout coasters.* Invite the children to draw or paint artwork that would fit under glasses, such as handprints to hold drinks, drawings of animals, people, faces, or flowers. Cover the designs on both sides with clear contact paper and cut them out with enough of a plastic margin to keep liquids off the table.

- *A pomander ball.* Shape aluminum foil into a ball, making a little knob on top. Have the children add glue to the ball and then put cinnamon, nutmeg, cloves, or allspice on the glue.

- *A picture.* Take each child's picture. Have the children glue their photo on construction paper and help them fold it so that it stands. Then have the children make a decorative frame for the picture.

2 Hold a May celebration to honor Mary. Have the children put flowers before her picture or statue. Have the children repeat after you:

> Mary, my mother in heaven above,
> This day I thank you and show you my love.
> Help me to grow up to be like your Son,
> Kind and loving to everyone.
>
> *Mary Kathleen Glavich, S.N.D.*

PREPARING THE FAITH EXPERIENCE

LISTENING

"Righteous Father, the world also does not know you, but I know you, and they know that you sent me. I made known to them your name and I will make it known, that the love with which you loved me may be in them and I in them."

John 17:25–26

REFLECTING

Jesus revealed God to us and showed us that the eternal, infinite, and almighty God is also our Father, a Father of love and mercy. Jesus himself addressed God as "Abba," a term of intimacy similar to "Papa" or "Daddy." In his teachings, Jesus made it clear that God is our Father too. He repeatedly spoke of "your Father" or "your heavenly Father."

A father loves his children. He cares and provides for them, protects and nurtures them. By calling God our Father, Jesus taught us that God does these things for us. He is not someone far removed from us but someone vitally interested in our well-being. God has shared divine life with us, and we are his children.

[T]hrough faith you are all children of God in Christ Jesus.

Galatians 3:26

As proof that you are children, God sent the spirit of his Son into our hearts, crying out, "Abba, Father!" So you are no longer a slave but a child, and if a child then also an heir, through God.

Galatians 4:6–7

Jesus had a foster father on earth: Saint Joseph, the husband of Mary. Scripture describes Joseph as a just man. He was someone you could trust, a man of integrity. Like his wife, Joseph was open to God's will for him. Although he did not understand why or how Mary was pregnant, at God's command he kept her as his wife. He obeyed the Jewish

laws and the mandates of government officials. He provided for his family when they were strangers in Bethlehem and refugees in Egypt. There and in Nazareth, Joseph made a living as a carpenter. He probably taught Jesus his trade.

It is not easy being responsible for the lives of others. On Father's Day and on other days, let us pray for the fathers of the world. We might pray to Saint Joseph, who knows what it means to be a father.

In everything, let us turn to our Father, praying as Jesus taught us:

> *Our Father, who art in heaven,*
> *hallowed be thy name;*
> *thy kingdom come;*
> *thy will be done*
> *on earth as it is in heaven.*
> *Give us this day our daily bread;*
> *and forgive us our trespasses*
> *as we forgive those who trespass against us;*
> *and lead us not into temptation,*
> *but deliver us from evil. Amen.*

RESPONDING

Having been nourished by God's Word, we are able to respond to God's great love for us. In prayer, respond to God's call to you to share his Word with others. You may also wish to respond in your prayer journal.

- How has God acted as a loving Father in my life?

Father, bless the children with good homes and loving parents.

Catechism of the Catholic Church

The themes of this lesson correspond to the following paragraphs: 239, 437, 2781.

THE FAITH EXPERIENCE

Child's Book pages 147–150

SCRIPTURE IN THIS LESSON
• *Matthew 6:32*

MATERIALS
• Father's Day Scripture card
• Bible
• Men's clothing and items that fathers use
• Option: Cutout #1, father
• Crayons or markers

PREPARATION
• Write the children's names on page 147.
• Place the Father's Day Scripture card for SHARING #2 in the Bible.
• If you wish, post Cutout #1.

ENRICHING THE FAITH EXPERIENCE
Use the activities at the end of the lesson to enrich the lesson or to replace an activity with one that better meets the needs of your group.

BOOKS TO SHARE
A Perfect Father's Day by Eve Bunting
  (Clarion Books, 1993)

My Daddy & I by P. K. Hallinan
  (Ideals Children's Books, 2006)

Daddy Makes the Best Spaghetti
  by Anna Grossnickle Hines (Clarion Books, 1989)

Papa, Please Get the Moon for Me by Eric Carle
  (Simon & Schuster, 1991)

SNACK
Suggestion: raisins

ALTERNATIVE PROGRAMS

DAILY PROGRAM
Day 1: Centering, Sharing A
Day 2: Enriching the Faith Experience choice
Day 3: Sharing B, Acting #1
Day 4: Enriching the Faith Experience choice
Day 5: Acting #2 and #3

THREE-DAY PROGRAM
Day 1: Centering, Sharing A
Day 2: Sharing B, Acting #1
Day 3: Acting #2 and #3

LEARNING OUTCOMES

The children will

• know that God gave them fathers.

• appreciate what their fathers do for them.

• show love for their fathers.

COMMENTS

1. Be sensitive to those children who do not live with their fathers. Children whose mothers are single parents may make cards for men who are like fathers to them—or they may give the cards to their mothers if they are like mothers and fathers to them.

2. Jesus instructed us to call God "Father." A father loves and nurtures his children. Children who have caring fathers are able to understand God's attitude toward them. Those who do not must depend on other people to show them paternal love and care.

CENTERING

Have the children play house in small groups, allowing them to choose their own roles.

SHARING [A]

❶ Distribute page 147 and talk about the picture of the father and child.

• *God gave us fathers to love and care for us.*

• *What are some things fathers do to show love for their families?*

• *How does your father show love for you?*

❷ **SCRIPTURE** Tell the children about God the Father. Read the adaptation of Matthew 6:32 from the Scripture card in the Bible.

• *Jesus told us that God is our Father in heaven. Listen to what Jesus says in the Bible: "Your heavenly Father knows everything you need."*

• *God loves us and cares for us like a father.*

❸ Recall Saint Joseph.

• *Who was Jesus' foster father on earth?* (Joseph)

• *Saint Joseph was a good father to Jesus. He took good*

Name_____

147 God Made the World

care of Jesus and Mary, Jesus' mother.

• Saint Joseph is in heaven now with Jesus and Mary. You can ask Saint Joseph to help your father be a good father.

4 Have the children circle on page 148 what their father does for them.

SHARING [B]

5 Ask the children to tell how they can show love for their fathers. Let them pantomime acts such as helping prepare dinner, bringing him the newspaper, or weeding the garden.

6 **PRAYER** Lead the children in prayer for their fathers. (Alternative prayer idea: Have the children pass around Cutout #1, father, and let each child who holds it pray for his or her father.)

• We can also pray for our fathers. Let's ask God the Father to bless our fathers and those who are like fathers to us.

Dear Father in heaven, please bless my father or someone who takes care of me like a father.

Circle what your father does for you.

148 God Made the World

Family Time

Special Lesson 10:
Father's Day
In this lesson the children talked about ways in which fathers show love. They were encouraged in return to show love for their fathers by words and actions. They learned that God is our Father in heaven.

Your Child
Families grow closer by spending time together. Take the opportunity to share daily activities as well as special time together. Speak to your child about God as a loving Father who cares for us and loves us.

Reflect
Jesus said, "Your heavenly Father knows everything you need."
(adapted from Matthew 6:32)

Pray
Father, help us trust you always.

Do
• Let your child share in some of the tasks of the father in your family: working in the yard, cleaning the garage, washing windows, cooking.
• Visit, call, or write the grandfathers in your family.
• Have a special meal in honor of the father in your family.
• Read to your child *Daddy Makes the Best Spaghetti* by Anna Grossnickle Hines. Ask your child to describe some of the ways that a father shows love for his children. Ask God to bless your father and all those who love and care for others.

For more family resources, refer to the Family Activity Booklet and visit www.loyolapress.com/preschool.

© Loyola Press.

ACTING

1 Have the children sing the following words to the tune of "London Bridge":

> God the Father, I love you,
>   I love you, I love you.
> God the Father, I love you,
>   my good Father.
>
> God the Father, I thank you,
>   I thank you, I thank you.
> God the Father, I thank you,
>   for my father.

2 Have the children make the Father's Day card on page 149. Read them the card and then help them follow these directions:

- Draw a picture in the frame of something your father does for you.

- Write your name.

- Fold the card to stand up.

3 Tell the children to give their cards to their mothers to save for them until Father's Day.

Have the children take home their pages and show their family the Family Time section.

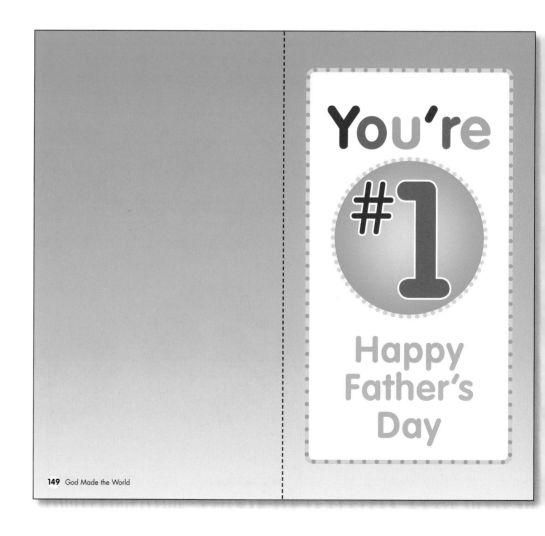

ENRICHING THE FAITH EXPERIENCE

Use the following activities to enrich the lesson or to replace an activity with one that better meets the needs of your group.

1 Have the children make a gift for their fathers for Father's Day. They could make a paperweight or knickknack out of a rock or piece of wood.

2 Help the children make sheets of butcher paper into wrapping paper for a Father's Day gift. They might decorate it with rubbings or use objects dipped in tempera paint.

3 Choose a day when the children will not be involved in making these gifts and invite fathers to the class. The children could present a short program, incorporating some of the songs and finger plays they have learned.

Thank you,

Love,

150 God Made the World © LOYOLAPRESS.

We thank God for the gift of life.

Psalm 139; Isaiah 43:1; John 10:10

PREPARING THE FAITH EXPERIENCE

LISTENING

You formed my inmost being;
 you knit me in my mother's womb.
I praise you, so wonderfully you made me;
 wonderful are your works!
My very self you knew;
 my bones were not hidden from you,
When I was being made in secret,
 fashioned as in the depths of the earth.

Psalm 139:13–15

REFLECTING

Every year on her birthday, a woman gave her mother a present in gratitude for the gift of life. It is fitting on each birthday to thank not only our mothers but also God, who called us into being and sustains us from day to day.

Because of God's gift of life, we are able to know the thrill and satisfaction of running, dancing, watching a sunrise, mastering a new skill, producing a painting or poem, and loving others. Moreover, God has shown tremendous love in treating us as family and offering us a share in his divine life.

Throughout the centuries God has guided the combinations of genes to make us the unique people we are. Irreplaceable creations, we are each special and precious. As a member of the Body of Christ, each of us has definite work to do. When we celebrate someone's birthday, we celebrate the person and his or her gifts, talents, graces, and contributions to humanity.

God has given us the freedom to live life to the hilt or to squander it. We may treasure it or take it for granted. We may live it selflessly or selfishly. In Deuteronomy, God challenges, "I have set before you life and death . . . Choose

life, then, that you and your descendants may live, by loving the LORD, your God, heeding his voice, and holding fast to him." (Deuteronomy 30:19–20)

In addition to celebrating the day we were born, we can also celebrate the day we were baptized. On that day we were reborn in the Holy Spirit and became members of God's family. At the end of our lives, we will have a new birthday to celebrate—the day we are born into eternal life. Usually the feast day the Church assigns to a canonized saint is the day of his or her death. Although we will not all be formally canonized, if we live with faith in God and follow Jesus, we can hope that someday we will also be raised to life to enjoy a celebration that lasts forever.

RESPONDING

God's Word moves us to respond in word and action. Let God's Spirit work within you as you prayerfully consider how you are being called to respond to God's message to you today. Responding through your journal may help to strengthen your response.

- What blessings since my last birthday can I celebrate this year?

Jesus, give the children an appreciation of life.

Catechism of the Catholic Church

The themes of this lesson correspond to the following paragraphs: 256–257, 2288.

THE FAITH EXPERIENCE

Child's Book pages 151–154

SCRIPTURE IN THIS LESSON
• *Psalm 139:14*

MATERIALS
• Birthdays Scripture card
• Bible
• Gift-wrapped present to be shared by all, such as a snack for the party
• Option: personal photo of a birthday party
• Crayons or markers
• Large sheets of paper
• Tape
• Music for SHARING #4
• Prizes, at least one per child
• Scissors
• Transparent tape

PREPARATION
• Write the children's names on pages 151 and 153.
• Place the Birthdays Scripture card for SHARING #2 in the Bible.
• "Hide" the present for CENTERING #2 where it can be seen.
• Draw or glue pictures of cakes on one or a few of the sheets of paper.
• If you wish, use a paper cutter to cut apart the strips on page 153 for the children.

MUSIC 'N MOTION

Use *Music 'n Motion* page T289 and CD Track 17 "Happy Birthday! It's Your Day" for this lesson. For a list of additional music, see page T320.

ENRICHING THE FAITH EXPERIENCE
Use the activities at the end of the lesson to enrich the lesson or to replace an activity with one that better meets the needs of your group.

BOOKS TO SHARE
When I Was Little: A Four-Year-Old's Memoir of Her Youth by Jamie Lee Curtis (HarperTrophy, 1995)

On the Day You Were Born by Debra Frasier (Harcourt Children's Books, 1991)

Happy Birthday to You! by Dr. Seuss (Random House Books for Young Readers, 1959)

A Birthday for Frances by Russell Hoban (HarperTrophy, 1995)

SNACK
Suggestion: candy and cupcakes

ALTERNATIVE PROGRAMS

DAILY PROGRAM
Day 1: Centering, Sharing A
Day 2: Enriching the Faith Experience choice
Day 3: Sharing B, Acting #1
Day 4: Enriching the Faith Experience choice
Day 5: Acting #2–4

THREE-DAY PROGRAM
Day 1: Centering, Sharing A
Day 2: Sharing B, Acting #1
Day 3: Acting #2–4

LEARNING OUTCOMES

The children will

• realize that their lives are a gift from God.

• thank God for their lives.

• celebrate their lives.

COMMENTS

1. Respect for life can be instilled in children at an early age. This lesson presents a good opportunity for deepening the children's reverence for life—their lives and those of others. Children who love themselves and consider themselves worthy of love will find it easier to reach out to God and others in love. At every meeting with the children, increase their self-acceptance by affirming them whenever possible. By loving the children, you will make them more loving.

2. You might hold a more elaborate birthday party that includes decorations, favors, place mats, balloons, and noisemakers.

CENTERING

❶ Gather the children in a circle for *Music 'n Motion* time. Play Track 17. Invite the children to do motions to the song along with you, using *Music 'n Motion* page T289.

❷ Have the children play "Huckle-Buckle Beanstalk." Tell the children that when they find the present you have hidden in the room, they should call "huckle-buckle beanstalk" and, without touching the present, sit down. After all the children have seen the gift and are seated, let the first child who found it open it.

❸ Talk about gifts.

• *When do you get gifts?* (Birthdays, Christmas)

• *Why do you give gifts to people?* (To show that you like them)

Name

151 God Made the World

SHARING [A]

❶ Distribute page 151. Have the children talk about the birthday party in the picture.

• *What's happening in the picture?* (The children are having a birthday party.)

• *What will the children do at the party?* (Sing "Happy Birthday," eat birthday cake and ice cream, play games)

• *Let's count the candles on the cake.* [Count.]

• *What do you think the presents will be?*

• *What are the children celebrating?* (The life of their friend or family member) [Option: Show and explain the photo.]

❷ **SCRIPTURE** Tell the children that life is a gift. Read the adaptation of Psalm 139:14 from the Scripture card in the Bible.

• *Our life is a gift from God. Life is a wonderful gift. What can you do because you are alive?*

• *Listen to this prayer from the Bible: "I praise you, God, for the wonder of myself."*

• *Once a year we celebrate our lives on our birthdays. Today let's celebrate the life of everyone here.*

SHARING [B]

❸ Have the children decorate the cake and add flames to the candles on page 152.

❹ Let the children play "Cakewalk." Tape sheets of paper in a circle on the floor. One or more of the sheets should have a picture of a cake on it. Have the children walk from sheet to sheet as music is played. When the music stops, the children who are on a sheet with a cake win a prize. At the end give consolation prizes to the children who didn't win.

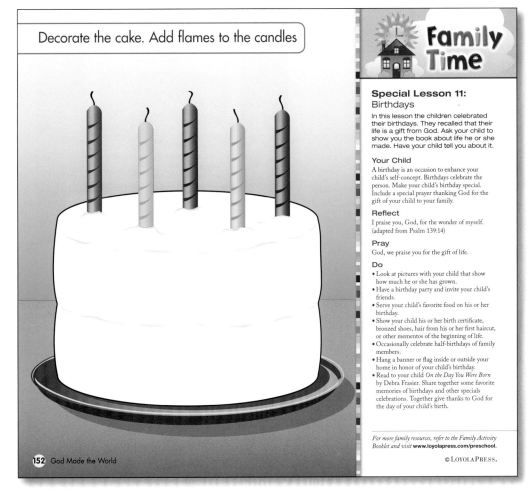

Decorate the cake. Add flames to the candles

Family Time

Special Lesson 11:
Birthdays

In this lesson the children celebrated their birthdays. They recalled that their life is a gift from God. Ask your child to show you the book about life he or she made. Have your child tell you about it.

Your Child
A birthday is an occasion to enhance your child's self-concept. Birthdays celebrate the person. Make your child's birthday special. Include a special prayer thanking God for the gift of your child to your family.

Reflect
I praise you, God, for the wonder of myself. (adapted from Psalm 139:14)

Pray
God, we praise you for the gift of life.

Do
• Look at pictures with your child that show how much he or she has grown.
• Have a birthday party and invite your child's friends.
• Serve your child's favorite food on his or her birthday.
• Show your child his or her birth certificate, bronzed shoes, hair from his or her first haircut, or other mementos of the beginning of life.
• Occasionally celebrate half-birthdays of family members.
• Hang a banner or flag inside or outside your home in honor of your child's birthday.
• Read to your child *On the Day You Were Born* by Debra Frasier. Share together some favorite memories of birthdays and other specials celebrations. Together give thanks to God for the day of your child's birth.

For more family resources, refer to the Family Activity Booklet and visit www.loyolapress.com/preschool.

152 God Made the World

© LOYOLAPRESS.

ACTING

1 **PRAYER** Invite the children to pray by singing the following verse to the melody of "Happy Birthday." See Enriching the Faith Experience #1 for additional verses.

> God, we thank you for life.
> God, we thank you for life.
> Our life is your good gift.
> God, we thank you for life.

2 Have the children make the accordion book from page 153. Tell them that they are making a birthday book to help celebrate their lives. Help them follow these directions:

- Cut the strips apart on the solid black line.

- Fold the strips on the dotted lines so that the lines on the front of the card are on the peaks.

- Place pages 2 and 3 next to each other and tape them together.

- Fold together pages 2 and 3 so that they are face-to-face.

- Fold up the book.

3 Read aloud the accordion book aloud and have the children follow along.

4 Gather the children in a circle for *Music 'n Motion* time. Play Track 17. Invite the children to do motions to the song along with you, using *Music 'n Motion* page T289.

Have the children take home their pages and show their family the Family Time section.

I Thank God I'm Alive!

I can see sunsets and skyscrapers, daisies and stars, and people who love me.

Name_____

1

I can hear music, wind in the trees, raindrops on the roof, and my mother calling me.

2

I can feel a kitten's fur, the warm sun, and a hug.

153 God Made the World   3

I can run down the street, into the lake, or to Grandma's house.

4

- *Were the learning outcomes achieved?*
- *Are the children showing more respect for one another?*

ENRICHING THE FAITH EXPERIENCE

Use the following activities to enrich the lesson or to replace an activity with one that better meets the needs of your group.

1 Have the children sing the following verse to the tune of "Happy Birthday." Insert the names of children whose birthdays are close to the day or insert every child's name.

> God, we thank you for [name].
> God, we thank you for [name].
> [Name] is your good gift.
> God, we thank you for [name].

2 Measure or weigh the children twice during the year to show them how much they are growing.

3 Have the children bring in pictures of their birthday parties. Post the pictures.

I can eat turkey, pizza, peas, chocolate chip cookies, strawberries, and popcorn.

7

I'm alive and I'm five. Life is great. Let's celebrate.

8

I can shout for joy, whisper a secret, and sing a song.

154 God Made the World   5

I can play hide-and-seek, watch movies, feed ducks, and snuggle under blankets on a cold night.

6   © LOYOLAPRESS.

FAITH FOCUS

Summer is a time to enjoy the world God made for us. Genesis 2:1–3

PREPARING THE FAITH EXPERIENCE

LISTENING

So God blessed the seventh day and made it holy, because on it he rested from all the work he had done in creation.

Genesis 2:3

REFLECTING

In these days of concern about stress and burnout, it is good to consider the example that God, the first worker, set for us. According to Scripture, after six days of creating, God "rested." Jesus sometimes invited his disciples to come away from the crowds and rest. He said, "Come away by yourselves to a deserted place and rest a while." (Mark 6:31) As a human being, Jesus needed periods of relaxation too and benefited from the Jewish sabbaths.

Ecclesiastes 3:1 states, "There is an appointed time for everything." One might add, "A time to work and a time to play." We need respites from our labor in order to be refreshed and strengthened. After a break we resume our work with renewed vigor. Collective human wisdom supports the need for recreation in the adage "All work and no play makes Jack a dull boy."

One word for *rest* in the Bible is *menuha.* This word signifies more activity than our word. It involves contemplation, becoming quiet in order to see more deeply into life. *Menuha* conveys the ideas of the good life—inner tranquility, the opportunity for reflection, and the absence of strife. In Psalm 23 the shepherd leads us to green pastures where he gives us rest, *menuha.*

Summer vacation is a time of rest. But it is also a time to think back on what has happened,

to enjoy God's world, and to plan for the future. It is a time to be with others and to be with God. Those who are accustomed to real rest will better be able to enjoy life in heaven, also known as eternal rest.

Let us pray this prayer written by Erasmus:

> *Lord Jesus, the Way,*
> *the Truth,*
> *and the Life,*
> *we pray,*
> *do not let us stray from you,*
> *the Way,*
> *nor distrust you,*
> *the Truth*
> *nor rest in anything else but you,*
> *the Life.*
> *Teach us by the Holy Spirit*
> *what to do,*
> *what to believe,*
> *and where to take our rest.*

RESPONDING

Having reflected upon God's Word, take some time now to continue to respond to God in prayer. You might wish to record your responses in your journal.

- What plans for this summer will enable me to enjoy a real rest?

  God, this summer keep the children and me safe, happy, and close to you.

Catechism of the Catholic Church

The themes of this lesson correspond to the following paragraphs: 2172, 2184–2185.

THE FAITH EXPERIENCE

Child's Book pages 155–158

SCRIPTURE IN THIS LESSON

• *Psalm 57:10–11*

MATERIALS

• Last Class/Summer Scripture card
• Bible
• Cutout #20, sun
• Option: a pair of sunglasses
• Crayons and markers

PREPARATION

• Write the children's names on page 155.
• Place the Last Class/Summer Scripture card for SHARING #4 in the Bible.
• Fill out the children's certificates on page 157.

MUSIC 'N MOTION

Use *Music 'n Motion* page T290 and CD Track 18 "God Is Great" for this lesson. For a list of additional music, see page T320.

ENRICHING THE FAITH EXPERIENCE

Use the activities at the end of the lesson to enrich the lesson or to replace an activity with one that better meets the needs of your group.

BOOKS TO SHARE

Curious George Goes to the Beach
by Margret and H. A. Rey (Houghton Mifflin, 1999)

Summersaults by Douglas Florian (Greenwillow, 2002)

Summer by Alice Low
(Random House Books for Young Readers, 2007)

SNACK

Suggestion: crispy rice treats

ALTERNATIVE PROGRAMS

DAILY PROGRAM

Day 1: Centering, Sharing A
Day 2: Enriching the Faith Experience choice
Day 3: Sharing B, Acting #1
Day 4: Enriching the Faith Experience choice
Day 5: Acting #2–4

THREE-DAY PROGRAM

Day 1: Centering, Sharing A
Day 2: Sharing B, Acting #1
Day 3: Acting #2–4

LEARNING OUTCOMES

The children will

• anticipate summer fun.

• thank God for the experiences of preschool.

COMMENTS

1. This lesson prepares the children for the idea of Sunday as a day of rest. God's Third Commandment (like all the other commandments) is psychologically healthy for us. In our hectic, fast-paced age, it is more necessary than ever to plan "holy pauses" for spiritual celebration and physical and mental rest, times for God and for the family. Leisure time affords us the opportunity to glory in God's gift of creation.

2. You might invite the parents for an end-of-the-year celebration during which the children perform the songs and finger plays that they learned in preschool. Include a display of the children's art and provide refreshments.

CENTERING

❶ Gather the children in a circle for *Music 'n Motion* time. Play Track 18. Invite the children to do motions to the song along with you, using *Music 'n Motion* page T290.

❷ Have the children do a finger play they especially like.

SHARING [A]

❶ Distribute page 155 and have the children talk about the summer activities in the pictures.

• *Summer is coming, and there will be no more preschool classes. During the summer you will do all kinds of exciting things at home. What are the children doing in the pictures?*

❷ Point out our need for rest.

• *God knows that we need to rest sometimes. God gave us summer vacation so that we will have time to play and have fun. The sun shines most of the time.* [Post Cutout #20, sun.] *Sometimes we have to wear sunglasses.* [Option: Put on sunglasses.]

• *What do you think you will do this summer?*

Name

3 Have the children finish coloring the picture on page 156.

SHARING [B]

4 SCRIPTURE PRAYER Lead the children in a prayer to thank God for the summer, reading the adaptation of Psalm 57:10–11 from the Scripture card in the Bible.

• *Let's thank God for giving us summer. I'll say part of a prayer from the Bible, and you repeat what I say.*

I will give thanks to you, O Lord. [Repeat.]

I will sing your praise before the world. [Repeat.]

For your kindness is as high as the sky. [Repeat.]

• *Let's pray that again, and this time when we say "as high as the sky," let's stretch our arms toward the sky.* [Repeat the prayer.]

ACTING

1 Ask the children what they learned in preschool. Show pictures, cutouts, and crafts to jog their memories.

2 Give each child the certificate from page 157 for completing the preschool course. Congratulate them for their hard work during the year.

3 Remind the children to thank God when they are having a good time during the summer or when they see something beautiful that God made.

4 Remind the children to thank God when they learn something new. Also remind the children and their families that they can refer to the Family Activity Booklet to recall the activities and songs they learned during the year.

Finish coloring the picture.

156 God Made the World

Family Time

Special Lesson 12:
Last Class/Summer

In this lesson the children talked about the coming summer activities. They also recalled what they have learned in preschool. Ask your child to show you the certificate he or she received. Congratulate your child and display the certificate.

Your Child
During the summer, bring out some of the cards and crafts from this preschool program and review with your child what he or she learned. Do several of the finger plays and songs from the Family Activity Booklet.

Reflect
I will give thanks to you, O Lord. I will sing your praise before the world. For your kindness is as high as the sky.
(adapted from Psalm 57:10–11)

Pray
God, may we praise you with joy forever.

Do
• Continue to pray spontaneously with your child during the summer as you enjoy beautiful times together.
• Plan family activities, such as picnics, games, or attending local festivals and fairs.
• Keep a family scrapbook of the summer's activities.
• Have your family portrait taken.
• Read to your child *Summer* by Alice Low. Talk about some of the fun things you will do this summer. Pray for God's blessing on your family and on your summertime activities.

For more family resources, refer to the Family Activity Booklet and visit **www.loyolapress.com/preschool.**

© Loyola Press.

5 Gather the children in a circle for *Music 'n Motion* time. Play Track 18. Invite the children to do motions to the song along with you, using *Music 'n Motion* page T290.

Have the children take home their pages and show their family the Family Time section.

CHECKPOINT

- *Were the learning outcomes achieved?*
- *Do the children seem to be looking forward to the summer?*

ENRICHING THE FAITH EXPERIENCE

Use the following activities to enrich the lesson or to replace an activity with one that better meets the needs of your group.

1 Give each child a small gift to use during the summer, such as liquid for blowing bubbles, a ball, a sand toy, or a holy card as a reminder of God.

2 Ask the children what songs or games they liked best in preschool and have them sing or play them.

3 Invite the children to tell about plans their families have for the summer or what they have done in past summers.

This is to certify that

_____

has completed the *God Made the World* preschool program.

_____   _____
Catechist's Signature   Date

157 God Made the World   © LOYOLAPRESS.

Page 158 is blank.

Music ♪n Motion

Contents

Songs for Units 1–5

Songs for Special Seasons and Days

Tracks 1–5 and 16 are used with the *God Made Me* (Age 3) program.

From the earliest days of a child's life, there is music and movement. Even before birth, a child hears the mother's heartbeat varied by tempo and accompanied by a range of sounds. Gently rocking their newborn babe in their arms, parents instinctively sigh, hum, and sing. The infant seems to understand this music, and the music is magic! Toddlers continue to use music to soothe and calm, for fun and play, and for prayer. Gestures accompany favorite melodies as children twirl on tippy toes, bend and leap, responding to the mood and meaning of the music. As preschoolers, children remain rooted in rhythm, movement, and facial expression as the primary means of communication. Preschool children love to imitate, to mime, and to dance hand in hand with a partner. They light up at the sound of music.

Preschool children are eager to learn about God, but are not yet able to grasp the abstract concepts of faith. For them, the gifts of music and dance can help communicate the fullness of faith. By placing their hand over their heart and singing "I've got peace in my heart," children sense that peace finds a home deep within. As they extend their hand and bow toward a classmate, they learn that peace is meant to be shared, joy is to be celebrated, and the love within us is to be given to others. Reaching arms high as they praise God in song, children discover that it takes energy to pray, and they also learn that prayer energizes their spirits. Singing with folded hands and heads bowed, children express reverence. Even if unable to offer a definition, they intuit prayer's meaning through movement and music.

Through movement, children learn that peace is meant to be shared.

Exercise of the creative imagination lays the groundwork for development of the religious imagination. These aesthetic elements—movement, music, and drama—promote empathy, solidarity, courage, and kindness as they enhance prayer. As catechists lead children in prayer, using music and movement, children can see the joy of the Lord on their catechist's face as they hear it in the catechist's voice. Music and movement, dance and drama are precious jewels in the treasure chest of every catechist, providing a means of communication that is deep, spiritual, memorable, and fun.

For the glory of God and the edification of his little ones,

Nancy Seitz Marcheschi

Come Together
by Michael Mangan

TRACK 6 | Use with Unit 1

Come together, let's celebrate. Sing a joyful song.

We are part of one family,

and God's love for us is so strong.

[Join hands with people standing on either side of you.]

[Gently swing joined hands forward and back.]

[Swing joined hands high above head.]

Verse 1:

Baptized we are called, (clap, clap)

as children of the Lord (clap, clap)

gathering here to worship and adore. (clap, clap, clap, clap, clap, clap)

[Clap hands over head.]

[Clap hands over head.]

[Lower hands, bring together, folded in prayer. Bow head, then lift head. Clap four times quickly, then two times.]

Verse 2:

Calling us by name, (clap, clap)

[Clap hands over head.]

diff'rent yet the same (clap, clap)

[Lower hands and clap hands.]

gathering here to praise God's holy name. (clap, clap, clap, clap, clap, clap)

[Slowly raise arms and look up. Clap four times quickly, then two times.]

Verse 3:

Blest with such great things, (clap, clap)

[Clap hands over head.]

we come to praise and sing (clap, clap)

[Clap hands over head.]

gathering here with thanks for what God brings. (clap, clap, clap, clap, clap, clap)

[Lower hands, bring together, folded in prayer. Bow head, then lift head. Clap four times quickly, then two times.]

Stand Up! By Michael Mangan

TRACK 7 | Use with Unit 2

Oh

[Place hands on bent knees.]

stand up!

[Straighten knees and stand tall, hands at sides.]

And sing to God.

[Reach hands out.]

Oh

[Place hands on bent knees.]

stand up!

[Straighten knees and stand tall, hands at sides.]

And praise God's name.

[Raise arms. Look up.]

Come on

[Place hands on bent knees.]

stand up!

[Straighten knees and stand tall, hands at sides.]

Stand up and sing praise to God.

[Slowly reach arms to sides and raise hands with palms up, elbows bent. Clap three times.]

Oh

[Place hands on bent knees.]

stand up!

[Straighten knees and stand tall, hands at sides.]

The final refrain repeats two times.

Windy Days by Jack Miffleton

TRACK 8 | Use with Unit 3

Invite the children to imagine they are outside. As you teach this song, encourage them to look and see with the eyes of the imagination, to hear with the ears of the imagination, to feel and smell, taste and even touch, all the while using the gift of their imagination.

Verse 1:

On windy days we sing God's praise, and we let the Spirit blow, blow,
and we let the Spirit blow. we let the Spirit blow.
Clouds roll by, kites fly high,

[Reach hands up high overhead. Feel the wind gently pushing and pulling you around. (Catechist models are changing direction every six beats.) Bend from side to side, back and forth, and twirl around.]

Verse 2:

On rainy days we sing God's praise, and we let the Spirit blow, blow,
and we let the Spirit blow. we let the Spirit blow.
Rivers flow, wheat fields grow,

[Open your hands and feel the rain wetting your palms. Turn your face up to the sky and feel the drops gently falling on your face. Open your mouth and take a little drink. Jump over the puddle in front of you.]

Verse 3:

On stormy days we sing God's praise,
and we let the Spirit blow.
Thunder shouts, lights go out,

and we let the Spirit blow, blow,
we let the Spirit blow.

[Hold your umbrella tightly. Try to walk home in the pouring rain. Uh-oh, thunder! Thank goodness you made it home! Hurry. Get in the door. Shake off the rain. But look! All the lights are out! Reach out your arms in front of you so you won't run into anything.]

Verse 4:

On sunny days we sing God's praise,
and we let the Spirit blow.
Robins sing, children swing,

and we let the Spirit blow, blow,
we let the Spirit blow.

[Look around and see how beautiful everything looks in the sunlight. Skip to the music. Imitate the robin spreading its wings and looking for worms. Take your partner's hands and dance.]

Praise and Glorify by Julie Howard

TRACK 9 | Use with Unit 4

Bless our God, all creation!

[Lean to left and clap hands, lean to right and clap hands, continuing back and forth to beat.]

Praise and glorify!

[Palms up, hands apart, then lower arms slightly, then raise arms straight up high.]

Bless our God, every nation!

[Lean to left and clap hands, lean to right and clap hands, continuing back and forth to beat.]

Praise and glorify!

[Palms up, hands apart, then lower arms slightly, then raise arms straight up high.]

Bless our God, sun and moon!

[Lean to left and clap hands, lean to right and clap hands, continuing back and forth to beat.]

Praise and glorify!

[Palms up, hands apart, then lower arms slightly, then raise arms straight up high.]

Bless our God, rain and dew!
Praise and glorify!
Bless our God, frost and cold!
Praise and glorify!
Bless our God, ice and snow!
Praise and glorify!
Bless our God, day and night!
Praise and glorify!
Bless our God, stars so bright!
Praise and glorify!

Bless our God, fish and fowl!
Praise and glorify!
Bless our God, stream and hollow!
Praise and glorify!
Bless our God, hills and mountains!
Praise and glorify!
Bless our God, rocks and fountains!
Praise and glorify!

Bless our God, oh bless our God.

[Lean to left and clap hands, lean to right and clap hands, continuing back and forth to beat.]

Bless our God, oh bless our God.

[Lower hands and arms.]

These two lines repeat as a background refrain while additional lyrics are sung.

Cats and dogs, snakes and frogs. Flowers and trees, birds and bees.

Snails and crabs, moms and dads. Earth and sky, you and I . . .

Care for Life by Michael Mangan

TRACK 10 | Use with Unit 5

Invite the children to imagine they are looking out at the whole beautiful world that God has made.

Care for all of God's creation.

[Reach right hand across body to left, then sweep it forward, then around to right.]

Care for ev'ry living thing.

[Reach left hand across body to right, then sweep it forward, then around to left.]

Care for the treasure we've been given.

[Reach right hand across body to left, then sweep it forward, then around to right.]

Care for life.

[Reach both hands forward, then sweep them out to sides, then lower slowly.]

Verse 1:

Hear the humpback singing from the sea
with a message for you and for me:
the dolphins and the coral reef,

the fishes in the ocean deep,
they won't survive unless we hear their
plea to . . .

[Make a triangle out of your hands and arms with elbows bent. Imagine you are a huge humpback whale . . . a playful dolphin. Move your arms/hands up and down and from side to side, while bending your body in different directions. Imagine jumping out of the water and back in again.]

Verse 2:

An eagle in a clear blue sky
soars above a mountain high
the dancing streams and forest trees,

so much life depends on these
we'll be sorry if we do not try to . . .

[Imagine you are an eagle. Stretch out your arms and raise them slowly up and down, bending your body from side to side. Look down at the earth from high in the sky. What do you see?]

Verse 3:

We must gather side by side.
People of the earth unite,
our sisters and brothers,

our fathers and our mothers,
the time has come now,
we must decide to . . .

[Take the hand of the person next to you. Gently swing your hands back and forth while you sing.]

Songs for
Special Seasons and Days

When the Saints Go Marching In

TRACK 11 | Use with Halloween/Feast of All Saints

Have the children take turns being the leader of the procession of saints (in Dixieland style).

March in place during the instrumental parts of the song.

Verse 1:

Oh, when the saints go marching in.
Oh, when the saints go marching in.

Oh, Lord, I want to be in that number
when the saints go marching in.

[Bend from side to side while you march to the beat. Shake "jazz hands" and reach arms from shoulder height.]

Verse 2:

And when the stars refuse to shine.
And when the stars refuse to shine.

Oh, Lord, I want to be in that number
when the stars refuse to shine.

[Alternate reaching arms straight up high over head while shaking "jazz hands."]

Verse 3:

Oh, when I hear that trumpet sound.
Oh, when I hear that trumpet sound.

Oh, Lord, I want to be in that number
when I hear that trumpet sound.

[Imagine you are playing a trumpet. Continue to step to the beat while moving the trumpet up and down and from side to side.]

Repeat verse 1:

Choose any instrument you wish to play . . . a clarinet, a saxophone, a flute, a guitar, or a drum. Pantomime playing your instrument while you step to the beat in the procession.

No Place to Stay

TRACK 12 | Use with Christmas

Clop, clop, clop went the
donkey's feet.
Clop, clop clop down the
stony street.

Nod, nod, nod went Mary's
head.

Nod, nod, nod she needed a
bed.

[Stomp right foot, then left,
then right.]

[Drop head, lower, then lower
again.]

[Yawn, then lean head on
folded hands.]

Knock, knock, knock went
Joseph at the door.

Knock, knock, knock is there
room for more?

No, no, no the innkeeper said.

[Pretend to knock on a door.]

[Pretend to knock on a door,
then open hands and reach
forward.]

[Shake head from side to side.]

No Place to Stay, music by Mary Beth Kunde Anderson
Music copyright © 2008, World Library Publications. www.wlpmusic.com

No, no, no not even one bed.

[Shake head from side to side, then hold up index finger.]

Wait, wait, wait the innkeeper said.

[Flex both hands, with palms facing out.]

Wait, wait, wait use my stable instead.

[Flex both hands, with palms facing out. Then point or thumb behind you.]

Sh, sh, sh what do I hear?
Sh, sh, sh Baby Jesus so dear!

[Place right index finger over lips.]

Oh, oh, oh what do I see?

[Imagine seeing Baby Jesus in the manger. Kneel down on left knee.]

Oh, oh, oh Jesus born for me!

[Kneel on both knees, fold hands, then bow head and body.]

Easter Alleluia by Michael Mangan

TRACK 13 | Use with Easter

Alleluia! He is risen!

[Reach right arm across body, then make an arc up high and bring back to right.]

Alleluia! He's alive!

[Reach left arm across body, then make an arc up high and bring back to left.]

Alleluia! Sing for joy now.

[Reach right arm across body, then make an arc up high and bring back to right.]

Jesus is alive!

[Place hands on heart, then reach arms forward.]

Verse 1:
Open up your hearts. See the empty tomb.

[Place hands over heart.]

Though he died on Calvary,

[Bow head reverently.]

Jesus is alive!

[Raise head, then reach arms forward.]

Verse 2:

Sing your songs of joy. Lift your voices high.

[Tilt head and body side to side on beat.]

His glory fills the earth.

[Reach both hands forward, then smoothly move them to sides.]

Jesus is alive!

[Raise head, then reach arms forward.]

Verse 3:

Go and tell the world. Go and sing Good News.

[Cup hands around mouth. Lean to right, then lean to left.]

Spread this message everywhere,

[Reach both hands forward, then smoothly move them to sides.]

"Jesus is alive!"

[Raise head, then reach arms forward.]

The final refrain repeats two times.

Thank You, Jesus by Mary Ann Renna

TRACK 14 | Use with Thanksgiving

Thank you, Jesus, thank you,
Jesus, thank you, Jesus.
Thank you, Jesus, thank you,
Jesus, thank you, Jesus.

[Tilt head from side to side
and clap on beat.]

Verse 1:

I thank you, Jesus, for my
hands

[Shake "jazz hands."]

'cause I can shake them as fast
as I can.

[Shake "jazz hands" twice,
then shake as fast as possible.]

And thank you for my fingers,
too,

[Wiggle fingers to beat.]

'cause I can wave right back
at you.

[Alternate waving hands, right
and left, to beat.]

Verse 2:

Thank you, Jesus, for my eyes
'cause I can close them shut or
open wide.

[Open eyes wide, close eyes,
then open wide again.]

And thank you for my elbows, too,

[Lift arms with bent elbows pointing to sides.]

because I like the way they move.

[Alternate lifting elbows, right and left, to beat.]

Verse 3:
Thank you, Jesus, for my hips 'cause I can move from side to side like this.

[Put hands on hips, then wiggle hips from side to side.]

And thank you for my legs so strong

[Lift right leg, then left leg, alternating to beat.]

'cause I can run and jump along.

[Run in place, then jump in place.]

The final refrain repeats two times.

God Is Love
by James V. Marchionda, O.P.

TRACK 15 | Use with Valentine's Day

God is love. God is love.
The living God is love.
And when we live in love,
we live in God and God lives in us.

Verse 1:
Our God has loved us so.
Now we can love each other.
And in the love we share,
our God will be made known.

[Form a large circle. Join hands with the people next to you. When the song begins, walk slowly counterclockwise in the circle. As the refrain ends, turn to your partner standing next to you.]

Verse 2:
The way we live in God
is through the Holy Spirit.
And we know this is true,
because of Jesus Christ.

Verse 3:
All people who know Christ
have God alive within them.
And we have come to trust
the love God has for us.

[Take your partner's hands and walk slowly in place, making your own little circle. When the refrain begins again, return to the large circle and begin walking counterclockwise.]

Happy Birthday! It's Your Day

TRACK 17 | Use with Birthdays

Happy Birthday, it's your day.
We're so glad you're five today.

[Join hands and form a large circle around the "birthday child," who is seated in a chair in the middle of the circle. All sing while walking counterclockwise in the circle.]

God made you, so stand up now.

[Children in the circle stop walking and stand still.]

Turn around and take a bow.

[Birthday child stands, turns in place, and then bows.]

God is Great by Michael Mangan

TRACK 18 | Use with Last Class/Summer

Verse 1:

Clap your hands.

[Clap hands three times.]

Sing "Jubilee!" ("Jubilee!")

[Reach arms forward.]

This is a time to celebrate.

[Twist hands at wrists.]

Clap your hands.

[Clap hands three times.]

Sing "Jubilee!" ("Jubilee!")

[Reach arms forward.]

God is good and God is great!
(God is good and God is great!)

[Raise arms slowly, looking up.
Then bring arms down slowly
and fold hands in prayer.]

Verse 2:

Stamp your feet.

[Stamp feet three times.]

Sing "Jubilee!" ("Jubilee!")

[Reach arms forward.]

This is a time to celebrate.

[Twist hands at wrists.]

Stamp your feet.

[Stamp feet three times.]

Sing "Jubilee!" ("Jubilee!")

[Reach arms forward.]

God is good and God is great!
(God is good and God is great!)

[Raise arms slowly, looking up.
Then bring arms down slowly
and fold hands in prayer.]

Verse 3:

Pat your knees.

[Pat right knee, then left, then right.]

Sing "Jubilee!" ("Jubilee!")

[Reach arms forward.]

This is a time to celebrate.

[Twist hands at wrists.]

Pat your knees.

[Pat right knee, then left, then right.]

Sing "Jubilee!" ("Jubilee!")

[Reach arms forward.]

God is good and God is great! (God is good and God is great!)

[Raise arms slowly, looking up. Then bring arms down slowly and fold hands in prayer.]

Verse 4:

Click your tongue.

[Click tongue three times.]

Sing "Jubilee!" ("Jubilee!")

[Reach arms forward.]

This is a time to celebrate.

[Twist hands at wrists.]

Click your tongue.

[Click tongue three times.]

Sing "Jubilee!" ("Jubilee!")

[Reach arms forward.]

God is good and God is great! (God is good and God is great!)

[Raise arms slowly, looking up. Then bring arms down slowly and fold hands in prayer.]

Verse 5:

Shout "Hip hooray!"
("Hip hooray!")

[Bend knees, then straighten
knees, and raise hands high.]

Sing "Jubilee!" ("Jubilee!")

[Reach arms forward.]

This is a time to celebrate.

[Twist hands at wrists.]

Shout "Hip hooray!"
("Hip hooray!")

[Bend knees, then straighten,
and raise hands high.]

Sing "Jubilee!" ("Jubilee!")

[Reach arms forward.]

God is good and God is great!
(God is good and God is great!
Yeah!)

[Raise arms slowly, looking
up. Then bring arms down
slowly, then slowly raise arms.
On final beat, reach arms even
higher.]

Sharing the Good News

Effective catechists are people who live their faith and share the Good News of Jesus with others, inviting them to develop and deepen their relationship with Christ. Catechists attend to their own faith and spiritual growth. In addition, catechists seek to increase their knowledge and skills in a variety of areas.

Effective catechists are

- sensitive to the developmental characteristics of those they will teach.

- aware of the process of faith and spiritual growth.

- knowledgeable about the role of the catechist in faith formation.

- grounded in the Church's faith tradition, including the *Catechism of the Catholic Church.*

- familiar with a variety of effective teaching methods, tools, and techniques.

This Catechist's Handbook provides essential information to help catechists craft their lessons with confidence and skill.

Four-year-olds . . .
• are energetic • like to make choices • are self-confident • are full of wonder

Physical Characteristics
- have developed large muscle control; can hop and gallop; a few can skip; are prone to hit and kick
- are developing small muscle control; are interested in materials that can be manipulated
- are full of energy; are incapable of sitting still for any length of time unless highly motivated
- have a short attention span
- are developing a sense of rhythm

Socioemotional Characteristics
- test their "world" and themselves against peers and siblings
- are nearly self-dependent in routines; focus on tasks with little interaction with others
- are brashly self-confident in their abilities
- need help to handle feelings and relate to others; can be aggressive and short-tempered
- like to make choices; resist regulations that limit freedom but begin to see the wisdom of rules
- are still self-centered but may share with a friend; like group work, games, and parties
- are becoming less sensitive, vulnerable, and demanding
- are sensitive to the feelings and attitudes of adults; can show sympathy; appreciate humor

Intellectual Characteristics
- wonder about everything; desire to learn more
- understand analogies; are imaginative and creative; like silliness, rhyming, and long words
- have fluent expression through play
- have animistic and anthropomorphic views
- draw symbolically; pictures have meaning for them; ideas are conveyed through color and design
- are intuitive

Religious Characteristics
- begin to understand God's love by experiencing human love
- need to see that God made them and every other child unique and special
- need to experience success
- want to do kind things for others and like to be recognized for doing them
- experience awe and wonder at creation and at their own powers
- are meditative, naturally contemplative, and prayerful; can be absorbed in ritual, song, and drama
- are hindered by viewing God as a means of correction
- observe how adults handle religious matters

Faith

God Made the World was designed for four-year-old children, recognizing that young children possess the gift of faith from Baptism and, therefore, have an innate readiness for religion. It engages them in experiences that prepare them to hear God's message and helps them respond to it in their lives. Through the *God Made the World* program, children come to see the religious dimension of their everyday lives and realize that life and religion are an integrated whole. They are also initiated into Catholic traditions and prepared for a life within the Christian community.

God is presented to the children as the good God who made them and the world. They learn that the Bible is a holy book in which God tells us "I love you" and are introduced to stories of faith from the Bible. The program helps children see Jesus as a friend who wants them to be happy. They learn a little about his life on earth with Mary, his mother; Joseph, his foster father; and his friends. They learn that Jesus died and rose from the dead.

Prayer

An ultimate purpose of catechesis is to enable the children to sense God's loving presence, to encounter him, and to enter into communion with him. In the *God Made the World* program, the children learn how to be silent and are introduced to the traditional prayer posture of kneeling with hands folded. They take part in a variety of prayer experiences to help them respond to God, including

- vocal prayer.
- spontaneous prayer.
- dance prayer.
- psalm responses.
- litanies.
- silent prayer of the heart.
- song.
- celebrations.

Liturgical Life

The *God Made the World* program initiates children into the liturgy by

- familiarizing them with the church building and sacred objects.
- introducing the use of symbols, gestures, music, and rituals.
- teaching them that they may ask for and receive forgiveness.

- leading them to express gratitude.
- giving them an appreciation of silence, which they use to enter within themselves.
- leading them to participate in celebrations.
- encouraging them to share food with others.
- helping them experience a sense of mystery and of the sacred.
- teaching them reverent church behavior.
- introducing them to the special seasons and feasts of the liturgical year. For reference, a calendar showing the seasons of the Church year is found on page T193.

Morality

The preschool years are a crucial time for building attitudes and dispositions upon which a good Christian moral life can develop. The foundation for good decision making is also laid in a child's early years. The *God Made the World* program also fosters the awakening of a Christian conscience in the children by leading them to

- appreciate God's goodness and personal love for them.
- sense that they are loved by the important people in their lives.
- know how to express sorrow by saying "I'm sorry."
- respect all people and all forms of life.
- value God's world and care for it.
- develop self-discipline and form good habits.
- sense solidarity with people everywhere.
- desire to share with those in need.

Social Justice and Service

In the *God Made the World* program, the children engage in activities that nurture kindness, honesty, forgiveness, and concern for others. Some of these activities are

- discussing and role-playing how kindness, forgiveness, and concern for others can be shown in their everyday lives.
- listening to stories of saints who have shown concern for others and for God's world.
- engaging in music and art activities that promote a spirit of sharing and caring for others.

The effectiveness of religious instruction is closely tied to the personal witness given by the teacher; this witness is what brings the content of the lessons to life. . . . A teacher who has a clear vision of the Christian milieu and lives in accord with it will be able to help young people develop a similar vision, and will give them the inspiration they need to put it into practice.

Congregation for Catholic Education,
The Religious Dimension of Education in a Catholic School, 96 (April 7, 1988)

Spiritual and Professional Growth as a Catechist

The *National Directory for Catechesis* names six tasks in catechesis:

- to promote knowledge of the faith
- to promote knowledge of the meaning of the Liturgy and the sacraments
- to promote moral formation in Christ
- to teach the Christian how to pray with Christ
- to prepare the Christian to live in community and to participate actively in the life and mission of the Church
- to promote a missionary spirit that prepares the faithful to be present as Christians in society (*NDC,* 20)

In accomplishing this sixfold task, catechists are aided by the Holy Spirit. However, to reflect effectively the teaching and the life of Jesus in their words and behavior, catechists need to grow continually in their faith. They should

- know and study further the teaching of the Church's Magisterium through lectures, courses, and Catholic publications.
- become imbued with the thought and spirit of the Bible through prayerful reflection.
- have a profound spirit of prayer and a deep sacramental life, for only union with Christ gives the light and strength needed for authentic catechesis.
- give service to others and encourage the children to serve.
- become more aware of the missionary nature of the Church and educate the children in global problems and needs.
- become better trained for the task of catechizing by always seeking better methods.

Ways to Build a Faith Community as a Catechist

- Communicate with parents and value their primary role in their children's faith formation.
- Share goals, values, projects, and ideas with fellow catechists and parish leaders.
- Be familiar with guidelines for parish and diocesan catechetical programs.
- Cooperate with others in making the parish a focal point of the community, especially in grade-level planning and projects.
- Participate in meetings and prayer services for catechists.
- Seek out opportunities for spiritual enrichment.
- Accept the strengths and weaknesses of the faith community and strive together to witness the Gospel.

A Catechist Is

confident, but dependent on God.

knowledgeable, but open to children's ideas.

efficient, but relaxed.

spiritual, but practical.

professional, but caring.

enthusiastic, but calm.

Professional Ethics for Catechists

- Keep comments about the children and their families on a professional level.
- Use information about the children and their families prudently and discreetly. Observe professional confidentiality.
- Hold conferences with or about the children at appropriate times and places.
- Inform the coordinator, a priest, or other appropriate person when you discern unusual needs or problems of the children.
- Strive to make your daily living reflect your faith.
- Prepare thoroughly for each lesson.

A Guide for Self-Improvement

As a catechist, you are a minister of the Word of God. Every child hopes to see and hear the kindness, the warmth, and the love of Jesus reflected in your facial expressions, your voice, and your very life. If you are receptive to God each day, if you take time to ponder his Word and deepen your relationship with God, if you are convinced of the power of the Gospel message, then the children will hear the Lord reveal the mystery of his love through you. You will discover that as you share your faith, you are personally enriched. Reflect on the following questions periodically to examine your effectiveness as a catechist and to determine areas for improvement:

- Do I present the message with the conviction, joy, love, enthusiasm, and hope that come from a commitment to Christ?
- Do I pray for light to understand what I am teaching and to know how to present God's Word persuasively?
- Do I reflect on Scripture as part of my preparation for each lesson?
- Do I have all materials ready before class time?
- Do I share my heart, my spirit, and my personal faith story as I convey the Christian message?
- Do I lead the children in prayer? Do I use a variety of prayer forms?
- How sensitive am I to the individual needs of the children?
- Have I communicated with the parents?
- Do I make an evaluation after each lesson and use it in future planning?
- Am I willing to spend time to promote my own growth in faith and understanding?

The *Catechism of the Catholic Church* is a marvelous tool for catechists. It provides information that can be useful in preparing lesson plans, and it also serves as a reference book. Each chapter in *God Made the World* includes references to paragraphs in the *Catechism* that are related to it.

Catechists are cautioned, however, that the *Catechism* is not intended to be used as a student textbook.

In addition to being a source of background material, the *Catechism* contains messages specifically for catechists. Paragraphs 426 through 429 are the centerpiece of what it says to us. They contain our mission statement, our goal, and our job description. The boldface title for this passage says it all—"At the heart of catechesis: Christ." Paragraph 426 states, "'At the heart of catechesis we find, in essence, a Person, the Person of Jesus of Nazareth, the only Son from the Father . . . who suffered and died for us and who now, after rising, is living with us forever.' To catechize is 'to reveal in the Person of Christ the whole of God's eternal design reaching fulfillment in that Person. It is to seek to understand the meaning of Christ's actions and words and of the signs worked by him.'" Only Christ "'can lead us to the love of the Father in the Spirit and make us share in the life of the Holy Trinity.'"

Our call is to bring people to the person of Jesus Christ, who lives and who is with us and who loves us. Religion class is a community of people who are journeying together, sharing faith in Jesus Christ, and growing in it. Religion class is a matter of formation—changing lives to be more Christlike. The room where it is held is sacred space, as holy as the catacombs where the first Christians gathered to deepen their relationship with Christ and their commitment to him.

We cannot give what we do not have. It was only after Paul encountered the risen Lord for himself that he was enflamed with a passion for teaching the world about him. The more we ourselves come to know Jesus Christ, the more zealous and convincing we will be in persuading others to live for him. The more we enter into the mystery of Christ's Death and Resurrection in our daily lives, the more we will be able to persuade others to live like him.

We can take heart that when we teach in the name of Jesus, he teaches through us, because we have been mandated and commissioned by him. Through his Spirit he is our invisible partner.

Seven essential messages from the *Catechism* are listed here, along with with their paragraph numbers for reading and reflection:

131–133	**Teach Scripture.** By reading it we learn "'the surpassing knowledge of Jesus Christ.'"
282	**Teach Creation.** It is of major importance because it concerns the very foundations of human and Christian life.
426–429	**Teach Christ.** Put people in communion with him.
1072	**Teach Liturgy.** In the sacraments, especially in the Eucharist, Christ Jesus works in fullness for our transformation.
1697	**Teach the Way of Christ.** Reveal the joy and the demands of the way of Christ.
1917	**Teach Hope.** "[T]he future of humanity is in the hands of those who are capable of providing the generations to come with reasons for life and optimism."
2663	**Teach Prayer.** Explain its meaning, always in relation to Jesus Christ.

Recent Church Documents for Catechesis

1979   *On Catechesis in Our Time* (Pope John Paul II)

1992   *Catechism of the Catholic Church*

1997   *General Directory for Catechesis*

2005   *National Directory for Catechesis*

2005   *Compendium of the Catechism of the Catholic Church*

2006   *United States Catholic Catechism for Adults*

Other Papal and Vatican Documents

1963   *Peace on Earth* (Pope John XXIII)

1963–1965   *Documents of the Second Vatican Council*

1987   *On Social Concern* (Pope John Paul II)

1991   *The Hundredth Year* (Pope John Paul II)

1991   *Dialogue and Proclamation* (Pontifical Council for Interreligious Dialogue and the Congregation for the Evangelization of Peoples)

1993   *The Splendor of Truth* (John Paul II)

1994   *Letter to Families* (Pope John Paul II)

1998   *Towards a Better Distribution of Land* (Pontifical Council for Justice and Peace)

1998   *The Day of the Lord* (Pope John Paul II)

1998   *The Dignity of Older People and Their Mission in the Church and in the World* (Pontifical Council for the Laity)

1999   *The Family and Human Rights* (Pontifical Council for the Family)

1999   *Memory and Reconciliation: The Church and the Faults of the Past* (International Theological Commission)

2001   *Directory on Popular Piety and the Liturgy* (Congregation for Divine Worship and the Discipline of the Sacraments)

2001   *The Jewish People and Their Sacred Scriptures in the Christian Bible* (Pontifical Biblical Commission)

2003   *The Eucharist in Its Relationship to the Church* (Pope John Paul II)

2006   *God Is Love* (Pope Benedict XVI)

2007   *On Christian Hope* (Pope Benedict XVI)

Other Documents of the United States Bishops

1991   *Putting Children and Families First: A Challenge for Our Church, Nation, and World*

1992   *Go and Make Disciples: A National Plan and Strategy for Catholic Evangelization in the United States*

1995   *Called and Gifted for the Third Millennium*

1998   *Sharing Catholic Social Teaching: Challenges and Directions*

1999   *Our Hearts Were Burning Within Us: A Pastoral Plan for Adult Faith Formation in the United States*

1999   *In All Things Charity: A Pastoral Challenge for the New Millennium*

2000   *Welcoming the Stranger Among Us: Unity in Diversity*

2001   *The Real Presence of Jesus Christ in the Sacrament of the Eucharist: Basic Questions and Answers*

2003   *General Instruction of the Roman Missal*

Most of these documents are available from www.usccb.org.

Prepare the Learning Space

- Divide the room into several areas.

  1. A free-play area supplied with picture books, wooden blocks, a carton of dress-up clothes, beads to string, toys, housekeeping materials, sand (or large kosher-size salt), cartons and large packing boxes, cereal boxes, shoe boxes, and cardboard cylinders

  2. An area where children may sit in a circle on a rug or carpet squares

  3. A large, clear space to play games and dance

  4. An activity area supplied with low tables and craft supplies, such as glue sticks, paints, scissors, crayons, and markers

Although the classroom setting is important, keep in mind that much can be done with little. The catechist's care, love, and acceptance far outweigh any benefits that the physical surroundings alone might offer.

- Arrange and decorate the room so that it is bright, interesting, and safe as well as aesthetically inviting and attractive.

- Keep the room neat and clean. Avoid a lot of distracting clutter. Reduce the noise level by hanging draperies, carpeting the floor, or using other sound-muffling devices.

- Arrange a prayer center with a cloth-covered table. Place there a Bible, a cross, flowers, and other items that might be suggested in the lesson. For more information about praying with the children, see Prayer on pages T297 and T314.

- Provide a special-interest table for displaying objects related to the lesson and for objects the children bring in.

- Post pictures related to the theme of the day at the eye level of the children.

- Designate a special table or space as a quiet place for children who need to calm down, deal with their emotions, or withdraw from the group for another reason. Never force a child to join the group.

- Display the work of all the children. If there is no bulletin board, string a line across the room and hang up the children's work with clip clothespins.

- Note whether there is adequate light, heat, and ventilation in the room.

- Have recorded music playing as the children enter each day.

- Imagine how the children will move about in the room. Plan where they will carry on activities, keep their belongings, and eat their snacks.

Recruit Helpers

- Arrange for teacher assistants, parents, and grandparents to help with lessons. Young children need individual attention. Two adults or older helpers should be in the room for all classes, not only to help with the activities but to also take charge if there is an emergency and you must leave the room. Send a volunteer chart to parents before the preschool classes begin or ask them to sign up during a parent-catechist meeting.

Gather Supplies

- Use simple containers for supplies and keep them in the same place so that the children know where they belong. You might keep supplies on a cart and wheel it to the work area when needed.

- Make sure that scissors have blunt ends and that they work easily. A drop of oil fixes scissors that are difficult to use. Teach the children to carry scissors with the blunt ends down. Provide left-handed scissors and mark them as such.

- Put petroleum jelly on the threads of paint jars so that the lids come off easily.

- Keep newspapers on hand to protect surfaces during art activities.

- Keep magazines in the room to place under the lesson pages if the children use crayons and pencils on a carpeted floor.

- Have equipment for cleaning up after art activities and snacks: pails or dishpans, paper towels, soap, large sponges, mop, broom, and dustpan.

Plan for the Year

- If you wish, tear out the pages of the Child's Book and sort them for the children according to lesson, keeping together the pages for each chapter, including the lesson page, activity page, and story booklet if there is one. Fold a sheet of paper around the top of each set of pages or insert a divider to separate them. Store the pages in a file, a desk drawer, or a carton until needed.

- Separate the cutouts and the Scripture cards in the back of this manual and store them in an envelope or file.

- Obtain the Spanish translations of the Family Time (Tiempo en familia) sections of the Child's Book and have them ready to photocopy for parents who may benefit from them. Visit www.loyolapress.com/preschool.

- Return to this Catechist's Handbook throughout the year, especially as you evaluate your lessons.

- Decide which lessons you will teach and fill in the chart on page OV-12.

Prepare the Lesson

- Plan and prepare well. Prayerfully read the Faith Focus and the Preparing the Faith Experience sections for the lesson. Consider using a journal to record your responses.

- Arrive for the lesson at least a half hour before the children arrive.

- Have everything set up for the lesson ahead of time, including materials for free play.

- Cut out the items on the activity pages as required to save class time and especially if the children have difficulty using scissors.

- Write the children's names on the appropriate Child's Book pages.

- Hand out name tags as long as you need them.

- Find out whether any child is celebrating a birthday during the week and if so, plan to celebrate in class. Seat the child in a specially decorated birthday chair and have the group sing "Happy Birthday." You may wish to establish additional birthday traditions, such as displaying a birthday banner or having the child wear a birthday crown.

Establish a Climate for Growth

- Address the children by name. Be sure to pronounce and spell their names correctly.

- Make the lesson a joyful experience for the children. Be warm and encouraging. Smile often.

- Be calm in your manner, reverent in your gestures, and joyful in your presentation.

- Demonstrate respectful behavior.

- Speak in a well-modulated voice, loud enough for everyone to hear you but soft enough to convey the wonder of the message you share.

- Be animated. Children will catch your enthusiasm.

- Ask the children about their families and interests.

- Listen to what the children are saying verbally and nonverbally. Be eager to understand their fears, worries, plans, stories—even their complaints.

- Express confidence in the children.

- Give words of encouragement for the children's efforts. Avoid giving too much or insincere praise for the end product. For young children, process is more important than product.

- Seek to provide the children with a sense of security. Reassure them of your care and acceptance with hugs and pats on the head. Avoid favoritism.

- Convey happiness to the children by your words and your tone of voice.

- Use frequent eye contact so each child feels you are speaking personally to him or her.

- Play music as the children work.

- See the children as individuals. Try not to generalize, but see each child as gifted by God. Make allowances for individual circumstances.

- Love your work. Teaching is hard work, but it is also a privilege. Show the children that you like teaching because you like them. Even more importantly, love your work as a person who shares the work of Jesus the Teacher.

Maintain a Healthy Classroom Discipline

- Establish routines at the beginning of the year.

- Establish a few simple classroom ground rules and review them with the children at the start of each class until they know the rules well. Word the rules positively. For example, state the rule "We always walk in this room" rather than "Don't run in this room." When someone doesn't follow a rule, ask the child to recall it and repeat it.

- Determine a signal to get the children's attention for a change of activity. This can be having a child ring a bell, whispering a phrase, or clapping one's hands to a specific rhythm.

- Do not expect all the children to participate in all group activities. Allow them the freedom to wander in and out of the group at will if necessary.

- Use special techniques if you want only a small number of children in the group to move at one time to form a line or to come to the front of the room. For example, have those who are wearing red clothing go first, those wearing blue go second, and so forth. You might sing or call children's names.

- Stress the positive by commenting on good behavior.

- Be observant while you are teaching.

- Expect good behavior. Don't tolerate misbehavior.

- When a problem arises, use a pleasant but firm tone of voice. In order to win over the child or children involved, keep calm and avoid becoming angry.

- Avoid letting one child prevent others from learning and cooperating. Suggest an alternative activity if a child's behavior is inappropriate.

- Plan for handling and putting away materials.

- Warn the children a few minutes ahead of time when an activity is drawing to a close so that they can finish the task.

- Show the children where the restroom is located. If it is outside the classroom, have a specific time for the group to go together.

- Pray for the children.

Teaching Tips

- Have the children sit in a circle on the floor.

- Include as many of the children as you can in the activities and discussions.

- Allow sufficient thinking time for children when they are responding to a question.

- Some unplanned experiences present opportunities for teaching a lesson. Take advantage of them.

- When the children are restless, adapt your plan.

- Let the children use pencils instead of crayons or markers on the Child's Book pages when appropriate.

- Repetition is important for children. Do not be afraid to repeat activities.

- Remember that young children learn through play and hands-on activities.

Prepare for Arts and Crafts

- Have the children sit at low tables for craft activities. If your room has no tables, children may work on the floor. For water and art activities, cover the carpet with a plastic tablecloth.

- Set rules about splashing paints, dropping clay, and washing hands.

- Encourage creativity and allow for choices.

- Provide smocks, aprons, or old shirts for the children to wear when they are painting. Cover the work area with newspapers.

- For a gluing activity, tell the children to apply glue to the area to be covered and then place the object on that area. Demonstrate that a small amount of glue is sufficient. Glue sticks are easier for the children to control than liquid glue.

- Give concise, simple directions, one step at a time.

- Prepare a model of the craft for the children if it will not hinder their creativity.

- In commenting on a child's work, do not ask "What is it?" Instead say "Tell me about your picture."

- Give children specific directions for cleanup. Make it every child's responsibility.

- Remedy mistakes and accidents as inconspicuously as possible. Use a blow dryer if necessary to dry paint before the children are dismissed.

- Send potentially messy projects home in paper bags or rolled up and fastened with a rubber band.

- Recipes for homemade materials for arts and crafts are provided beginning on page T325.

Plan for Physical Activities and Games

- Balance physical activities with quiet activities. Young children love action poems, finger plays, dancing, games, and physical exercises. Moreover, they cannot sit still longer than five minutes.

- Play games in which no child loses or is out. Young children have difficulty with losing games.

- Join in the children's games.

Prepare for Snacks

- Provide or have parents provide nutritious snacks for the lesson. Be aware of and communicate to others any food restrictions or allergies.

- Set up the snacks on trays ahead of time, with portions for each child.

- Begin the snack period with a prayer of thanks. A meal prayer is taught on page T76.

- Encourage the children to keep their cups in the center of the table to avoid spills.

- Let the children assist in preparing and distributing snacks and in the cleanup.

Each person is created in God's image, yet there are variations in individual abilities. Positive recognition of these differences discourages discrimination and enchances the unity of the Body of Christ.

Statement of the U.S. Bishops: Welcome and Justice
for Persons with Disabilities (1998)

By choosing a variety of teaching techniques, catechists make use of the strengths of children's various learning styles and also attend to the needs of exceptional children. These children can include both those with some form of learning difficulty, as well as those who are considered gifted. Efforts made in this area enhance the learning experience for all children.

Use of Scripture Stories

- Tell some stories as an eyewitness, using direct address. Be dramatic.

- Use the Bible and pictures during storytelling.

- After the story is read, have the children dramatize it, perhaps by using pantomime.

Use of Music and Gesture

- Provide silent, reflective time to draw the children into a sense of the sacred.

- Play peaceful, calming music to help the children quiet themselves for prayer.

- Engage the children with echo-type songs and prayers. Use songs with direct, simple messages about the faith to help the children retain the basic truths. Suggested songs are found on the CD. For a list of additional music, see page T320.

- Use simple gestures for refrains to promote the children's participation. Use *Music 'n Motion* beginning on page T265 to incorporate gestures and music into the lessons.

Questioning Techniques

- State questions in their entirety, and then break them down into basic components.

- Use simple questions to increase group participation, for example, use repeat-after-me questions or statements or use simple completion questions.

- Ask questions immediately following what was taught.

- Use critical-thinking questions for those children who can handle them.

Physical Impairment

- Adapt your teaching to fit the needs of the child with a physical disability, using individualized instruction.

- Use devices or a buddy system to help the child with materials and group activities.

- If a child has symptoms that at times might be disruptive, be prepared to address the situation in a way that will minimize embarrassment to the child.

- Encourage social interaction through verbal activities and other opportunities.

Visual Impairment

- Consider range of vision and lighting needs when seating the child.

- Permit the child to move for closer views of charts or demonstrations.

- Provide large-print books, audio materials, and materials he or she can touch.

- Plan lessons that involve other senses besides sight.

- Assign a partner for visual activities.

- Keep the learning area clear of hazards.

Hearing Impairment

- Face the child when you talk to him or her.
- Seat the child near the front of the room or close to audio equipment.
- Seat a child who has a hearing loss in one ear so that the impaired ear is toward the wall.
- Avoid standing where glare from light might inhibit the child's ability to read your lips.
- Speak clearly, using a normal tone and pace.
- Reword directions often. Some sounds are heard better than others.
- Encourage verbal interaction.
- Make arrangements for a sign-language interpreter to work with you as needed.

Speech Impairment

- Speak distinctly and in short phrases.
- Use visual as well as oral instruction.
- Work individually in a separate area with the child whose oral work needs attention.
- Allow extra time for the child to respond to your questions and comments.

Handling Social and Behavioral Problems

- Arrange the room to minimize distractions. Carpeting, sound-absorbing materials, and room dividers can help.
- Structure the schedule to avoid last-minute changes and to allow mastery of content within the child's attention span.
- Help the child develop routines.
- Prepare change-of-pace activities between learning periods and give the child opportunities to move about the room.
- Give specific tasks that are interesting to the child.
- Plan stimulating activities for after—not before—periods of concentration.
- Explain the rationale for what the child is learning.
- Establish a plan of action for completing work.
- Reward the child for demonstrating self-control and responsibility and for completing a task in the appropriate length of time.
- Use strategies that provide immediate feedback, such as hand-raising and flash cards.

Learning Disabilities

- Provide routine and orderly procedures. Minimize distractions.

- Keep lessons short and varied, introduce skills one at a time, and review often. Allow extra time.

- Use books and materials with large print and a simple setup.

- Reinforce verbalized concepts with visual and kinesthetic cues.

- Set up situations in which the child will experience success. Frequently compliment the child on his or her strengths.

- Review and clarify directions.

- Ask questions often to assess the child's understanding of the lesson.

Mental Impairment

- Adjust class work to the child's attention span and level of coordination and skill.

- Individualize learning and use teacher aides.

- Simplify concepts, overteach in a concrete manner and with a variety of forms, and repeat periodically.

- Allow the children to assist one another as appropriate.

Giftedness

- Suggest independent study, small-group work, enrichment activities, and discovery learning that is related to the child's interests.

- Provide supplementary resources and direct the child to pursue more challenging topics.

- Capture the child's interest with puzzles and games.

- Ask the child to help with preparing materials and demonstrations and with teaching other children.

- Encourage high-level thinking skills and persistence in difficult learning.

From the beginning, this one Church has been marked by a great diversity which comes from both the variety of God's gifts and the diversity of those who receive them. Within the unity of the People of God, a multiplicity of peoples and cultures is gathered together. Among the Church's members, there are different gifts, offices, conditions, and ways of life.

Catechism of the Catholic Church, 814

Convinced of this truth, the Church urges its catechists to

- incorporate the cultures of the people in their catechesis.

- address the needs of various groups of people.

- respect and cherish the uniqueness of different groups.

- lead others to know and respect cultures different from their own.

The following suggestions can help catechists teach more effectively as they promote multicultural awareness and respect.

Responding to the Needs of Various Cultures

- Understand and be sensitive to both the home and the community of each child.

- Learn about the history, traditions, and values of the ethnic groups to which the children belong.

- Make sure that your teaching takes into account the life experiences of the children.

- Make the effort to have all written communications to parents or guardians translated into the language spoken at home.

- Be aware that there are subgroups within larger groups. For example, Spanish-speaking people come from Mexico, Puerto Rico, Cuba, and other countries. Each has a distinct culture. The same is true for people of Native American, African American, Asian, and other ancestries.

- Consider your group's special needs in relation to justice and peace. Prepare the children to assume responsibility for achievement of their goals.

- Become familiar with popular devotions unique to the ethnic groups that make up your class.

- Read books with positive reflections of multicultural diversity to the children.

Incorporating the Gifts of Various Cultures

- Encourage the children to share their customs and family celebrations with one another.

- Integrate cultural holidays and feasts, special events, and neighborhood celebrations into the life examples you use in your teaching.

- In liturgical and social celebrations, especially on important occasions, incorporate the language and symbols of the groups that make up your learning community.

- Encourage liturgical and social celebrations that express the spirit, history, and traditions of the cultural groups in your learning community.

Educating Children to Know and Respect Various Cultures

- Watch for unjust or stereotypical treatment of sexes, races, and cultures in the materials you use and in your own words as you teach. Raise the consciousness of those around you.

- Do not use racial, ethnic, or cultural nicknames or make jokes that label or stereotype.

- Be alert to ways of acknowledging contributions made by various cultural groups to the rich traditions of the Catholic Church.

- Share stories about saints from a variety of cultures and social conditions.

- Be understanding of the present struggle of various cultural groups in finding their place in U.S. society and in the Church.

Art

Throughout history, faith has been expressed in painting and sculpture. Art is a concrete expression of a person's thoughts and feelings. When children see their inner religious thoughts and feelings expressed visually, they can grow spiritually. Art helps them become more aware of religious concepts and relates the messages they have heard to their own lives. Young children express their ideas through drawing and painting, using lines and forms that will later develop into writing.

- Give clear directions. Provide a sample.
- Create a quiet, reflective atmosphere by playing appropriate background music as the children work. Encourage them to think about what they have just experienced or learned.
- Give the children who wish to do so an opportunity to talk about their work.
- Display the work at the children's eye level so that it can be appreciated.
- Be aware that coloring books and patterns do not stimulate creativity. For a drawing activity, stimulate ideas and guide the children by making comments such as "I wonder whether you will draw green grass in the background" or "I wonder whether you will make your picture fill the whole sheet."

Audiovisuals

Audiovisuals (movies, videotapes, DVDs, slides, audio CDs, and audiotapes) can lead the children to a deeper appreciation of the message in each chapter.

- Preview the entire audiovisual and read the guide that comes with it. Determine whether it is appropriate for your lesson and your group. Decide how you will use the audiovisual—to introduce a subject or to review it.
- Prepare to introduce audiovisual presentations. Give adequate background information and tell the children what to look for, focusing attention on the main purpose for listening or viewing.
- Plan discussion questions and activities to follow the presentation.
- Introduce new vocabulary and concepts before showing the audiovisual.
- After the presentation, provide time for quiet reflection or written response.

Bulletin Boards

An effective bulletin-board display is simple, timely, and catches people's attention. Its unity, with emphasis on the more important elements, and its balanced arrangement, with movement (or flow), make it educational as well as attractive. It is an easily understood teaching aid.

- Think of a caption that draws attention, such as a question, a three-dimensional device, a current idiom, or "big" or stylized words.
- Create an overall effect to hold interest.
- Plan the movement of the board. Displays are usually viewed left to right, top to bottom. Figures of people and animals draw attention. Repeat shapes, textures, and colors—or related variations—for unity.
- Achieve balance, which can be symmetrical or asymmetrical. For informal balance, use two or more small shapes with a larger one, a small colorful shape with a larger dull one, a small shape near the bottom with a larger shape near the top, or a small eye-catching shape with a larger common shape.
- Make objects touch one another, or connect them with yarn, paper, or colored lines. An odd number of items is better than an even number.
- Use wallpaper, wrapping paper, construction paper, shelf paper, velour, felt, or burlap as a background for letters and pictures.
- Arrange the children's papers so that they can be easily seen; never place one on top of another.

Celebrations

Celebrations, including song, prayer, Scripture, ritual, and symbol, draw the children more deeply into the message of the lesson. Through communal prayers and private reflections in the celebrations, the children are imbued with the mystery of faith celebrated and come to appreciate liturgical elements. The impressions that celebrations make on the children justify the time, preparation, and practice they entail.

- Create an atmosphere of beauty, peace, and prayer through the use of candles, flowers or plants, cloth, religious art, music, and symbols. (Check with the proper authority regarding local regulations for using candles in a classroom setting.)

- Make sure all the children know what to do and say. Practice the songs used.

- Remind the children that they are praising and thanking God through their celebration.

Children's Literature

Books are highly effective tools for shaping attitudes and imparting values. Through stories, the children come to understand themselves and others, and they learn to relate to others and to their world in a better way. Good literature confronts readers with basic human problems and helps them deal with these problems. Stories can reinforce the Christian message presented in class and help children apply Christian principles to their lives. Jesus was conscious of the power of stories and used them in his teaching. Recommended books are listed for each chapter under the feature title "Books to Share."

- As you read a story, make your voice and face full of expression.

- Show the pictures and call attention to certain features in them. Give the children the opportunity to respond to the story and pictures.

- Involve the children in the story by asking questions or by having them add sounds, words, or gestures. Prepare props ahead of time.

Dramatization

Dramatization effectively reinforces the Christian message and helps children internalize it. Role-playing enables children to apply religious truths to their daily life.

- Maintain an atmosphere of security and seriousness needed to give the children self-confidence. Use role-playing only when the children are comfortable with one another.

- Ignore giggles and awkwardness.

- Allow the children to choose their roles. Have them take turns.

- Use simple props and costumes.

- Prepare the performers sufficiently.

- Put signs on the participants for identification if necessary.

- Accept the children's interpretations and praise their efforts. However, if their interpretations lack insight, guide them to understand the feelings of the people in the situations.

- Discuss the activity with the children in the light of Christian values.

Visit www.loyolapress.com/preschool for suggestions about using storybooks in prayer and catechesis.

Flannel Board

Flannel-board figures add another dimension to storytelling. Sets of flannel figures can be purchased, or you can make your own. Glue small pieces of flannel or felt to the back of paper figures, or use flannel or felt to make the figures.

- Arrange the figures in order of use.

- Practice telling your story until you feel at ease with the story and the movement of the figures.

- Use the figures for review. For example, distribute them to the children and have them tell the story, or have them give clues about their figure and ask the group to guess which one they have.

Group Projects

As the children work together to reach a common goal, qualities needed in community are fostered: consideration, understanding, cooperation, patience, initiative, and responsibility. Small-group activities afford the children an experience of interdependence and provide a welcome change from the classroom routine.

- Explain the directions clearly and demonstrate when appropriate.

- Show interest in the groups' work by encouraging them, offering suggestions, and asking questions.

- Make sure that all the children are participating.

Games

Playing games is fun for children and also contributes to their development. Games provide practice in mental, physical, and social skills; offer opportunities for problem solving and creativity; stimulate imagination; and increase attention spans.

- Remove potential hazards from the play area.

- Explain the game clearly and simply. Establish ground rules. Demonstrate when necessary.

- Let the children take turns being the leader. Assist children who need help.

- Have several groups play a game to allow the children to have more turns. Avoid games that eliminate children, or plan something to occupy those who are out of the game.

- Replay the children's favorite games.

Memorization

Knowledge of certain elements of Catholic belief is best acquired by memorizing them. Pope John Paul II pointed out that "the blossoms . . . of faith and piety do not grow in the desert places of a memoryless catechesis. What is essential is that the texts that are memorized must at the same time be taken in and gradually understood in depth, in order to become a source of Christian life on the personal level and the community level." (*On Catechesis in Our Time,* 55)

- Lead the way by memorizing the material first. Children memorize easily and will naturally repeat psalm verses prayed as a group.

- Integrate memorized material into the lesson in a meaningful way. The children should understand the material they are memorizing.

Music

Music can set the mood for the lesson and predispose the children to receive God's message. Besides introducing the lesson, music can be used to review and reinforce the message. It can serve as a prayer before or after class. Music unites the group, provides an enjoyable opportunity for self-expression, and stirs up feelings of love and loyalty to Christ and his Church. Both singing and listening to music have the power to open hearts to the Lord.

- As you teach a song, consider the following steps:

  1. Give a general introduction and ask the children to listen to the song.

  2. Have them listen again for specific ideas. Discuss difficult lyrics.

  3. Have them sing the song softly or hum along as you sing or play it.

- Ask the children to sing with enthusiasm and make the song a prayer. Suggest that they think about the meaning of the song and sing with all their hearts.

- Invite the children to add gestures or interpretive dance steps. See *Music 'n Motion,* beginning on page T265.

- If you lack musical talent, find ways to compensate. For example, use recorded music or invite assistance from other members of the community.

- Encourage the children to sing spontaneous original songs and create your own.

Pictures and Visuals

The icons of the Eastern Churches are treasured because of their power to sweep us up to God. Stained-glass windows have been a medium of religious instruction for centuries. Similarly, pictures such as art masterpieces and the photos and illustrations in the Child's Book can influence the children's response to the catechesis. They can stimulate learning, awaken an appreciation of the message, and lead to prayer.

- Use visuals to arouse interest, to raise questions, and to clarify concepts.

- Choose visuals that are artistically good, convey an accurate religious message, and are large enough to be seen by all.

- Use questions or comments to lead the children to share insights. Ask them how the picture makes them feel and how it relates to the lesson. Have them create a story based on the picture or role-play the situation depicted.

Play

Children learn through play as they investigate the world, master themselves, and build interpersonal relationships. Children's toys should encourage thinking, exploration, creativity, and communication. Provide a variety of toys for the children. Share play experiences with the children to understand their world better.

- Provide toys that allow children to engage in free-form, open-ended play: wooden blocks, play-houses, puppets, dolls, and trucks. Allow freedom for the children in their play.

- Select toys that encourage the children's creativity. A nonspeaking doll engages the children's imaginations better than a doll that talks. A toy that the children move is better than a battery-run toy. Rotate toys to maintain the children's interest.

- Make sure that the toys are safe. Do not give the children toys with sharp edges, small parts or projectiles, or toys that may present potential danger if they are broken. Check to make sure that fabric is labeled "flame-retardant" or "flame resistant." Painted toys should have nontoxic paint.

- Create toys with the children.

Prayer

Prayer opens children's hearts to God's message. It gives them the time and space they need to reflect on God's words and the meaning the words have for their lives. Most important, it provides an avenue for God to touch the children and to change them by his love.

- Be a person of prayer yourself, and share your own prayer life with the children as appropriate.

- Respect each child's needs. Some will feel comfortable praying aloud and spontaneously. Others will prefer to pray silently. Show respect and appreciation for the various types of prayer.

- Prepare the children for prayer. Provide time for them to settle down and focus on God. Teach them to adopt a posture that is conducive to prayer.

- Create an attractive prayer center. Place there a Bible, a crucifix, a banner, a candle, religious statues, or pictures related to the feast, season, or topic of study. Regularly gather the group in the prayer center for prayer experiences. Encourage the children to use the area for personal prayer. Suggest that they have their families arrange similar prayer centers at home.

Puppets

Puppets are a valuable teaching aid, especially for young or shy children. Since puppets are merely toys, they should not pray or speak the religious message. The faith message should be grounded in reality.

Puppets can be made in the following ways:

- Lunch bags—Draw, paint, or glue on features. The bags may be stuffed and tied or left open so that a hand can be inserted.

- Paper—Mount paper cutouts on pencils, rulers, craft sticks, kitchen utensils (such as spoons or spatulas), or even brooms. Paper plates make good puppet faces.

- Socks and mittens—Fabric scraps and other decorations can be sewed or glued to them to make faces and clothing.

- Finger puppets—These can be cut from paper and taped together to fit a finger, or they can be made from felt or old gloves.

- Puppets with arms—Use a paper cup or a cardboard tube, cutting holes on the sides for a thumb or finger.

- Wooden clothespins—Decorate them with felt-tipped pens, yarn, and fabric.

Questions

Posing questions is a time-honored technique for leading children to the truth. Both Socrates and Jesus relied heavily on questions when they taught. Asking questions keeps the children's attention.

- Vary the types of questions you ask, from simple recall questions to those that require some explanation. Address questions to the entire group before calling on a child to answer.

- Be comfortable with the silence as the children reflect on the question. To encourage children to give more thoughtful responses, avoid calling on the first child who raises his or her hand.

- Implement strategies that allow all children to participate. For example, give a child an object such as a beanbag to hold while answering. Then have the child pass the object to the next speaker.

Storytelling

Through Bible stories and stories from the lives of Christians past and present, we share the heritage of our faith. Storytelling can also be used to share one's personal faith. Sharing one's faith journey gives witness to the faith. Both forms of storytelling deepen the children's understanding of Jesus and their relationship with him.

- Make a story your own by adapting it to the children and to your message.

- Practice telling the story by using facial expressions, animated gestures, and expression in your voice for effect and emphasis.

- Use visuals to enhance the telling: pictures, puppets, chalkboard, flannel board, and so forth.

- Relate personally to each child as you tell the story. Establish eye contact with individuals and be sensitive to how each is responding to the story.

- Let the story speak for itself. Its message may be less effective if you moralize.

GUIDELINES FOR MEETING WITH PARENTS

REASONS FOR THE MEETING

1. To help parents realize their important role in shaping their children's religious lives

2. To suggest ways parents can make the most of ordinary opportunities to nurture family faith and to celebrate God's presence in their lives

3. To help parents understand their children's development and become aware of factors that contribute to their religious development

4. To explain the *God Made the World* program for four-year-old children and to describe how parents can be involved

NUMBER OF MEETINGS

Opportunities for parent education can be an important component of a preschool program. The number of meetings will vary according to the parents' needs and interests. The following suggestions are for one meeting, which you might schedule for two different times to provide an added opportunity for parents to attend.

PRACTICAL POINTS TO CONSIDER

1. Schedule a meeting near the beginning of the year. Select a convenient time (or times) for the parents. Invite a parish priest to participate.

2. Create a comfortable atmosphere for the meeting.

- Select a suitable meeting place.
- Plan to welcome each person individually, while volunteers take care of registration, name tags, and so forth.
- Plan refreshments.

3. Decide how to publicize your meeting. Announce the meeting in letters to parents and in parish bulletins. Visit www.loyolapress.com/preschool for sample meeting publicity. Highlight its benefits to parents and clearly state the following details:

- Why the meeting is being held
- Who is involved
- What will be included
- When and where the meeting will take place
- How long it will last

- Whom to contact for further information

Follow written announcements with personal invitations.

4. Create an environment for prayer by arranging a prayer center in your meeting space. Include a Bible, a copy of the *God Made the World* Child's Book, flowers and other objects from nature to represent the themes of the preschool program, and a candle. (Confirm with the proper authority regarding use of candles in your meeting space.) Use lighting and music to set apart the prayer time.

5. Allow time for an adequate exchange of thoughts and feelings.

6. Make available a chart for volunteers to sign up to help during lessons and, if you wish, a chart for volunteers who offer to supply snacks for the lessons. Visit www.loyolapress.com/preschool for volunteer chart templates.

7. Include parents in an evaluation of the meeting. Visit www.loyolapress.com/preschool for a sample evaluation form.

PARENT MEETING
YOUR FOUR-YEAR-OLD COMES TO KNOW GOD

PROPOSED MEETING OUTLINE

I. Introduction

   A. Welcome

   B. Affirm the parents' role in shaping children's religious life.

   C. Overview of the meeting

   D. Prayer

II. Presentation: "Your Child's Spirituality and the Preschool Program"

III. Refreshment Break

IV. Presentation: "Fostering Your Child's Spirituality at Home"

V. Discussion

VI. Closing prayer

CONSIDERATIONS WHEN PLANNING THE PRESENTATIONS

1. Families come in many forms and styles. One thing all participants will have in common is a strong love for their children.

2. Respect the parents' time by preparing well and starting and ending as scheduled.

3. Parents typically value gaining insight into how families function and the developmental stages their children are going through.

4. Raising children in the faith often demands a willingness to make choices as a family that go against the culture.

5. Many parents seek support and authorization to step into their role as spiritual leaders in their families.

6. Some adults in attendance will not have had a thorough catechetical formation, and some may be indifferent to religion.

7. Parents want what's best for their children, but they may need help to see how good moral and spiritual development are essential elements in providing what's best.

8. Families will benefit from understanding their noble mission to bring Christ to their homes, workplaces, neighborhoods, and the world.

SAMPLE MEETING

Part I: Introduction (15 minutes)

A Welcome the parents.

- Introduce yourself and any other catechists in the preschool program. Tell why you are happy to be a preschool catechist.

- Thank the parents for coming; acknowledge the difficulties they may have met in arranging to be present. Invite them to settle quietly in their seats, take a few deep breaths, and let go of the cares of the day.

- Have the parents introduce themselves.

B Affirm the parents' role in shaping their children's religious life.

- Express your awareness of the parents' deep concern for their children. Give specific examples of ways parents show this by providing for a child's needs and guiding and teaching every day.

- Remind the parents that their children received the gift of faith in Baptism and are open to God and capable of perceiving his presence.

- Discuss the parents' role as their children's first teachers of the faith and their importance to their children's religious development. Describe ways they have helped shape their children's faith through actions of love, acceptance, and respect, as well as by praying and worshiping together. Remind them of the help they receive from God in the grace offered throughout each day, and especially in the sacraments—Baptism first of all, Eucharist, Reconciliation, Confirmation, and Matrimony.

- Explain that parents teach the faith in many ways, most powerfully through their example. When they respond to Christ's call in their daily lives, their children learn to love and follow Christ.

C Briefly outline the meeting and the expectations you have for it.

D Pray together.

- Call attention to the prayer center and note the objects from nature representing the themes of the preschool program. Invite all to join in a time of prayer.

- Light the candle, then pause to allow everyone to enter into the spirit of prayer.

- Begin with the Sign of the Cross and lead prayer using this prayer or your own:

    Loving God, we praise you for the splendor of the world you created and for creating us in your image. As we teach the faith to the children, may we experience anew the wonder of your creation. Bless us as we journey together and seek to grow in your love. We ask this through Christ, our Lord. Amen.

Part II: Your Child's Spirituality and the Preschool Program (20 minutes)

A Ask the parents to think about some characteristics that describe their preschool child. Invite a few volunteers to name one of the characteristics. Encourage the parents to keep these in mind as you share with them the characteristics of a four-year-old child as given on page T296. Visit www.loyolapress .com/preschool to offer this as a parent handout.

B Explain a child's spirituality. You might include the following ideas:

- Four-year-old children are developing a sense of God and of the sacred.

- Children discover God's love through the love of their family and come to trust God.

- Children learn about love and reconciliation in the family. Their experiences there extend later to the community and to the whole human race.

- Children absorb their family's faith, attitudes, values, and vision of life.

- Children adopt the behavior of their parents: their reverence at prayer and at Mass as well as their actions on behalf of those in need.

- Since children respond to the world with wonder, prayers of praise and thanks come easily to them.

- The religious experiences of childhood greatly determine the spirituality of the mature adult.

C Present the preschool program:

- Goals

- Topics

- Examples of different types of activities (See examples in the Family Activity Booklet in the Child's Book.)

- Allow parents to review lesson materials, including the Child's Book and resources found in the Catechist's Guide.

D Show resources available to parents, such as those listed here. Let the parents look through them during the refreshment break. Visit www.loyolapress.com/preschool for a handout listing resources and for order information.

Raising Faith-Filled Kids: Ordinary Opportunities to Nurture Spirituality at Home. Tips and tools for nurturing family spirituality by Tom McGrath. Published by Loyola Press (also available in Spanish).

52 Simple Ways to Talk with Your Kids About Faith. A guide for family conversations about faith by Jim Campbell. Published by Loyola Press.

A Prayer Book for Catholic Families. Introduces traditional prayers and family prayer traditions. Published by Loyola Press.

Catholic Household Blessings & Prayers. A resource for family prayer. Published by the United States Conference of Catholic Bishops.

The Spiritual Life of Children. A popular book by Robert Coles. Published by Houghton Mifflin.

Your Four-Year-Old: Wild and Wonderful. A helpful book by Louise Bates Ames and Frances L. Ilg, M.D. Published by Dell Publishing.

Various children's Bibles and Bible storybooks, such as the following:

All About Jesus. Bible stories selected by Martine Blanc-Rerat. Published by Loyola Press.

The Greatest Story Ever Told. A pop-up activity book of stories of Jesus by Linda and Alan Parry. Published by Loyola Press.

Part III: Refreshment Break (10 minutes)

Part IV: Fostering Your Child's Spirituality at Home (20 minutes)

A Describe resources for families in the preschool program.

- Show the Family Time section of a lesson from the Child's Book. Mention that this section contains the message of the lesson, tells what the children were taught and how, and suggests Scripture, prayer, and home activities to reinforce and extend the concepts and experiences of the lesson. Indicate if Spanish translations of Family Time (Tiempo en familia) will be made available for parents who may benefit from them. Note that these can be found at www .loyolapress.com/preschool.

- Explain that each Family Time concludes with a storybook suggestion, a discussion prompt, and a prayer suggestion related to the theme of the lesson. Propose to parents that this could be incorporated into their child's bedtime routine or another part of the day. Visit www.loyolapress.com/ preschool for additional information about using this feature, including a handout for parents.

- Distribute and explain the Family Activity Booklet. Encourage the parents to use this resource to repeat a newly learned poem, finger play, or song at home with the children after each appropriate lesson. They can also use the directions provided for completing crafts at home as needed. Visit www.loyolapress.com/ preschool to download additional copies of this resource.

B Suggest ways to foster faith in the home.

- Worship together as a family at Sunday Mass.

- Establish time each day for family prayers and blessings.

- Share meals together and pray Grace Before Meals. Consider meal prayer traditions, such as holding hands around the table while praying meal prayers.

Look for additional suggestions for making the most of family meals in the pamphlet *Mealtime Matters,* published by Loyola Press.

- Display sacred objects in the home, such as a Bible, a crucifix, or an image of Mary with her Son.

- Celebrate Catholic holy days and feasts, as well as family members' birthdays and name days and anniversaries of Baptisms and First Holy Communions.

- Maintain open channels of communication.

- Look for opportunities for teaching in everyday experiences.

Part V: Discussion (15 minutes)

Divide the parents into groups and suggest one or more of the following questions for discussion:

- What are some of your memories of your earliest religious experiences?

- How do you talk to your children about God?

- How does your family pray?

- What opportunities do you foresee for developing your child's faith?

- In what practical ways can your child see faith lived in your family?

- What religious traditions do you have at home? What ideas do you have for starting some?

- What difficulties might you meet in fostering faith in your child?

Conclude the discussion time by asking volunteers to describe their hopes for their child as they participate in this year's preschool program.

Part VI: Closing (10 minutes)

A Evaluation

- Ask the parents which part of the meeting they found most valuable. Provide an evaluation form with a checklist showing the various parts of the meeting and ask for feedback. Encourage additional comments and use the responses to improve future meetings. Visit www.loyolapress.com/preschool for a sample evaluation form.

B Closing prayer

Give parents a copy of the following prayer (available at www.loyola press.com/preschool). Invite them to join you in a closing prayer.

- Leader: Let us pray for God's help as we seek to nourish the faith of our children and our families. Let us begin our prayer in the name of the Father, and of the Son, and of the Holy Spirit.

- All: Amen.

- Leader: Generous God, you fill us with your love and grace. Open our hearts that we may receive your many blessings to us. Guide us as we seek to nourish our own faith and help us as we share the faith with our children. We ask this through Christ, our Lord. Amen.

- Reader: A reading from the Gospel of Saint Luke. (Luke 2:51–52)

- Leader: Let us pause for a moment and reflect silently on our hopes for the children as they grow in God's love. [*Pause.*] Let us pray for ourselves, our families, and our children. Our response is "Lord, hear our prayer."

- May the example of the Holy Family of Jesus, Mary, and Joseph inspire our family life, we pray . . .

- May all parents and catechists be strengthened by God's grace, we pray . . . May the children grow in wisdom, age, and favor before God and all people, we pray . . .

- Leader: Let us pray together in the words that Jesus taught us: Our Father . . .

- Leader: God, bless us and keep us faithful to you. Bless the children you have given to our care and guide them in the ways of your love. Send your blessing on all parents and catechists and make us signs of your love. We pray this in Jesus' name.

- All: Amen.

Song	Collection	Publisher
Chapter 1: God Made Me		
Every Person Is a Gift of God	Hi God 3	OCP
Children of God	Rise Up and Sing 2d edition	OCP
Anatome	Music for Kids Vol. 1: Best of Joe Wise	GIA
This Little Light of Mine	Wee Sing Bible Songs	Price Stern Sloan
God Is So Good	Wee Sing Bible Songs	Price Stern Sloan
Chicken Lips	Fingerprints	Big Steps 4 U Publishing
Chapter 2: God Made My Family		
Jesus, I Will Stay with You	Stories and Songs of Jesus	OCP
Yes, We Will Do What Jesus Says	Stories and Songs of Jesus	OCP
Show Me Your Smile	Pockets: Songs for Little People	GIA
A Dad Like You	Big Steps for Little Feet	Big Steps 4 U Publishing
Gramma's House	Fingerprints	Big Steps 4 U Publishing
Chapter 3: God Made My Friends		
I'll Need a Friend Like You	Take Out Your Crayons	WLP
When I'm Crying, You Hear Me	Take Out Your Crayons	WLP
Show Me Your Smile	Pockets: Songs for Little People	GIA
Jesus Loves the Little Children	Stories and Songs of Jesus	OCP
Jesus Always Helps Us	Stories and Songs of Jesus	OCP
Take My Hand	Stories and Songs of Jesus	OCP
Chapter 4: God Made My Helpers		
When I'm Crying, You Hear Me	Take Out Your Crayons	WLP
Don't Look for Jesus in the Sky	I See a New World	WLP
What Makes Love Grow?	Hi God!	OCP
Spending	Mugwumps and Important Things	Jennie Flack
Be with Us, O Lord	A Wonderful Song of Joy	OCP
Chapter 5: God Made My Church Family		
God Has Made Us a Family	Hi God 3	OCP
You Gather a Family	Rise Up and Sing	OCP
We Are the Church	Calling the Children	OCP
Jesus, I Will Stay with You	Stories and Songs of Jesus	OCP
Yes, We Will Do What Jesus Says	Stories and Songs of Jesus	OCP
Chapter 6: God Made Churches		
God Likes to Play	Take Out Your Crayons	WLP
I Hear a Song in My Heart	Take Out Your Crayons	WLP
Wherever I Am, God Is	Hi God 3	OCP
In the House of Our God	Rise Up and Sing 2d edition	OCP
Chapter 7: God Made the Bible		
Giant Song	Mugwumps and Important Things	Jennie Flack
We Hear God's Word	Rise Up and Sing 2d edition	OCP
God Made Me	Wee Sing Bible Songs	Price Stern Sloan

Song	Collection	Publisher
Chapter 8: God Made Music		
Little David, Play on Your Harp	*Wee Sing Bible Songs*	Price Stern Sloan
Sing a Simple Song	*Hi God 2*	OCP
Old MacDonald Had a Band	*Singable Songs for the Very Young*	Rounder
Celebration Song	*Big Steps for Little Feet*	Big Steps 4 U Publishing
Chapter 9: God Made Water		
All Your Gifts of Life	*Hi God 2*	OCP If All the Raindrops,
Rain	*My Toes Are Starting to Wiggle*	Miss Jackie Music Company
Water in the Rain Clouds	*My Toes Are Starting to Wiggle*	Miss Jackie Music Company
Chapter 10: God Made Food		
Kinds of Food	*Learning Basic Skills Through Music Vol. 1*	Educational Activities
Peanut Butter Sandwich	*Singable Songs for the Very Young*	Rounder
The Epic of Peanut Butter and Jelly	*Music for Kids: The Best of Joe Wise*	GIA
Thank You, Lord	*Stories and Songs of Jesus*	OCP
Chapter 11: God Made Land		
God Made Mud	*Take Out Your Crayons*	WLP
I've Got the Spirit	*Take Out Your Crayons*	WLP
My God, How Great You Are	*Spirit & Song 2*	OCP
Chapter 12: God Made Air		
Wherever I Am, God Is	*Hi God 3*	OCP
Everywhere	*Big Steps for Little Feet*	Big Steps 4 U Publishing
Chapter 13: God Made Light		
Children of the Lord	*Hi God 2*	OCP
Jesus, Come to Us	*Rise Up and Sing 2d edition*	OCP
The Light Song	*Mugwumps and Important Things*	Jennie Flack
Chapter 14: God Made Color		
I Love to Color	*Pockets: Songs for Little People*	GIA
Colors	*Learning Basic Skills Through Music Vol. 1*	Educational Activities
Parade of Colors	*Learning Basic Skills Through Music Vol. 2*	Educational Activities
Chapter 15: God Made Weather		
Mr. Sun	*Singable Songs for the Very Young*	OCP
Jesus Always Helps Us	*Stories and Songs of Jesus*	OCP
Goobers	*Big Steps for Little Feet*	Big Steps 4 U Publishing
My Pout Can't Come Out	*Fingerprints*	Big Steps 4 U Publishing
Chapter 16: God Made Flowers		
People Worry	*Stories and Songs of Jesus*	OCP
Count It All Joy	*Big Steps for Little Feet*	Big Steps 4 U Publishing
Chapter 17: God Made Trees		
The Tiny Seed	*Stories and Songs of Jesus*	OCP
Hip Hip Hooray Hippopotamus	*Fingerprints*	Big Steps 4 U Publishing

Song	Collection	Publisher
Chapter 18: God Made Animals		
God Loves the Animals	*Take Out Your Crayons*	WLP
If I Were a Butterfly	*Hi God 2*	OCP
All Living Things	*Rise Up and Sing*	OCP
The Grizzleback Snookerhog	*Pockets: Songs for Little People*	GIA
Down by the Bay	*Singable Songs for the Very Young*	Rounder
Going to the Zoo	*Singable Songs for the Very Young*	Rounder
Hip Hip Hooray Hippopotamus	*Fingerprints*	Big Steps 4 U Publishing
Chapter 19: God Made Birds		
Children Everywhere	*Rise Up and Sing*	OCP
You Are Always with Me	*Rise Up and Sing 2d edition*	OCP
Robin in the Rain	*Singable Songs for the Very Young*	Rounder
People Worry	*Stories and Songs of Jesus*	OCP
Count It All Joy	*Big Steps for Little Feet*	Big Steps 4 U Publishing
Birds	*Learning Basic Skills Through Music Vol. I*	Educational Activities
Chapter 20: God Made Fish		
Children Everywhere	*Rise Up and Sing*	OCP
And It Was Good	*Young People's Glory and Praise Vol. 2*	OCP
Fishing for People	*Stories and Songs of Jesus*	OCP
Chapter 21: God Made Butterflies		
The Butterfly Song	*Best of Mary Lu Walker*	Paulist
Signs of New Life	*Bloom Where You're Planted*	OCP
Chapter 22: God Made Big Things		
If I Had a Dinosaur	*More Singable Songs*	Rounder
Chapter 23: God Made Little Things		
Children Everywhere	*Rise Up and Sing*	OCP
Spider on the Floor	*Singable Songs for the Very Young*	Rounder
Chapter 24: God Made Countries		
Don't Look for Jesus in the Sky	*I See a New World*	WLP
Chapter 25: God Made Laughter		
Joy, Joy, Joy	*Hi God!*	OCP
The Joy of the Lord	*Hi God!*	OCP
The Grizzleback Snookerhog	*Pockets: Songs for Little People*	GIA
Sharing	*Mugwumps and Important Things*	Jennie Flack
Joy Is My Strength	*Fingerprints*	Big Steps 4 U Publishing

Song	Collection	Publisher
Halloween/Feast of All Saints		
Have a Good Old Time on Halloween Night	*Holiday Songs & Rhythms*	Hap Palmer Music Company
Halloween Is Coming	*My Toes Are Starting to Wiggle*	Miss Jackie Music Company
What Do You Like About Halloween?	*My Toes Are Starting to Wiggle*	Miss Jackie Music Company
God's Love	*Big Steps for Little Feet*	Big Steps 4 U Publishing
Sharing Comes 'Round Again	*Fingerprints*	Big Steps 4 U Publishing
Give It Away	*Fingerprints*	Big Steps 4 U Publishing
Advent		
Alleluia! Hurry, the Lord Is Near	*Rise Up and Sing 2d edition*	OCP
Light the Advent Candle	*Rise Up and Sing*	OCP
An Angel Came from Heaven	*Stories and Songs of Jesus*	OCP
Christmas		
O Come, Little Children	*Rise Up and Sing 2d edition*	OCP
Go Tell It on the Mountain	*Rise Up and Sing 2d edition*	OCP
Calling the Children	*Calling the Children*	OCP
Glory to God	*Stories and Songs of Jesus*	OCP
How Much God Loves Us	*Stories and Songs of Jesus*	OCP
The Little Baby	*Big Steps for Little Feet*	Big Steps 4 U Publishing
Lent		
God's Love	*Sing a Song of Joy!*	WLP
Easter		
Thank You, Lord	*Hi God!*	OCP
Jesus Lives	*Stories and Songs of Jesus*	OCP
We Believe	*Calling the Children*	OCP
Easter Rise Up	*Big Steps for Little Feet*	Big Steps 4 U Publishing
Pentecost		
Go Now in Peace	*Singing Our Faith*	GIA
Prayer of Peace	*Singing Our Faith*	GIA
Peace Is Flowing Like a River	*Hi God 2*	OCP
Thanksgiving		
Thank You, Lord	*Hi God!*	OCP
All Your Gifts of Life	*Hi God 2*	OCP
Thank You, Lord	*Stories and Songs of Jesus*	OCP
It Is Good	*Big Steps for Little Feet*	Big Steps 4 U Publishing

Song	Collection	Publisher
Valentine's Day		
The Sharing Song	*Singable Songs for the Very Young*	Rounder
I Hear a Song in My Heart	*Take Out Your Crayons*	WLP
One Red Valentine	*My Toes Are Starting to Wiggle*	Miss Jackie Music Company
Will You Be My Valentine?	*My Toes Are Starting to Wiggle*	Miss Jackie Music Company
God's Circle of Love	*Hi God 3*	OCP
God's Love	*Big Steps for Little Feet*	Big Steps 4 U Publishing
Sharing Comes 'Round Again	*Fingerprints*	Big Steps 4 U Publishing
Give It Away	*Fingerprints*	Big Steps 4 U Publishing
Mother's Day		
Yes, We Will Do What Jesus Says	*Stories and Songs of Jesus*	OCP
Immaculate Mary	*Rise Up and Sing 2d edition*	OCP
Father's Day		
A Dad Like You	*Big Steps for Little Feet*	Big Steps 4 U Publishing
Birthdays		
I Wonder If I'm Growing	*Singable Songs for the Very Young*	Rounder
How Much God Loves Us	*Stories and Songs of Jesus*	OCP
Last Class/Summer		
I Hear a Song in My Heart	*Take Out Your Crayons*	WLP
Wherever I Am, God Is	*Hi God 3*	OCP
Celebration Song	*Big Steps for Little Feet*	Big Steps 4 U Publishing

Flannel Board

Cover a sheet of cardboard with flannel. Attach sandpaper or felt strips to the back of pictures.

PAINT

Simple Finger Paint

Add tempera paint to liquid starch.

Finger Paint

- 2 cups flour
- 2 teaspoons salt
- 3 cups cold water
- 2 cups hot water
- food coloring or powdered tempera

Combine flour, salt, and cold water and beat until smooth. Add hot water and boil mixture, stirring constantly until clear. Beat until smooth. Mix in color.

Cornstarch Finger Paint

- 3 tablespoons sugar
- ½ cup cornstarch
- 2 cups cold water
- food coloring or powdered tempera

Combine sugar, cornstarch, and water. Cook over low heat, stirring constantly until mixture thickens. Let cool. Add coloring.

Soap Flake Finger Paint

- 1 cup cornstarch
- 2 cups cold water
- 2 envelopes unflavored gelatin
- 1 cup soap flakes
- food coloring or powdered tempera

Dissolve the cornstarch in 1½ cups cold water. Soften gelatin in remaining cold water and add to cornstarch mixture. Cook over medium heat, stirring occasionally until mixture is thick. Stir in soap flakes. Add coloring. Store in an airtight container.

Easy Soap Flake Finger Paint

- ½ cup soap chips
- 6 cups water
- 1 cup liquid starch
- powdered tempera

Dissolve soap chips in water. Mix water with starch. Add tempera.

Easiest Soap Flake Finger Paint

Mix soap flakes with a little water. Beat with an eggbeater. Add color.

Face Paint

- 1 cup solid vegetable shortening
- 1 cup cornstarch
- water (if necessary)
- food coloring

Mix shortening and cornstarch until smooth. If thick, add water; if thin, add shortening. Add food coloring. If sealed in plastic and refrigerated, this paint will keep for three days.

CLAY AND DOUGH

Uncooked Modeling Dough

- 3 cups flour
- 1 cup salt
- 1 cup water with coloring
- 1 tablespoon oil
- 1 tablespoon alum (as a preservative)

Mix dry ingredients. Add water and oil gradually.

Reusable Clay

- 2 tablespoons oil
- 1 cup water
- food coloring
- 1½ cups salt
- 4 cups flour

Mix oil, water, coloring. Mix salt and flour. Add water mixture to salt and flour. Knead. Store in plastic bags or sealed container.

Cooked Modeling Dough

- 1 cup cornstarch
- 2 cups baking soda
- 1¼ cups water
- food coloring or powdered tempera

Combine cornstarch, baking soda, water, and coloring. Cook over medium heat until thick. Cool and knead.

Baker's Clay

- 1 cup salt
- 4 cups flour
- 1½ cups water
- liquid tempera

Mix salt and flour with hands, adding water. Knead five minutes. Add liquid tempera. Bake finished products on foil-covered sheets at 350°F until hard and brown.

Salt Ceramic

- 1 cup salt
- ½ cup cornstarch
- ⅔ cup water
- food coloring

Combine ingredients. Cook over medium heat and stir until thick. Remove from heat. Knead in coloring. Refrigerate.

Cooked Play Dough

- 1 cup flour
- ½ cup salt
- 1 cup water
- 1 tablespoon cooking oil
- 1 teaspoon cream of tartar
- food coloring

Mix ingredients except for food coloring. Cook the mixture over medium heat until it forms a ball. Knead it on waxed paper. Store dough in an airtight container or plastic bag. Shape the dough into balls. Poke a deep hole in each and add a drop or two of food coloring. The children will be surprised to see the dough change color as they work with it.

Uncooked Play Dough

- 2 cups flour
- 1 cup salt
- 6 teaspoons alum powder
- 2 tablespoons salad oil
- 1 cup water
- food coloring or tempera paint

Mix all ingredients.

Finger Gelatin

- 4 envelopes unflavored gelatin
- 3 packages (3-ounce size) flavored gelatin
- 4 cups boiling water

Combine gelatins. Add water and stir until dissolved. Pour into 9-inch by 13-inch baking pan. Chill. Cut with a cookie cutter. Eat with fingers.

BUBBLES

Bubbles

- ¼ cup dishwashing liquid
- ½ cup water
- 2 drops glycerin
- 1 drop food coloring

Stir the ingredients. Store the mixture in a tightly closed container.

Giant Bubbles

- 6 cups water
- 2 cups dishwashing liquid
- 1 cup corn syrup

Mix the ingredients about four hours ahead of time. Pour the solution into shallow pans. Make a wand with about a 6-inch diameter out of pipe cleaners or wire coat hangers with the sharp ends covered. Dip the wand in the solution and wave it once with a long, sweeping motion. Let the children chase the bubbles.

Alternative Recipe

- 1 gallon water
- ¼ cup dishwashing liquid
- 1 tablespoon corn syrup

Mix the ingredients. Cut off the bottom of a plastic water bottle. Dip the large open end into the solution and blow into the mouth of the water bottle.

Warning: The solution may damage carpeting, floors, and grass.

Ave Maria Press
P.O. Box 428
Notre Dame, IN 46556
(800) 282-1865
www.avemariapress.com

The Center for Learning
P.O. Box 910
2105 Evergreen Road
Villa Maria, PA 16155
(800) 767-9090
www.centerforlearning.org

Coronet, the Multimedia Company
A Division of Phoenix Learning
2349 Chaffee Dr.
St. Louis, MO 63146-3306
(800) 221-1274
www.phoenixlearninggroup.com

The Crossroad Publishing Company
16 Penn Plaza, Suite 1550
New York, NY 10001
(212) 868-1801
www.cpcbooks.com

Daughters of St. Paul
See Pauline Books & Media

Educational Activities, Inc.
P.O. Box 87
Baldwin, NY 11510
(800) 797-3223
www.edact.com

Franciscan Communications
See St. Anthony Messenger Press

Liguori Publications
One Liguori Drive
Liguori, MO 63057-9999
(800) 325-9521
www.liguori.org

Liturgical Press
Saint John's Abbey
P.O. Box 7500
Collegeville, MN 56321-7500
(800) 858-5450
www.litpress.org

Liturgy Training Publications
1800 N. Hermitage Avenue
Chicago, IL 60622-1101
(800) 933-1800
www.ltp.org

Live Oak Media
P.O. Box 652
Pine Plains, NY 12567-0652
(800) 788-1121
www.liveoakmedia.com

Loyola Press
3441 N. Ashland Avenue
Chicago, IL 60657
(800) 621-1008
www.loyolapress.org

National Catholic Educational Association
1077 30th Street, NW, Suite 100
Washington, DC 20007-3852
(800) 711-6232
www.ncea.org

National Conference for Catechetical Leadership
125 Michigan Ave., NE
Washington, DC 20017
(202) 884-9753
www.nccl.org

New City Press
202 Cardinal Rd.
Hyde Park, NY 12538
(800) 462-5980
www.newcitypress.com

Oblate Media and Communication
4126 Seven Hills Dr.
St. Louis, MO 63033
(800) 233-4629
www.videoswithvalues.org

Orbis Books
Price Building
Box 302
Maryknoll, NY 10545-0302
(800) 258-5838
www.maryknollmall.org

Pauline Books & Media
50 Saint Paul's Ave.
Boston, MA 02130
(800) 876-4463
www.pauline.org

Paulist Press
997 Macarthur Boulevard
Mahwah, NJ 07430-9990
(800) 218-1903
www.paulistpress.com

Paulist Productions
Box 1057
17575 Pacific Coast Highway
Pacific Palisades, CA 90272
(310) 454-0688
www.paulistproductions.org

Resource Publications, Inc.
160 E. Virginia St. #290
San Jose, CA 95112
(888) 273-7782
www.rpinet.com

Sacred Heart Kids' Club
869 South Rimpau Blvd.
Los Angeles, CA 90005
(323) 935-2372
www.sacredheartsisters.com/
sacredheartkidsclub

St. Anthony Messenger Press
Franciscan Communications
28 W. Liberty Street
Cincinnati, OH 45202-6498
(800) 488-0488
www.catalog.americancatholic.org

Sheed & Ward
Rowman & Littlefield Publishers, Inc.
4501 Forbes Blvd., Suite 200
Lanham, MD 20706
(800) 462-6420
www.rowmanlittlefield.com/Sheed

Sophia Institute Press
P.O. Box 5284
Manchester, NH 03108
(800) 888-9344
www.sophiainstitute.com

Spoken Arts, Inc.
195 South White Rock Road
Holmes, NY 12531
(800) 326-4090
www.spokenartsmedia.com

Treehaus Communications, Inc.
P.O. Box 249
906 West Loveland Ave.
Loveland, OH 45140
(800) 638-4287
www.treehaus1.com

Twenty-Third Publications
1 Montauk Ave., Suite 200
New London, CT 06320
(800) 572-0788
www.twentythirdpublications.com

United States Conference of Catholic Bishops
3211 Fourth Street, NE
Washington, DC 20017
(800) 235-8722
www.usccbpublishing.org

Vision Video
P.O. Box 540
Worcester, PA 19490
(800) 523-0226
www.visionvideo.com

Weston Woods Studios
143 Main Street
Norwalk, CT 06851
(800)-243-5020
www.teacher.scholastic.com/products/
westonwoods

MUSIC SOURCES

G.I.A. Publications, Inc.
7404 South Mason Avenue
Chicago, IL 60638
(800) 442-1358
www.giamusic.com

Mary Lu Walker Albums & Songbooks (MLW)
http://home.stny.rr.com/maryluwalker

Oregon Catholic Press Publications (OCP)
P.O. Box 18030
Portland, OR 97218-0030
(800) 548-8749
www.ocp.org

Pauline Books & Media
50 Saint Paul's Ave.
Boston, MA 02130
(800) 876-4463
www.pauline.org

World Library Publications (WLP)
J.S. Paluch Company, Inc.
3708 River Rd., Suite 400
Franklin Park, IL 60131
(800) 566-6150
www.wlp.jspaluch.com

SCRIPTURE

GAMES

B

"Bigger Than, Stronger Than," T165
"Bluebird, Bluebird," T142
"Blue Catcher," T147
"Butterfly—Fly," T158

C

"Cakewalk," T257
"Color Hunt," T108

D

"Doggie and Bone," T48
"Duck, Duck, Goose," T146

F

"The Farmer in the Dell," T19
"Feed the Baby," T75
"Follow Simon," T32, T61
"Follow the Leader," T85, T215

G

"Guess the Animal," T133

H

"Hot Potato," T189
"Huckle-Buckle Beanstalk," T256

I

"I Can Make You Smile," T190
"I Spy," T101

L

"Love Around the World," T181

M

"Mother May I?", T245
"Musical Chairs," T64

N

"Name Game," T7

P

"Pass the Ring," T27
"Pin the Tail on the Turkey," T235
"Put a Smile on the Pumpkin," T199

R

"Ring-around-the-Rosy," T120

S

"Simon Says," T227
"Stop and Go," T106

T

"Thank–You Relay," T232
Tug-of-war, T153

FINGER PLAYS

E

"The Elephant Goes Like This and That," T169

F

"Five Little Monkeys Jumping on the Bed," T136

H

"Here Is the Church," T49

I

"The Itsy, Bitsy Spider," T172

P

"Pitter–pat, Pitter–pat," T71

S

"Silent Night," T211

T

"There Was a Little Turtle," T137
"This Is My Garden." (to the tune of "On Top of Old Smokey"), T123
"This Is My Turtle," T176
"Two Little Blackbirds Sitting on a Hill," T146

POEMS

C

"Colors," T109

G

"God, We Thank You for Life" (to the tune of "Happy Birthday"), T258, T259
"God Is There," T229
"The Grand Old Duke of York," T88

I

"I Am a Fish in the Great Blue Sea," T152
"I Have Two Eyes That Wink and Blink" (to the tune of "Hark the Herald Angels Sing"), T11
"I Know An Old Lady Who Swallowed a Fly," T190
"I Love to Watch God's Birds Fly By," T147
"I Saw a Little Bird Go Hop, Hop, Hop," T147

L

"Little Arabella Miller," T161
"Little Jack Horner," T77
"Little Miss Muffet," T77

M

"The March Wind," T95

R

"Roses Are Red, Violets Are Blue," T246

S

"Sharing Poem," T217
"Sing a Song of Sixpence," T77

T

"Teddy Bear, Teddy Bear," T137
"This is the Way We Set the Table" (to the tune of "Here We Go 'Round the Mulberry Bush"), T226
"Turkey Time," T235

W

"Way Down South Where Bananas Grow," T169
"The Wind Tells Me," T95

SONGS

A

"Animal Fair," T138

"The Ants Came Marching" (to the tune of "When Johnny Comes Marching Home Again"), T177

"Away in a Manger," T209

B

"Bluebird, Bluebird," T143

F

"The Farmer in the Dell," T19

"Frère Jacques," T180

G

"God, We Thank You For" (to the tune of "Happy Birthday"), T259

"God's Family" (to the tune of "Row, Row, Row Your Boat"), T38

"God the Father, I Love You" (to the tune of "London Bridge"), T252

"Growing Is Good" (to the tune of "God Is So Good"), T216

H

"He's Got the Whole World," T88

"His Banner over Me Is Love," T62

I

"If You're Happy and You Know It," T187

"I Had a Little Nut Tree," T129

"I'm a Child of God" (to the tune of "I'm a Little Teapot"), T10

"I'm Going to Sing When the Spirit Says Sing," T229

"I'm Gonna Sing When the Spirit Says Sing," T228

J

"Jesus Loves Me," T54

L

"Looby Loo," T69

"Love, Love," T215, T241

M

"The More We Are Together," T25

Music List, T320

Music 'n Motion, T7, T9, T14, T17, T22, T26, T27, T30, T32, T36, T39, T44, T47, T52, T56, T60, T63, T68, T71, T74, T76, T84, T87, T92, T94, T98, T101, T104, T107, T112, T115, T120, T122, T126, T128, T132, T135, T142, T146, T147, T150, T153, T158, T160, T164, T167, T172, T174, T180, T183, T186, T189, T196, T199, T208, T211, T220, T222, T232, T234, T238, T240, T256, T258, T262, T264, T265–294

"My God Is So Great," T89, T166

O

"Oh, Do You Know the Police Officer" (to the tune of "The Muffin Man"), T33

"Oh, How I Love Jesus," T27

"Oh, My Darling, Oh, My Darling" (to the tune of "Clementine"), T241

"Oh, We Thank You, We Do" (to the tune of "Happy Birthday"), T235

P

"Praise the Lord Together," T95

R

"Rejoice in the Lord Always," T191

"Ring-around-the-Rosy," T120

"Rise and Shine," T99

T

"This Is the Way We Set the Table" (to the tune of "Here We Go 'Round the Mulberry Bush"), T226

"This Is the Way We Wash Our Clothes" (to the tune of "Here We Go 'Round the Mulberry Bush"), T71

"Twinkle, Twinkle, Little Star," T10

W

"We Wish You a Merry Christmas," T211

"Where is Thumbkin?" (to the tune of "Frère Jacques"), T19

CHILD'S BOOK ART CREDITS

Credits are supplied in sequence, left to right, top to bottom. Page positions are abbreviated as follows: (t) top, (c) center, (b) bottom, (l) left, (r) right.

The stapler, glue bottle, and scissors icons throughout this book were illustrated by Kathryn Seckman Kirsch.

Unit 1 **1** Kathryn Seckman Kirsch, **3** Claudine Gevry, **4** Kathryn Seckman Kirsch, **5** Phyllis Pollema Cahill, **6** Nan Brooks, **7–8** Ginna Hertenstein, **9** Kathryn Seckman Kirsch, **11–12** Claudine Gevry, **13** Robert Voigts and Kathryn Seckman Kirsch, **15–16** Claudine Gevry, **17** iStock/Ivanov, **19** Phyllis Pollema Cahill, **20** Nan Brooks, **21**(tl,tr) Renée Daily, **21**(cl) © Bill Wittman Photography, **21**(bl) © The Crosiers/Gene Plaisted OSC, **21**(br) Phil Martin Photography

Unit 2 **23** Kathryn Seckman Kirsch, **24** Robert Voigts and Kathryn Seckman Kirsch, **25–27** Phyllis Pollema Cahill, **28** Cheryl Arnemann, **29–30** Kathryn Seckman Kirsch, **31**(tl) Phyllis Pollema Cahill, **31**(bl) iStock/meldayus, **31**(r) iStock/Jolanta Vaitkeviciene, **32** Phyllis Pollema Cahill, **33** Claudine Gevry, **34** Cheryl Arnemann, **37**(illustrations) Robert Voigts and Kathryn Seckman Kirsch, **37**(l) iStock/Julie Hagan, **37**(tc) iStock/Pathathai Chungyam, **37**(cc) iStock/Alison Trotta-Marshall, **37**(bc) iStock/Jaimie D. Travis, **37**(tr) iStock/Thomas Perkins, **37**(br) iStock/Franky De Meyer, **38**(tl) iStock/Charles Shapiro, **38**(cl) iStock/zimmytws, **38**(tr) iStock/Christian J. Stewart, **38**(cr) iStock/William Freeman, **39** Nan Brooks, **41** Claudine Gevry, **42** Phyllis Pollema Cahill, **45**(tl) iStock/Sharon Day, **45**(cl) iStock/Vasko Miokovic, **45**(bl) iStock/Michael Irwin, **45**(tc,cc) iStock/Uyen Le, **45**(bc) iStock/Edyta Pawłowska, **45**(tr) iStock/Patrick Laverdant, **45**(br) iStock/Tomas Bercic, **45**(l) iStock/Uzi Tzur, **45**(r) Phil Martin Photography

Unit 3 **47** Nan Brooks, **48** Kathryn Seckman Kirsch, **49** iStock/Viviyian, **51–52** Ginna Hertenstein, **53** Robert Voigts and Kathryn Seckman Kirsch, **55** iStock/Jill Fromer, **55** Yoshi Miyaki, **57**(Jesus) Renée Daily, **57** Robert Voigts and Kathryn Seckman Kirsch, **58** Kathryn Seckman Kirsch, **58** iStock/Sherri Camp, **60** Robert Voigts and Kathryn Seckman Kirsch, **61–62**(balloons) Kathryn Seckman Kirsch, **61**(l) Robert Voigts and Kathryn Seckman Kirsch, **61**(r) Robert Voigts and Kathryn Seckman Kirsch, **62** Kathryn Seckman Kirsch, **63** Ginna Hertenstein, **64**(tl,cl,bl) iStock/Marc Brown, **64**(tr) iStock/Jani Bryson, **64**(cr) iStock/Sharon Dominick, **64**(brl) iStock/Jose Maria Bouza, **64**(br2) iStock/Danny Hooks, **64**(br3) iStock/Fred De Bailliencourt, **65** Robert Voigts and Kathryn Seckman Kirsch

Unit 4 **67** iStock/Brent Melton, **68** iStock/Olga Chernyak, **69**(l) Kathryn Seckman Kirsch, **69**(r)–**70** iStock/Bill Noll, **71**(tl) iStock/Hilary Brodey, **71**(bl) iStock/Appletat, **71**(tc) iStock/Rhienna Cutler, **71**(bc) iStock/Ekaterina Monakhova, **71**(tr) iStock/Derek Thomas, **71**(br) iStock/Scott Feuer, **71**(tree) iStock/Christine Balderas, **72** Ginna Hertenstein, **73** iStock/John Woodcock and polygraphus, **75–76** Robert Masheris, **77–80** Don Wilson, **81–82** Ginna Hertenstein, **83**(tl) iStock/Kiyoshi Takahase, **83**(bl) iStock/David Hutchison, **83**(ccl) iStock/Valeriy Kalyuzhny, **83**(bcl) iStock/Greg Cooksey, **83**(tcr) iStock/Douglas Allen, **83**(ccr) iStock/Rick Wylie, **83**(bcr) iStock/Andrew Howe, **83**(tr) iStock/EricIsselee, **84** Robert Masheris, **85–86** iStock/totallyJaimie, **87**(sea anemone) iStock/Robert Simon, **87**(starfish) iStock/Jurjen Draaijer, **87**(jellyfish) iStock/Klaas Lingbeek vanKranen, **87**(yellow fish) iStock/Kevin Phillips, **87**(octopus) iStock/Herve Lavigne, **87**(seahorse) iStock/Kristian Sekulic, **87**(eel) iStock/Heike Loos, **87**(sea turtle) Stock/Second Shot, **87**(whale) iStock/John Pitcher, **87**(coral) iStock/Rich Ellec, **87**(crab) iStock/Martijn van de Laar, **87**(clam shells) iStock/Kevin Miller, **88** Robert Masheris, **85**(fish) iStock/totallyJaimie, **89**(background)–**90** iStock/bulent gutek

Unit 5 **92** iStock/Olga Chernyak, **93–94** iStock/totallyJaimie, **95** Claudine Gevry, **97**(tl) iStock/Jose Quintana, **97**(bl) iStock/Angel Rodriguez, **97**(r) iStock/Dawn Nichols, **98**(r) iStock/Bart Sadowski, **102** Ginna Hertenstein, **103** Kathryn Seckman Kirsch, **104** iStock/totallyJaimie, **105**(tl) iStock/Lynwood Lord, **105**(cl) iStock/Nilesh Bhange, **105**(tc) Ben Molyneux People/Alamy, **105**(bc) iStock/Knighterrant, **105**(tr) iStock/Tanya Lug, **105**(cr) iStock/Robert Churchill, **105**(br) iStock/Alberto Fanelli, **105**(globe) Len Ebert, **106**(tl) iStock/Nikolay Titov, **106**(bl) iStock/Manuel Gelpi Diaz, **106**(c) iStock/Jeffrey Smith, **106**(tr,br) iStock/Justin Horrocks, **109** Phyllis Pollema Cahill, **110** Ginna Hertenstein, **111** Robert Voigts and Kathryn Seckman Kirsch

Special Lessons **113** Sally Schaedler, **114–115** Robert Voigts and Kathryn Seckman Kirsch, **117** Sally Schaedler, **118** Robert Voigts, **119–120** iStock/George Manga, **121** Sally Schaedler, **122**(branch) iStock/Igor Smichkov, **122**(ornament) Kathryn Seckman Kirsch, **123** Robert Voigts and Kathryn Seckman Kirsch, **124** Robert Voigts, **125** iStock/Monika Adamczyk, **126**(tl) iStock/Kathye Killer, **126**(cl) iStock/Ozg Ur Donmazr, **126**(bl) iStock/Leslie Banks, **126**(tr) iStock/Jason Lugo, **126**(cr) iStock/Monika Adamczyk, **126**(br) iStock/Jill Chen, **127**(feet) Kathryn Seckman Kirsch, **127**(tl) iStock/Carrie Bottomley, **127**(cl) iStock/Glenda Powers, **127**(bl)iStock/Ekaterina Monakhova, **127**(tr) iStock/Ron Chapple, **127**(cr) iStock/Aldo Murillo, **127**(br) iStock/Ann Marie Kurtzh, **127**(feet) Kathryn Seckman Kirsch, **129** iStock/Randy Plett, **130** Mia McGloin, **131–132** Claudine Gevry, **133**(tl) iStock/Olga Solovei, **133**(tc) iStock/Greg Cooksey, **133**(bc) iStock/Jeffrey Smith, **133**(tr) iStock/Aldo Murillo, **134** Phil Martin Photography, **137** Kathryn Seckman Kirsch and iStock/Olga Chernyak, **139**(tl) Veer/LWA-Stephen Welstead, **139**(bl) iStock/Robert Kirk, **139**(br) iStock/Marzanna , Syncerz, **140** Ginna Hertenstein, **141** Robert Voigts and Kathryn Seckman Kirsch, **143** iStock/Miroslav Ferkuniak, **144** Claudine Gevry, **145–146** Kathryn Seckman Kirsch, **148** Claudine Gevry, **151** Nan Brooks, **152** Robert Voigts and Kathryn Seckman Kirsch, **153–154** Ginna Hertenstein, **155**(tl) iStock/Ron Chapple, **155**(bl) Stock/Jason Lugo, **155**(br) iStock/Izabela Habur, **156** Claudine Gevry, **157** Susan Tolonen

Family Activity Booklet **159**(tl) Meg Elliott Smith, **159**(tc) iStock/Ron Chapple, **159**(br) iStock/Thomas Perkins, **160**(cr) Meg Elliott Smith, **161**(bl) iStock/Olga Chernyak, **161**(br),**162**(cr,br) Meg Elliott Smith, **161**(bl) iStock/Angel Rodriguez, **164**(tr) iStock/Christoph Ermel, **164**(br) iStock/Miroslaw Andrzej Oslizlo, **164**(tr) iStock/Stefan Klein, **165**(butterflies) Mia McGloin, **165**(tr),**166**(tl,cr,br) Meg Elliott Smith

Art Credits **167–168** iStock/Olga Chernyak

Photos and illustrations not acknowledged above are either owned by Loyola Press or from royalty-free sources including but not limited to Agnus, Alamy, Comstock, Corbis, Creatas, Fotosearch, Getty Images, Imagestate, iStock, Jupiter Images, Punchstock, Rubberball, and Veer. Loyola Press has made every effort to locate the copyright holders for the cited works used in this publication and to make full acknowledgment for their use. In the case of any omissions, the Publisher will be pleased to make suitable acknowledgments in future editions.

MUSIC 'N MOTION CD CREDITS

Track 1: "I Am Wonderfully Made," words and music by Jack Miffleton. Copyright © 1978, World Library Publications, Franklin Park, IL 60131-2158. www.wlpmusic.com. From the recording *Sing a Song of Joy,* ℗© 1999, World Library Publications. All rights reserved. Used by permission.

Track 2: "Helping," words and music by Jack Miffleton. Copyright © 1978, World Library Publications, Franklin Park, IL 60131-2158. www.wlpmusic.com. From the recording *Sing a Song of Joy,* ℗© 1999, World Library Publications. All rights reserved. Used by permission.

Track 3: "Peace in My Heart," words and music by Mary Ann Renna. Copyright © 2004, World Library Publications, Franklin Park, IL 60131-2158. www.wlpmusic.com. All rights reserved. Used by permission. From the recording *Kids Sing for Jesus,* ℗© 2004, AvilaRose, Inc. All rights reserved. Used by permission.

Track 4: "Jump Up, Get Down," words and music by Mary Ann Renna. Copyright © 2004, World Library Publications, Franklin Park, IL 60131-2158. www.wlpmusic.com. All rights reserved. Used by permission. From the recording *Kids Sing for Jesus,* ℗© 2004, AvilaRose, Inc. All rights reserved. Used by permission.

Track 5: "You Are the Light," words and music by Michael Mangan. Copyright © 2004, Litmus Productions. Exclusive licensing agent in North America: World Library Publications, Franklin Park, IL 60131-2158. www.wlpmusic.com. From the recording *Forever Will I Sing,* ℗© 2004, Litmus Productions. Exclusive licensing agent in North America: World Library Publications. All rights reserved. Used by permission.

Track 6: "Come Together," words and music by Michael Mangan. Copyright © 1993, Litmus Productions. Exclusive licensing agent in North America: World Library Publications, Franklin Park, IL 60131-2158. www.wlpmusic.com. All rights reserved. Used by permission.

Track 7: "Stand Up!," words and music by Michael Mangan. Copyright © 2001, Litmus Productions. Exclusive licensing agent in North America: World Library Publications, Franklin Park, IL 60131-2158. www.wlpmusic.com. From the recording *Setting Hearts on Fire,* ℗© 2001, Litmus Productions. Exclusive licensing agent in North America: World Library Publications. All rights reserved. Used by permission.

Track 8: "Windy Days," words and music by Jack Miffleton. Copyright © 1979, World Library Publications, Franklin Park, IL 60131-2158. www.wlpmusic.com. From the recording *Sing a Song of Joy,* ℗© 1999, World Library Publications. All rights reserved. Used by permission.

Track 9: "Praise and Glorify," words and music by Julie Howard. Copyright © 1995, World Library Publications, Franklin Park, IL 60131-2158. www.wlpmusic.com. From the recording *Here I Am, God!,* ℗© 1995, World Library Publications. All rights reserved. Used by permission.

Track 10: "Care for Life," words and music by Michael Mangan. Copyright © 1997, Litmus Productions. Exclusive licensing agent in North America: World Library Publications, Franklin Park, IL 60131-2158. www.wlpmusic.com. From the recording *True Colors Shine,* ℗© 2007, Litmus Productions. Exclusive licensing agent in North America: World Library Publications. All rights reserved. Used by permission.

Track 11: "When the Saints Go Marching In," traditional.

Track 12: "No Place to Stay," music by Mary Beth Kunde-Anderson. Music copyright © 2008, World Library Publications, Franklin Park, IL 60131-2158. www.wlpmusic.com. All rights reserved. Used by permission.

Track 13: "Easter Alleluia," words and music by Michael Mangan. Copyright © 1993, Litmus Productions. Exclusive licensing agent in North America: World Library Publications, Franklin Park, IL 60131-2158. www.wlpmusic.com. From the recording *This Is the Time,* ℗© 2005, Litmus Productions. Exclusive licensing agent in North America: World Library Publications. All rights reserved. Used by permission.

Track 14: "Thank You, Jesus," words and music by Mary Ann Renna. Copyright © 2004, World Library Publications, Franklin Park, IL 60131-2158. www.wlpmusic.com. All rights reserved. Used by permission. From the recording *Kids Sing for Jesus,* ℗© 2004, AvilaRose, Inc. All rights reserved. Used by permission.

Track 15: "God Is Love," words and music by James V. Marchionda, O.P. Copyright © 1988, World Library Publications, Franklin Park, IL 60131-2158. www.wlpmusic.com. From the recording *Let the Children Come to Me,* ℗© 1988, World Library Publications. All rights reserved. Used by permission.

Track 16: "Happy Birthday! It's Your Day" (age 3), traditional melody.

Track 17: "Happy Birthday! It's Your Day" (age 4), traditional melody.

Track 18: "God Is Great," words and music by Michael Mangan. Copyright © 1998, Litmus Productions. Exclusive licensing agent in North America: World Library Publications, Franklin Park, IL 60131-2158. www.wlpmusic.com. All rights reserved. Used by permission.

#1 father
(Mr. Riley)

#2 mother
(Mrs. Riley)

#4 Joe Riley

#3 Patty Riley

#5 Buttercup

#6 Dizzy Bee

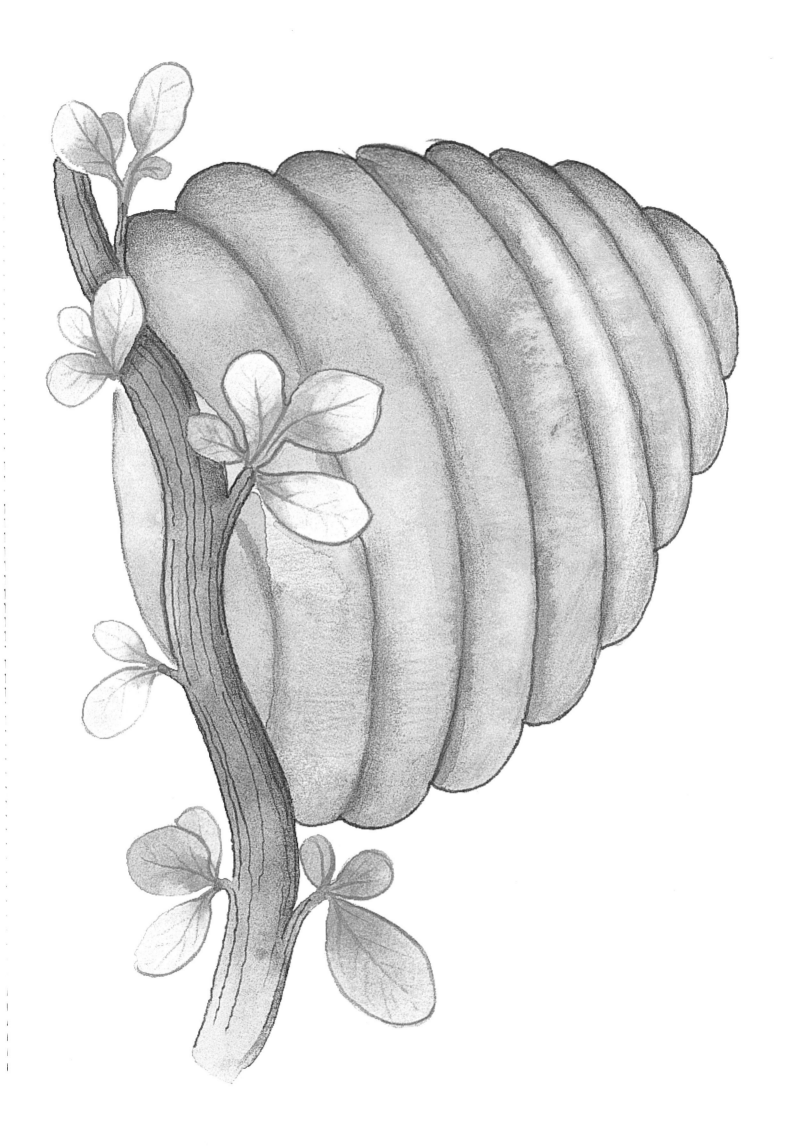

#7 beehive

© LOYOLA PRESS.

#9 priest

© LOYOLA PRESS.

#8 Jesus

© LOYOLA PRESS.

#10 Mary

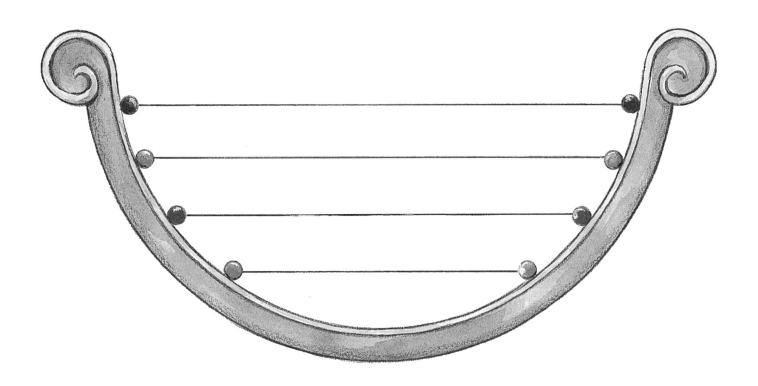

#11 Tillie Mouse

#12 harp

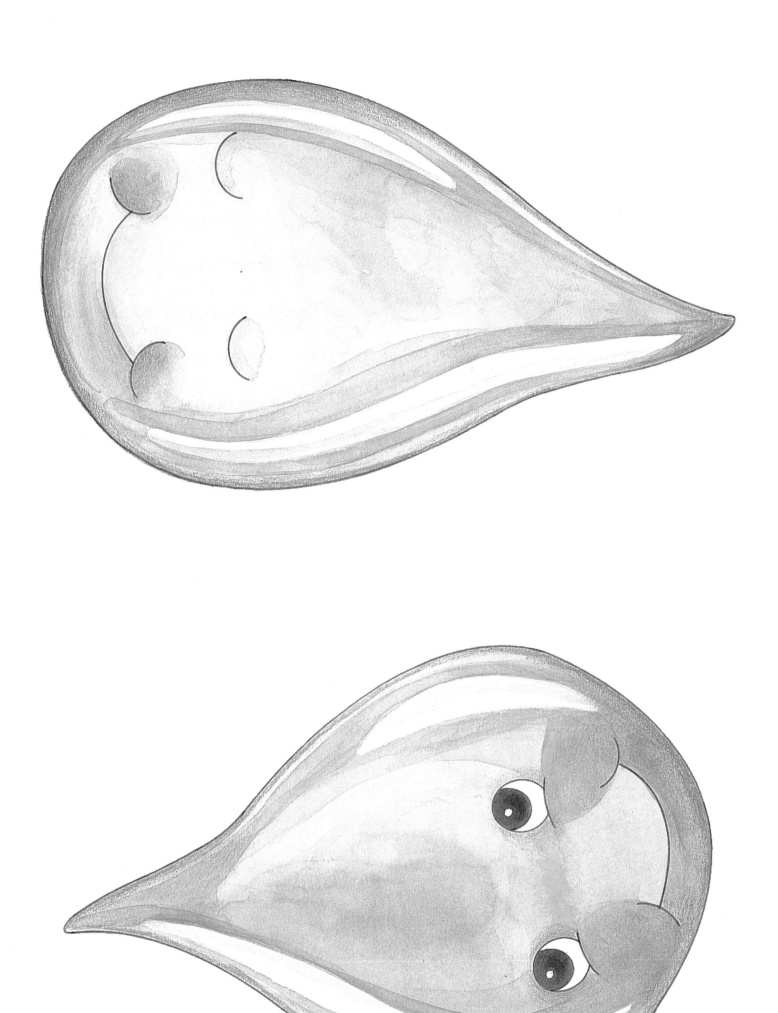

#13 raindrop
(one of five)

© LOYOLAPRESS.

#14 raindrop
(one of five)

© LOYOLAPRESS.

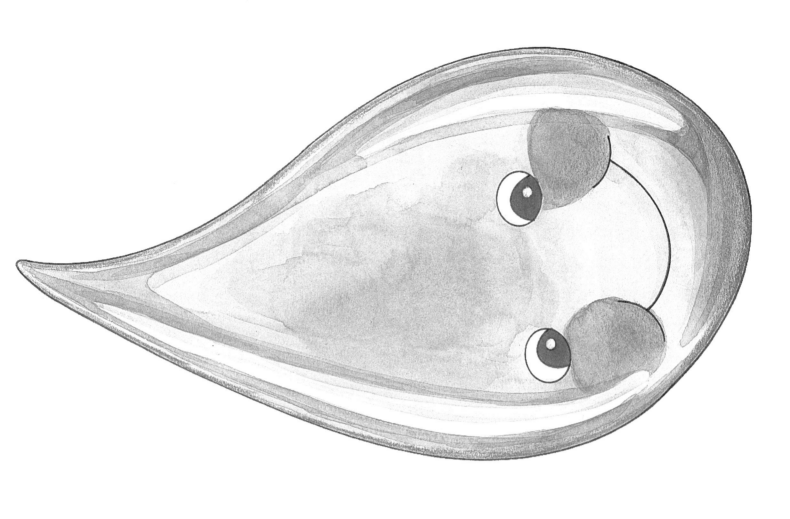

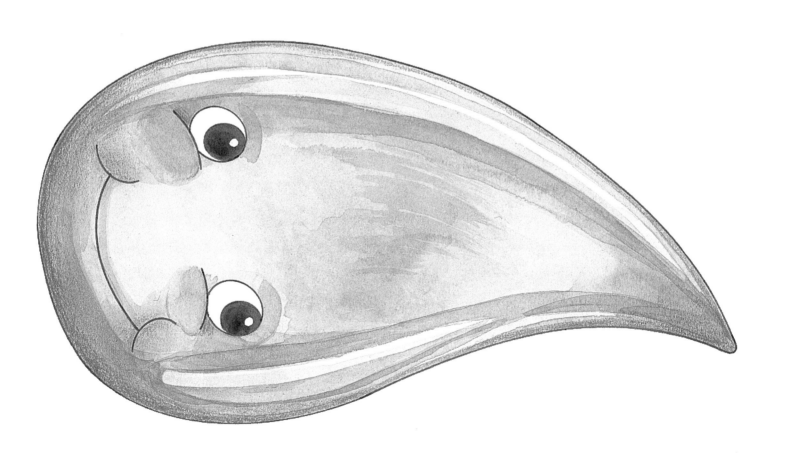

#15 raindrop
(one of five)

© LOYOLAPRESS.

#16 raindrop
(one of five)

© LOYOLAPRESS.

#18 baby

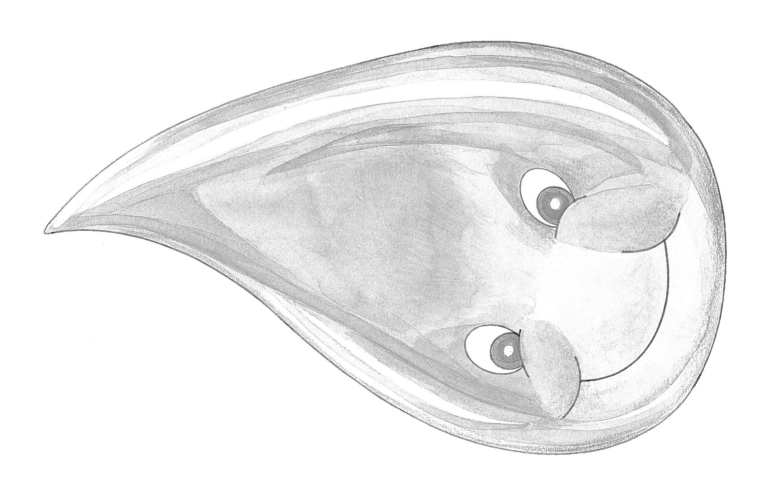

#19 Mr. Sparrow

#20 sun

#21 red/green circle

© LOYOLA PRESS.

#22 red
(one of seven color cards)

© LOYOLA PRESS.

#23 orange
(one of seven color cards)

#24 yellow
(one of seven color cards)

#25 green
(one of seven color cards)

#26 blue
(one of seven color cards)

#27 pink
(one of seven color cards)

#28 purple
(one of seven color cards)

#29 snowflake

#30 cloud

#31 rose

#32 bouquet

#33 monkey

#34 lion

#35 elephant

#36 horse

#37 turtle

#38 bear

#39 rabbit

#40 dog

#42 fish
(one of ten)

#41 fish
(one of ten)

#44 fish
(one of ten)

#43 fish
(one of ten)

#46 fish
(one of ten)

#45 fish
(one of ten)

#48 fish
(one of ten)

#47 fish
(one of ten)

#50 fish
(one of ten)

#49 fish
(one of ten)

#51 monarch butterfly

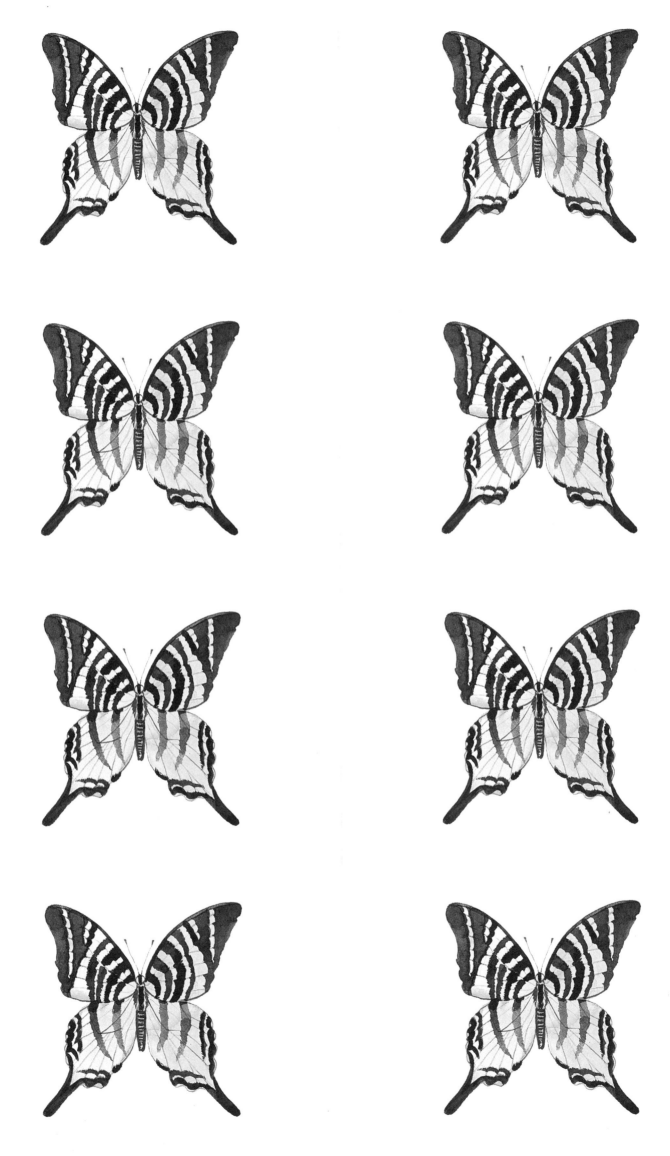

#53 butterfly
(one of eight)

#52 butterfly
(one of eight)

#55 butterfly
(one of eight)

#54 butterfly
(one of eight)

#57 butterfly
(one of eight)

#56 butterfly
(one of eight)

#59 butterfly
(one of eight)

#58 butterfly
(one of eight)

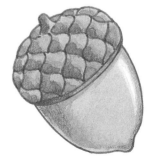

#60 acorn/oak tree

#62 Ali, boy from Kenya

#61 Veena, girl from India

#64 pumpkin

#65 Baby Jesus

#66 star

#63 smile/frown

#67 heart

Scripture Cards

You may wish to separate the Scripture cards and store them in a separate folder. Before presenting a lesson in which Scripture is quoted, place the corresponding card in your Bible.

As you read the card from the Bible during the lesson, you will be reinforcing for the children that the words are from "God's book."

Chapter 3

"You are my friends."

adapted from John 15:14

Chapter 2

Jesus went with Mary and Joseph to Nazareth and was obedient to them. Jesus grew in wisdom and age and favor before all.

adapted from Luke 2:51–52

Chapter 1

I have called you by name: you are mine. You are precious in my eyes, and I love you.

adapted from Isaiah 43:1,4

When [God] calls [the stars], they answer, "Here we are!" shining with joy for their Maker.

Baruch 3:35

Chapter 7

One day Jesus set a child before all the people. He said, "Only people who are like this child will be with me in heaven forever."

adapted from Matthew 18:2–3

I will love you forever and ever.

adapted from Isaiah 54:10

© LOYOLA PRESS.

Chapter 6

I am glad when I go to God's house.

adapted from Psalm 122:1

Once Jesus went to God's house to pray. Some people were doing things there that they shouldn't have been doing. Jesus chased those people out. Jesus said, "God's house should be a place of prayer."

adapted from John 2:13–17

© LOYOLA PRESS.

Chapter 5

"Everyone will know you are my followers, if you love one another."

adapted from John 13:35

© LOYOLA PRESS.

Chapter 11

[T]he LORD is the great God,

the great king over all gods,

Whose hand holds the depths of the earth;

who owns the tops of the mountains.

The sea and dry land belong to God,

who made them, formed them by hand.

Psalm 95:3–5

© LOYOLA PRESS.

Chapter 10

The earth is full of the goodness of the LORD.

adapted from Psalm 33:5

© LOYOLA PRESS.

Chapter 8

Sing to the LORD a new song.

Sing joyfully to the LORD, all the earth.

adapted from Psalm 98:1,4

© LOYOLA PRESS.

Chapter 14

Look at the rainbow! Then bless God who made it.

adapted from Sirach 43:11

Chapter 13

God said, "Let there be light," and there was light. God saw how good the light was.

Genesis 1:3–4

Chapter 12

The LORD God formed man out of the clay of the ground. Then God blew breath into the man, and the man came to life.

adapted from Genesis 2:7

Chapter 17

Out of the ground the LORD God made different kinds of trees grow that were delightful to look at and good for food.

adapted from Genesis 2:9

Chapter 16

One day Jesus was telling people about how God loves us. He said, "Look at the flowers. They don't work, but God clothes them in clothes more beautiful than a king's. God will take care of you just as God takes care of the flowers. You don't have to worry."

adapted from Luke 12:27–28

Chapter 15

Sun and moon,
bless the Lord . . .

Every shower and dew,
bless the Lord . . .

All you winds,
bless the Lord . . .

Cold and chill,
bless the Lord . . .

Dew and rain,
bless the Lord . . .

Frost and chill,
bless the Lord . . .

Ice and snow,
bless the Lord . . .

Lightnings and clouds,
bless the Lord . . .

Daniel 3:62–73

Chapter 20

God created huge creatures and all kinds of swimming creatures to fill the water.

adapted from Genesis 1:21

Chapter 19

God said, "Let birds fly in the sky." And God made all kinds of winged birds. God blessed them.

adapted from Genesis 1:20–22

Chapter 18

God formed animals and birds out of the ground and brought them to the first man to give them names. Whatever the man called each animal was its name.

adapted from Genesis 2:19

Chapter 23

God looked at everything he had made and called it very good.

adapted from Genesis 1:31

Chapter 22

God is greater than all his works.

adapted from Sirach 43:29

Chapter 21

God has made a home for us in heaven.

adapted from 2 Corinthians 5:1

Lent

Our love for God is shown in our deeds.

adapted from 1 John 3:16–18

© LOYOLA PRESS.

Halloween/ Feast of All Saints

"You are the light of the world. Let your light shine so people see the good things you do and praise our Father in heaven."

adapted from Matthew 5:14,16

© LOYOLA PRESS.

Chapter 25

"Your hearts will be happy and your joy will last forever."

adapted from John 16:22

© LOYOLA PRESS.

Thanksgiving

Give thanks to the Lord, who is good, whose love lasts forever.

adapted from Psalm 118:29

© LOYOLA PRESS.

Pentecost

"Peace be with you. Receive the Holy Spirit."

adapted from John 20:21–22

© LOYOLA PRESS.

Easter

"I am the resurrection and the life; whoever believes in me will live forever."

adapted from John 11:25

© LOYOLA PRESS.

Father's Day

"Your heavenly Father knows everything you need."

adapted from Matthew 6:32

Mother's Day

"Children, obey your parents in everything . . ."

Colossians 3:20

Valentine's Day

"As I have loved you, so you also should love one another."

John 13:34

Last Class/Summer

I will give thanks to you, O LORD. [Repeat.]

I will sing your praise before the world. [Repeat.]

For your kindness is as high as the sky. [Repeat.]

adapted from Psalm 57:10–11

Birthdays

I praise you, God, for the wonder of myself.

adapted from Psalm 139:14